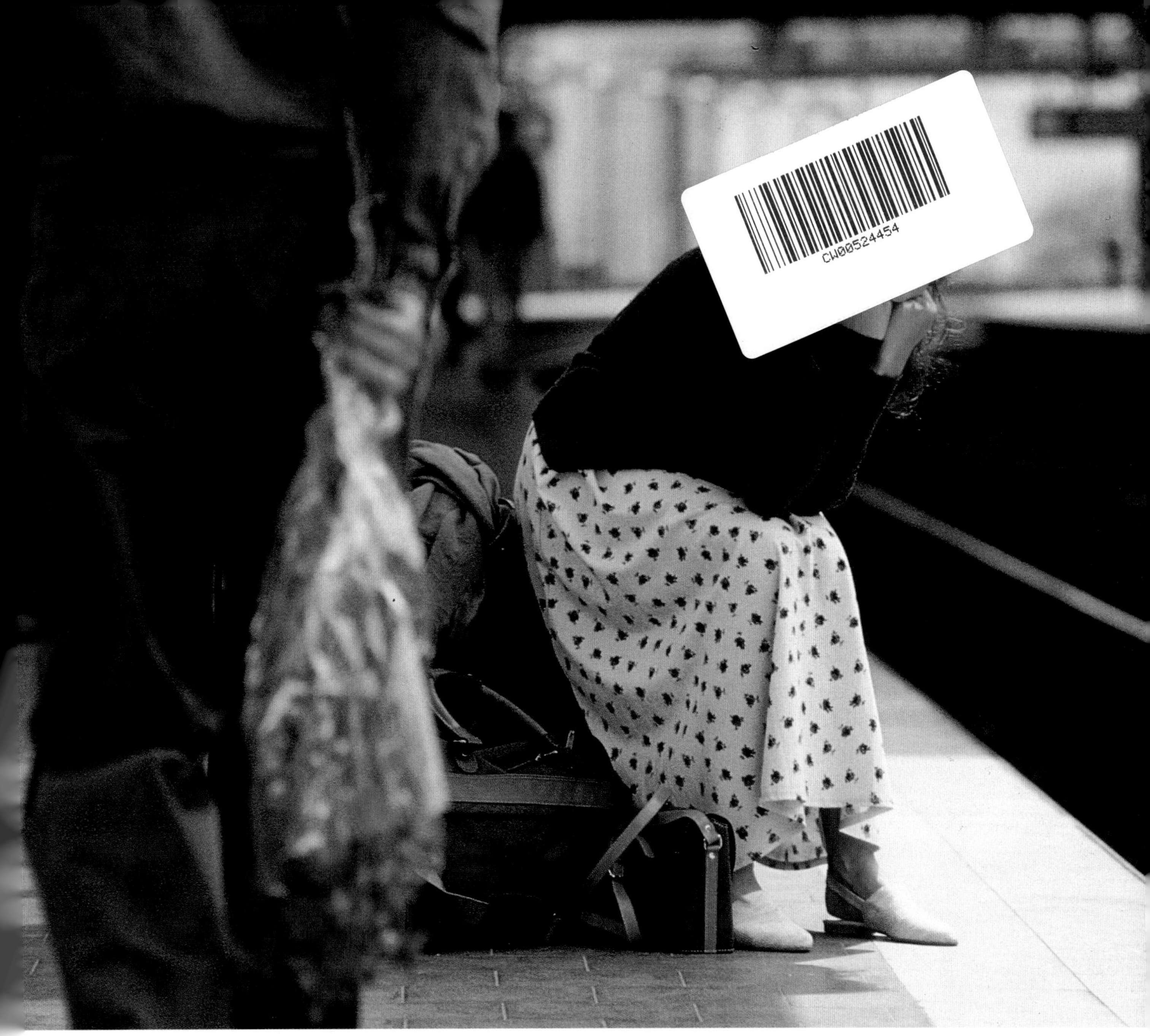

(don't keep 'em waiting)

AT&T Direct® Service

AT&T Direct is a great way to reach those you care about back home. It provides quick access to English-speaking operators and fast connections with clear sound quality.

For easy dialing instructions and access numbers, please find a wallet guide in the back of this publication.

For more information, check out the AT&T Worldwide Traveler Web Site at http://www.att.com/traveler/

INTRODUCTION

From The Inn at Whitewell, Lancashire
Winner of the 1998 Johansens Most Excellent Inn Award

Like so many of my colleagues who personally run country inns and small hotels, I became a hotelier and started my own business as a second career. Fifteen years ago I retired as Managing Director of one of the larger operating companies of a well-known national brewer, responsible for three breweries and hundreds of pubs and hotels. The first major surprise at Whitewell was to find that, in spite of my professional background, I knew so little about the front-line realities of running an inn. For one thing I completely underestimated the physical and mental commitment that was required.

Building up a soundly successful inn probably takes at least five years and it is consequently essential that the work is something which you actually enjoy. It is therefore very exciting and an honour to be judged by the Johansens team as the 1998 Inn of the Year. To feature in this way in such a successful and prestigious guide is a recognition of the outstanding contribution of the staff and my family.

Lastly may I thank all the guests who have stayed with us and have taken the trouble to report to Johansens that they enjoyed their visit to the Inn at Whitewell. The staff, my family and I look forward to greeting warmly all Johansens guests who come to Whitewell in the future.

Richard Bowman, Proprietor

WELL ... DE GUSTIBUS
NON EST DISPUTANDUM
HILDON
AN ENGLISH
NATURAL MINERAL WATER
OF EXCEPTIONAL TASTE
GENTLY CARBONATED
Composition in accordance with the results of the officially
recognized analysis 26 March 1992.
Hildon Ltd., Broughton, Hampshire SO20 8DG, ☏ 01794 301 747
750ml e
"FOR BEST BEFORE DATE SEE CAP"
Bottled at source, Broughton, Hampshire
Bottled at source, Broughton, Hampshire
"FOR BEST BEFORE DATE SEE CAP"

INTRODUCTION

From The Sea Crest, St. Brelade, Jersey
Winner of the 1998 Johansens Most Excellent Restaurant Award

Martha and I are thrilled and not a little shocked to have won the Johansens Most Excellent Restaurant Award. It is the culmination of many years of effort and we are most grateful to the team at Johansens for their support and encouragement.

We started at the Sea Crest in 1990 and over the last eight and a half years we have developed a marriage of our own tastes with those of the customers and, of course, the Chef. We have decorated the restaurant with our own collection of 20th century pictures including works by such artists as John Piper, Picasso, Buffet, John Hoyland, Patrick Caufield and Bert Irvin. We also regularly have guest artists who show a collection of their own paintings and often come and talk about art in general. The picture above is an original by Emma Faull.

We are a Restaurant with rooms but we make sure that all our guests have a warm welcome and the rooms are exceedingly comfortable, just as Johansens guests would expect, in fact we have over the last two years won the Gold Merit Award from Tourism, the only hotel in our category to have done so. Most of our rooms have uninterrupted views over the sea and at night the sun sets over the sea in front of the hotel. Petit Port is one of the least spoilt beaches in Jersey and so we are an ideal place to rest and relax.

The Sea Crest specialises in local seafood, we almost always have lobster (only not available when the weather is too bad for the fishermen to go out to their pots) and usually have sea bass, Dover sole and brill. We aim to provide traditional dishes with a twist and offer a variety of food suitable for all ages and tastes. We also offer special vegetarian dishes and try to use local produce as much as possible.

We are especially pleased to welcome Johansens guests and look forward to showing them just what it is that makes us the Most Excellent Restaurant of the Year.

Julian and Martha Bernstein

WELL … DE GUSTIBUS
NON EST DISPUTANDUM

HILDON

AN ENGLISH
NATURAL MINERAL WATER
OF EXCEPTIONAL TASTE

DELIGHTFULLY STILL

Composition in accordance with the results of the officially recognized analysis 26 March 1992.
Hildon Ltd., Broughton, Hampshire SO20 8DG. ☎01794-301 747

750ml ℮

"FOR BEST BEFORE DATE SEE CAP"
Bottled at source, Broughton, Hampshire

Bottled at source, Broughton, Hampshire
"FOR BEST BEFORE DATE SEE CAP"

Photograph reproduced with the kind permission of the ETB

Johansens Recommended Traditional Inns, Hotels and Restaurants in England

Castles, cathedrals, museums, great country houses and the opportunity to stay in areas of historical importance. England has so much to offer. Whatever your leisure interests, there's a network of around 560 Tourist Information Centres throughout England to give you friendly, free advice on places to visit, entertainment, local facilities and travel information.

English Heritage
Keysign House
429 Oxford Street
London W1R 2HD
Tel: 0171 973 3396
Offers an unrivalled choice of properties to visit.

Historic Houses Association
2 Chester Street
London SW1X 7BB
Tel: 0171 259 5688
Ensures the survival of historic houses and gardens in private ownership in Great Britain.

The National Trust
36 Queen Anne's Gate
London SW1H 9AS
Tel: 0171 222 9251
Cares for more than 590,000 acres of countryside and over 400 historic buildings.

Regional Tourist Boards

Cumbria Tourist Board
Ashleigh
Holly Road
Windermere
Cumbria LA23 2AQ
Tel: 015394 44444
England's most beautiful lakes and tallest mountains reach out from the Lake District National Park to a landscape of spectacular coasts, hills and dales.

East of England Tourist Board
Toppesfield Hall
Hadleigh
Suffolk IP7 5DN
Tel: 01473 822922
Cambridgeshire, Essex, Hertfordshire, Bedfordshire, Norfolk, Suffolk and Lincolnshire.

Heart of England Tourist Board
Woodside
Larkhill Road
Worcester
Worcestershire WR5 2EF
Tel: 01905 763436
Gloucestershire, Hereford & Worcester, Shropshire, Staffordshire, Warwickshire, West Midlands, Derbyshire, Leicestershire, Northamptonshire, Nottinghamshire and Rutland. Represents the districts of Cherwell and West Oxfordshire in the county of Oxfordshire.

London Tourist Board
6th floor Glen House
Stag Place
London SW1E 5LT
Tel: 0171 932 2000
The Greater London area
(see page 13)

Northumbria Tourist Board
Aykley Heads
Durham DH1 5UX
Tel: 0191 375 3000
The Tees Valley, Durham, Northumberland and Tyne & Wear

North West Tourist Board
Swan House
Swan Meadow Road
Wigan Pier, Wigan
Lancashire WN3 5BB
Tel: 01942 821222
Cheshire, Greater Manchester, Lancashire, Merseyside and the High Peak District of Derbyshire

South East England Tourist Board
The Old Brew House
Warwick Park
Tunbridge Wells
Kent TN2 5TU
Tel: 01892 540766
East and West Sussex, Kent and Surrey

Southern Tourist Board
40 Chamberlayne Road
Eastleigh
Hampshire SO5 5JH
Tel: 01703 620006
East and North Dorset, Hampshire, Isle of Wight, Berkshire, Buckinghamshire and Oxfordshire

West Country Tourist Board
60, St David's Hill
Exeter
Devon EX4 4SY
Tel: 01392 425426
Bath and NE Somerset, Bristol, Cornwall and the Isles of Scilly, Devon, Dorset (Western), North Somerset and Wiltshire

Yorkshire Tourist Board
312 Tadcaster Road
York YO2 2HF
Tel: 01904 707961
Yorkshire and North & North East Lincolnshire

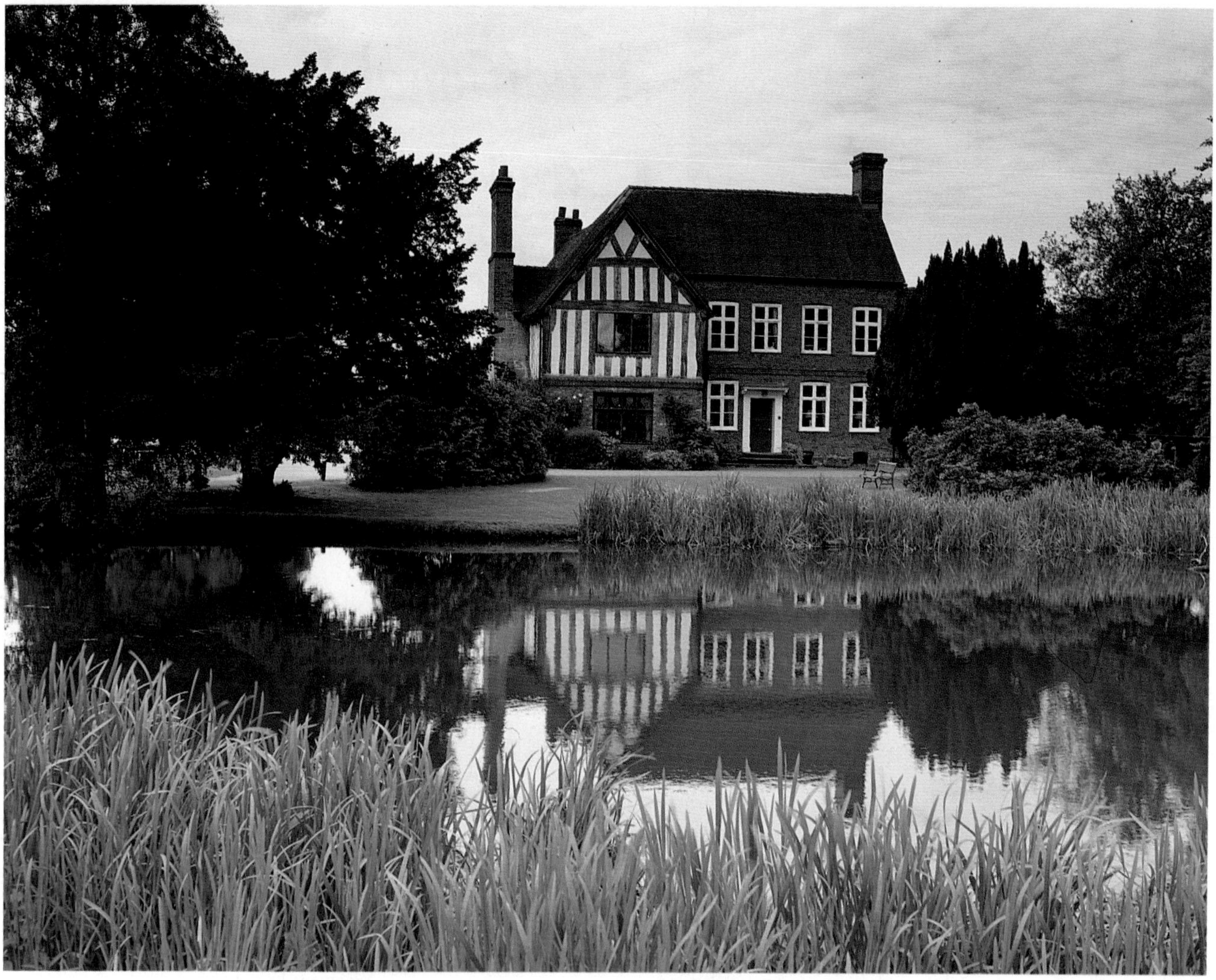

THE MOAT HOUSE

ACTON TRUSSELL, STAFFORD, STAFFORDSHIRE ST17 0RJ
TEL: 01785 712217 FAX: 01785 715344 E-MAIL: info@moathouse.co.uk

This impressive, oak-beamed and moated manor house is excellent in every way. History, luxurious comfort, warmth, superb food, ultra modern amenities and a spectacular canal side setting all combine in a picturesque village in the heart of rural Staffordshire. Built in the 15th century, the Moat House is the perfect retreat for those seeking peace, tranquillity and leisurely enjoyment. There are 21 luxury en suite bedrooms, including two suites, with facilities to suit the most discerning guest. Most are air-conditioned. The bar retains the character and charm of the hotel's past with exposed beams and a magnificent inglenook fireplace. Dining is an experience, with chef Matthew Davies producing sophisticated and imaginative dishes in the elegant, AA Rosetted restaurant. The Moat House is also a first-class business venue, offering seven meeting rooms including a suite. Local attractions include Alton Towers, The Potteries, Weston Hall, Shrugborough Hall, and Cannock Chase Country Park. Clay pigeon shooting, fishing, archery and off road driving facilities are close by. Uttoxeter racecourse is within easy reach. **Directions:** From the M6, exit at junction 13 and take the A449 towards Stafford. At the first island turn right, signposted Acton Trussell. The Moat House is at the far end of the village. Price guide: Single £65–£120; double/twin £80–£130; suite £140–£160.

For hotel location, see maps on pages 212-218

THE RED LION INN

THE GREEN, ADDERBURY, NR BANBURY, OXFORDSHIRE OX17 3LU
TEL: 01295 810269 FAX: 01295 811906

Situated in the historic village of Adderbury and overlooking the picturesque village green, The Red Lion is a magnificent example of a traditional coaching inn. This ancient royalist hostelry pre-dates the Civil War and local folklore pinpoints it as a Royalist bolt hole and the secret tunnel which was used to flee from the Parliamentarians is now part of the wine vaults. Devotees of English heritage will delight in the wealth of old oak and stone chimney pieces which have been carefully preserved and visitors cannot fail to be impressed by the tasteful interior decoration which is consistent throughout. Each of the bedrooms is individually appointed drawing inspiration from a bygone era yet still offering all the modern amenities. Individual rooms are available for private functions, also separate meeting rooms and a board room suitable for business meetings or conferences in a propitious environment for special occasions. The Red Lion is recommended for the quality in addition to its general ambience. Formal and informal meals are available in bars or the restaurant. Traditional inn food is presented generously and without fuss in a friendly, stylish atmosphere. Oxford, Blenheim Palace, Stratford-upon-Avon and the Cotswolds are all nearby. **Directions:** The Red Lion is three miles south of Banbury on the A4260 Oxford road (formerly the A423), six miles from the M40 junction 10 or four miles from junction 11. Price guide: Single: £55; double £65–£80.

13 rms MasterCard VISA AMERICAN EXPRESS M 25

THE GREYHOUND INN

STOCKS ROAD, ALDBURY, NR TRING, HERTFORDSHIRE HP23 5RT
TEL: 01442 851228 FAX: 01442 851495

Set in the glorious village of Aldbury, this former coaching inn overlooking a charming duck pond is now a popular location for film makers. The Greyhound Inn is surrounded by the beautiful Chiltern Hills with its wealth of footpaths and bridle paths, bird and nature attractions. The individually decorated bedrooms combine traditional décor such as antiques and pine furnishings with modern day comforts including television and en suite facilities. Breakfast, either continental or full English, is served in the oak-beamed restaurant. Guests may dine here in the evening and savour the creations of the chef, Damien Ng. The frequently changing menu is mainly based on fine English dishes with a strong emphasis on quality and the freshness of ingredients. During the summer months, the locally renowned bar snacks may be enjoyed in the beer garden by the honeysuckle-covered pergola. They are complemented by a local brew, Aldbury, made by the neighbouring Vale Brewery Company. Nearby attractions include the Rothschilds Museum, Whipsnade Zoo and Stocks, an excellent base for golf and horse riding. **Directions:** From the M1, leave at junction 5 or 8. Exit the M25 at junction 20 and take the new A41. Leave at the Tring exit and follow the signs for Aldbury. Price guide: Single £39.50; double £46. Weekend packages are also available.

10 rms MasterCard VISA AMERICAN EXPRESS M 20

For hotel location, see maps on pages 212-218

The Boathouse Brasserie

HOUGHTON BRIDGE, AMBERLEY, NR ARUNDEL, WEST SUSSEX BN18 9LR
TEL: 01798 831059 FAX: 01798 831063

This delightful informal restaurant is on the River Arun at the site of the ancient Houghton Wharf. It is under the same private ownership as the White Horse Inn at Sutton. The restaurant is Edwardian in style, full of character and strewn with charts and maritime bric-a-brac. Weather permitting, you may prefer to enjoy your meal out on the open wooden deck or under the verandah. The attractive staff are friendly and attentive. The Carvery, is without doubt, the speciality here – succulent roast meats are on display, carved for you by the chefs. There is a small but impressive à la carte menu and the fresh fish is a tempting alternative. Extra seasonal dishes are shown on the blackboard in the bar. There is a fine selection of sweets, a good cheeseboard and coffee of the highest class. The set price lunch (two-courses and coffee) is good value and very popular. On Sunday it is advisable to book well ahead. The wine list is well chosen and reasonably priced. Arundel Castle, Petworth House, Parham House, Chichester (Festival Theatre) and Goodwood Racecourse are all nearby. Being on the Southdowns Way there are some good walks to be had. The Amberley Chalkpits Industrial Museum is nearby. **Directions:** The Boathouse is on the B2139 (Arundel to Storrington Road) where it crosses the River Arun.

For hotel location, see maps on pages 212-218

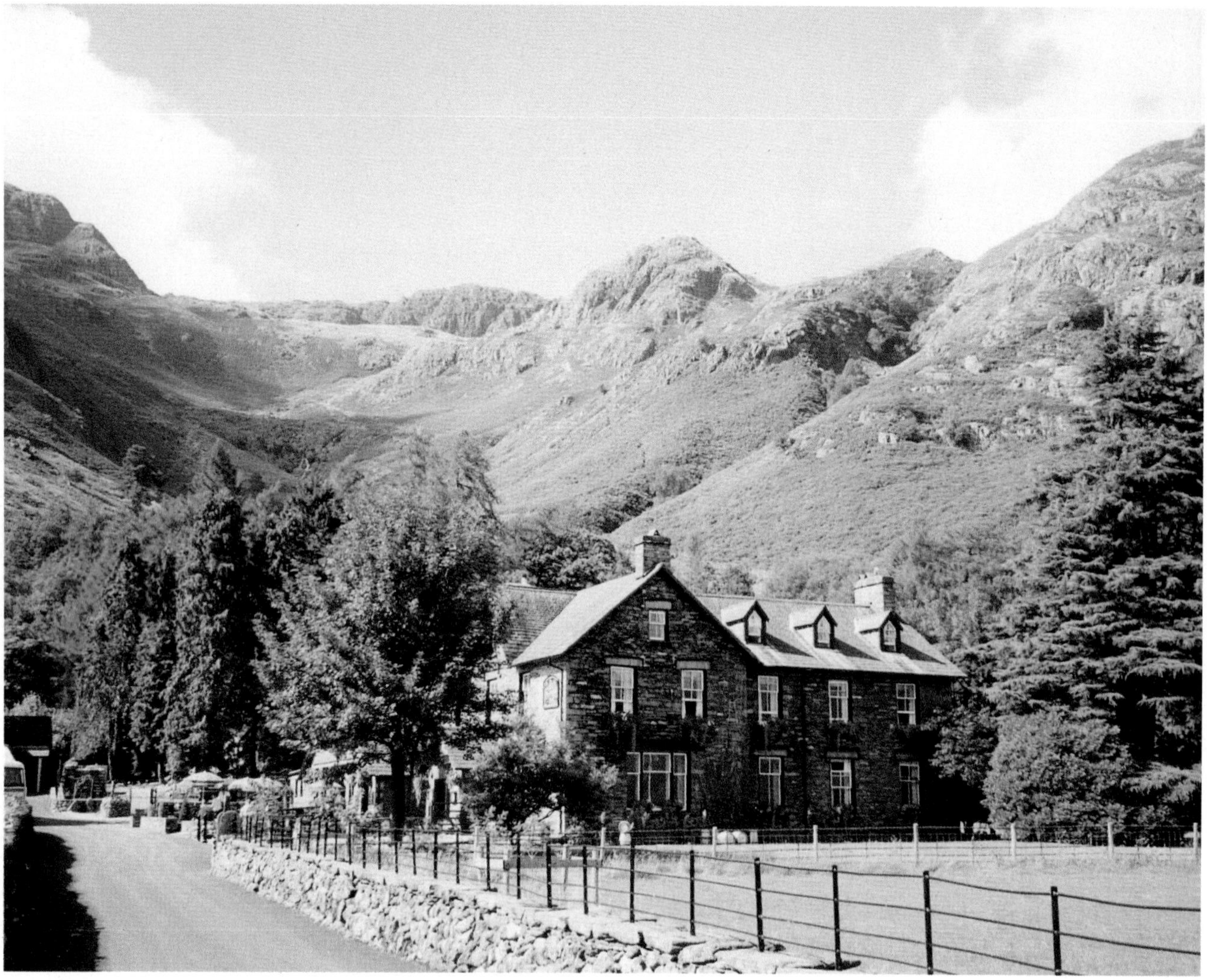

THE NEW DUNGEON GHYLL HOTEL

GREAT LANGDALE, AMBLESIDE, CUMBRIA LA22 9JY
TEL: 015394 37213 FAX: 015394 37666

The splendour of Lakeland's most majestic fells is the setting for The New Dungeon Ghyll Hotel. It is built on the site of an ancient Norse settlement, but was rebuilt as a Victorian Hotel in the 1830s. Bought by John Smith in 1991 and completely refurbished, the hotel stands in its own lawned gardens in a spectacular position beneath the Langdale Pikes and Pavey Ark. The comfortable bedrooms are all en suite and offer colour television, tea and coffee making facilities and direct dial telephones. There are two bars with open fires and the Residents' Bar has an original slate floor. The dining room enjoys panoramic views of the Valley and the Fells beyond. A table d'hôte menu is offered and includes a varied choice of both English and continental dishes. Generous portions are served to satisfy the hearty appetite of a keen walker. A good selection of wines is available to complement the cuisine. The Langdale Valley offers wonderful walking and climbing opportunities in England's most beautiful corner, with abundant wildlife and many places of historical and literary importance. From the hotel guests can walk up Stickle Ghyll to Stickle Tarn and onwards to Pavey Ark, Harrison Stickle and numerous other pikes. **Directions:** M6 junction 36 A591. Through Windermere to Ambleside. Follow A593 towards Coniston, turn right onto B5343 to Langdale. The hotel is two miles past Chapelstyle on the right. Price guide: Single £40–£45; double £59–£70.

For hotel location, see maps on pages 212-218

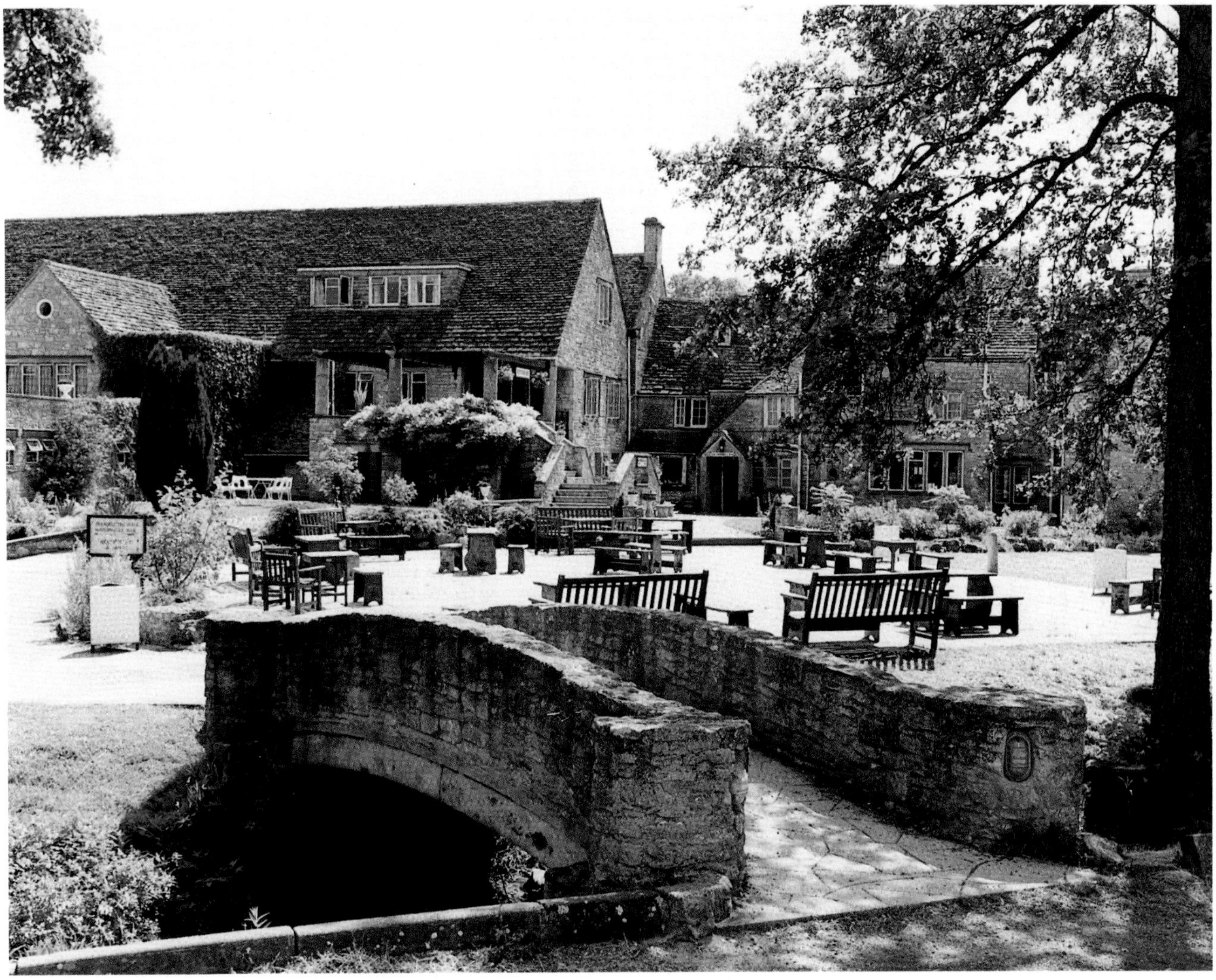

The Frogmill Hotel

SHIPTON, ANDOVERSFORD, NR CHELTENHAM, GLOUCESTERSHIRE GL54 4HT
TEL: 01242 820547 FAX: 01242 820237

Set amidst five acres of beautiful grounds with the River Coln running through them and the rolling Cotswolds beyond, The Frogmill is a very individual hotel renowned for its welcoming and friendly atmosphere. Its character is underlined by the old world charm of original beamed ceilings, centuries old honey-coloured and iron-grey stone walls, huge open log burning fireplaces and polished antique furniture. The Frogmill is mentioned in the Doomsday Book as a working mill in 1087 and was converted into a coaching inn during the 1600's. A water wheel still turns slowly beside the Terrace Restaurant where excellent à la carte and table d'hôte menus are prepared to suit the most discerning diner. The freshest of local produce, game and fish are used in their creation. During summer months a large patio beside the river is an ideal place to wine and dine alfresco. The bar also serves a variety of award-winning dishes. The hotel has a mixture of 16 old world and more modern bedrooms. All are en suite and have every modern comfort and convenience. A 9-hole golf course is adjacent and clay pigeon shooting and archery can be arranged. **Directions:** Six miles east of Cheltenham and 200 yards south of the junction of the A40 and the A436 at Shipton. Price guide: Single £50; double/twin £60.

For hotel location, see maps on pages 212-218

THE ROYAL OAK INN

BONGATE, APPLEBY-IN-WESTMORLAND , CUMBRIA CA16 6UN
TEL: 017683 51463 FAX: 017683 52300 E-MAIL: ApplebyInn@aol.com

The Royal Oak has been a coaching inn since the 1600s and parts of the building are 750 years old. It is a well cared for, traditional hostelry, situated in the oldest part of the north Pennine town of Appleby-in-Westmorland. The oak panelling, beams, stone walls and open fires combine to give the inn its warm, inviting atmosphere. The bedrooms are all individually furnished and all have a private bathroom. Facilities for ironing and clothes-drying are available. Guests will find the owners hospitable and their staff attentive, providing an efficient service. An extensive selection of fresh fish, local meat and vegetarian dishes, together with some unusual specialities, are offered to suit all tastes. There are two dining rooms, one of which is non-smoking and an extensive wine list of over 70 bins. A full Westmorland breakfast is served to set visitors up for a day of sightseeing. The Royal Oak has held an AA rosette for its food since 1996. Hand-pumped ales plus malt whiskies are offered in the Snug and Taproom bars. The inn is well placed for visitors wishing to explore the celebrated scenery of the high moorlands, as well as the numerous castles and historic houses in the area. Running through Appleby is the Settle to Carlisle railway which traverses spectacular remote countryside. **Directions:** The inn can easily be located on the south-east approach to Appleby from the A66 Penrith-Scotch Corner road. Price Guide: Single £44–£55; double £78–£88.

9 rms MasterCard VISA AMERICAN EXPRESS M 20

For hotel location, see maps on pages 212-218

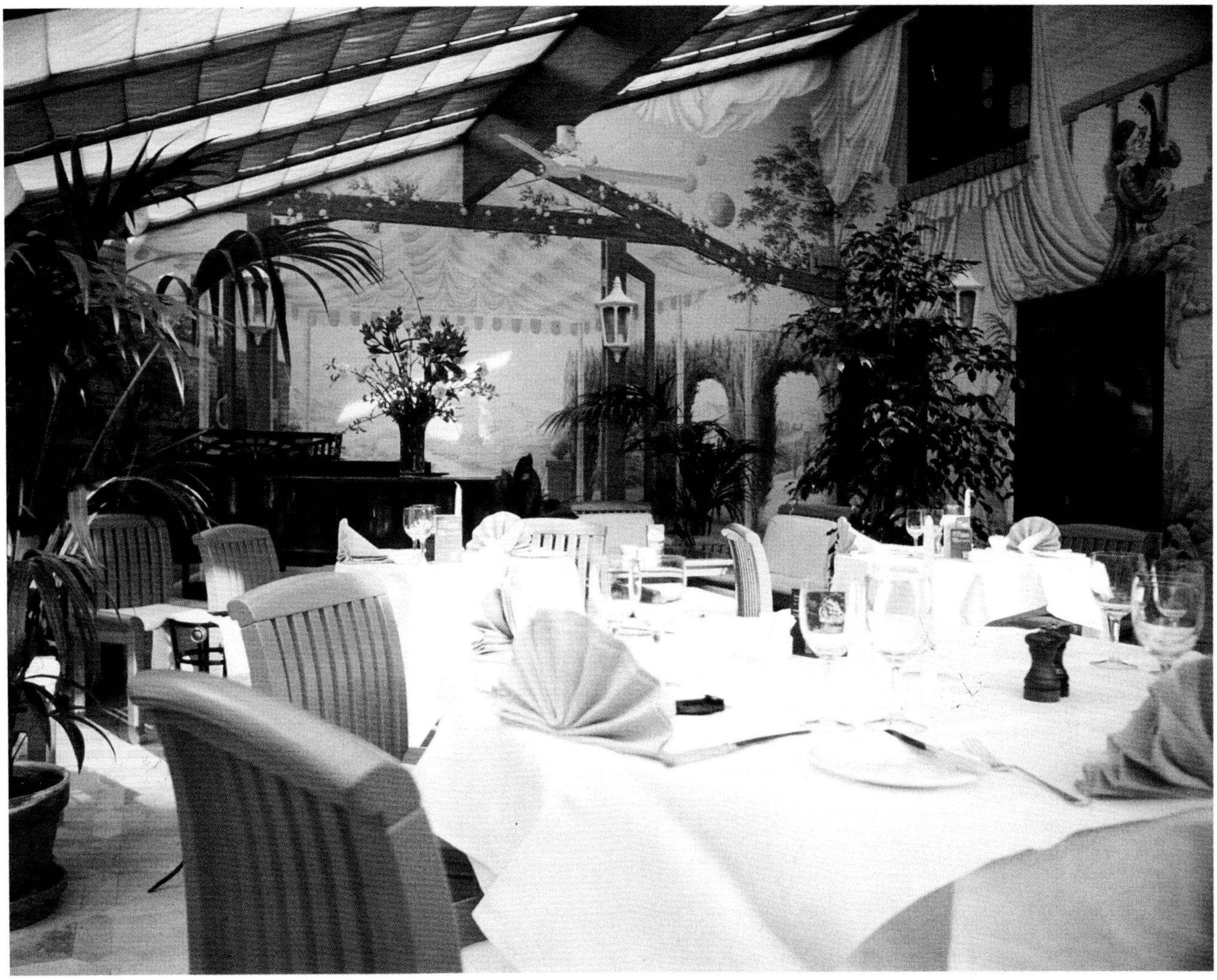

OLD BEAMS

WATERHOUSES, STAFFORDSHIRE ST10 3HW
TEL: 01538 308254 FAX: 01538 308157

Nigel and Ann Wallis' lovely home, dating back to 1746, has developed under their ownership since 1980 to become one of England's top-class provincial restaurants. There is an oak-beamed reception and bar area where pre-dinner drinks can be enjoyed by an open fire, and an enchanting garden comes into play in summer for alfresco drinks and coffee. A converted smithy across the road houses beautifully decorated and individually styled bedrooms, several with four-poster beds. Each named after one of the famous Staffordshire potteries has the luxury of hand-made beds and provides all the little extras to make your stay a memorable one. Meals can be enjoyed in the main restaurant or in the conservatory with its lush foliage and splendid mural. Here Nigel's well-deserved reputation for superb cuisine is truly represented in a succession of exceptional dishes. From grilled lobster served whole to Aberdeen Angus beef and rump of Herdwick lamb only the finest ingredients are used and all are presented with inspired sauces and garnishes. An award-winning wine list of over 130 bins has informative tasting notes and is augmented by a fine selection of whiskies and brandies. The Old Beams Restaurant is ideally situated for visiting the Peak National Park, Alton Towers, Chatsworth and the Staffordshire potteries' visitor centres. **Directions:** Old Beams is on A523 Ashbourne–Leek road, about 35 minutes' drive from M6 or M1. Price guide: Single from £65; double from £75.

5 rms MasterCard VISA AMERICAN EXPRESS M 12

RED LION INN

MAIN STREET, HOGNASTON, ASHBOURNE, DERBYSHIRE DE6 1PR
TEL: 01335 370396 FAX: 01335 370961 E-MAIL: lionrouge@msn.com

The Red Lion is a typical country inn which offers a traditional welcoming atmosphere of good hospitality and homely service. It is situated on the fringe of The Peak District in the main street of the tiny village of Hognaston, just a short drive from the attractive old market town of Ashbourne. With a log fire in the bar, cosy corners, good ales and rustic character, this is a welcome retreat for those wanting a relaxing break or for visitors seeking the opportunity to walk through beautiful countryside. Three individually styled and traditionally furnished bedrooms offer comfortable accommodation. Each bedroom has en suite facilities with a shower. Guests dine in a delightful, sunny conservatory or in the L-shaped bar where the menu is entirely "chalkboard". The choice is extensive and the food is good. Chef Hilary Heskin and her team show considerable expertise in the interesting and imaginative choice of ingredient combinations and sauces that they create and in the way they present them. This wonderful walking country is home to some of England's finest stately homes and National Trust properties such as Sudbury Hall and Kedleston Hall. Other attractions include boating and fishing at Carsington Water, Crich Tramway Museum and Alton Towers. **Directions:** From M1, exit at junction 25 and take A52 towards Derby and Ashbourne. Hognaston is situated on B5035 Ashbourne-Wirksworth road. Price guide: Single £40; double £65.

For hotel location, see maps on pages 212-218

THE KINGS ARMS HOTEL AND RESTAURANT

MARKET PLACE, ASKRIGG-IN-WENSLEYDALE, NORTH YORKSHIRE DL8 3HQ
TEL: 01969 650258 FAX: 01969 650635 E-MAIL: rayliz@kahaskrigg.prestel.co.uk

Ray and Liz Hopwood will welcome you to their country Georgian manor house set amid some of Britain's most emotive scenery, as captured on canvas by Turner during his stay in the early 1800s. Originally built in 1760, the building became an inn in 1810 and it established a tradition of warm hospitality and good food, winning the Yorkshire Life Hotel of the Year award for "outstanding culinary credentials and highly individual period ambience". There are three distinctive bars: one is better known as The Drover's Arms from the BBC television series All Creatures Great and Small. In each of the comfortable bars guests can enjoy an award-winning meal with ales from the cask. Beautifully styled bedrooms include richly draped four-poster, half-tester and brass beds; all thoughtfully appointed to ensure the utmost comfort. The panelled Clubroom Restaurant epitomises elegance and sophistication. The fixed price à la carte menu comprises the freshest of produce, fish and game in season. Special dinners are held regularly to celebrate events in the calendar. An extensive wine list complements the menu. The Silks Grill, also available for private functions, offers steaks, game and fresh fish. The Yorkshire Dales, Settle-Carlisle Railway, Aysgarth Falls and Brontë country are nearby. **Directions:** In the centre of Askrigg, ½ mile from A684 near Bainbridge. This road links A1 at Leeming Bar with M6 at Sedbergh (Jct37). Price Guide: Single £50–£75; double £79–£125.

For hotel location, see maps on pages 212-218

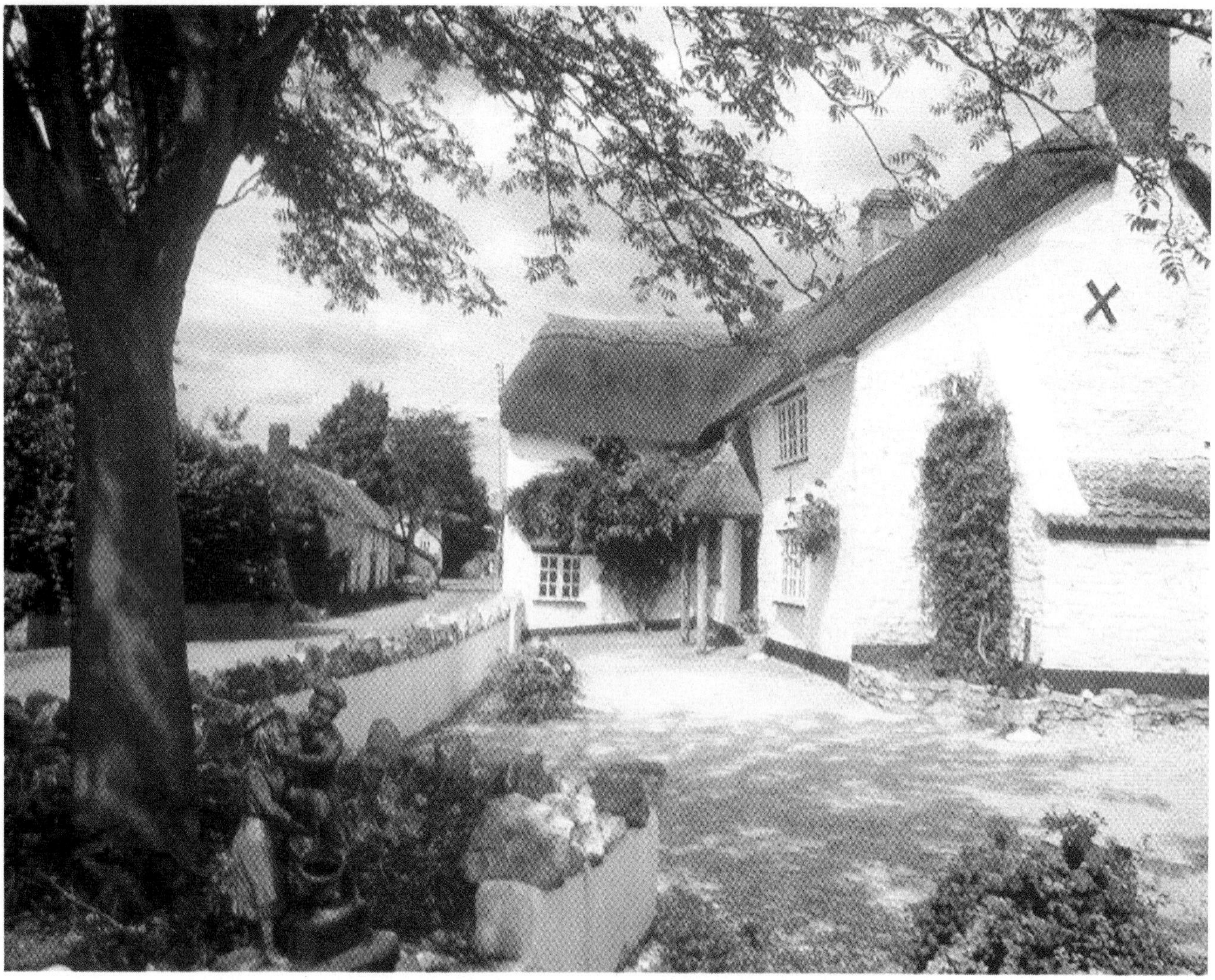

TYTHERLEIGH COT HOTEL

CHARDSTOCK, AXMINSTER, DEVON EX13 7BN

TEL: 01460 221170 FAX: 01460 221291

Originally the village cider house, this 14th century Grade II listed building has been skilfully converted into a spacious modern hotel, idyllically situated in the secluded village of Chardstock on the Devon/Dorset/Somerset borders. The bedrooms, converted from former barns and outbuildings, are all individually designed, some with four-poster or half-tester beds and double Jacuzzis. The beautifully designed award winning restaurant is housed in a Victorian-style conservatory, overlooking an ornamental lily pond with cascading fountain and wrought-iron bridge. Special house parties are held at Christmas and New Year and bargain break weekends can be arranged. The hotel has an outdoor heated swimming pool, sauna, solarium and mini-gym. Riding, tennis, golf and clay pigeon shooting can be arranged locally. The hotel is ideally located for guests to explore the varied landscape of the South West with many historic houses and National Trust properties nearby, such as Forde Abbey, Shute Barton and Parnham House. **Directions:** From Chard take A358 Axminster road; Chardstock signposted on the right about 3 miles along. Price guide: Single £55; double/twin £65–£85.

For hotel location, see maps on pages 212-218

THE WINDMILL AT BADBY

MAIN STREET, BADBY, NR DAVENTRY, NORTHAMPTONSHIRE NN11 6AN
TEL: 01327 702363 FAX: 01327 311521

The Windmill Inn Hotel was first established as an inn in the 17th century and is situated in the heart of the pretty village of Badby. A traditional thatched country pub, complete with log fires, The Windmill offers good food and a range of cask-conditioned ales. The owners, with their extensive experience of hotel and pub management, have plenty of ideas for regular activities. Winter Sportsmen's Dinners and theme nights with entertainment are popular events. The en suite bedrooms provide comfortable accommodation and the whole hotel is ideally suitable for house party weekends from 12–14 guests. Under the skilled eye of Gavin Baxter, the kitchen prepares a varied range of freshly cooked dishes. Many specialities are made and these include Stilton mushrooms, char-grilled Cajun chicken, steak and kidney pie and poached salmon with new potatoes. Weddings, functions and business conferences are catered for with ease. The surrounding woods and meadows provide excellent walking (Badby is the start of both the Knightley and Nene Ways). Places to visit include Althorp Park (only 7 miles), Canons Ashby, Sulgrave Manor (home of the Washingtons), Blenheim Palace, Silverstone Circuit, Warwick and Stratford-upon-Avon. **Directions:** The Windmill is in the centre of Badby, a village located off the A361, three miles south of Daventry on the Banbury road. Price Guide: Single £45–£49; double £69–£79.

8 rms MasterCard VISA AMERICAN EXPRESS M 50

THE PHEASANT

BASSENTHWAITE LAKE, NR COCKERMOUTH, CUMBRIA CA13 9YE
TEL: 017687 76234 FAX: 017687 76002

This famous 17th century coaching inn is set in lovely gardens and woodlands just 100 yards from the shores of Bassenthwaite Lake. Renowned for its friendly hospitality, The Pheasant has 20 light and airy bedrooms, each comfortably furnished and with private facilities. Three are located in the bungalow next to the hotel. Guests have three sitting rooms to choose from when they want to enjoy a quiet morning coffee or a real Cumbrian afternoon tea with home-made specialities including scones with brandy butter. The bar, with its polished walls and oak settles, is said to be one of the best known in the Lake District. With its traditional setting and convivial atmosphere, this is the perfect place to enjoy a drink before moving on to dinner. The cuisine served in the lovely beamed dining room includes many local Cumbrian specialities, in addition to traditional English food and a wide selection of fine wines. A daily changing menu includes culinary delights to cater for all. The Pheasant is within easy reach of the whole Lake District. Usually chosen for its idyllic and peaceful location, the hotel makes a convenient base for guests on fishing, bird-watching or sporting expeditions. **Directions:** Just off the A66, The Pheasant is 6 miles east of Cockermouth and 8 miles north-west of Keswick. Price guide: Single £59–£79; double £90–£112.

For hotel location, see maps on pages 212-218

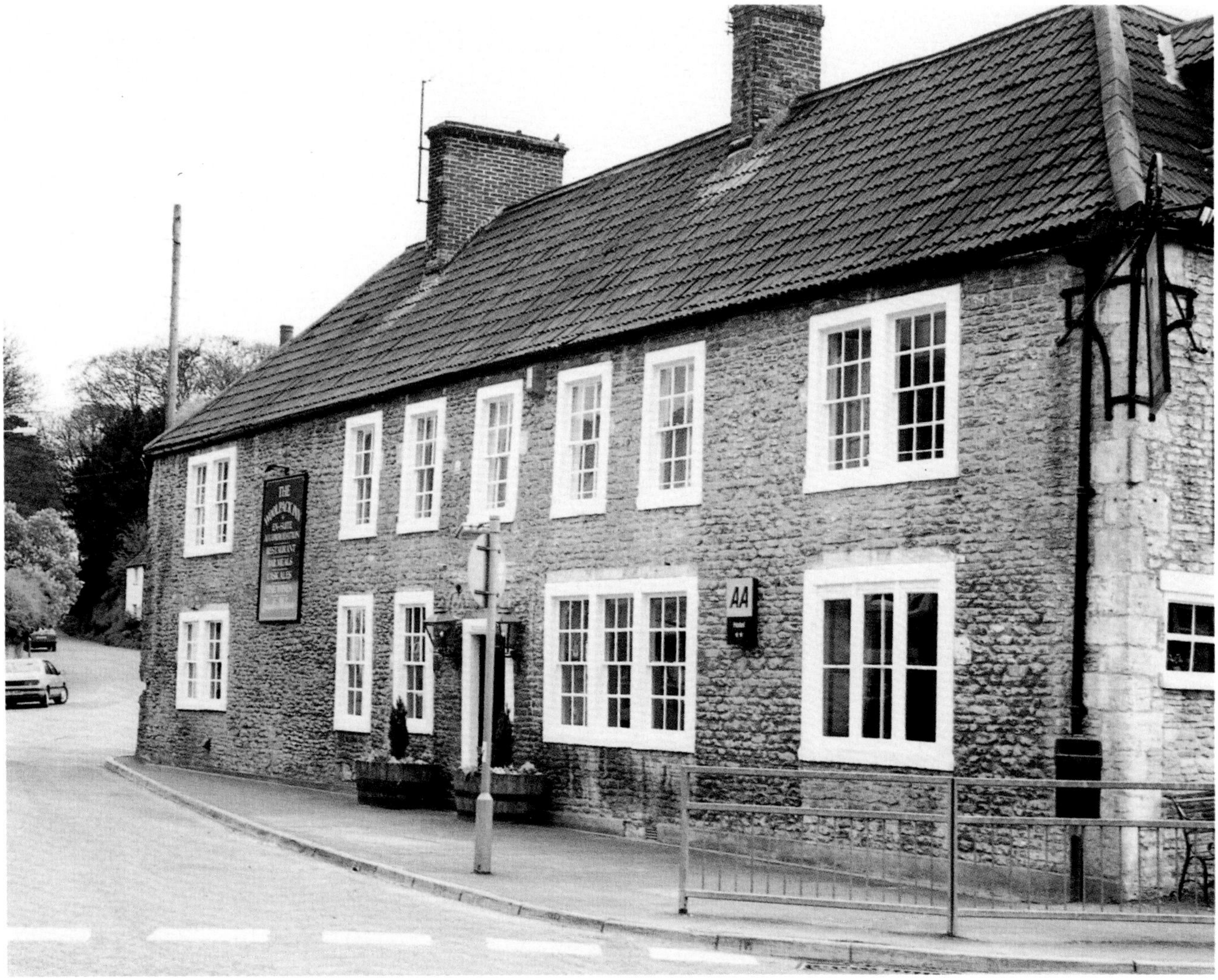

THE WOOLPACK INN

BECKINGTON, NR BATH, SOMERSET BA3 6SP
TEL: 01373 831244 FAX: 01373 831223

Situated in the centre of the village of Beckington, on the borders of Somerset, Avon and Wiltshire, The Woolpack is a small coaching inn dating from the 16th century. Legend has it that condemned criminals were allowed a final drink here before being led away to the local gallows. The inn has been thoughtfully decorated and furnished to recapture the original character of the building. On the ground floor is the bar area, with its stone floor and open log fire, where fine traditional ale is served. There is also a small lounge. Each of the 12 bedrooms has been individually renovated, each having an en suite bathroom and all modern comforts. There are places to visit nearby in abundance: the Georgian city of Bath, the cathedral cities of Salisbury and Wells, Longleat House and Safari Park, Lacock, Glastonbury, Stourhead, Cheddar Gorge and Wookey Hole, the stone circles at Stonehenge and Avebury, and the tropical bird gardens at Rode. **Directions:** Beckington, recently bypassed, is on the A36 Bath–Southampton road on the borders of Somerset and Wiltshire. Price guide: Single £55; double £65–£85.

For hotel location, see maps on pages 212-218

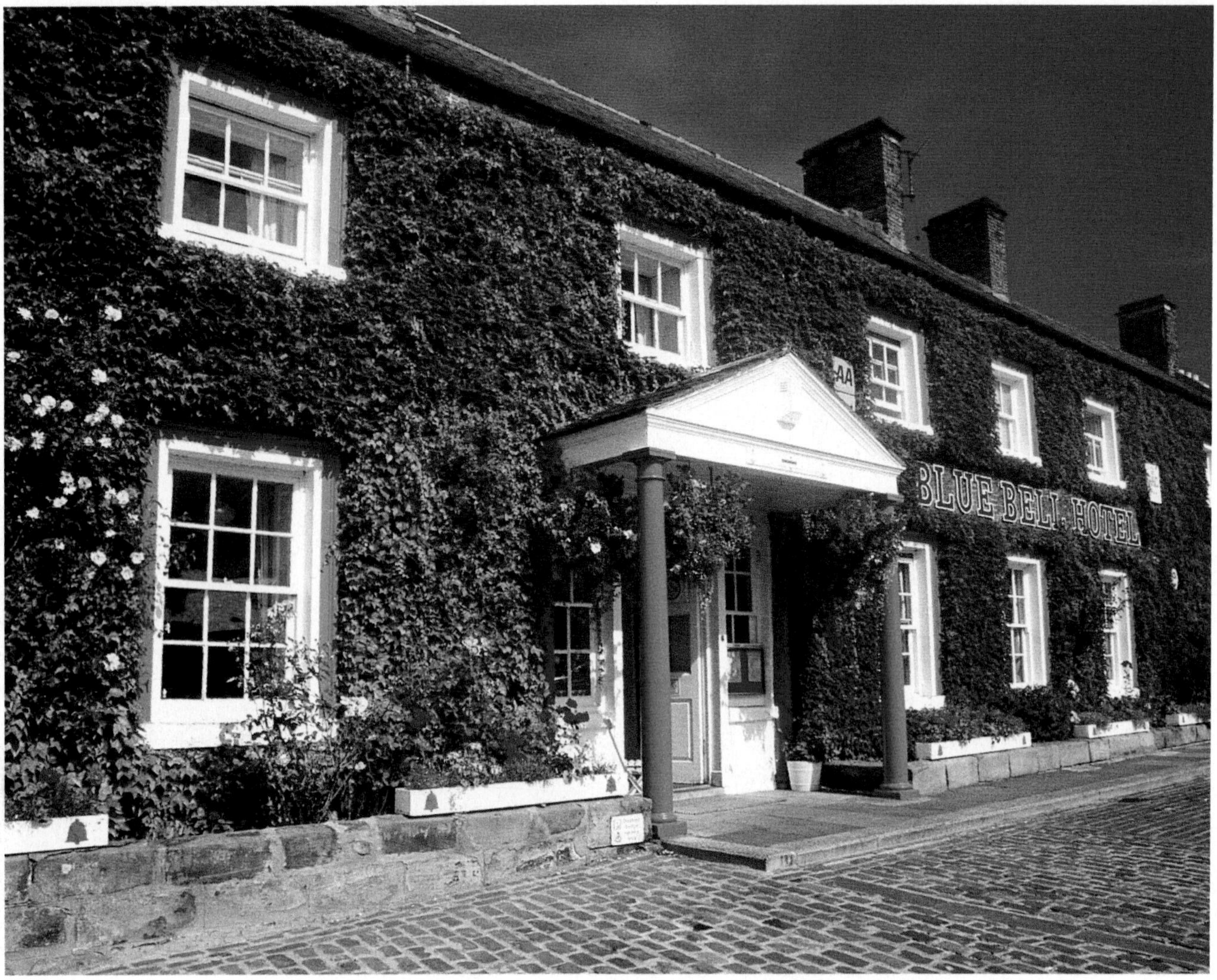

THE BLUE BELL HOTEL

MARKET PLACE, BELFORD, NORTHUMBERLAND NE70 7NE
TEL: 01668 213543 FAX: 01668 213787 E-MAIL: bluebel@globalnet.co.uk

This beautifully restored old coaching inn stands in the centre of Belford, near the old Market Cross. The sophisticated Georgian-style interiors are decorated to complement the original features. Luxurious bedrooms provide every modern comfort and are all unique. There is an elegant residents' lounge and two bars, well stocked with fine malts, rare brandies and vintage ports. The hotel also has three acres of walled terraced grounds, with a putting lawn and an organic vegetable and herb garden. The emphasis is on freshness with fruit and vegetables from the hotel gardens, combined with an excellent supply of fresh local produce such as Cheviot lamb, Tweed salmon and Craster kippers, creating a range of delicious seasonal dishes. Frequently changing à la carte and table d'hôte menus are served in the garden restaurant, which is furnished with locally crafted tables. For a more simple but substantial menu, try the Buttery. There is much to discover along Northumberland's scenic coastline – the Farne Islands, Lindsifarne and Berwick-upon-Tweed are among the many interesting attractions. Sporting activities which can be enjoyed locally include shooting, fishing, riding and golf. Directions: Midway between Berwick and Alnwick, about 14 miles south of Berwick and two minutes from the A1. From A1 turn off at Belford/Wooler junction to join the B6349. The hotel is situated in the centre of the village. Price guide: Single £38–£60; double £76–£98.

For hotel location, see maps on pages 212-218

CATHERINE WHEEL

BIBURY, NR CIRENCESTER, GLOUCESTERSHIRE GL7 5ND
TEL: 01285 740250 FAX: 01285 740779

The 15th century Catherine Wheel is located centrally in Bibury, the Cotswold village described by William Morris as "the most beautiful in England". Straddling the River Coln, this pre-Roman settlement was listed in the Domesday Book: amongst today's attractions are the trout farm and Arlington Mill Museum, just a stroll down the hill from the inn. In the main bar area there is clear evidence of former 15th century dwellings and recent refurbishment has retained many original features entirely in keeping with its history, including the many exposed ships' timber beams. The Arlington Bar commemorates Old Bibury in fine prints and old photographs and its warm hospitality is reflected in the large open fires that blaze in wintertime. Equally popular in summer is the ancient apple and pear orchard which provides plenty of shaded seating for a refreshing drink. The two double and two family bedrooms have thoroughly modern en suite bathrooms, colour televisions and complimentary hot drink trays. The extensive dining areas are run on informal lines, offering a wide choice of traditional British Pub fare. The fresh Bibury trout are perennially popular: fine roast beef for Sunday lunch and daily chef's special dishes provide an array of alternatives. Nearby are the ancient cottages of Arlington Row and the wonderful gardens of Barnsley House. **Directions:** Bibury stands on B4425 between Cirencester and Burford. Price guide: £40 per room plus £5 per head for breakfast.

For hotel location, see maps on pages 212-218

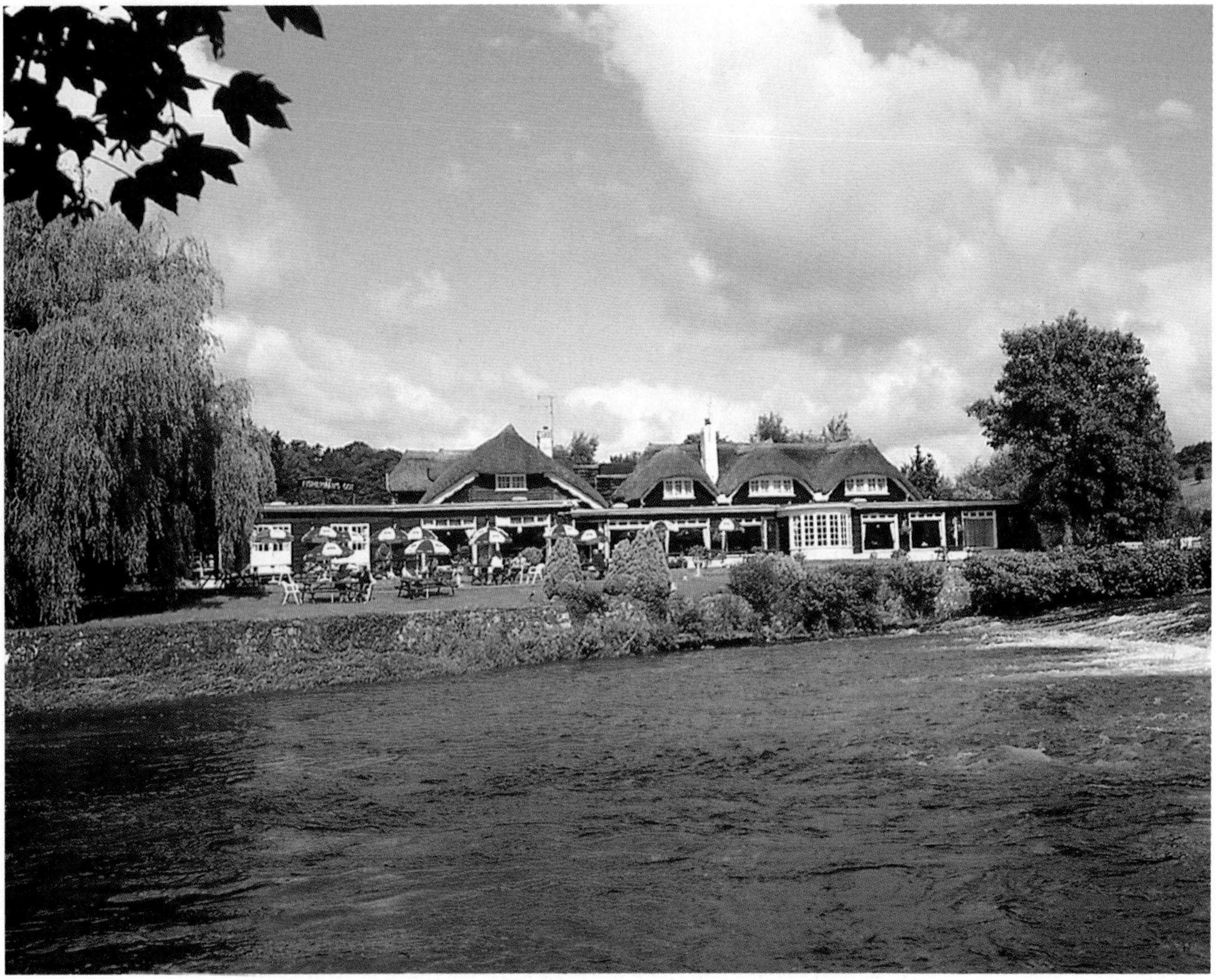

THE FISHERMAN'S COT

BICKLEIGH, NR TIVERTON, DEVON EX16 8RW
TEL: 01884 855237/855289 FAX: 01884 855241

This picturesque, rambling, thatched inn, surrounded by thickly wooded hillsides, stands on the west bank of the River Exe. Bickleigh Bridge nearby dates from the middle ages. The charming traditional bars and comfortable, rooms combined with tasteful furnishings create a relaxing atmosphere which tempts guests to return again and again. The Fisherman's Cot is excellent value for money with the 21 en suite bedrooms having every home-from-home facility. They vary in size, but all enjoy the character of old world charm. Superbly prepared cuisine can be enjoyed in the warmly panelled restaurant which in the summer months opens onto a terrace overlooking the river. The inn is an ideal base for guests who enjoy walking, riding and fishing. For those who like history, Bickleigh Castle is nearby along with Tiverton Castle and Tiverton Canal with its horse-drawn barges are all within easy reach. Directions: From the M5 exit at junction 27. At Tiverton take the A396 to Bickleigh. Alternatively, follow the A 396 from Exeter city centre. Price guide: Single from £46; double/twin from £66. Bargain short breaks available.

For hotel location, see maps on pages 212-218

STAG & HOUNDS

FOREST ROAD, BINFIELD, NR BRACKNELL, BERKSHIRE RG12 9HA
TEL: 01344 483553 FAX: 01344 423620

The Stag & Hounds is a charming 14th century inn with a fascinating history. It has strong hunting connections and was a favourite with Henry VIII on his regular hunting trips to Great Windsor Park and the surrounding areas. It is also believed that Elizabeth I enjoyed watching the locals dancing round the maypole from the windows of the inn. A tree stump in front of the inn marks the original centre of the Great Park and it is now a protected monument. Visitors to the Stag & Hounds can expect a very warm welcome and excellent hospitality. It is full of character, tastefully decorated, comfortably furnished and has retained many original features - all that is best in a British pub, complemented by delicious dishes from a comprehensive menu and a superb selection of beers and wines. Binfield village, with its 14th century church, is ideally situated for exploring the many delights of Berkshire. Nearby is Ascot and its popular racecourse, Eton with its famous college and historic Windsor. **Directions:** From the M4, exit at junction 10. Take the A329 towards Bracknell and at the first exit turn left onto the B3408. Continue through Binfield village and turn left at the mini roundabout, signed Bracknell and Warfield. The Stag & Hounds is approximately half a mile further on.

For hotel location, see maps on pages 212-218

WHITE HORSE HOTEL

4 HIGH STREET, BLAKENEY, HOLT, NORFOLK NR25 7AL
TEL: 01263 740574 FAX: 01263 741303

The White Horse was formerly a 18th century coaching inn and in the early 1900s became the first hotel in Blakeney, a popular boating centre with a main street of brick and flint buildings and a waterfront crowded with sailing craft and cruisers. Set around a shady courtyard, the hotel has ten simple and uncluttered en suite bedrooms, some with good views across the harbour, the National Trust reserve and marshes. All have colour television, telephone and tea and coffee making facilities. A comfortable residents sitting room is available. The area is much favoured by artists and the hotel has its own gallery with regularly changing exhibitions. No dogs. Situated in the former stables which overlook the walled garden, the restaurant is light and airy and has an attractive relaxed style. Chef Christopher Hyde offers a seasonal à la carte menu using local fare. Lobsters, sea bass, pheasant and pigeons are favourites with special dishes introduced daily on the restaurant blackboard. Bar food includes whitebait, herring roes, crab salads and mussels. The meals are complemented by a good choice of wines and ales. The sandy resorts of Sheringham and Cromer, boat trips to Blakeney Point Nature Reserve, the Norfolk Coast Path, Blickling Hall and Holkham Hall are all nearby. There is sailing, fishing, riding and golf ar Cromer and Sheringham. **Directions:** From Norwich, take A140 to Cromer and then A149 coastal road west for approx. 12m. Price guide: Single £35; double £70; suite £80.

10 rms MasterCard VISA AMERICAN EXPRESS M 25

For hotel location, see maps on pages 212-218

DIAL HOUSE

THE CHESTNUTS, HIGH STREET, BOURTON-ON-THE-WATER , GLOUCESTERSHIRE GL54 2AN
TEL: 01451 822244 FAX: 01451 810126

In the heart of the Cotswolds lies Dial House Hotel, a small 17th century country house which combines the charm and elegance of a bygone era with all the facilities of a modern hotel. Proprietors Lynn and Peter Boxall have 26 years experience in the hotel industry and extend a warm welcome to their guests. The hotel is open throughout the year and roaring log fires burn throughout the winter months. In the summer, lunches are served in the delightful and secluded walled garden. Chef Callam Williamson creates delicious, freshly-cooked food for the à la carte restaurant, which creates an aura of old England with its inglenook fireplace and oak beams. Dial House has received 2 AA Rosettes for its cuisine and every care is taken by friendly staff to provide guests with an interesting choice of dishes and good quality wines. An open fire in the comfortable lounge creates an ideal setting to finish off an evening with coffee and liqueurs. The décor of the bedrooms is light and cheery. Some have antique four-poster beds and overlook the garden. All are en suite, centrally-heated and equipped with tea and coffee making facilities. Bargain breaks available. Stratford-Upon-Avon, Bath and Cirencester, Warwick Castle, Blenheim Palace, Cheltenham, Slimbridge Wildfowl Trust and Oxford are all nearby. **Directions:** Bourton-on-the-Water is 4 miles south west of Stow-on-the-Wold off A429. Price Guide: Single from £48; double from £96.

For hotel location, see maps on pages 212-218

THE MANOR HOTEL

WEST BEXINGTON, DORCHESTER, DORSET DT2 9DF
TEL: 01308 897616 FAX: 01308 897035

The Manor Hotel, winner of the 1997 Johansens Most Excellent Inn Award and also mentioned in the Domesday Book, is in a wonderful setting, overlooking the beautiful Dorset countryside and spectacular Lyme Bay. The friendly atmosphere is apparent immediately on entering the inn, while the oak-panelling, stone walls and original fireplaces remind guests they are in the midst of history. The restaurant is brilliant, with two or three course menus that include wonderful choices - smoked duck breast and mango salad, lobster and scallop ragout, roast salmon and prawns with a lime and avocado salsa or roast pork with sage crust and apple sauce. Vegetarian dishes also feature, and there is a children's menu. The wine list is exciting. Buffet meals, also including seafood, are served in the cosy cellar bar. There is an attractive conservatory for relaxing while children have their own play area outside. There are twelve charming en suite bedrooms and those at the top of the house have splendid views over the sea. This is Thomas Hardy country and there are famous gardens and historic houses to visit. Chesil Beach and Abbotsbury Swannery are nearby and water sports and country pursuits can be enjoyed. **Directions:** West Bexington is on the B3157, 5 miles east of Bridport, 11 miles from Dorchester and Weymouth. Price guide: Single £49–£54; double £98–£108.

12 rms

For hotel location, see maps on pages 212-218

THE BOARS HEAD

MAIN ROAD, AUST, BRISTOL BS12 3AX
TEL: 01454 632581 FAX: 01454 632278

The delightful, welcoming 16th century Boars Head is situated remotely down a maze of narrow lanes just outside the tiny village of Aust. It is almost too comfortable and special to be an inn. Beautifully decorated and furnished, its interior is broken up with lots of intimate areas which feature soft seating, large sofas and armchairs. The Boars Head is enthusiastically run by Brian Holder and Mary May who say that many visitors apologise after stepping through the front door because they believe they have wandered into someone's private home. There is no public bar, just comfortable armchairs where visitors can relax over their newspapers or a friendly chat. Open fires burn logs resembling small tree trunks during winter months. The inn is a favourite lunchtime venue with business executives from Bristol, Avonmouth, Chepstow and Newport and an evening attraction for the locals. All are drawn by the hospitable atmosphere and excellent traditional food. Tempting dishes include such delights as River Severn salmon, trout from Cirencester and plaice served with Evesham asparagus when in season. A short drive away, at Thornbury, is the unfinished "castle" of the Duke of Buckingham, one of the most imposing Tudor buildings in the west of England. There are no bedrooms. **Directions:** M4 to M48 turn off at Junction 1 and join the A403 to Aust.

For hotel location, see maps on pages 212-218

The New Inn

BADMINTON ROAD, MAYSHILL, NR FRAMPTON COTTRELL, BRISTOL BS17 2NT
TEL/FAX: 01454 773161

Built as a rest-stop for travellers on the road north from Bristol via Chipping Sodbury, this lovely 17th century inn has a unique rustic charm. It is a superb example of a historic coaching inn and the hospitality afforded to those early passengers and coachmen is just as generous today. It is a delightfully unspoilt tavern. A plaque discovered inserted above the fireplace in an upstairs room bears the date 1655 and it is now displayed in the main bar. Although renovated and sympathetically modernised, many of the fitments and the unevenness of the floors and ceilings ensure that much of the New Inn's 300-year-old character remains. A rotating hook for supporting a baby's cradle away from the fire hangs from the ceiling in the traditionally furnished Says Court Lounge. Popular with locals, the inn's fine range of beers, good homely food and conviviality also attracts visitors from miles around. The shopping and entertainment delights of Bristol are close by. It is worth visiting the 14th century church of St James at Iron Acton to see stained glass from the Middle Ages. Popular daytime excursions also include trips to Dyram Park, a country mansion with extensive parkland overlooking the valley of the Severn. **Directions:** The New Inn is situated a just few miles north of Bristol, off the A342 road to Yate.

For hotel location, see maps on pages 212-218

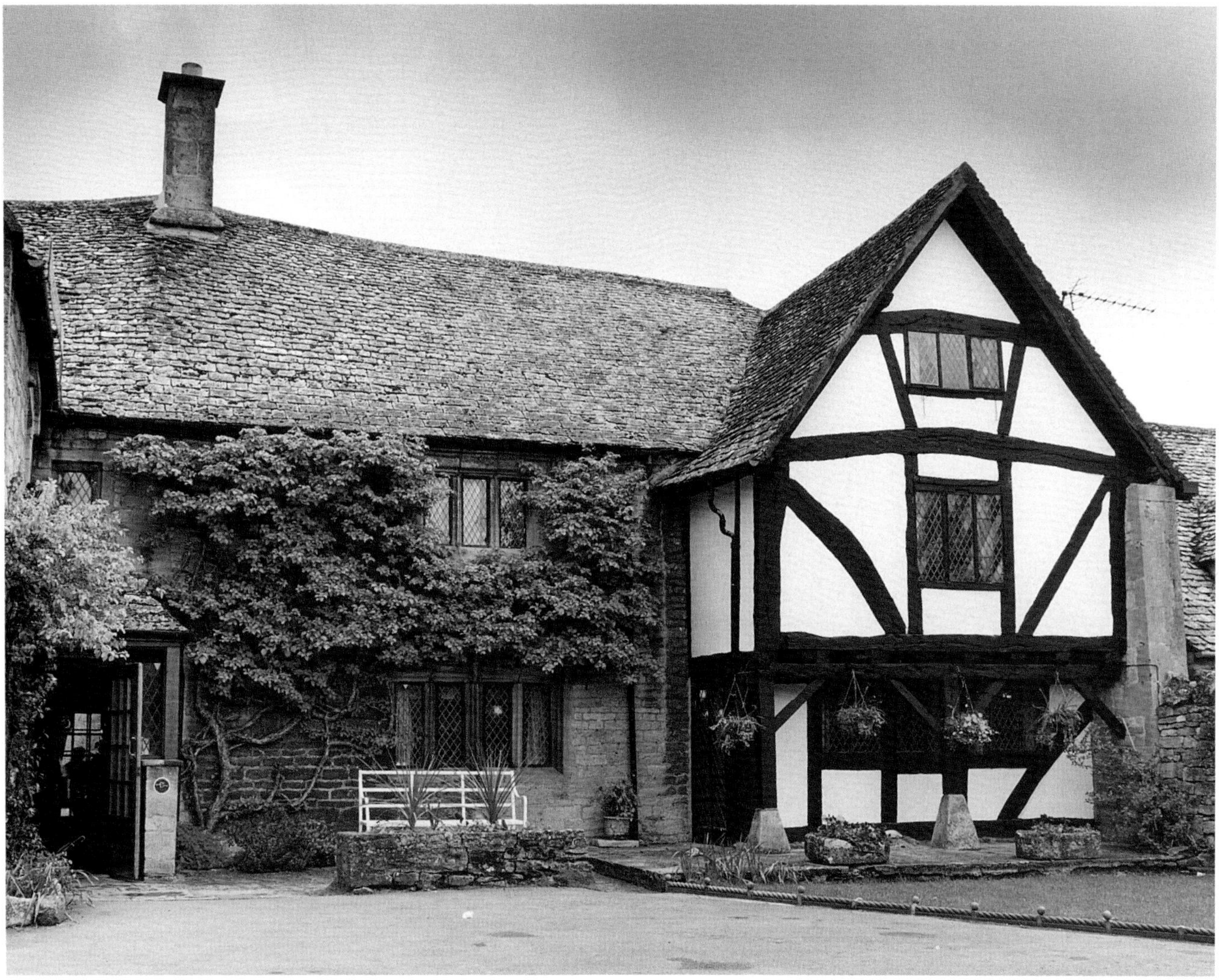

THE BROADWAY HOTEL AND RESTAURANT

THE GREEN, BROADWAY, WORCESTERSHIRE WR12 7AA
TEL: 01386 852401 FAX: 01386 853879

The delightful Broadway Hotel stands proudly in the centre of the picturesque Cotswold village of Broadway where every stone evokes memories of Elizabethan England. Once used by the Abbots of Pershore, the hotel was formerly a 16th century house, as can be seen by its architecture which combines the half timbers of the Vale of Evesham with the distinctive honey-coloured and grey stone of the Cotswolds. It epitomises a true combination of old world charm and modern day amenities with friendly efficient service. All of the bedrooms provide a television, telephone and tea and coffee making facilities. Traditional English dishes and a peaceful ambience are offered in the beamed Courtyard Restaurant. There is an impressive variety of à la carte dishes complemented by a good wine list. The cosy and congenial Jockey Club bar is a pleasant place to relax and enjoy a drink. The inn overlooks the village green at the bottom of the main street where guests can browse through shops offering an array of fine antiques. On a clear day, 13 counties of England and Wales can be viewed from Broadway Tower. Snowhill, Burford, Chipping Campden, Bourton-on-the-Water, Stow-on-the-Wold and Winchcombe as well as larger Cheltenham, Worcester and Stratford are within easy reach. **Directions:** From London M40 to Oxford, A40 to Burford, A424 through Stow-on-the-Wold, then A44 to Broadway. Price guide: Single £58.50–£60; double £95–£110.

For hotel location, see maps on pages 212-218

THE SNAKECATCHER

LYNDHURST ROAD, BROCKENHURST, HAMPSHIRE SO42 7RL
TEL: 01590 622348 FAX: 01590 624155

The Snakecatcher is one of the New Forest's most delightful inns and incorporates buildings used as stabling for coaching traffic before the arrival of the railway in 1847. Then they were converted into The Railway Inn and in 1983 it was renamed after a local customer, Harry "Brusher" Mills, who roamed the Forest catching adders for payment and brushed the wicket of the nearby cricket pitch. Refurbishment has extended and enhanced The Snakecatcher's facilities but much of the traditional character and features remain, including a skittle alley in Brusher's Bar. The furniture, fittings and décor are in keeping with the inn's history and an excellent range of beers is complemented by good, wholesome, home-cooked food. There are open fires to comfort winter visitors while during the summer months they can sip refreshments in a charming little garden and, on occasions, enjoy the inn's brass band concerts. Although a lot of the village dates from the railway age there are some 17th century cottages and The Church of St Nicholas is mentioned in the Domesday Book of 1086. It is an ideal base from which to explore the New Forest and for visiting such places as Beaulieu, Broadlands, Salisbury and Winchester. **Directions:** The Snakecatcher is on the A337 between Lyndhurst and Lymington, reached from the M27 via junction 1.

For hotel location, see maps on pages 212-218

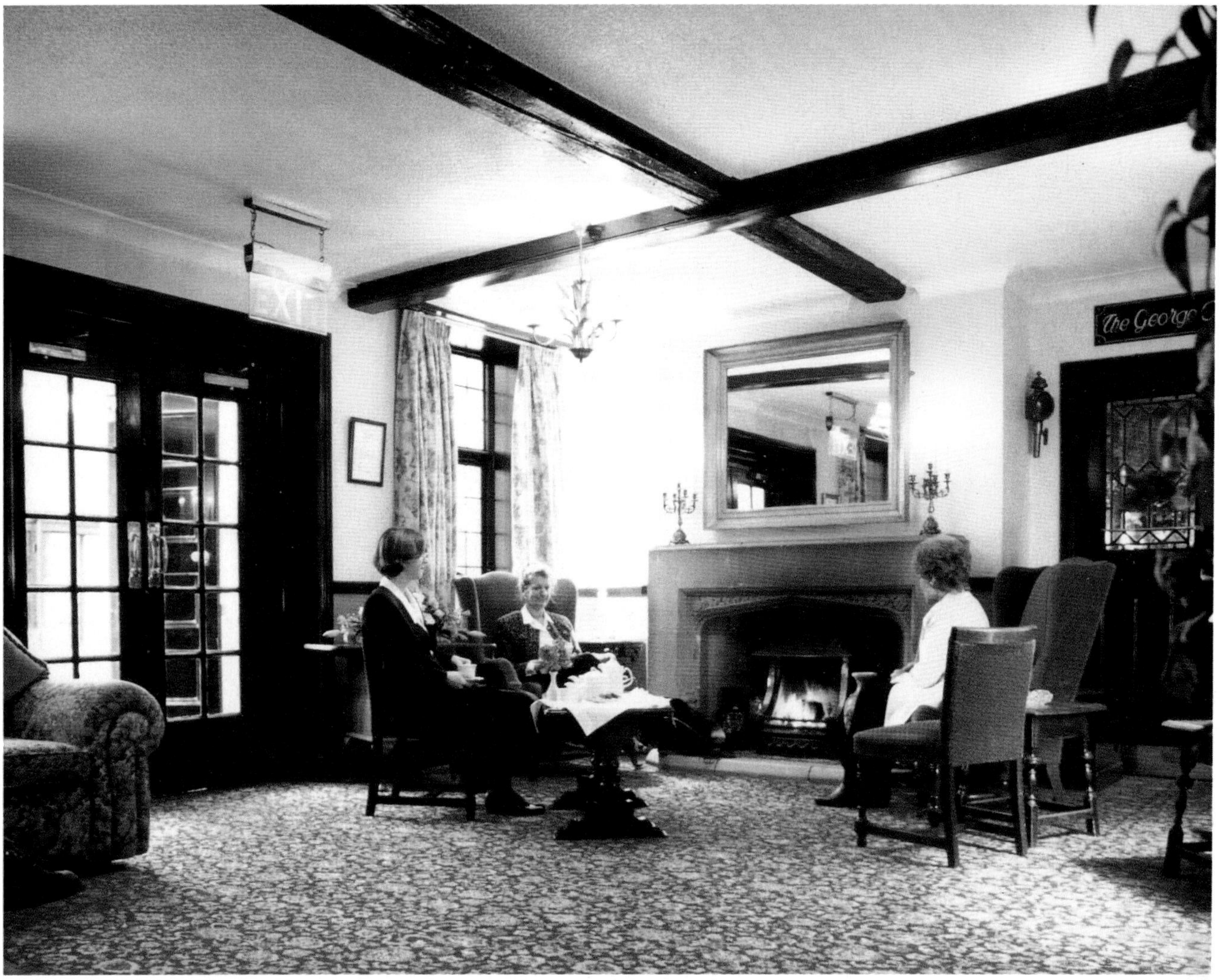

THE GEORGE COACHING INN

THE OLD GREAT NORTH ROAD, BUCKDEN, HUNTINGDON, CAMBRIDGESHIRE PE18 9XA
TEL: 01480 810307 FAX: 01480 811274

The historic village of Buckden stands deep in Cromwell country and at its heart the 17th-century George Coaching Inn reflects its former importance as a staging post on the York to London mail route. There is a warm welcome here from the friendly staff and this is echoed in the log fire and comfortable sofas that greet guests in the reception lounge. The adjacent George Cartwright Bar is equally convivial with its beams and open fire. There are chef's daily suggestions offered in the bar and an alternative menu, should diners prefer something light. In The Georgian Restaurant à la carte meals and Sunday lunches of excellent quality are freshly prepared and cooked to order by chef Stephen Lewis. High quality ingredients, both traditional and contemporary, are presented in a modern style. The bedrooms are bright and welcoming, with up-to-date appointments and well-equipped bathrooms. Some, including the bridal suite, feature lace-draped four-poster beds and on special occasions guests can expect to be greeted by fresh flowers and champagne. Nearby are Grafham Water for sailing, canoeing and water-skiing, Buckden Manor and horse-racing at Huntingdon. Within easy reach is the university city of Cambridge and the cathedrals of Ely and Peterborough. **Directions:** Buckden is signposted off A1 two miles south of its junction with A14. The George is on the village High Street. Price guide: Single £63–£72; double/twin £84–£88.

For hotel location, see maps on pages 212-218

THE DARTBRIDGE INN

TOTNES ROAD, BUCKFASTLEIGH, DEVON TQ11 0JR
TEL: 01364 642214 FAX: 01364 643977

This is one of Devon's loveliest inns, famed for its magnificent, award-winning external floral displays and its picturesque location on the banks of the beautiful River Dart at the gateway to the mountains, moors, valleys and woods of Dartmoor National Park. Luxurious furnishings, oak panelling, open fires and superb cuisine combine to create a charming and restful atmosphere. Diners can enjoy chef Paul Ralph's extensive à la carte menu or choose from a 'Daily Special' board offering up to 25 dishes that includes guinea fowl, pheasant, turkey and veal. Bar snacks are served either inside or on the long, flower filled terrace. There are 11 tastefully decorated and comfortably furnished bedrooms. All are en suite, centrally heated and have television and tea and coffee making facilities. Guests can easily stroll to the nearby famous Salmon Leap and close by is Buckfast Abbey, a butterfly farm and otter sanctuary. The historic town of Totnes with its Norman castle is a 10 minutes drive and the picturesque little towns and villages of Dartmoor National Park are within easy reach. **Directions:** Take the A38 from Exeter towards Plymouth. Turn left at the Totnes exit onto the A384 and The Dartbridge Inn is on the left after approximately 300 yards. Price guide: Single £45; double £65.

For hotel location, see maps on pages 212-218

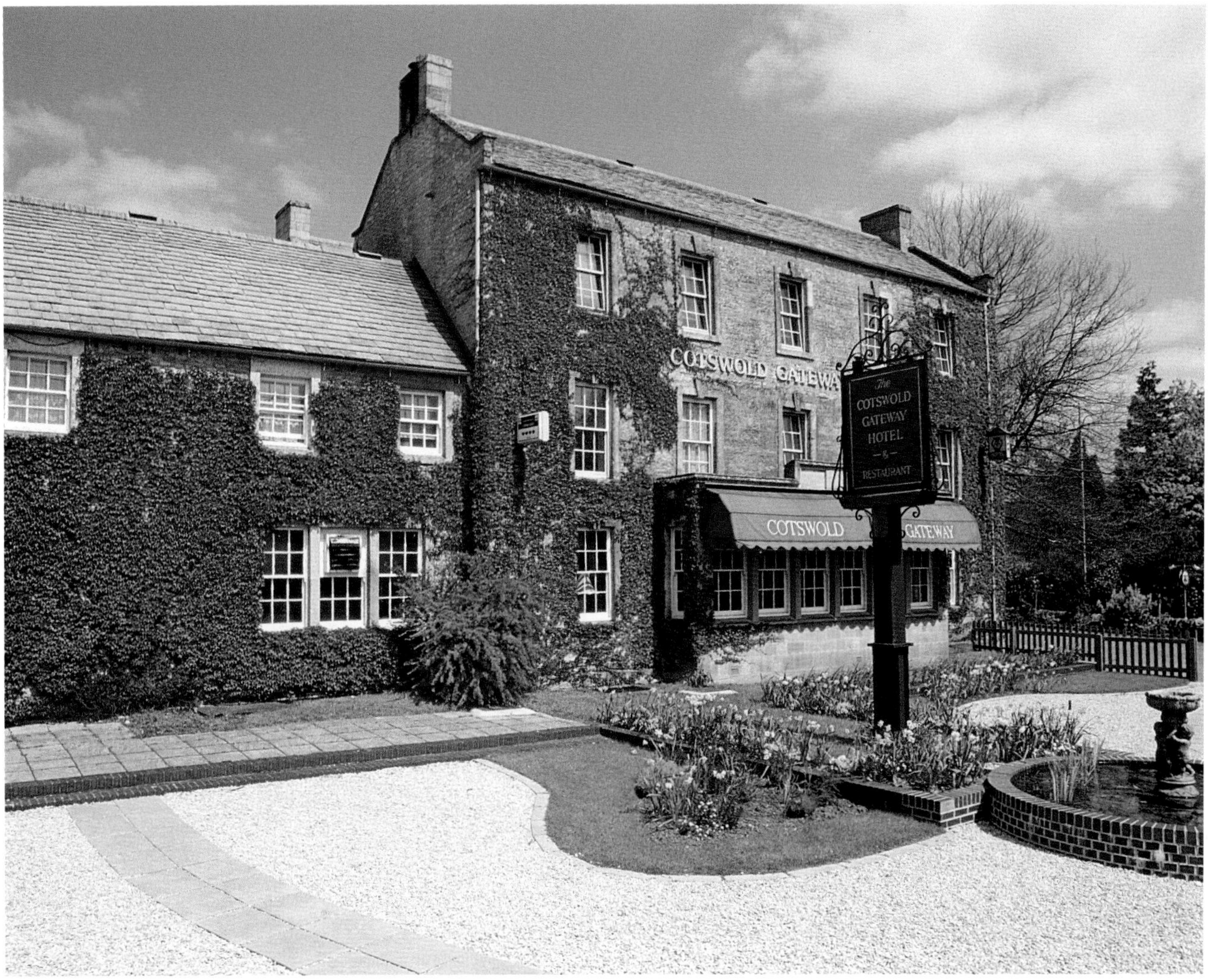

Cotswold Gateway Hotel

CHELTENHAM ROAD, BURFORD, OXFORDSHIRE OX18 4HX

TEL: 01993 822695 FAX: 01993 823600 E-MAIL: cotswold.gateway@dialpipex.com.l.c

In the days of horse drawn coaches Cotswold Gateway Hotel was a welcome stopover for travellers visiting Burford. Today, this 18th century inn, which has recently been lavishly renovated, offers its guests every modern comfort and amenity. A friendly and intimate service is offered by the highly trained staff, equal to any found in a family run hotel. All of the bedrooms have been individually designed and furnished and provide a trouser press, alarm clock, television, telephone and tea and coffee making facilities. Deservedly awarded its first AA rosette, the spacious and pleasantly furnished restaurant has an extensive menu comprising of English and Continental dishes supported by a good wine list. The bar, where an exciting range of English and continental fare is served, has undergone a complete refurbishment. It is a pleasant place to relax and enjoy a drink, while the coffee shop serves informal meals, tea and refreshments. Adjacent to the hotel is a mews of specialist antique shops offering an array of fine antique pieces. Burford itself has changed little since the end of the 17th century and its streets are lined with exquisite buildings in the honeyed, locally quarried limestone. There are many other pretty Cotswold villages to explore. **Directions:** Burford is on the A40 where it crosses the A361, halfway between Oxford and Cheltenham. Price guide: Single £60; double £80.

For hotel location, see maps on pages 212-218

THE GOLDEN PHEASANT HOTEL & RESTAURANT

THE HIGH STREET, BURFORD, OXFORDSHIRE OX18 4QA
TEL: 01993 823417/823223 FAX: 01993 822621

Much favoured by Queen Elizabeth I, the town of Burford is often referred to as the Gateway to the Cotswolds. At its heart, the Golden Pheasant has an unbroken history as a coaching inn dating back to the 15th century. Unpretentious yet atmospheric, the property is full of character with authentic beams and open log fires. The welcome here is equally warm and families particularly are made to feel at home. Bedroom accommodation is shared between the main building and former outhouses that enclose a rear courtyard, soft furnishings and up-to-date amenities render them both cosy and comfortable. Some of the larger rooms and suites boast traditional four-poster beds and all have en suite bathrooms. Morning coffees, light lunch and afternoon teas are always on offer in the lounge and bar: yet it is the restaurant dinners that are the Golden Pheasant's crowning glory. An extensive à la carte offers modern interpretations of classical fare. Burford is the ideal base for visits to the famous Cotswold villages of Broadway, Bourton and Lower Slaughter and is equally convenient for Oxford and Cheltenham. Nearby places of interest include Blenheim Palace, Gloucester Cathedral and Berkeley Castle. **Directions:** Burford is signposted from A40 Oxford to Cheltenham road at its junction with A361. The Golden Pheasant is in the High Street. Price guide: Single £65; double £85–£105.

For hotel location, see maps on pages 212-218

THE LAMB INN

SHEEP STREET, BURFORD, OXFORDSHIRE OX18 4LR
TEL: 01993 823155 FAX: 01993 822228

The Lamb Inn, in the small Cotswold town of Burford, is everyone's idea of the archetypal English inn, where it is easy to imagine that time has slipped back to some gentler age. The inn is set in a quiet location with a pretty walled garden. To step inside is to recapture something of the spirit of the 14th century: flagged floors, gleaming copper, brass and silver reflect the flicker of log fires and the well-chosen antiques all enhance the sense of history here. The bedrooms, which have recently been refurbished, offer comfortable accommodation, with oak beams, chintz curtains and soft furnishings. Guests can enjoy the best of British cooking. Dinner, chosen from a three-course table d'hôte or à la carte menu, is taken in the candlelit pillared dining room and might include such dishes as fresh grilled sardines with lime butter sauce, followed by roast tenderloin of pork wrapped in smoked bacon with a blue cheese cream sauce. Light lunches are served in the bar or in the garden. On Sundays, a traditional three-course lunch is served. Packed lunches and hampers can be provided. The inn is near the heart of the town, where guests can browse through antiques shops or laze by the waters of the River Windrush. Burford is within easy reach of Oxford, Cheltenham, Stow-on-the-Wold and the many attractive Cotswold villages. **Directions:** Sheep Street is off the main street in Burford. Burford is 20m W of Oxford. Price guide: Single £60–£75; double £95–£115.

For hotel location, see maps on pages 212-218

THE HOSTE ARMS HOTEL

THE GREEN, BURNHAM MARKET, NORFOLK PE31 8HD
TEL: 01328 738777 FAX: 01328 730103

Overlooking the green in the picturesque village of Burnham Market, The Hoste Arms dates back to the 17th century. Deservedly The Hoste has received many awards including Johansens Inn of the Year, Egon Ronay Pub of the Year and the Inn of the Year César Award from the Good Hotel Guide. All 20 bedrooms are individually decorated and all en suite, some offering views of the village, others of the landscaped garden. Paul Whittome continues his quest constantly to improve and upgrade services and facilities, recently enhancing the enjoyment of his guests with the addition of a very stylish and relaxed lounge and also the new Gallery Restaurant. A small panelled restaurant offers scope for private dinner parties and conferences. The Hoste Arms offers an excellent menu, created by head chef Stephen David and his team, which features an extensive amount of seafood and has British, French and Oriental touches. The wine list contains well priced wines and Paul has a private collection of his favourites which are offered to guests. The Hoste Arms is well situated to cater for most interests. There are several stately homes in the area, including Holkham Hall and Sandringham. For nature lovers there are bird sanctuaries and boat trips. Golf enthusiasts have Hunstanton, Brancaster and Cromer. **Directions:** Burnham Market is about two miles from the A149 on the B1155. Price guide: Singles £50–£60; doubles £60–£80.

For hotel location, see maps on pages 212-218

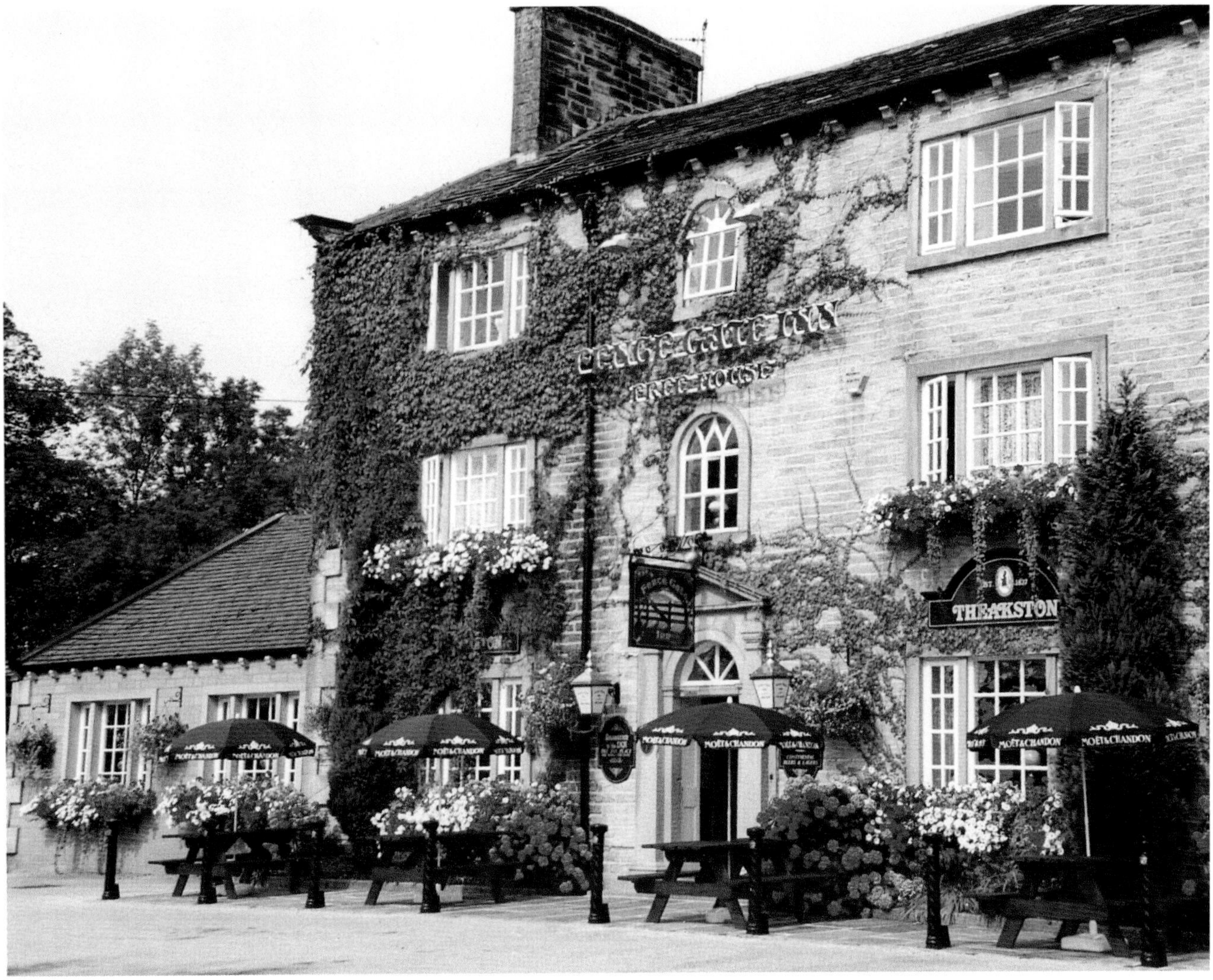

FENCE GATE INN

WHEATLEY LANE ROAD, FENCE, NR BURNLEY, LANCASHIRE BB12 9EE
TEL: 01282 618101 FAX: 01282 615432

Set within a collection of small villages a short distance from Pendle Hill in the picturesque village of Fence. The Fence Gate was originally a house used as a collection point for cotton delivered by barge and distributed to surrounding cottage dwellers to be spun into cloth. Owner Kevin Berkins has redesigned and refurbished the house into a stylish inn and an extensive banqueting centre for all occasions with two versatile suites and a brasserie. A large, restful conservatory overlooks beautifully landscaped gardens that incorporate waterfalls and fountains. The Brasserie menu boasts a variety of tempting dishes including breast of Cressingham duck cooked pink, with a gooseberry sauce and an apple chutney. English leg of lamb steak marinated and cooked in honey, flavoured with spices and garlic served on a bed of flageolet beans, grilled medallion of salmon presented on a bed of mange tout flavoured with a saffron and sweet pepper butter sauce. There are house specialities and a wide selection of vegetarian dishes. For Fence Gate diners new to the area, there are numerous places to visit, whether it be for shopping at the Boundary Mill Shop or other leisure facilities available nearby. **Directions**: From the M65 exit junction 13, take first left along the Padiham by-pass for 1½miles. Turn right at brown signs to Barley Picnic site then first left, the Fence Gate is set back on right.

For hotel location, see maps on pages 212-218

THE RED LION

BY THE BRIDGE AT BURNSALL, NEAR SKIPTON, NORTH YORKSHIRE BD23 6BU
TEL: 01756 720204 FAX: 01756 720292 E-MAIL: redlion@daelnet.co.uk

Beamed ceilings, creaky floors and roaring log fires in winter greet you at this former 16th century Ferryman's Inn on the banks of the River Wharfe in the picturesque Yorkshire Dales village of Burnsall. Owned and run by the Grayshon family, it is surrounded by glorious open countryside. Guests can step out for numerous walks straight from the front door. The hotel is actually on the "Dalesway". The 11 bedrooms are all slightly different yet traditionally furnished, many with antiques and most have wonderful views over the village green, river and Burnsall Fell. Large and attractive, it has been awarded an AA Rosette for serving food that is delicious and varied, imaginatively cooked and well-presented. Table d'hôte dishes such as local rabbit braised in ale and served with herb dumplings, or partridge with apricot seasoning and game chips, are complemented by a selection of wines from throughout the world. Special half-board terms and winter warmer breaks are available. Bolton Abbey and Priory, the historic market town of Skipton with its medieval castle and the Settle to Carlisle Railway. The Red Lion has private fishing on the River Wharfe and also 7 miles of trout and greyling fishing. Skipton and Ilkley golf courses are 11 miles away. **Directions:** Burnsall is north of Skipton on the B6160 between Grassington and Bolton Abbey. The Red Lion is in the centre of the village by the bridge. Price guide: Single £42–£70; double £84–£110.

11 rms MasterCard VISA AMERICAN EXPRESS M 60

For hotel location, see maps on pages 212-218

BOAR'S HEAD HOTEL

LICHFIELD ROAD, SUDBURY, DERBYSHIRE DE6 5GX
TEL: 01283 820344 FAX: 01283 820075

This 17th century house was lost from the famous Vernon estate through a game of cards! It is now a well known local hostelry, having been run by the Crooks family for many years. Guests arriving will be welcomed by the architectural beauty of this very old building. There is a warm bar, with natural brick walls, horse brasses and hunting horns. The residents' lounge looks onto a pretty patio where drinks are served in summer months. Much thought has been given to furnishing the delightful bedrooms which have every possible facility, including teletext and Sky television. Visitors enjoy a choice of real ales and excellent home-cooked dishes with the chef's specials listed on a blackboard. There are two restaurants, the elegant Royal Boar with an imaginative à la carte menu and the less formal Hunter's Table Carvery and Bistro offering fresh fish, pasta dishes and splendid roasts, both at lunchtime and in the evening. The Royal Boar is closed on Sunday evenings, but is famous for its Sunday lunch. A fascinating wine list covers vineyards worldwide, with 70 entries that include 6 house wines and a selection of 10 half-bottles! Alton Towers and Uttoxeter Racecourse are lively attractions nearby. Other guests will enjoy Chatsworth House, Sudbury Hall, Tutbury Castle and the Bass Museum. **Directions:** The hotel is on A515, just south of A50 from Stoke on Trent to Derby. Price guide: Single from £39.50; double from £49.50.

For hotel location, see maps on pages 212-218

THE CHEQUERS INN

FROGGATT EDGE, NR CALVER, DERBYSHIRE S30 1ZB
TEL: 01433 630231 FAX: 01433 631072

A Grade II listed building, The Chequers Inn originally comprised four 16th century houses, rebuilt in the 18th century and now extensively refurbished. It is situated on an old pack horse road in the heart of the Peak district National Park. Visitors will see plenty of reminders of the inn's history; a horse-mounting block still stands outside the main building and the old stables house the logs that fuel today's open fires. Behind the inn, acres of unspoiled woodland lead up to Froggatt Edge, with its panoramic views. Each of the six cottage-style bedrooms has its own identity and for an extra touch of romance, one room has a four-poster bed. Local chef Julie Presland creates a wide variety of European and British meals, with several fish dishes and local game in season. The menus are original, and healthy and are served in the extended bar areas, where quiet corners may be found. Amongst the many regular and popular dishes, Bakewell pudding, the local speciality, is a favourite dessert here – delicious served hot with cream. This is wonderful walking country: you can leave your car and follow the Derwent River or the Peak trails. Chatsworth House, Haddon Hall, the caverns of Castleton and the market town of Bakewell are all close by. **Directions:** The inn is situated on the old pack horse road, now the B6054 which links Bakewell and Sheffield, 6 miles from Bakewell on Froggatt Edge. Price guide: Single £48–£55; double £60–£70.

6 rms MasterCard VISA M 30

 For hotel location, see maps on pages 212-218

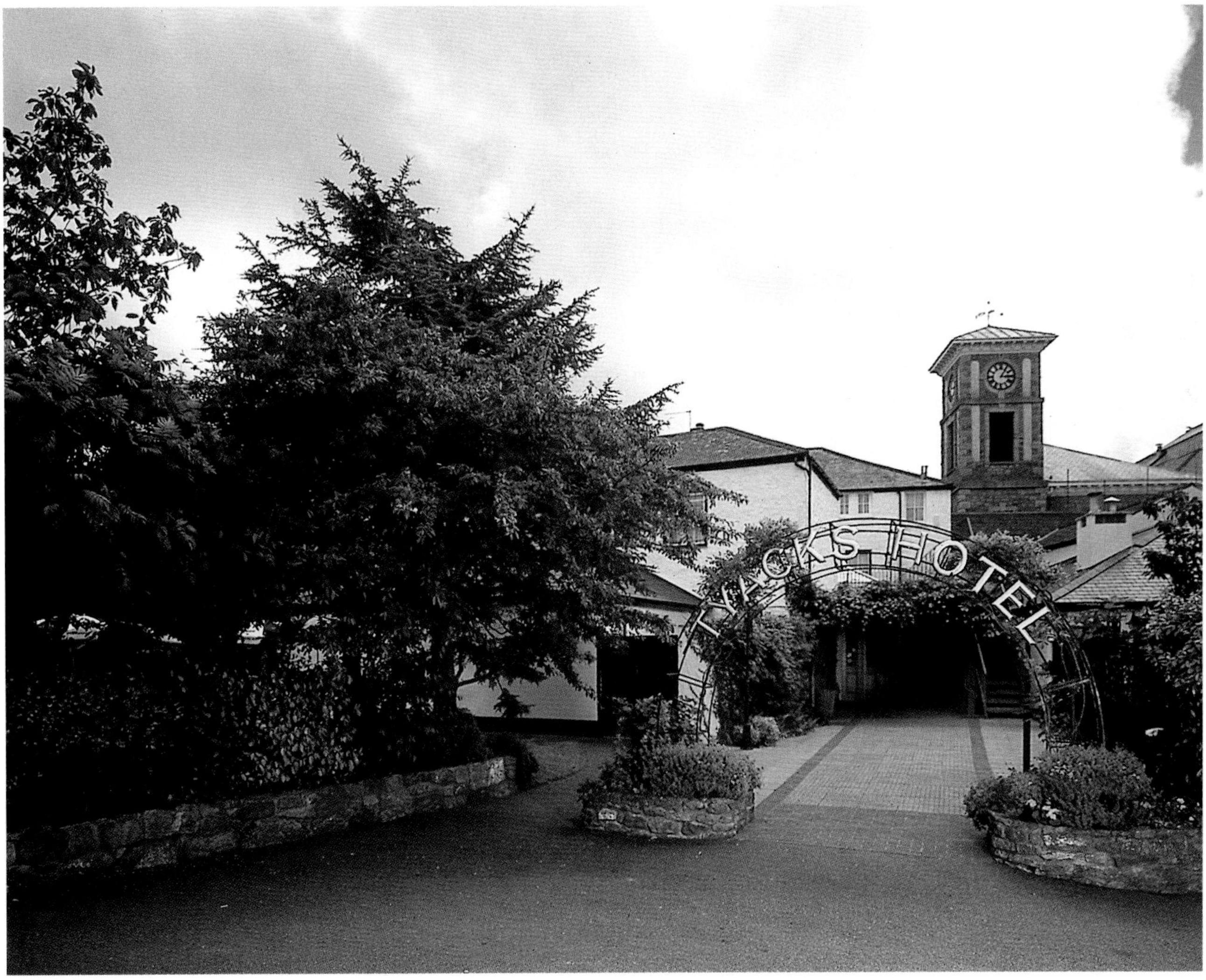

TYACKS HOTEL

27 COMMERCIAL STREET, CAMBORNE, CORNWALL TR14 8LD
TEL: 01209 612424 FAX: 01209 612435

This charming 18th century coaching inn, set in the heart of Camborne, is just three minutes drive from the main A30 road or less than five minutes from the bus or railway stations. The Tyacks is used by business men and women as well as tourists as a base for travelling in the west of Cornwall. Re-opened in 1992, having been totally refurbished to AA and RAC 3 Star standard, the inn has become popular with visitors from all over the world as is reflected in the restaurant's imaginative menus. Adjacent to the restaurant is an attractive lounge bar, ideal for a quiet drink or bar snack. For those who enjoy a lively pub atmosphere there is the Coach Bar. Beside the hotel entrance, opposite the old stables is a patio and beer garden where drinks and snacks can be enjoyed on a sunny day. The à la carte, table d'hôte and vegetarian menus offer a splendid choice of English and Continental fare using fresh Cornish fish, vegetables and meats. Guests can explore the Tate Gallery at St Ives, Camborne School of Mines and Geology Museum, Tehidy Country Park and Golf Club, Penzance and Lands End. The Engines Museum at Poole, the house of William Murdoch, founder of gaslighting, in Redruth are also worth a visit. **Directions:** From A30 turn off at the sign for Camborne West then follow signs for town centre. Tyacks Hotel is on the left-hand side. Price guide: Single £45; double £75–£80; suite £100–£110.

For hotel location, see maps on pages 212-218

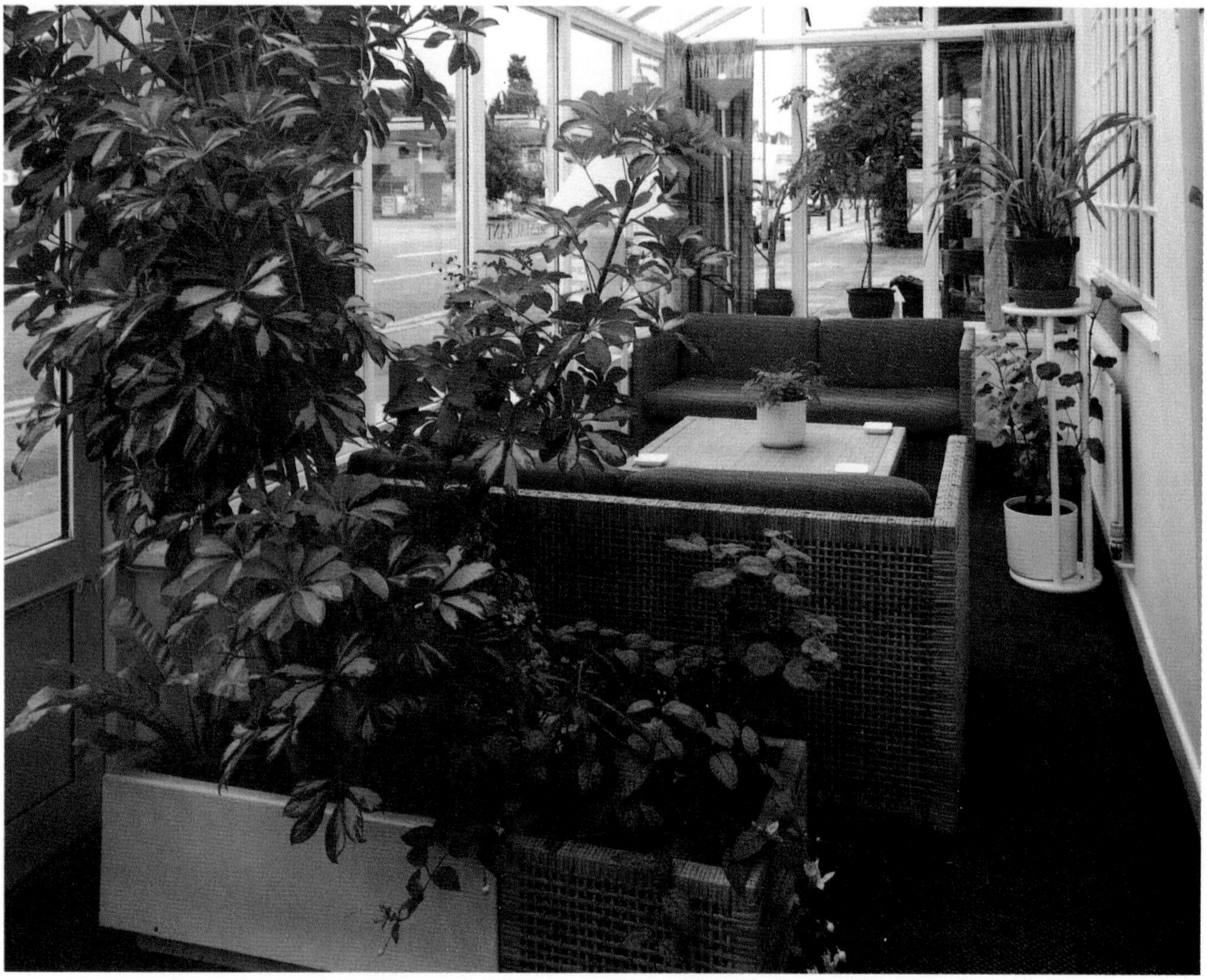

Panos Hotel & Restaurant

154–156 HILLS ROAD, CAMBRIDGE , CAMBRIDGESHIRE CB2 2PB
TEL: 01223 212958 FAX: 01223 210980

This small unpretentious and friendly hotel is managed by Genevieve Kretz. It is close to the centre of town and to the railway station and has a regular clientèle who return again and again, treating it as Cambridge's best kept secret. Guests enter the hotel through the attractive conservatory bar which, like the other reception rooms, is filled with fresh flowers arranged by Genevieve. The six bedrooms are comfortable and well appointed, all with en suite shower facilities, colour television, a radio alarm, writing desk, mini-bar and facilities to plug in personal computers. Full breakfast is included in the price. The restaurant is recognised to be one of the best in Cambridge, with menus supervised by the owner. The famous Panos charcoal-grilled steaks and flambé dishes are listed beside mezze and sword-fish kebabs. An excellent wine list is available too. Nearby attractions include punting on the River Cam and for those preferring dry land, the famous Cambridge Botanical Gardens. There are the historic colleges to admire, also the Fitzwilliam Museum. Ely Cathedral is not far away and for those who like more activity, there is the racing at Newmarket. **Directions:** From city centre follow signs to station and hospital as far as Hills Road. Once on Hills Road carry straight on to traffic lights and railway bridge avoiding fork to station. Panos is immediately on your right. Private car park at the rear. Price guide: Single £50; double £70.

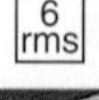

10

For hotel location, see maps on pages 212-218

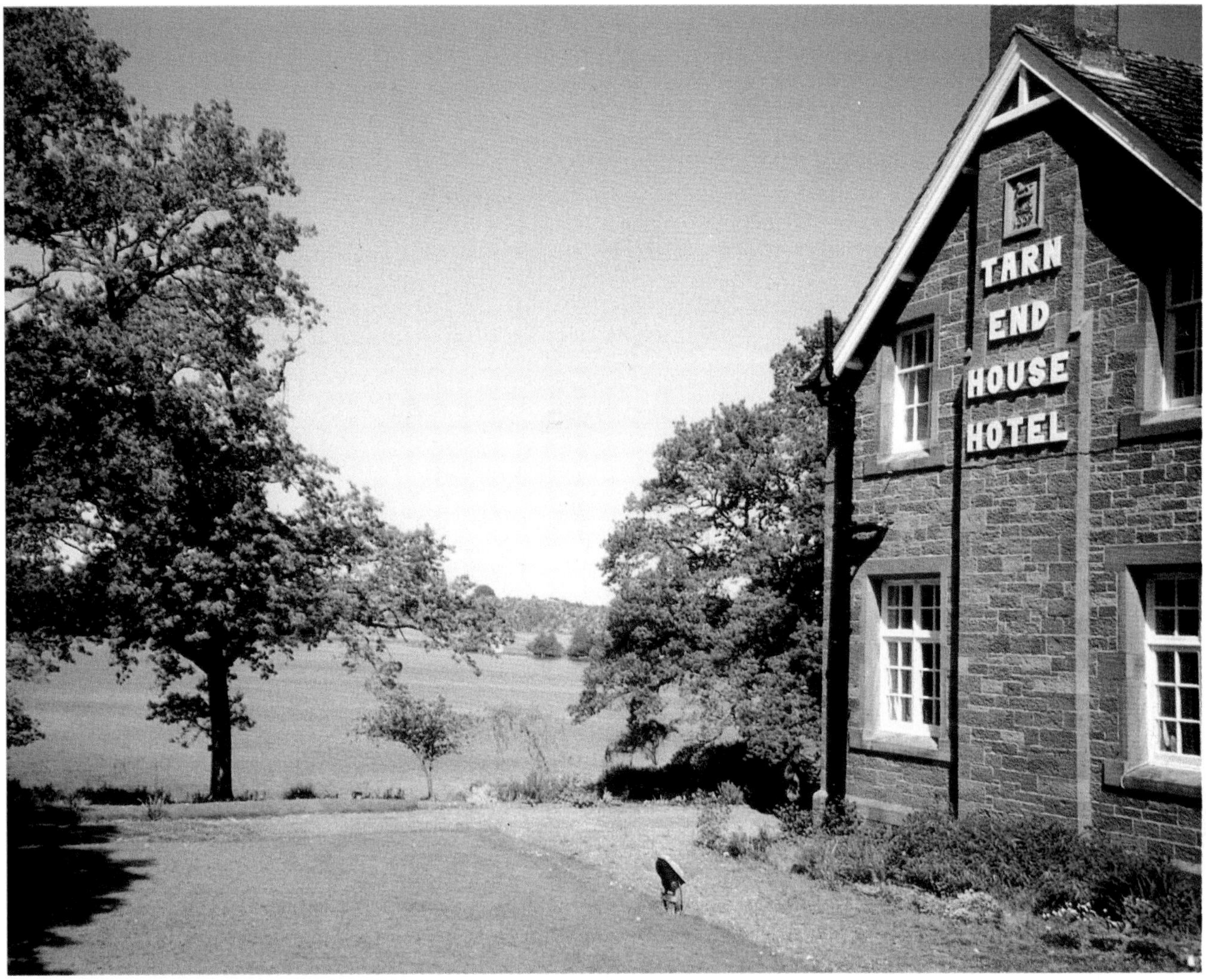

THE TARN END HOUSE HOTEL

TALKIN TARN, BRAMPTON, CUMBRIA CA8 1LS
TEL: 016977 2340 FAX: 016977 2089

The Tarn End House Hotel has idyllic surroundings at any time of year. This former estate farm house is over 100 years old and is set in its own grounds, with lawns running down to the shores of Talkin Tarn. A very warm welcome and traditional hospitality are guaranteed. The nicely furnished bedrooms have every modern facility and offer exceptional views. This is an ideal spot in which to escape from the world and there is a good choice of leisure activities. Long walks can be taken over the surrounding fells, or the more active can take advantage of rowing, wind-surfing or sailing on the Tarn. There are good golf courses nearby and river fishing and rough shooting can be arranged. The inn enjoys a very good reputation for its cuisine. Guests can savour a meal chosen from two menus – à la carte or table d'hôte. Bar snacks are also available at lunchtime. Hadrian's Wall, Lanercost Priory and the City of Carlisle with its historic castle. The River Gelt is an ideal place to visit for bird-watchers and the Scottish borders are within easy reach. **Directions:** From M6 junction 43 take A69 to Brampton. From the centre of Brampton take B6413 towards Castle Carrock and Talkin Tarn. Go over the railway and past Brampton Golf Club and take second left to Talkin village – the hotel is on the left. Price guide: Single £35–£49; double £55–£85.

For hotel location, see maps on pages 212-218

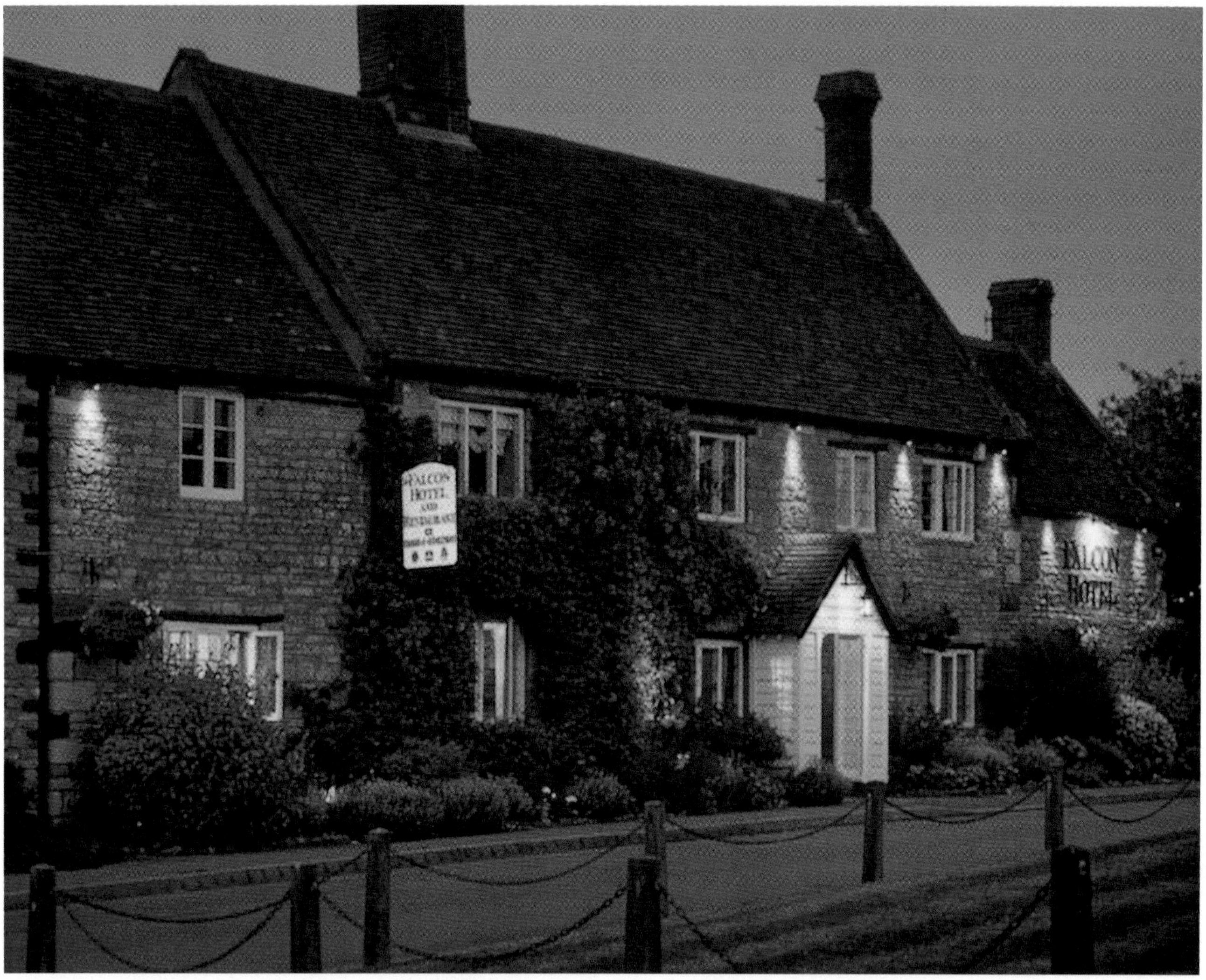

THE FALCON HOTEL

CASTLE ASHBY, NORTHAMPTON, NORTHAMPTONSHIRE NN7 1LF
TEL: 01604 696200 FAX: 01604 696673

Six miles south of Northampton, in the heart of the Marquess of Northampton's estate, The Falcon is a delightful country cottage hotel, secluded and tranquil, minutes away from the rambling acres of Castle Ashby House. The owners have invested energy and enthusiasm into transforming this once modest place into a haven of comfort, excellent food and attentive service. Bedrooms are beautifully furnished, cosy cottage style and the bathrooms have been recently upgraded. Lunch and dinner, which are created where possible from seasonal, home-grown produce, are served in the intimate restaurant which overlooks a lawn with willow trees. The excellent value-for-money cuisine, modern English in flavour, is prepared by chef Neil Helks. A fixed-price menu costs £19.50, including coffee and petits fours. There is also an interesting à la carte selection. The extensive wine list can be studied by guests at their leisure over preprandial drinks by a glowing log fire. Walk in the grounds of Castle Ashby estate. Further afield, visit Woburn, Althorp, Silverstone, Bedford and Stratford. **Directions:** Exit M1 junction 14 northbound or 15 southbound. Follow the signs to A428 where Castle Ashby and The Falcon are clearly signposted, six miles south-east of Northampton. Price guide: Single £77.50; double £92.50.

For hotel location, see maps on pages 212-218

The George Hotel

MARKET PLACE, CASTLE CARY, SOMERSET BA7 7AH
TEL: 01963 350761 FAX: 01963 350035

The George has played an important part in the history of this unspoilt Somerset town, having been a coaching inn since the 15th century. The charming bedrooms combine modern needs with individual furnishings: – special breaks throughout the year are included in the tariff. Guests will enjoy meeting the local residents in the snug bar (no smoking) and the George Bar which has an elm beam dating back to the 10th century in its inglenook fireplace. Traditional ales are served together with an excellent selection of bar meals. Awarded 2 AA Rosettes, this fine panelled restaurant offers an à la carte menu using the finest of local produce, prepared by chef. The menu is complemented by a well-selected wine list. There are many fine buildings to visit in the town mainly built of 'Cary gingerbread' stone including an 18th century town lock-up known as the 'Roundhouse'. Many National Trust properties and gardens, Wells, Glastonbury, Sherborne and Longleat are nearby. For sport, Wincanton races, various golf courses, horse riding and ballooning are within close proximity. **Directions**: Castle Cary is signposted off the A303 at Wincanton, reached via the M3 from London, or via Bath from the M4. There is also a direct train from London Paddington taking 90 minutes. Price guide: Single: £44–£55; double £70–£85.

For hotel location, see maps on pages 212-218

KINGSHEAD HOUSE RESTAURANT

BIRDLIP, GLOUCESTERSHIRE GL4 8JH
TEL: 01452 862299

Judy and Warren Knock have now been running their restaurant, a stone-built former coaching inn on the edge of the Cotswolds, for over ten years. In the welcoming oak-beamed dining-room Judy provides excellent modern English cooking. Her menu changes twice-weekly, offering up to four courses with perhaps five delicious choices for each course. She uses only fresh ingredients; fish is delivered from South Wales, meat is from a local butcher and vegetables from a nearby farm. Main courses range from chicken cooked in paprika and soured cream to rack of lamb with a garlic crust and a tomato and pesto sauce, while starters may include avocado gazpacho with prawns or foie gras. Puddings are equally appealing, with such delights as strawberry crème brulée and summer fruit bavarois. There is one en suite bedroom, well proportioned and comfortably furnished. The restaurant opens for lunch, Tuesday to Sunday and for dinner Tuesday to Saturday. Smoking is discouraged but not entirely banned. The wine list, compiled by Warren Knock, offers over seventy different wines and has a particularly useful selection of half-bottles. **Directions:** Kingshead House stands at the top of Birdlip Hill with its famous view. Birdlip is situated just off the A417 on the B4070, 8 miles from Gloucester and Cheltenham. Price guide: Double £70 including full breakfast.

CHEF'S SPECIALS

•••••••

Boudin blanc truffé
our own home-made sausage of chicken breast and truffles

Tagine of lamb with couscous
lamb marinated in spices and fresh coriander

Ballotine of salmon
with Champagne sauce

Orange meringue
with strawberries and a Cointreau sauce

For hotel location, see maps on pages 212-218

THE PHEASANT INN

HIGHER BURWARDSLEY, TATTENHALL, CHESTER, CHESHIRE CH3 9PF
TEL: 01829 770434 FAX: 01829 771097 E-MAIL: davelpheas@aol.com

This is a charming 300 year old inn, partly timbered, at the top of the Peckforton Hills looking out over the Cheshire Plains to Wales. The bar has a magnificent log fire and a resident parrot called Sailor. Recently a conservatory has been added which is used as an extension to the dining room at weekends. The bar is well stocked, there is an array of real ales and some fine wines to accompany meals. The Highland Room', popular with local inhabitants, has a daily menu chalked up, which includes a choice for vegetarians. At weekends there is a superb Sunday lunch menu for just £12.50, while on Saturday evenings they produce the most delicious four-course dinner for only £14.50. Eight of the ten en suite bedrooms are in converted barns, allowing peace and privacy – all rooms have modern amenities. For added interest the owner David Greenhaugh keeps a herd of prize-winning Highland cattle which graze in surrounding fields and the beef is a speciality of the house. Chester, Wrexham and Nantwich are within easy driving distance. Oulton Park motor racing is nearby. There is trout fishing and golf available and the health-giving Peckforton Hills are ideal for rambling. **Directions**: A41 from Chester. After six miles turn left for Tattenhall then left again in village, signed Burwardsley. Top of hill, left at Post Office and hotel is higher still on left. Price guide: Single £45–£50; double/twin £70–£85.

For hotel location, see maps on pages 212-218

THE CROWN INN

GIDDEA HALL, YATTON KEYNELL, CHIPPENHAM, WILTSHIRE SN14 7ER
TEL: 01249 782229 FAX: 01249 782337

This is a picturesque honey-coloured coaching inn, secluded and tranquil, in a tiny hamlet just a short drive from the attractive market town of Chippenham. Its origins can be traced to the 15th century and renovations and refurbishment reflect the owners' determination to combine history with discreet modernisation, creating an elegant small hostelry. The cosy front bar with an old open hearth fire sets the scene for visitors and the hospitable ambience continues into the interlinking dining areas. The Crown has a reputation for good English food. There are simple bar snacks or more varied and elaborate meals such as breast of pheasant stuffed with paté, wrapped in bacon and finished with sloe gin, casserole of venison in a red wine sauce, or skewered queen scallops and prawns marinated in ginger and lime juice. The Crown's eight adjacent en suite bedrooms have all modern conveniences, are furnished in style and are totally in keeping with expectations for a stay in this beautiful escapists' spot. Two have four-posters. The Castle Combe golf course and racecourse are nearby. Badminton is only twenty minutes away. Castle Combe, one of the most photographed of Wiltshire's many pretty villages, also lies close by. The inn is also central to Bath and the West Country. **Directions:** Exit the M4 at junction 17 for Chippenham. Then turn right onto the A420. After about two miles turn right onto the B4039 for Yatton Keynell. Price guide: Double/twin From £55.

For hotel location, see maps on pages 212-218

THE NOEL ARMS HOTEL AND RESTAURANT

HIGH STREET, CHIPPING CAMPDEN, GLOUCESTERSHIRE GL55 6AT
TEL: 01386 840317 FAX: 01386 841136

A long tradition of hospitality awaits you at the Noel Arms Hotel. In 1651 the future Charles II rested here after his Scottish army was defeated by Cromwell at the battle of Worcester and for centuries the hotel has entertained visitors to the ancient and unspoilt, picturesque Cotswold Village of Chipping Campden. Many reminders of the past; fine antique furniture, swords, shields and other mementoes can be found around the hotel. There are 26 en sùite bedrooms in either the main house or in the tastefully constructed new wing, some of which boast luxurious antique four-poster beds and all offering the standards you expect from a country hotel. The impressive oak panelled, restaurant, awarded 2 AA Rosettes, offers an excellent menu including a seasonal selection of fresh local produce. You may be tempted to choose from the extensive range of bar snacks available in the conservatory or Dovers Bar. The fine selection of wines from around the world are delicious accompaniments to any meal. Try some of the traditional cask ales and keg beers. Browse around the delightful array of shops in Chipping Campden or many of the enchanting honey-coloured Cotswold Villages, Hidcote Manor Gardens, Cheltenham Spa, Worcester, Oxford and Stratford-upon-Avon which are all close by. **Directions:** The Noel Arms is in the centre of Chipping Campden, which is on the B4081, 2 miles east of the A44. Price guide: Single £70–£75; double £99–120.

26 rms MasterCard VISA AMERICAN EXPRESS M 20

For hotel location, see maps on pages 212-218

The Codrington Arms

WAPLEY ROAD, CODRINGTON, NR CHIPPING SODBURY, BRISTOL BS37 6RY
TEL/FAX: 01454 313145

True West Country hospitality can be enjoyed at this attractive and welcoming old inn situated between historic Bristol and the picturesque Cotswolds. Renovated and modernised over the years it retains a great many of its original period features. The surrounding countryside has been the scene of history making it popular with sightseers who like to explore small villages, hamlets and market towns. Two miles north is the old town of Chipping Sodbury and a short drive east is Regency-style Dodington House whose grounds were landscaped by Capability Brown. Also close by is Badminton House, the Palladian mansion home of the Duke of Beaufort and the venue for the world famous annual horse trials. The Codrington Arms is believed to date back to the 15th century and to have been part of the nearby family estate of John de Codrington (1363–1425), who was Standard Bearer for King Henry V at Agincourt. A warm Cotswold atmosphere prevails throughout the inn's extensive and comfortable bars and dining areas. Fine ales and wines are served as well as an extensive bar menu including good and substantial dishes such as steaks, fresh trout and breaded plaice. The inn has no bedrooms. **Directions:** Leave Bristol on the M32 and join the M4 East to junction 18 and then take the second left.

For hotel location, see maps on pages 212-218

THE NEW INN AT COLN

COLN ST-ALDWYNS, NR CIRENCESTER, GLOUCESTERSHIRE GL7 5AN
TEL: 01285 750651 FAX: 01285 750657 E-MAIL: stay@new–inn.co.uk

In days of yore, when Queen Elizabeth I was giving royal assent to the import of tobacco from the new-found Americas, she was also initiating a travel boom in England, by instigating a network of coaching inns after the pattern already set on the Continent. One of the Cotswold inns that her initiative helped to create was The New Inn at Coln St-Aldwyns on Akeman Street, the old Roman Road, leading North East out of Cirencester. The New Inn, though old in years, is today utterly new in spirit, winning ever fresh awards for food and hospitality – its two Rosettes being in permanent flower as a second Queen Elizabeth reigns. Since Brian and Sandra-Anne Evans took over six years ago The New Inn at Coln has blossomed and Stephen Morey's skills in the kitchen have added a gastronomic dimension to the charm and comfort of the ancient but cleverly modernised bedrooms – perfect accommodation for an idyllic week in the Cotswolds, a useful stopover or as a timely resting place after an exceedingly fine dinner. For those whose minds may be more focussed on business, there is a charming meeting room. Close to this picturesque Cotswolds base are Stratford-upon-Avon, Bath, Oxford and Cheltenham and within healthy walking distance is Bibury with its photogenic Arlington Row. **Directions:** From Burford (A40), take B4425 towards Bibury, then turn left after Aldsworth. Price guide: Single £65–£80; double £90–£120.

14 rms MasterCard VISA AMERICAN EXPRESS M 10

For hotel location, see maps on pages 212-218

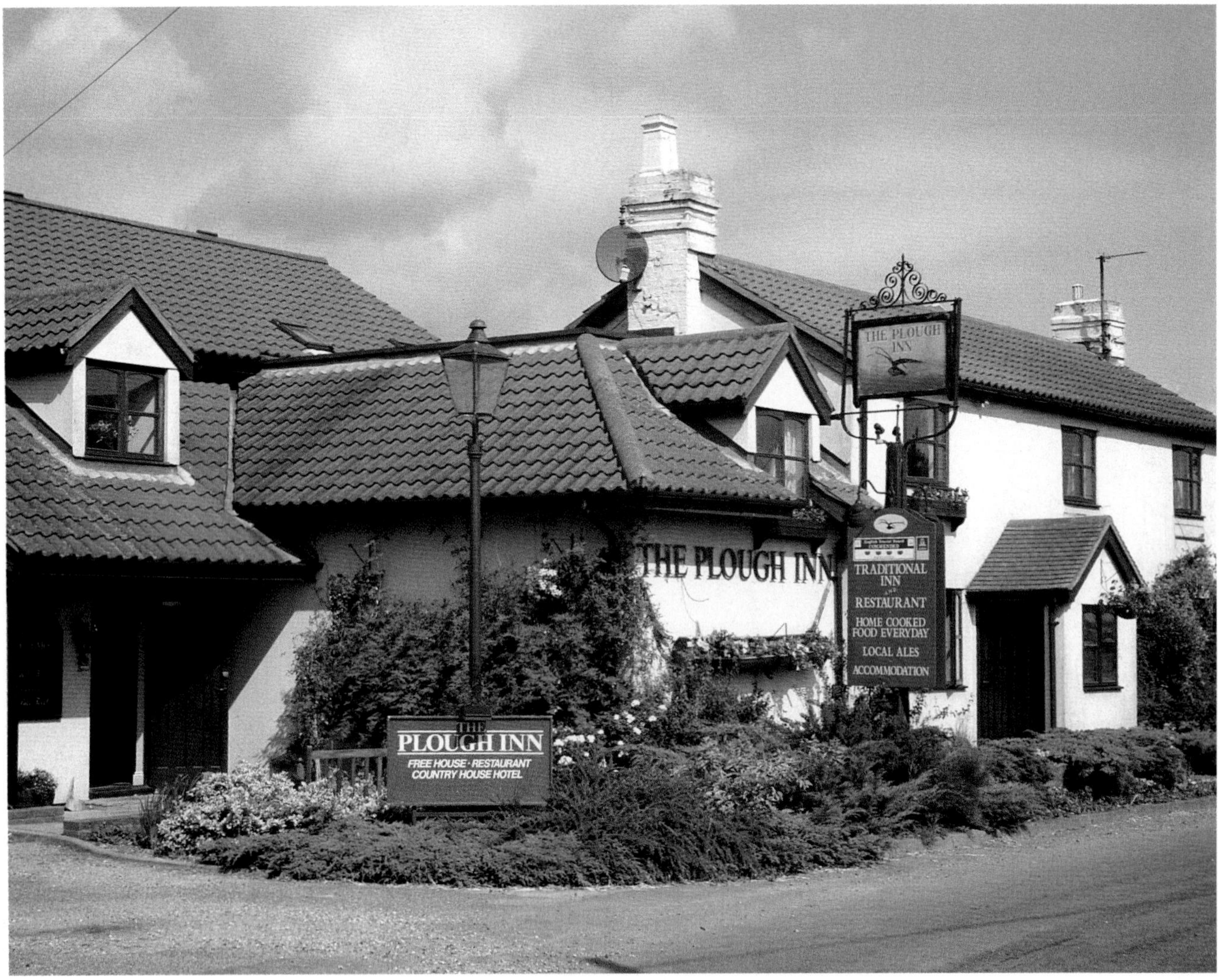

THE PLOUGH INN

BROCKLEY GREEN, NR HUNDON, SUDBURY, SUFFOLK CO10 8DT
TEL: 01440 786789 FAX: 01440 786710

The Plough is a typical, charming, early 19th century inn commanding superb, panoramic views from its windows over the beautiful Stour Valley and five acres of immaculate grounds. Old beams, exposed soft red brickwork, solid, heavy furniture and comfortable sofas and chairs contribute to the inn's welcoming ambience. There are eight comfortable, en suite bedrooms, all providing the comforts and quality expected of a hotel awarded four crowns from the English Tourist Board. The intimate, attractive bar is a restful delight offering an imaginative choice of bar meals and a good selection of traditional ales. Simms restaurant is highly regarded locally and serves superb English style cuisine. The Plough's peaceful rural location belies the presence of the many areas of interest within a short distance. Cycles are available for those seeking to explore the delightful picture-postcard villages nearby and landscape immortalised by painter John Constable. Within a 30 minutes drive there is the historic market town of Bury St Edmunds, the medieval wool towns of Lavenham and Long Melford, Constable's birthplace at Sudbury, Cambridge, Ely, Newmarket and the Imperial War Museum at Duxford. **Directions:** Exit the M11 at junction 9. Follow the A604 towards Haverhill. Turn left onto the A143 and after 2 miles turn right to Kedington and follow the signs to Clare. Price guide: Single £45; double/twin £65.

For hotel location, see maps on pages 212-218

The Cricketers

CLAVERING, NR SAFFRON WALDEN, ESSEX CB11 4QT
TEL: 01799 550442 FAX: 01799 550882

This attractive 16th century freehouse in the Essex countryside, just ten minutes from Stansted Airport, has responded to its popularity and reputation for good food by purchasing an adjacent residence to provide increased accommodation for guests. Known as The Pavilion, this new house provides six charming bedrooms, two with four-poster beds and one on the ground floor, ideal for those with mobility problems. All are en suite, colourful and well-appointed. Breakfast is served in the main building. The oak-beamed bar serving real ale and restaurant have cricket memorabilia on the walls. There is a non-smoking area. Guests enjoy the big log fire in the winter and alfresco refreshments in the garden in summer. The Restaurant menu, changing seasonally, has ten appetizing starters and ten succulent main courses, interesting interpretations of classic English cooking and the puddings are of the same calibre. A salad bar pleases slimmers. The wine list is diverse, from house wines through to champagnes, European vineyards alongside many New World names, and many half-bottles. Guests enjoy visiting Audley End with its renowned house and park, going racing at Newmarket, or exploring Cambridge, Saffron Walden and Duxford Air Museum. **Directions:** Leave M11 at junction 8, heading west, then right onto B1383, signed Newport and left at the B1038 to Clavering. Price guide: Single £60; double £80.

For hotel location, see maps on pages 212-218

Crown At Hopton

HOPTON WAFERS, CLEOBURY MORTIMER, SHROPSHIRE DY14 0NB
TEL: 01299 270372 FAX: 01299 271127

This enticing 16th century inn is situated in a hamlet dating back to the Norman Conquest, surrounded by the lush farmland, tumbling streams and wooded valleys of South Shropshire. Exposed beams and wooden floors characterise the bedrooms, which are decorated in an appropriate cottage style. All are spacious and most attractive. The bar, which offers a selection of cask- conditioned beers, adjoins an open terrace and like all the rooms, has many original features including an inglenook fireplace. Originally a 15th century smithy, the traditionally furnished restaurant – known as "Poacher's" – makes a fine setting in which to relax over dinner. There is a table d'hôte menu offering a choice of imaginatively cooked dishes prepared from fresh, seasonal ingredients and an extensive à la carte menu. The wine list is well compiled and dessert wines are available by the glass. A good selection of ports, cognacs and armagnacs is available. Apart from exploring the beautiful countryside, guests can visit Stokesay Castle, many National Trust properties and historic Ludlow. Another option is to take a romantic trip aboard a steam locomotive on the Severn Valley Railway. Ironbridge Gorge Museum is about 30 minutes drive away. **Directions:** The Crown Inn is by the A4117 between Ludlow and Kidderminster, two miles west of Cleobury Mortimer. Price guide: Single £45; double £75.

8 rms MasterCard VISA

For hotel location, see maps on pages 212-218

The Redfern Hotel

CLEOBURY MORTIMER, SHROPSHIRE DY14 8AA

TEL: 01299 270 395 FAX: 01299 271 011 E-MAIL: jon@red-fern.demon.co.uk

This country town hotel provides good value accommodation and a warm welcome in the heart of England. The Redfern Hotel stands in an attractive setting in Cleobury Mortimer – a market town dating back to the *Domesday Book*. Crisply decorated bedrooms have white-painted walls and floral fabrics, in keeping with the country house style. Draught ale is served in the cosy bar where memorabilia and pictures depicting the town's history are displayed. For parents' peace of mind, a baby-listening service is available. Breakfast is served in the conservatory throughout the morning. Freshly baked home-made bread each day. Redfern's English Kitchen Restaurant has a homely, welcoming atmosphere, with its home-cured hams and cider flagons hanging from the beams. The menu is changed daily to offer a variety of home-cooked dished such as Shropshire chicken stuffed with Shropshire Blue cheese and breadcrumbs, or fillet of pork in orange and ginger sauce. Golf is available at a local course with concessionary green fees. For the more adventurous the Redfern also has its own canal narrowboat for hire. Local attractions include the Ironbridge Gorge Industrial Museum or a scenic trip on the Severn Valley Railway. Other sights close by are Ludlow Castle and the beautiful countryside of the Welsh Marches. **Directions:** Cleobury Mortimer is on A4117 between Kidderminster and Ludlow, 11m from each. Price Guide: Single £45–£65; double £70–£85.

For hotel location, see maps on pages 212-218

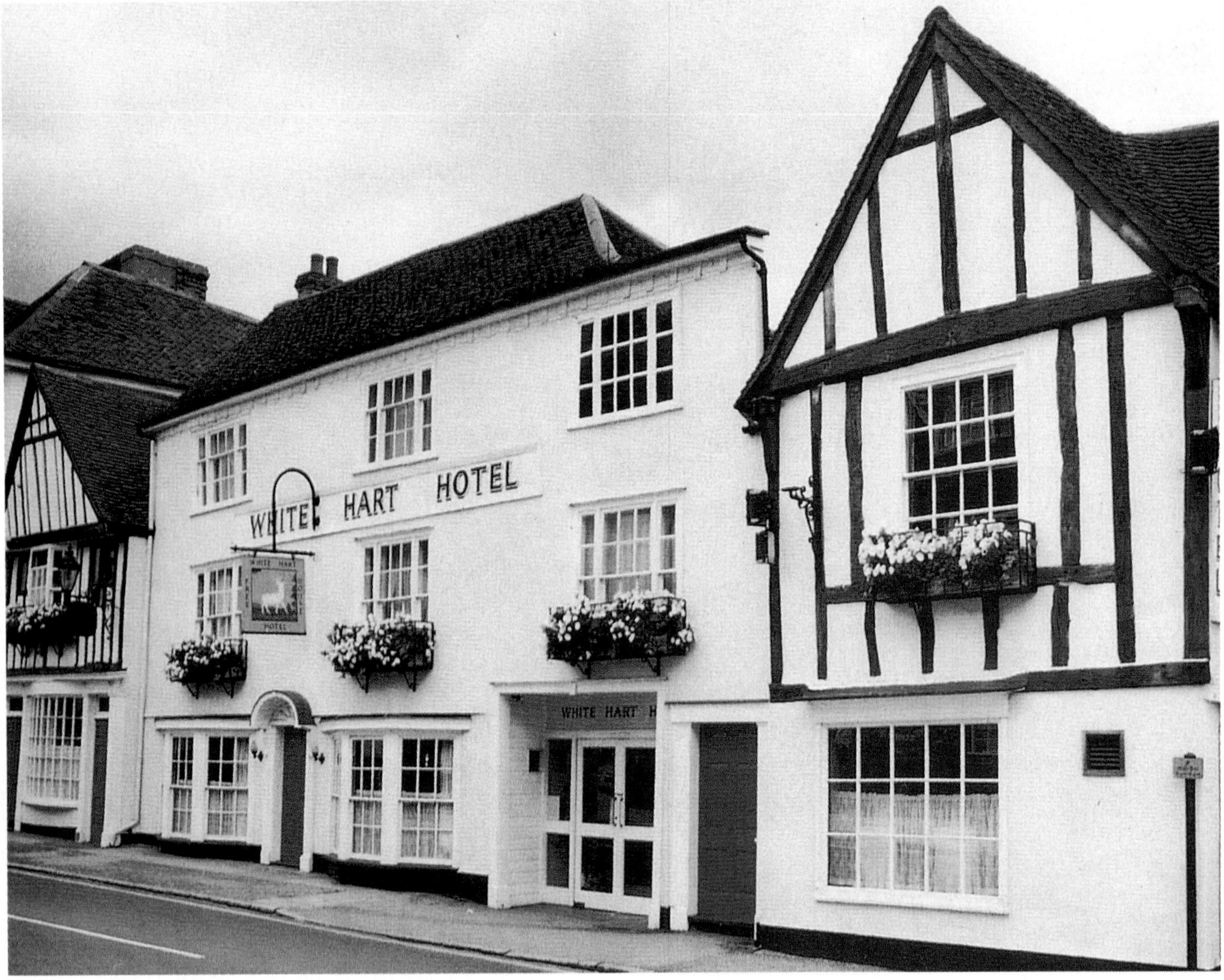

THE WHITE HART HOTEL & RESTAURANT

MARKET END, COGGESHALL, ESSEX CO6 1NH
TEL: 01376 561654 FAX: 01376 561789

A historic hotel, The White Hart is situated in the Essex town of Coggeshall, where it has played an integral part for many years. In 1489 The White Hart became the town's meeting place when most of the adjoining Guildhall was destroyed by fire. Part of that original Guildhall now forms the residents' lounge, and features magnificent roof timbers hewn from sweet chestnut. Sympathetically restored throughout, the hotel has been comfortably appointed with much attention to detail. All the en suite bedrooms have been decorated with bright fabrics to reflect the hotel's colourful character. Heavily timbered and spacious, the restaurant enjoys a good reputation locally. The table d'hôte and à la carte menus feature a choice of Italian dishes with a particular emphasis on seafood and shellfish. Pasta is freshly made and aromatic sauces and tender cuts of meat figure prominently on the menu. The hotel has recently received merit awards from the RAC for comfort and its restaurant, which already holds 2 AA rosettes and an Egon Ronay recommendation. Coggeshall is noted for its antiques shops. It is also convenient for Colchester and Chelmsford and the ferry ports of Felixstowe and Harwich. **Directions:** Coggeshall is just off the A120 between Colchester and Braintree. From the A12 follow signs through Kelvedon, then take B1024. Price guide: Single £61.50; double/twin £97.

For hotel location, see maps on pages 212-218

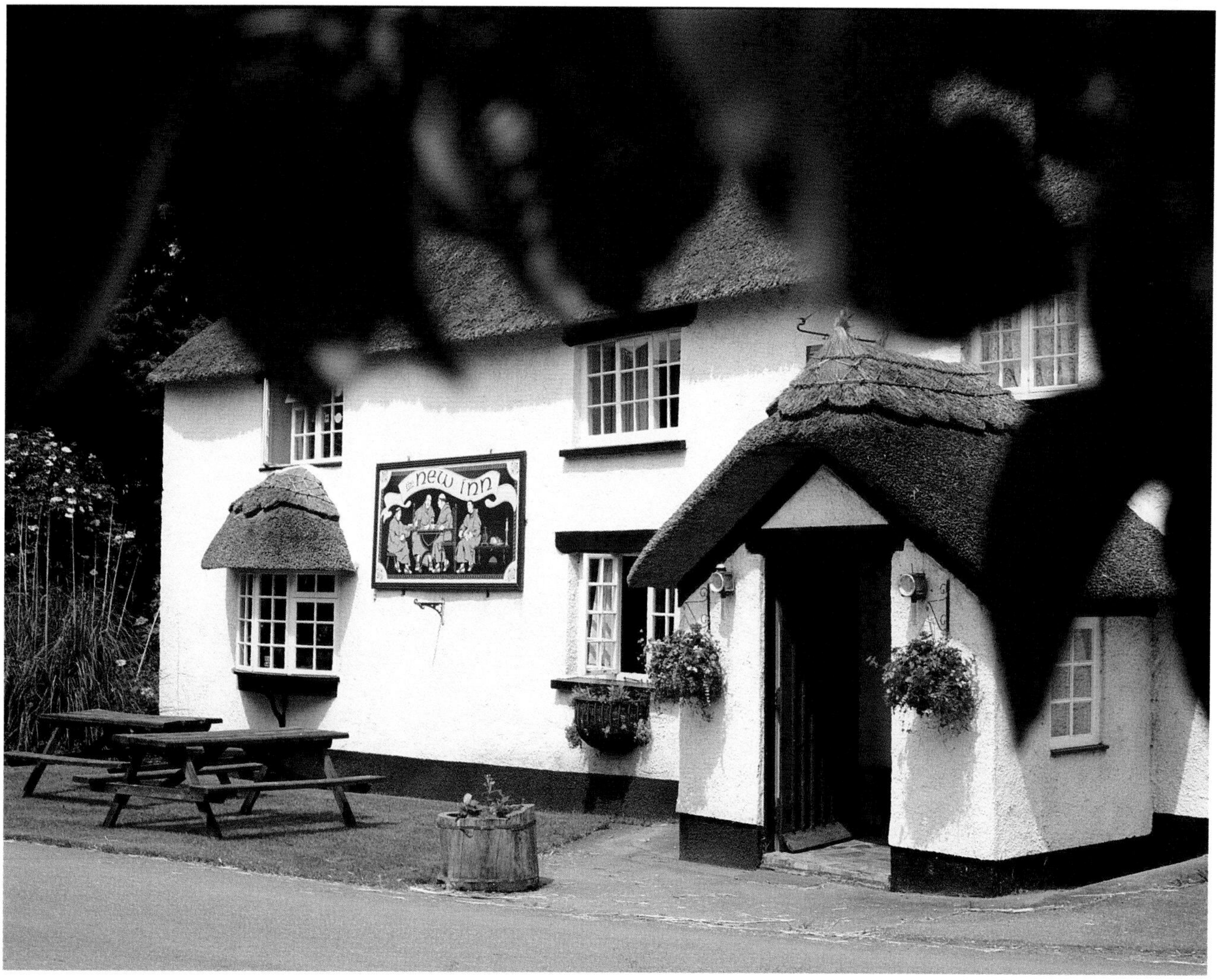

The New Inn

COLEFORD, CREDITON, DEVON EX17 5BZ
TEL: 01363 84242 FAX: 01363 85044 E-MAIL: new–inn@eurobell.co.uk

Those wishing to escape the hectic pace of everyday life will be delighted with this lovely 13th century thatched inn, located in a truly secluded valley beside a bubbling brook. The New Inn, a Grade II listed building of cob, has been tastefully renovated and refurbished over the years. Today it retains the character and ambience of a past era, featuring chintz curtains and interesting pictures and ornaments. A warm welcome is extended to guests from owners Irene and Paul Butt and their talkative parrot, Captain! The resident ghost, Sebastian, is also reputed to be friendly... The accommodation is excellent, with spacious and individually-appointed bedrooms offering every comfort. In the winter months, the lounge is the place to sit and enjoy the cosy warmth of a log fire. Two full-time chefs create memorable dishes, using the best and freshest local ingredients. The menu includes delicious starters, such as sherried kidney tart, cream of Devon crab soup or grilled goats cheese with walnuts and walnut oil salad, and a good selection of speciality dishes, grills, snacks and sweets. An extensive choice of drinks, including four traditional ales, is served in the bars. The wine list has been awarded many accolades for its selection. The cathedral city of Exeter, Dartmoor and Exmoor are all close by. **Directions:** Take the A377 Exeter-Barnstable Road. Coleford is signed two miles from Crediton. Price guide: Single £46–£56; double £60–£70.

For hotel location, see maps on pages 212-218

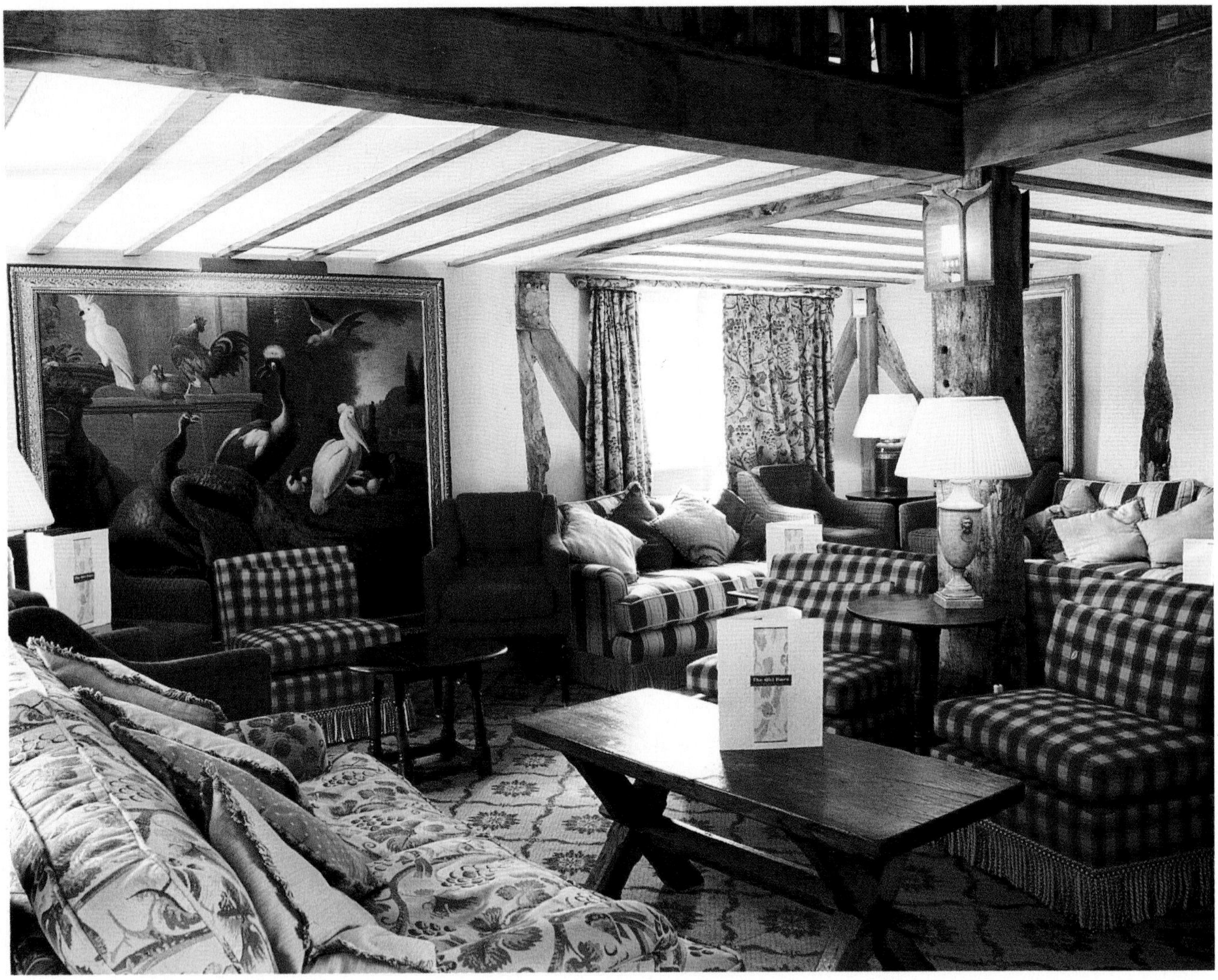

THE PLOUGH INN & OLD BARN RESTAURANT

MACCLESFIELD ROAD, EATON, NR CONGLETON, CHESHIRE CW12 2NH
TEL: 01260 280207 FAX: 01260 298377 E-MAIL: rpms96@focusnet.co.uk

Few inns can claim such a beautiful barn restaurant as that at The Plough, a lovely, half-timbered coaching inn built in 1602. Owners Clive and Christine Winkle discovered the impressive, 300-year-old timber framed barn where it stood on the Builth Wells hills, Wales, and had it dismantled, transported and rebuilt onto their hotel. It is now a restaurant enhanced by the award-winning cuisine of head chef Colin Starkey. He produces imaginative and intriguing menus that include dishes such as pan fried scallops on a bed of oriental deep fried vegetables, asparagus and orange salad and hot banana and chocolate tart tatin laced with a Seville orange tea and vanilla ice-cream. More informal meals can be enjoyed in the inn's bar. The Plough's eight en suite bedrooms are in converted stables. All have a delightful, individual character, are splendidly furnished and decorated with luxurious fabrics in the style of the famous Royal Doulton pottery ranges. The inn is situated on the edge of the Peak National Park and is an ideal base for touring and visiting many historic sites, Royal Doulton, Jodrell Bank and the Halls at Little Moreton, Capesthorne and Gawsworth. **Directions:** Exit the M6 at either junctions 17 or 18. Follow the directions to Congleton then take the A34 towards Manchester. After approximately half-a-mile turn onto the A536 towards Macclesfield. The Plough is one mile further on. Price guide: Single £45–£58; double/twin £55–£75.

For hotel location, see maps on pages 212-218

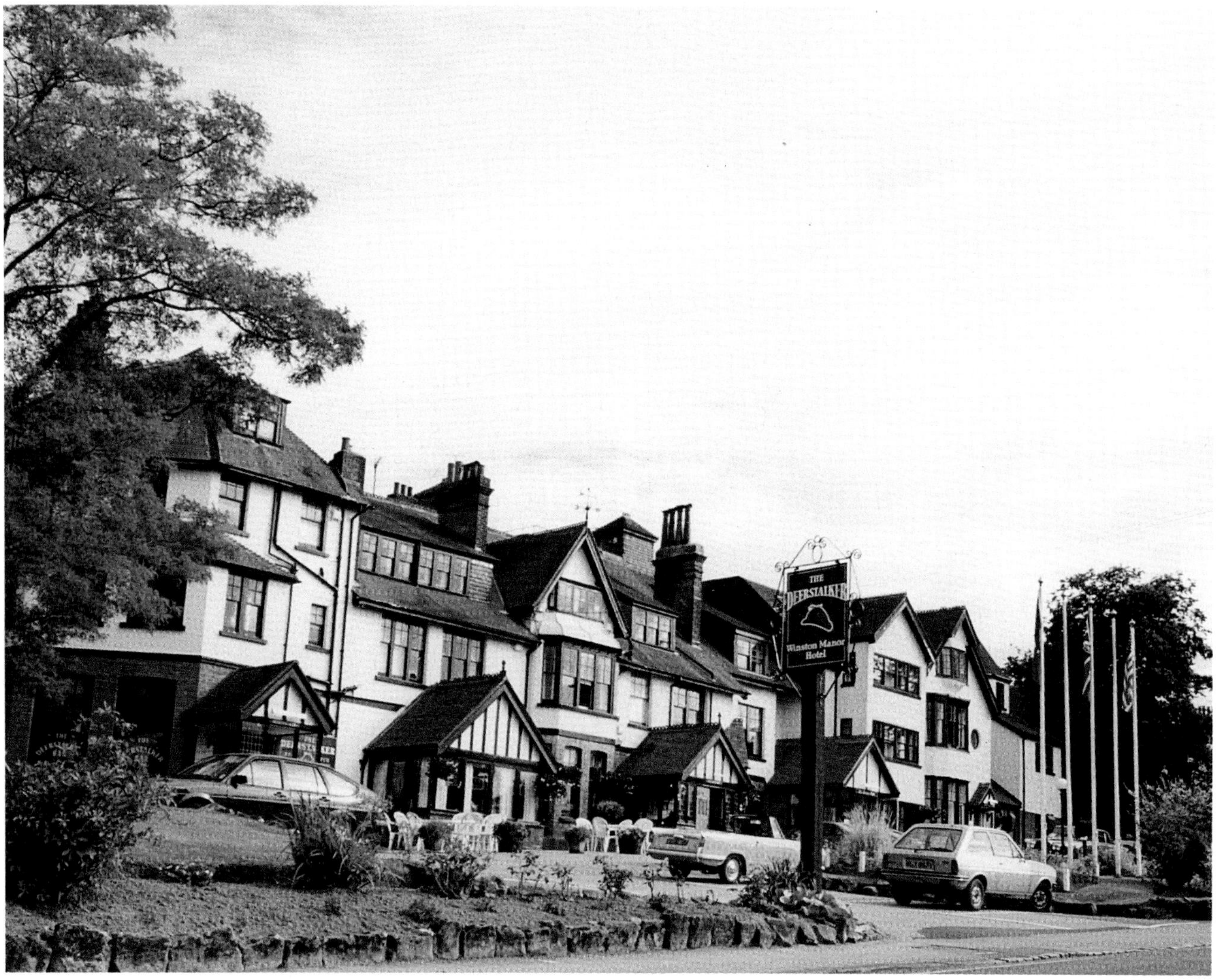

WINSTON MANOR

BEACON ROAD, CROWBOROUGH, EAST SUSSEX TN6 1AD
TEL: 01892 652772 FAX: 01892 665537 E-MAIL: WINSTON@CHASLEYHOTELS.CO.UK

Set on the edge of Ashdown Forest, Winston Manor lies in the heart of English wine growing country. This charmingly traditional hotel has 51 tastefully decorated bedrooms, fully equipped to meet the needs of today's guests. The elegant Edwardian lounge, warmed by a blazing log fire in the colder months, is the perfect place to read and relax after a day's business or pleasure. The deerstalker bar offers excellent pub food and speciality local beers. Guests are invited to take advantage of the excellent facilities offered by the Oasis Leisure Club. These include a swimming pool with jetstream, sauna, Jacuzzi, fully equipped state-of-the-art gym, sunbed and Beauty Room. In Le Petite Maison Restaurant, an award-winning team of chefs provides a superb range of dishes, complemented by an extensive range of fine wines. Sample the delicious roasted sea bream and grey mullet served with couscous and sun-dried tomato and coriander butter sauce or be tempted by the grilled Scottish sirloin steak au poivre, accompanied by a shallot brandy and green peppercorn sauce. Awarded 2 Rosettes for its cuisine. Glyndebourne, Chartwell, Hever and Leeds Castles and Penshurst Place are nearby. Golf enthusiasts are spoilt for choice with five first-class courses within easy reach. **Directions:** From M25, Jct5 via Tunbridge Wells. Winston Manor is set back from A26, between Tunbridge Wells and Uckfield. Price guide: Single £95; double £115.

For hotel location, see maps on pages 212-218

The Victoria Hotel

VICTORIA ROAD, DARTMOUTH, DEVON TQ6 9RT
TEL: 01803 832572 FAX: 01803 835815

The Victoria Hotel is situated just 150 yards from the River Dart and harbour in Dartmouth, a town steeped in history in an area of unspoilt natural beauty. In the elegant bedrooms, great attention has been paid to the quality of furnishings and lighting to provide an environment of total comfort and luxury. All rooms include an en suite shower or bathroom and full range of modern amenities. The lounge bar offers excellent food, traditional beers and fine wines. The range of leisure activities offered in this locality include sailing, boat trips to Totnes, sea fishing and golf. Every sumptuous meal produced in this intimate and inviting restaurant is cooked to order using first class local produce. A full à la carte menu is available for lunch and dinner and includes an excellent range of seafood such as local lobsters and crabs. There is also a good choice of local game and fine meals all prepared with flair. Over two dozen carefully selected wines are available to complement any meal. Dartmoor, Dartmouth Castle and South Hams are within easy reach. **Directions:** From the M5 join the A38, leave at the A384 signposted to Totnes and follow the signs to Dartmouth. Price guide: Single £45–£60; double £80–£110.

For hotel location, see maps on pages 212-218

THE GEORGE HOTEL

HIGH STREET, DORCHESTER-ON-THAMES, OXFORD OX10 7HH
TEL: 01865 340404 FAX: 01865 341620

In the heart of the Thames Valley lies The George. Dating from the 15th century, it is one of the oldest inns in the country. In the days of the stage coach, it provided a welcome haven for many an aristocrat including the first Duchess of Marlborough, Sarah Churchill. However, more recent times have seen famous guests of a different hue such as author DH Lawrence. The buildings of the George Hotel have changed little since their heyday as a coaching inn. It retains all the beauty and charm of those days, whilst offering every modern amenity. All the rooms are en suite and furnished with fine antiques and the owners have created a décor which suits the requirements of modern times whilst maintaining the spirit of the past. The menu changes daily allowing the chef to ensure that only the freshest and finest produce reaches your table. The imaginative cuisine, awarded 2 AA Rosettes, is beautifully presented and delicious. The beamed dining room provides a delightful setting in which to enjoy an excellent meal, served by friendly, professional staff. Dorchester-on-Thames provides easy access to the Cotswolds, Blenheim Palace and Oxford. Stratford-upon-Avon, Henley, Windsor and an inexhaustible source of beautiful walks and cultural and sporting activities. Excellent meeting facilities for up to 36 in the Stable Suite and two smaller rooms each for up to 8 people. **Directions:** On A4074, 9 miles south of Oxford. Price guide: Single £62.50; double £80; four poster £92.50.

18 rms MasterCard VISA AMERICAN EXPRESS M 36

For hotel location, see maps on pages 212-218

MANOR HOUSE HOTEL & RESTAURANT

HIGH STREET, OLD DRONFIELD, DERBYSHIRE S18 6PY
TEL: 01246 413971 FAX: 01246 412104

Dating from 1540, the Manor House offers a high standard of luxury for both business and social travellers. All ten en suite bedrooms are individually decorated in keeping with a 450 year old building and offer many facilities. There are two spacious luxury suites, one of which is sponsored by Champagne Piper Heidsieck and includes a complimentary half bottle of Piper with each stay. Both suites feature polished dining tables, crystal glassware and original beamed ceilings, combining the elegance of a bygone era with a luxury expected by today's discerning traveller. The critically acclaimed restaurant offers a tempting selection from both the blackboard and the extensive à la carte menus. Current delights include crisp garlic and herb tuile basket with sauteed duck livers and wild mushrooms followed by stuffed saddle of rabbit. Locally sourced produce features strongly alongside the superb 120 bin wine list, all of which are available by the glass. The hotel is ideally located as a business base supplying Sheffield and Chesterfield and for travellers visiting the Derbyshire Peaks, Chatsworth House, Bakewell, Blue John Mines and Dronfield Church. **Directions:** Old Dronfield is 5m south of Sheffield; 3m north of Chesterfield on A61 to Bowshaw roundabout, then take B6057 south. First right in the dip, left over bridge on to Wreakes Lane, the hotel is 100yards past the Peel Monument on the right. Price guide (incl extensive breakfast): Single £55; double £75; suite £115.

10 rms · MasterCard · VISA · AMERICAN EXPRESS · M 45

For hotel location, see maps on pages 212-218

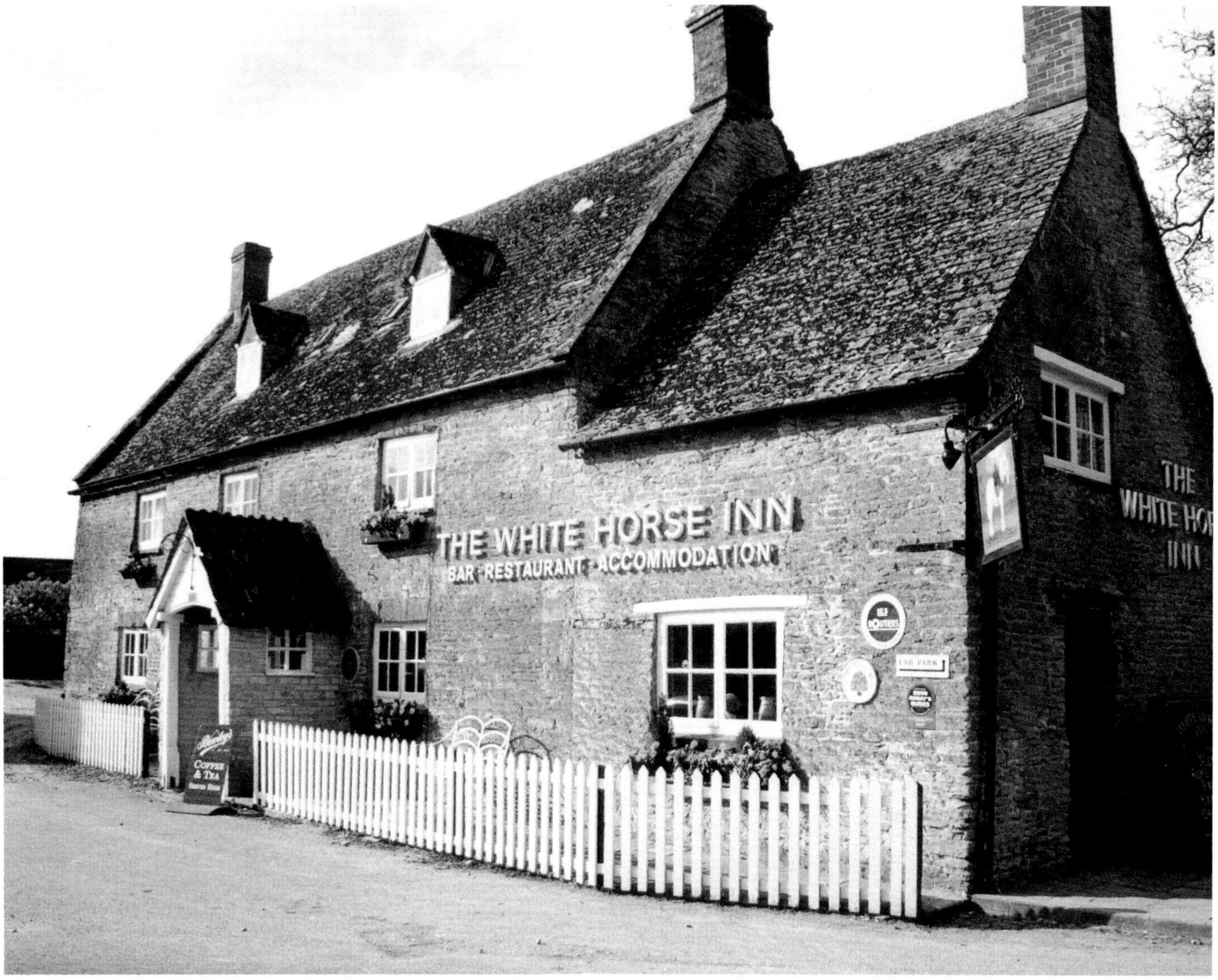

THE WHITE HORSE INN

DUNS TEW, NR BICESTER, OXFORDSHIRE
TEL: 01869 340272 FAX: 01869 347732

Built of warm, Cotswold honey stone this attractive, 17th century coaching inn is situated at the heart of the lovely little North Oxfordshire village of Duns Tew. Truly traditional is the welcome that awaits visitors as they step into its peaceful, country interior of flagstone floors, oak panelling, timber beams, wide open fireplaces and old oak furniture. A good choice of real ales and tasty, inexpensive hot and cold meals and light snacks are served in a bar full of character. The restaurant is non smoking and specialities of its varied and delicious menus are the chef's home-made dishes and local game in season. The cuisine is complemented by a thoughtfully chosen wine list. The ten, comfortably appointed bedrooms are all en suite with bath and shower fittings, colour television and tea and coffee making facilities. Some are air-conditioned and one has a four-poster bed. The beautiful Cotswold countryside is on the inn's doorstep and a short drive away is the 120-acre Cotswold Wildlife Park, Blenheim Palace, Silverstone motor racing track and Cheltenham racecourse. Golfing breaks are a speciality and microlight and glider flights can be arranged at the nearby Enstone airfield. **Directions:** The White Horse is just off the main Oxford to Banbury road, six miles from junction 10 of the M40. Price guide: Single £45; double/twin £55–£65.

For hotel location, see maps on pages 212-218

THE BLUE LION

EAST WITTON, NR LEYBURN, NORTH YORKSHIRE DL8 4SN
TEL: 01969 624273 FAX: 01969 624189

Heather moorlands, waterfalls, limestone scars and remote valleys surround the picturesque village of East Witton – the gateway to Wensleydale and Coverdale. The Blue Lion, a 19th century coaching inn, has much to entice visitors to its doors – lovely individually furnished bedrooms, welcoming public rooms with original flagstone floors and open fires, plus delicious food. Private functions for up to 45 people can be accommodated. Head Chef, John Dalby, provides an ample selection of well-compiled, innovative dishes with a frequently changing menu. Some interesting choices such as red mullet, monkfish or wild boar served with a rich port wine sauce are regularly available. The wine list that accompanies the menus offers a vast array of excellent wines from all over the world. The dining room is attractively decorated with candle-light creating an intimate atmosphere. In the bar there is a fine selection of hand-pulled traditional beers as well as an extensive menu of freshly prepared meals served at lunchtime and dinner. The spa towns of Ripon and Harrogate are within easy driving distance and well worth a visit. Jervaulx Abbey and many castles are in the area. There is an all-weather tennis court in the village. **Directions:** A6108, eight miles north of Masham and five miles south of Leyburn. Price guide: Single £48–£65; double £70–£90.

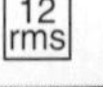

For hotel location, see maps on pages 212-218

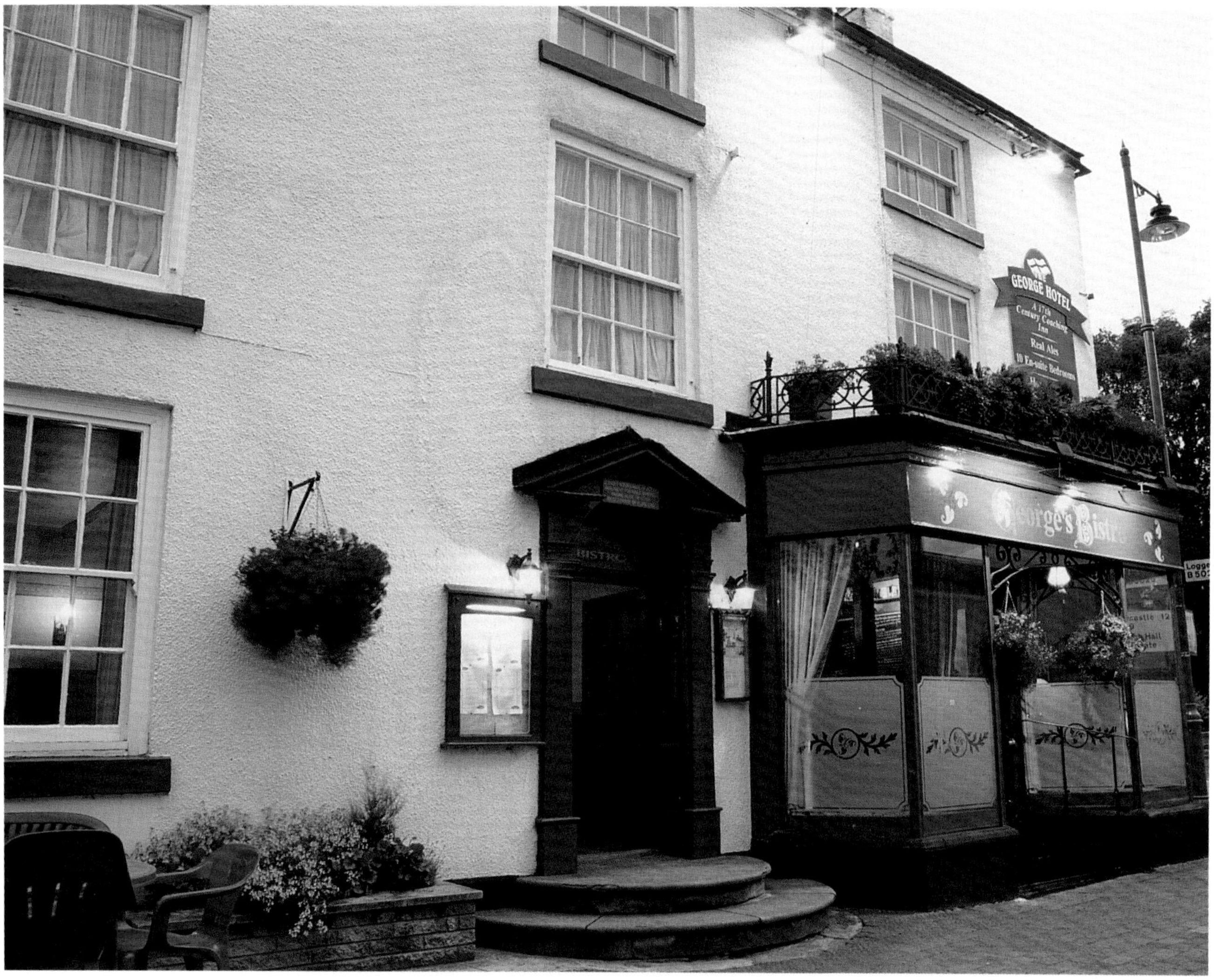

THE GEORGE HOTEL

ECCLESHALL, STAFFORDSHIRE ST21 6DF
TEL: 01785 850300 FAX: 01785 851452

This charming family-run 17th century coaching inn is set in the quaint Staffordshire market town of Eccleshall. Its nine bedrooms have been tastefully decorated in sympathy with the age and character of the building and are equipped with a full range of modern amenities. Freshly made teas and coffees are served throughout the day in the bar. With its oak beams, dried hops and Inglenook fireplace, this is also the place to enjoy fine traditional ales, malt whiskies and a selection of light lunches. The hotel also boasts its own micro brewery, producing four different ales for guests to sample. George's Bistro offers an impressive range of imaginative dishes. Tempt your palate with pan-fried breast of chicken, stuffed with a pork and capsicum mousseline and coated with a cream of onion sauce or maybe try the pot-roasted poussin, marinated in a chillied sweet and sour wild berry sauce. There is also an excellent range of fish, pasta and rice dishes to choose from, as well as various omelettes and mouth-watering grills. Shugborough Hall, Weston Park, Bridgemere Garden World, Wedgwood Visitor centre and Lichfield Cathedral. The hotel also lies within easy reach of Alton Towers and Ironbridge are nearby. **Directions:** From the M6 junction 14 turn left towards Eccleshall on the A5013. From junction 15 turn left towards Stoke, then right towards Eccleshall via the A519. Price guide: Single £55; double £90.

For hotel location, see maps on pages 212-218

Ye Old Crown

HIGH STREET, EDENBRIDGE, KENT TN8 5AR
TEL: 01732 867896 FAX: 01732 868316

This remarkably preserved old inn and staging post is unmissable in Edenbridge because it has a unique bridging sign spanning the High Street. Ye Old Crown is steeped in romantic history and tradition, having been host to thirsty and hungry wayfarers since the reign of Edward III (1327-1377). The inn's fascinating interior boasts a wealth of nooks and crannies and even a secret passage used by a notorious 17th century dynasty of smugglers, the Ramsey Gang. Although sympathetically added to, restored, renovated, refurbished and modernised over the centuries the Crown has retained many of its original features. These include a fine crown post, moulded roof plates, smoke blackened rafters and an inglenook fireplace in the bar. The six bedrooms are situated just a few yards from the inn. They are all en suite, beautifully furnished, with every facility to make a stay at the inn as comfortable and possible. Guests an enjoy bar meals or a more extensive and excellent restaurant menu that includes smoked salmon and champagne breakfast. Places of interest nearby include Hever Castle, Penshurst Place, Chiddingstone Castle, Royal Tunbridge Wells and Tonbridge. **Directions:** Exit the M25 at junctions 5 or 6. Take the A 25 to Westerham and then the B2026 south to Edenbridge. Price guide: Single from £54; double/twin from /£74.

For hotel location, see maps on pages 212-218

THE WHEATSHEAF INN

EGTON, NR WHITBY, NORTH YORKSHIRE YO21 1TZ
TEL: 01947 895271 FAX: 01947 895271

This traditional, stone-built inn is situated in a delightful part of North Yorkshire in the small village of Egton, just five miles from the sea. Proprietors of The Wheatsheaf, Susan and Michael Latus, create a welcoming atmosphere. With the emphasis on attentive service, guests receive good hospitality and excellent value for money. In the public rooms, the original character has been maintained and the small, cosy bedrooms, two of which are en suite, have been furnished in keeping with the style of an old country inn. Stone walls, oak beams and attractively laid tables are the setting for dinner. The mouth watering and varied menu is changed regularly using fresh seasonal variations. There is a good selection of starters including seafood choices. Main courses range from country pies to international dishes. There is also an extensive Lunch Menu available. The surrounding North York Moors National Park provides ample scope for walking, fishing, riding, canoeing, sailing and trips on steam trains. Captain Cook's birthplace at Great Ayton, Robin Hood's Bay, Staithes and Whitby, with its abbey, are a short drive away. **Directions:** Egton is close to Whitby. From Pickering, turn off the A169 to Grosmont and Egton in Esk Dale. Price guide: Single £30–£40; double £40–£50.

5 rms M 12

For hotel location, see maps on pages 212-218

The Christopher Hotel

HIGH STREET, ETON, WINDSOR, BERKSHIRE SL4 6AN
TEL: 01753 811677 / 852359 FAX: 01753 830914

Halfway between Eton College and Windsor Bridge, in Eton's High Street lies The Christopher Hotel, originally a coaching inn which for many years enjoyed somewhat of a racy reputation. The comfortable and elegantly furnished bedrooms are located in the main building and courtyard. A range of modern amenities includes satellite television, tea/coffee making facilities, hairdryer and direct-dial telephone. Guests may choose between having a continental breakfast served in their room or taking a full traditional English breakfast in the restaurant. Excellent food, which has a good local reputation, can be enjoyed in the relaxed atmosphere of the welcoming restaurant. The cuisine is prepared from the freshest organic produce and complemented by a fine selection of wines to suit all pockets. A traditional ambience and friendly service are the hallmarks of the Victoria Bar, offering a wide variety of food and drinks. The hotel has been awarded 3 AA Stars and 4 Crowns Commended. Windsor Castle, Eton College, Legoland, Thorpe Park and Cliveden are within easy reach. Outdoor attractions include trips on the Thames, golf at Wentworth and the Berkshire, Windsor Royal Horse Show and Driving Championships, Ascot and Windsor races. Guests may browse in the many good shops close by. **Directions:** Exit M4 at Jct5; follow signs to Eton. The hotel is in the High Street with its own car park through a carriage entrance. Price guide: Single from £90; double from £100; family rooms from £105.

33 rms MasterCard VISA AMERICAN EXPRESS M 35

For hotel location, see maps on pages 212-218

Acorn Inn

EVERSHOT, DORSET DT2 0JW
TEL: 01935 83228

Immortalised as "The Sow and Acorn" in the novels of Thomas Hardy, the history of today's inn is as rambling as the building itself. Originally known as The Kings Arms, it once brewed its own ales with water drawn from the source of the River Frome. All the original charm and character of 400 years exudes from the beamed bars and log fires that greet guests on arrival. An equally warm welcome from proprietors Martyn and Susie Lee serves as a reminder that this is one of England's classic inns. The nine en suite bedrooms, two with shower rooms only, are individually decorated and have their own style and character, each taking a name from Hardy's "Tess of the d'Urbervilles". "Tess" is a charming room with a feature bay window overlooking the village: "Silverthorn" boasts a four-poster bed, corner Jacuzzi bath and shower. All food is fresh and cooked to order by chef Gordon Sutherland who enjoys an excellent reputation. A choice of menus allows guests to choose meals either in the bar or the restaurant with a wide selection of traditional cuisine on offer, supplemented by a carefully selected wine list. The Acorn makes an ideal base for exploring Hardy country. Historic houses and gardens close by include Forde Abbey, Barrington Court and Montacute House. **Directions:** Evershot is south of A37 midway between Yeovil and Dorchester. Price guide: Single £55; double/twin £80–£120.

9 rms MasterCard VISA AMERICAN EXPRESS M 40

For hotel location, see maps on pages 212-218

Riverside Restaurant And Hotel

THE PARKS, OFFENHAM ROAD, NR EVESHAM, WORCESTERSHIRE WR11 5JP
TEL: 01386 446200 FAX: 01386 40021

The Riverside may not be a big hotel, but it has great style and a superb position, being perched high above the River Avon in the original Evesham Abbey's 15th century deer park. Three cleverly converted 17th century cottages blend with the main house to create an elegant 1920's residence. There are just seven enchanting bedrooms, all thoughtfully appointed. Lovely chintz fabrics and views over the gardens and terrace to the river add to guests' pleasure on arrival. Having a Chef-Patron, the restaurant is extremely important and a designated non-smoking area. The three frequently changing menus are reasonably priced for the exceptional range and style of choices offered. Interesting starters are followed by a selection of traditional and innovative dishes, including fresh monkfish and local pheasant. The tempting dessert list is shorter. The cellar holds 60 wines from £11.50 to £60. The restaurant is closed on Sunday evenings and all day Monday. The bar has big sofas, deep armchairs and large windows overlooking the river, the ambience being that of a country house drawing room. Guests may fish in the Avon, take a small boat out or visit the Royal Worcester Porcelain factory, go to Stratford-upon-Avon, or relax watching county cricket at Worcester. **Directions:** Take M5/junction 7 or M40/junction 16 to Evesham and approach the hotel from the B4510 to Offenham down a private drive through market gardens. Price Guide: Single £60; double £80.

7 rms MasterCard VISA M 8

For hotel location, see maps on pages 212-218

THE ROYAL OAK OF LUXBOROUGH

LUXBOROUGH, EXMOOR NATIONAL PARK, NR DUNSTER, SOMERSET TA23 0SH
TEL: 01984 640319 FAX: 01984 641298

The Royal Oak is a superb 14th century family run inn of immense charm and character. Tucked away in the folds of the Brendon Hills within the beautiful Exmoor National Park it offers the warmest of welcomes and a wealth of old world ambience. With its low, heavy, exposed beams, inglenook fireplaces, flagstone and cobbled floors, and small colourful garden it is the consummate rural retreat from today's busy world. All nine en suite bedrooms, most with Scandinavian pine furniture, are quiet and comfortable. The dining rooms and bars are a delight. No piped music, fruit machines nor glitzy fittings have intruded. Fine country prints and glass-cased fish catches decorate the walls. Chef Scott Fitzgerald produces exemplary country cooking. His menus are extensive, ranging from home-made soup or smoked duck to venison casserole served in a plum and cranberry sauce and fresh trout garnished with an almond, pernod and dill sauce. The surrounding countryside is a rambler's paradise. A network of footpaths radiates from the inn and there are innumerable picturesque villages to explore. Shooting, fishing, riding and off-road safaris can be arranged. **Directions:** Exit the M5 at junction 25. Take the A358 towards Minehead, turn left at Washford, then right at The White Horse for Roadwater. Luxborough is signposted. Price guide: Single £30; double/twin £50-£65.

9 rms M 10

For hotel location, see maps on pages 212-218

The Royal Oak Inn

WITHYPOOL, EXMOOR NATIONAL PARK, SOMERSET TA24 7QP
TEL: 01643 831506/7 FAX: 01643 831659

The Royal Oak Inn has a reputation for good food and hospitality spanning 300 years. Set in the pretty village of Withypool, it is ideal for exploring Exmoor. Today's visitors are offered comfortable accommodation in individually furnished bedrooms. A two bedroom self-contained cottage is also available. The Residents' and Rod Room Bars, with their beamed ceilings and crackling log fires, epitomise the character of an old country inn. 1998 Michelin Hostelry Award. The restaurant, open in the evenings, offers guests table d'hôte and à la carte menus. Dishes of the highest calibre are cooked to order with particular emphasis on preparation and presentation. To complement the meal, choose from a list of over 70 carefully selected wines. Extensive lunch and supper menus are available in the Rod Room Bar. The inn specialises in organising country sports for either groups or individuals. Arrangements can be made for riding, hunting, stabling, game shooting, fly-fishing and Exmoor Safaris. **Directions:** Withypool is seven miles north of Dulverton – just off the B3223 Dulverton–Exford road, or 10 miles off North Devon Link road A361 via North Molton. Price Guide: Single £33–£61; double £66–£92.

8 rms MasterCard VISA AMERICAN EXPRESS

For hotel location, see maps on pages 212-218

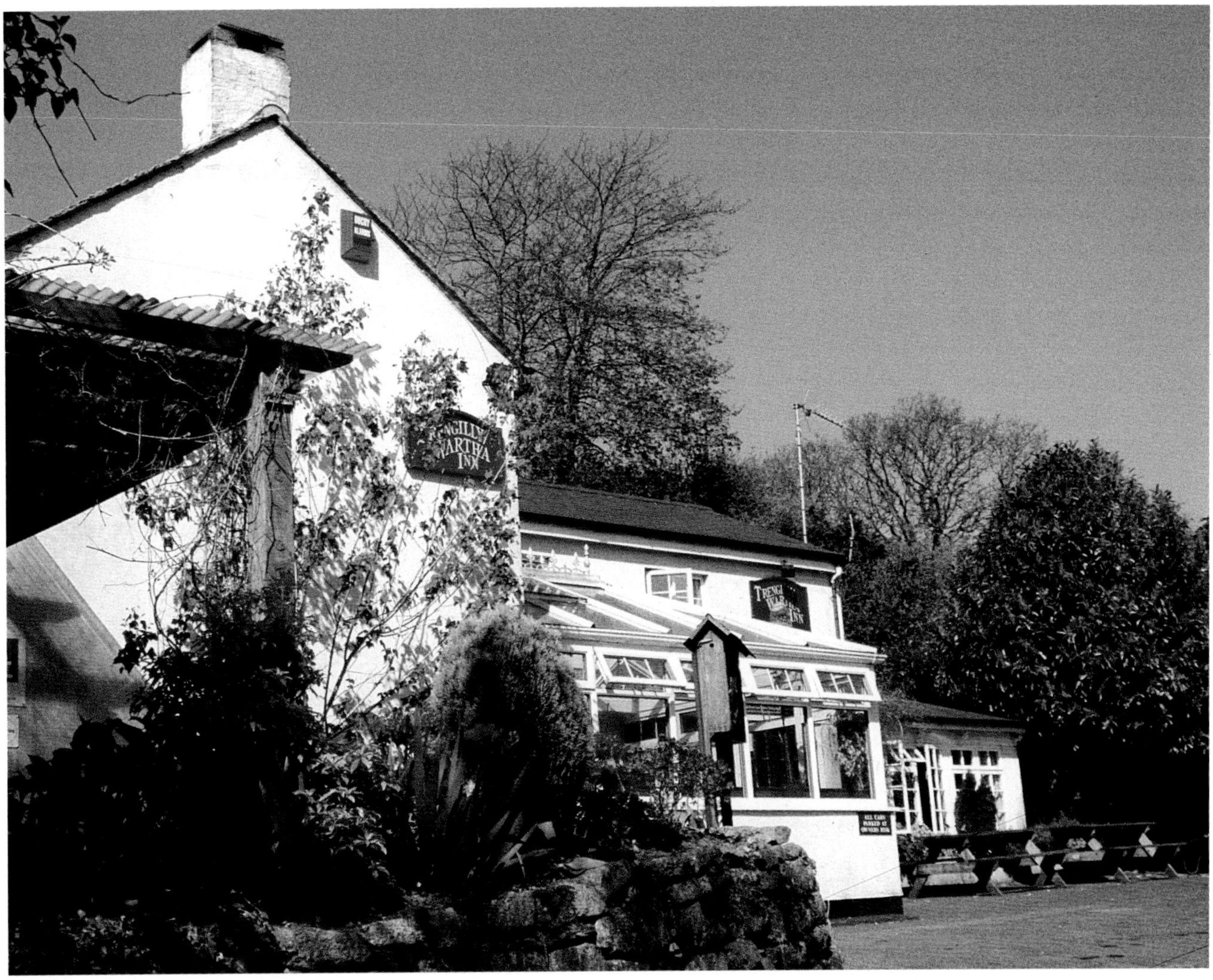

Trengilly Wartha Country Inn & Restaurant

NANCENOY, CONSTANTINE, FALMOUTH, CORNWALL TR11 5RP
TEL: 01326 340332 FAX: 01326 340332 E-MAIL: trengilly@compuserve.com

Trengilly Wartha is in "an area of outstanding natural beauty" near the village of Constantine, close to the Helford River. The location is romantic and famous. Daphne du Maurier's novel 'Frenchman's Creek' could have been written here about the local creek Polpenwith. The ambience is like staying in a private house that happens to be the local inn – there are newspapers in the attractive lounge and the Logan and Maguire families are very hospitable. The 'cottage' bedrooms are pristine, furnished in pine. Trengilly's Bar is cheerful, frequented by the locals. Being a freehouse a good range of real ales is available, together with farm ciders. The Beer Garden overlooks the valley and the vine shaded pergola offers escape from the sun. In winter a big fire blazes! The bar food is delicious. The restaurant has a Gallic theme, both in appearance and having an ever-changing inspired Prix-Fixé menu – local fish included – and the wines are superb (180 listed!) The substantial breakfast is very English. Energetic guests sail, golf, ride or surf off the nearby beaches. Cornish gardens, little harbours, the seal sanctuary, Falmouth harbour and the Lizard Peninsula must be explored. **Directions:** A39 to Falmouth, then head for Constantine on B3291, where the inn is signed. Price guide: Single £39–£44; double £52–£80.

For hotel location, see maps on pages 212-218

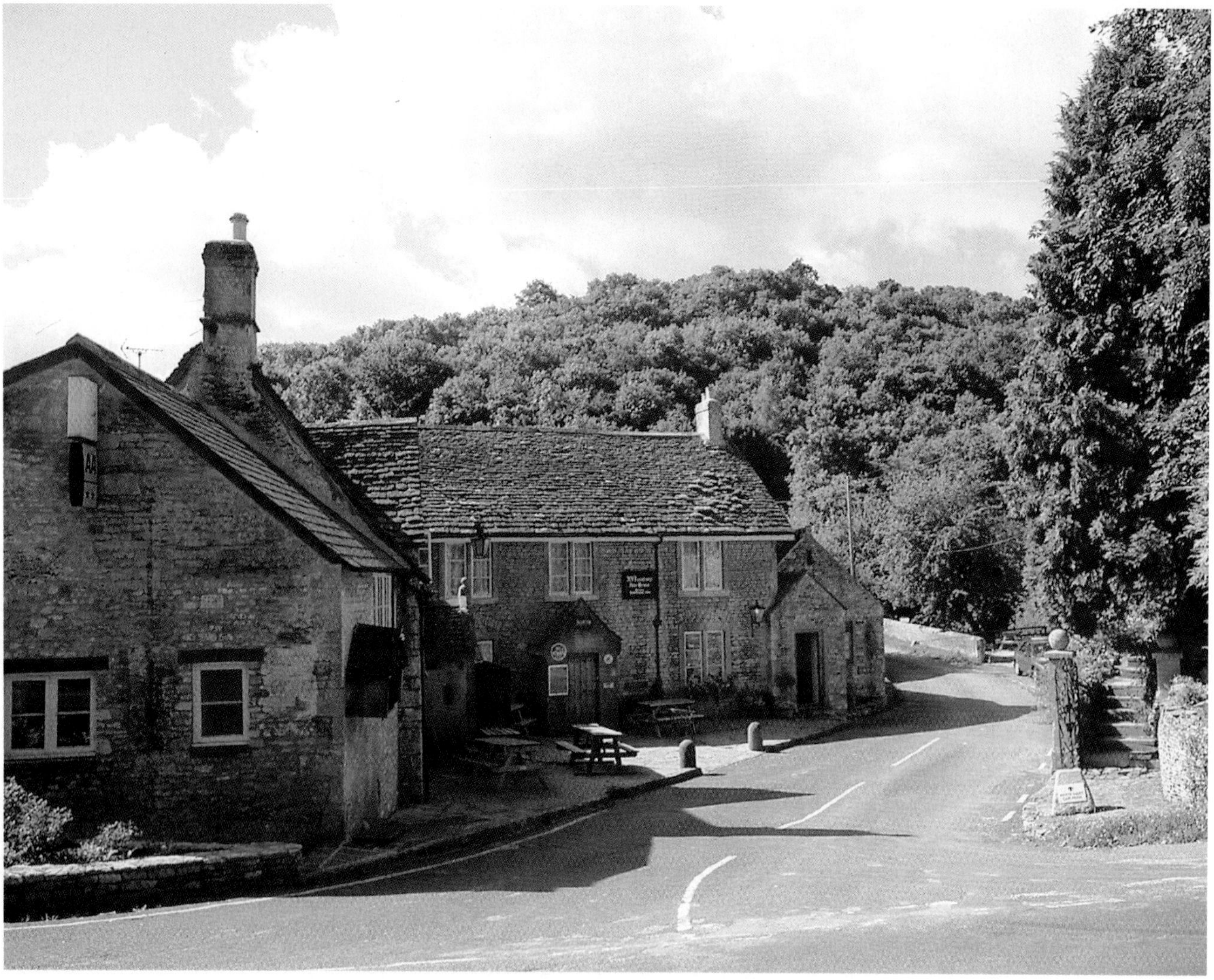

The White Hart

FORD, CHIPPENHAM, WILTSHIRE SN14 8RP
TEL: 01249 782213 FAX: 01249 783075

Believed to date back to 1553, the White Hart is made of stone and prettily situated alongside the Bybrook River. The terrace overlooking the water is the ideal spot to eat and drink while looking out for kingfishers, herons and wagtails. Despite its rustic character, country lanes and riverside walks, the small village of Ford is within easy reach of the M4, Chippenham and Bath. Four of the bedrooms have four-poster beds and two have half-testers. Whether your room is located in the old stable block or main building, it will be comfortable and well-equipped. The White Hart is renowned for its delicious home cooking: all meals are freshly prepared, carefully presented and offer very good value. In the Riverside Restaurant the extensive à la carte menu typically includes venison casserole, herb-roasted grouse, supreme of chicken with a crab and saffron sauce and rack of lamb with chestnut and leek stuffing. The bar menu includes hearty soups, pies and ploughman's lunches. As well as traditional scrumpy, the bar offers one of Wiltshire's widest selection of real beers. The Good Pub Guide 'Pub of the Year' 1995 and Les Routiers Inn of the Year 1996. There are a number of country walks nearby – you can walk through the Bybrook Valley to Castle Combe. Bath, Bowood House, Corsham Court and Lacock are also close by. **Directions**: Leave the M4 at junction 17 or 18. Ford is situated off the A420 Bristol–Chippenham road. Price guide: Single from £50; double from £75.

For hotel location, see maps on pages 212-218

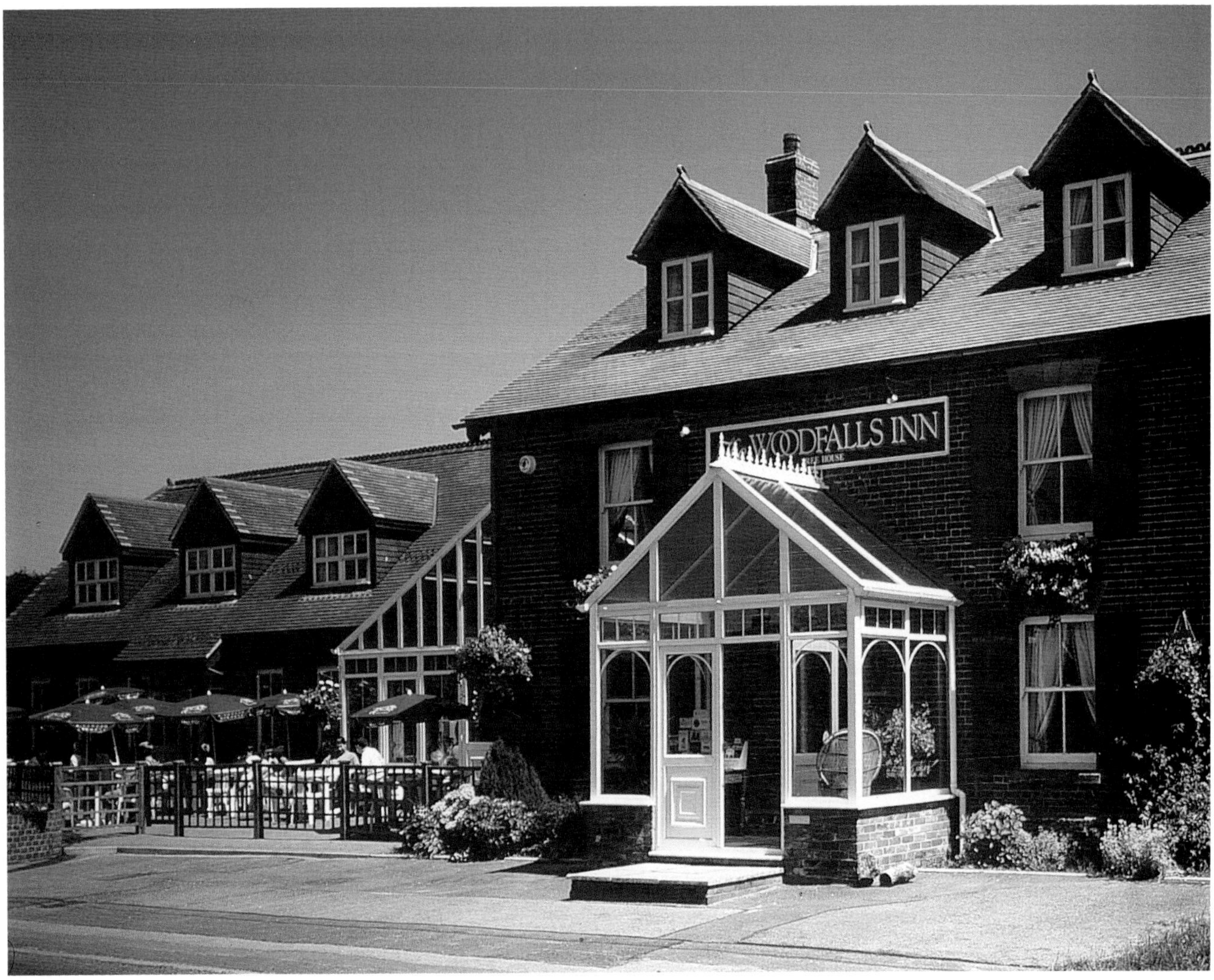

THE WOODFALLS INN

THE RIDGE, WOODFALLS, FORDINGBRIDGE, HAMPSHIRE SP5 2LN
TEL: 01725 513222 FAX: 01725 513220

Standing alongside the old coaching route from the beautiful New Forest to historic Salisbury, The Woodfalls Inn has provided rest and relaxation for travellers since 1870. Its welcome, hospitality, quality of service and traditional English ambience is such that owner Michael Elvis was honoured with the prestigious Innkeeper of the Year award by the British Institute of Innkeeping last year. All the bedrooms, named after flowers of the forest, are en suite, extremely comfortable and are tastefully and individually decorated in typically English fashion. Some have four posters. The inn also has a purpose-built conference and meetings suite with a capacity for up to 150 delegates. The standard of cuisine served in the intimate Lovers' Restaurant will satisfy every palate. Chef Paul Boyland produces excellent French dishes and interesting ethnic touches on his frequently changing table d'hôte and à la carte menus. More informal meals can be enjoyed in the conservatory or bar which has an extensive selection of properly stored cask conditioned ales. Picnic baskets can be arranged. Walking and riding in the enchanting New Forest, sailing on the Solent, golf and Salisbury with its cathedral is within easy reach. **Directions:** From the M27, exit at junction 1. Take the B3079, fork left at Brook onto the B3078, then fork right at Telegraph Corner onto the B3080 for Woodfalls. Price guide: Single £49.95; double £59.95–£95.

For hotel location, see maps on pages 212-218

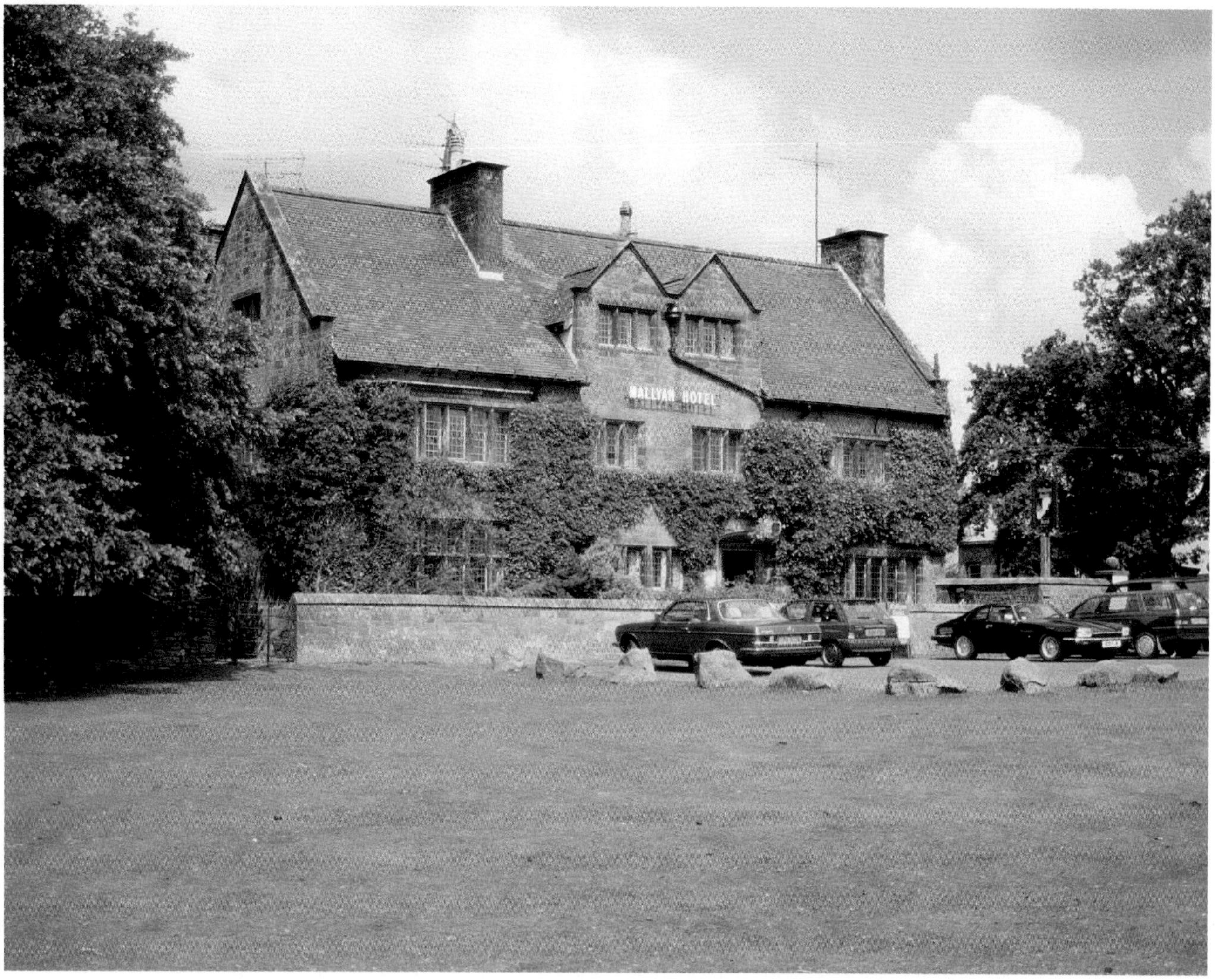

Mallyan Spout Hotel

GOATHLAND, NEAR WHITBY, NORTH YORKSHIRE YO22 5AN
TEL: 01947 896486 FAX: 01947 896327

Set in excellent walking country, this is a perfect spot from which to explore the beautiful North York Moors National Park, to cast for trout or salmon on the River Esk and to enjoy many country pursuits such as riding. The hotel occupies a fine position in the picturesque village and takes its name from the waterfall flowing through the wooded valley, just a short walk away. Behind the stone-built, ivy-clad exterior are comfortable rooms with a relaxing atmosphere. Three spacious lounges command views of the two acre garden and Esk valley beyond. Cottage-style bedrooms, decorated with lovely fabrics, provide every convenience. An impressive table d'hôte menu offers guests an extensive choice of dishes, making it easy to see why this restaurant is so popular locally. Freshly caught seafood from Whitby is a house speciality. An AA Rosette has been awarded for cooking. Take a scenic trip on the North York Moors Railway. Whitby Abbey, once a burial place for kings and Easby Abbey, a 12th century monastery are both close by. Magnificent Castle Howard is just 20 miles away. **Directions:** The hotel is situated 9 miles from Whitby and 38 miles from York. From the A169 Pickering-Whitby road, turn off to Goathland. The nearest railway station is Whitby. Price guide: Single £50–£65; double £65–£135.

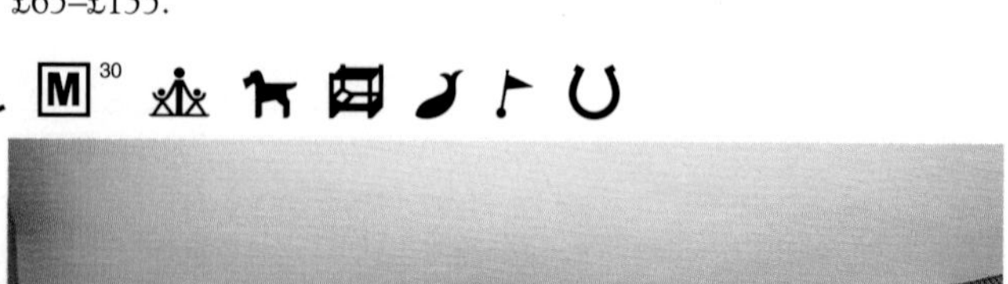

For hotel location, see maps on pages 212-218

THE LEATHERNE BOTTEL RIVERSIDE INN & RESTAURANT

THE BRIDLEWAY, GORING-ON-THAMES, BERKSHIRE RG8 0HS
TEL: 01491 872667 FAX: 01491 875308

Winner of the Johansens 1996 Most Excellent Restaurant Award. The setting is unique, on the banks of the Thames in a nature conservation area, overlooking water meadows and the Berkshire Downs. Self-taught chef-patron Keith Read has become widely acclaimed. The Times has awarded him a six-star rating and includes him among today's most accomplished chefs. Egon Ronay described him as unpretentious and imaginative, relying on fresh, quality produce. In summer, dine in the riverside terrace garden, ablaze with colour and scented with wild herbs. The menu may include sea bass with virgin olive oil, samphire and sweet ginger, or tuna with apple mint and a stew of plum tomatoes and basil. In winter, log fires glow and the smell of simmering game stock fills the air. Local pheasant flavoured with lemon thyme and pancetta, or wood pigeon with red chilli, chick peas and coriander, are among the choices. Puddings are simple and mouth-watering: ginger brandy snap baskets full of summer berries, or steaming cappuccino pudding with Mount Gay sauce. The dining rooms reflect the style and taste of the owner: strong colours, fresh flowers and faultless yet relaxed service. Each table has a view of the river and the bar is filled with cookery books and marble sculptures. **Directions:** Signed off B4009 Goring–Wallingford road. From M4 Jct12: 15 mins; from M40 Jct6: 15 mins. Oxford is 30 mins drive, London 60 mins. Price guide (dinner for two incl. wine): £90–£120.

For hotel location, see maps on pages 212-218

GRIMSTHORPE (Bourne)

THE BLACK HORSE INN

GRIMSTHORPE, BOURNE, LINCOLNSHIRE PE10 0LY

TEL: 01778 591247 FAX: 01778 591373 E-MAIL: blackhorseinn@saqnet.co.uk

The Black Horse Inn lies within a short detour off the A1. Skilful restoration work has preserved the charm of the old inn while upgrading the accommodation to a high standard of modern comfort. The traditional character of the bar creates a welcoming area for guests and local residents alike. The original beams, stone walls and open fires all add to the considerable charm of the inn. There is a delightful honeymoon/executive suite with its own small sitting room and a spa bath. Guests can chose between the innovative bar and dining room menus. The menu which won the Inn the award for Perrier Young Chef of the Year 1997/8 is offered – Cappaccino of puy lentil soup, tarragon stuffed fillet of lemon sole, pheasant breast stuffed with chicken, prunes and chestnuts with fondant potatoes and sautéed sprouts with lemon tart for dessert. There's something to tempt the most discerning of palates – with game and fish as in season – and the dishes are complemented by a very reasonably priced fine wine list. Grimsthorpe Castle, with its attractive park and nature trail around the lake, Burghley House, famous for its horse trials, Belvoir Castle and Belton House all lie close by. Golf, fishing and swimming are all within a 20 minute drive. **Directions:** Leave A1 between Grantham and Stamford, taking A151 at Colsterworth heading towards Bourne. Price Guide: Single £50–£55; double £60–£75; suite £85.

6 rms · MasterCard · VISA · AMERICAN EXPRESS · M 40 · 14

For hotel location, see maps on pages 212-218

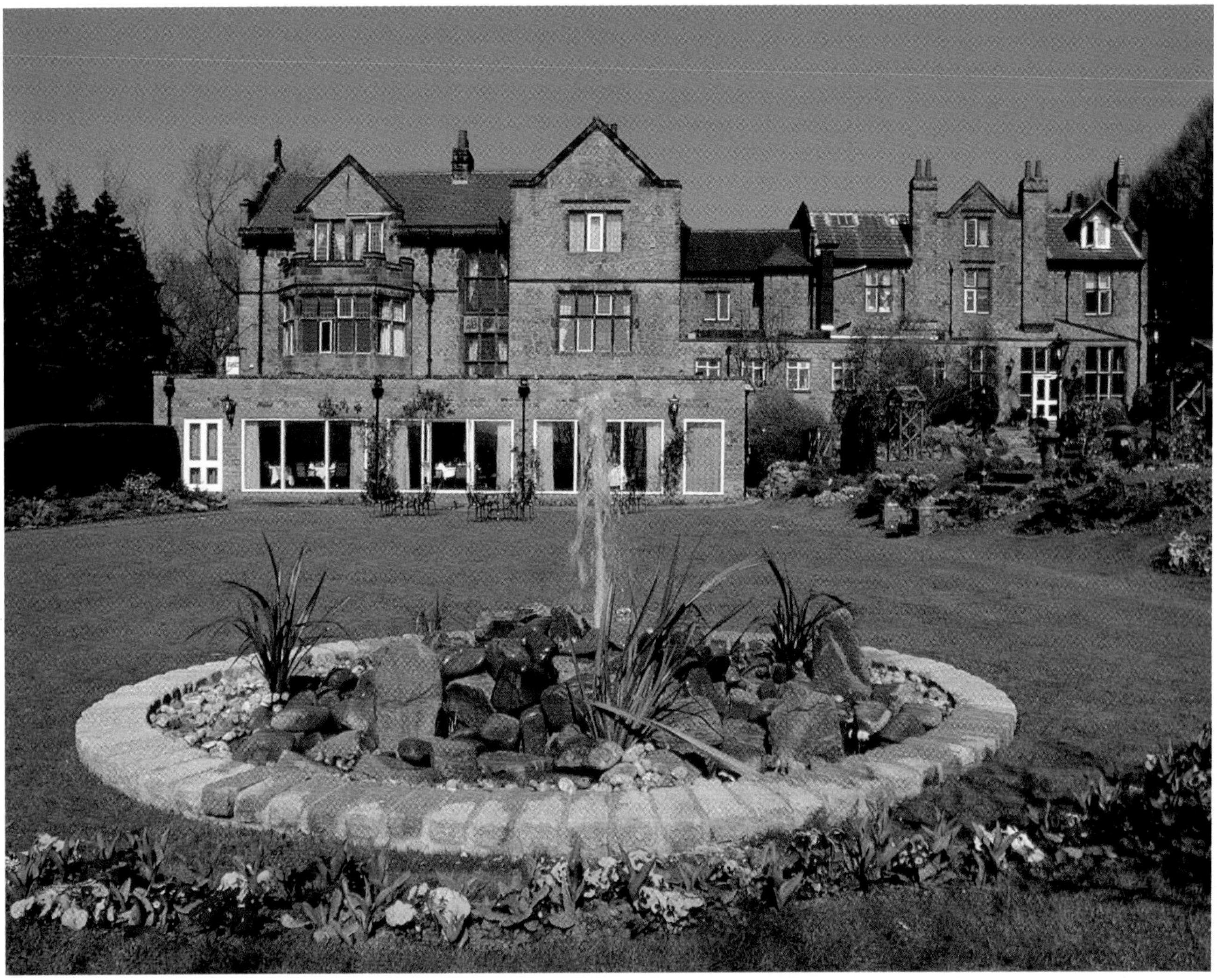

THE MAYNARD ARMS

MAIN ROAD, GRINDLEFORD, DERBYSHIRE S32 2HE
TEL: 01433 630321 FAX: 01433 630445

The owners of this Victorian inn have transformed its ambience and image into a very stylish small hostelry at this superb location overlooking the beautiful Derbyshire Peak National Park. The en suite bedrooms, which include two suites, are charming, comfortable and well equipped. Guests booking Friday and Saturday nights may stay in their room free on the Sunday night (except before Bank Holidays). The excellent restaurant offers a primarily traditional English fare featuring local game when in season, together with a carefully selected wine list. An extensive range of bar food is served at lunchtime and in the evenings in the Longshaw Bar – the busy hub of the inn. The second, quieter, bar is ideal for a drink before dinner and has a big log fire in winter months. There is a peaceful lounge with a view of the pretty gardens and the Dales. Chatsworth, Haddon Hall and Castleton are spectacular reminders of the heritage of the region. The market town of Bakewell is fascinating. Walkers have an endless choice of directions to take. Fishing is on the Derwent. Golf, pony-trekking and even gliding can be arranged locally. Regional theatres abound. **Directions:** Leaving Sheffield on the A625, The Maynard Arms is on the left just before reaching Grindleford. Price guide: Single £63; double £73.

The Rock Inn Hotel

HOLYWELL GREEN, HALIFAX, WEST YORKSHIRE HX4 9BS
TEL: 01422 379721 FAX: 01422 379110 E-MAIL: THE.ROCK@DIAL.PIPEX.COM

Situated in a tranquil valley, yet midway between the commercial centres of Halifax/Huddersfield and Manchester/Leeds, this superb hostelry offers all the attractions of a traditional wayside inn as well as the sophistication of a first-class hotel. Bedrooms are equipped to luxurious standards being en suite with baths and showers, remote-control satellite TV, mini-bar and tea/coffee making facilities. 12 new deluxe bedrooms open in September '98. The Victorian-style bar serves a range of hand-pulled ales and is open all day, every day, for meals and drinks. Superb conference facilities are available for up to 200 persons. Churchill's is a spacious restaurant, with a dance floor and a light and airy conservatory, opening out on to a large patio, overlooking a delightful rural aspect, where one can dine 'alfresco'. A variety of menus is available all day in any of the dining areas including the two conservatories, ranging from snacks to an 'East meets West' selection and daily blackboard specials. Romantic Brontë country and the spectacular Yorkshire countryside is ideal for rambling. The award-winning Eureka! Museum is a great favourite with families and the immediate area is a golfer's paradise. **Directions:** Leave M62 at Jct24 and follow signs for Blackley for approximately one mile, at the crossroads turn left for Holywell Green. The hotel is ½ mile along on the left. Price Guide: Single £45–£95; double £64–£104.

30 rms MasterCard VISA AMERICAN EXPRESS M 200

For hotel location, see maps on pages 212-218

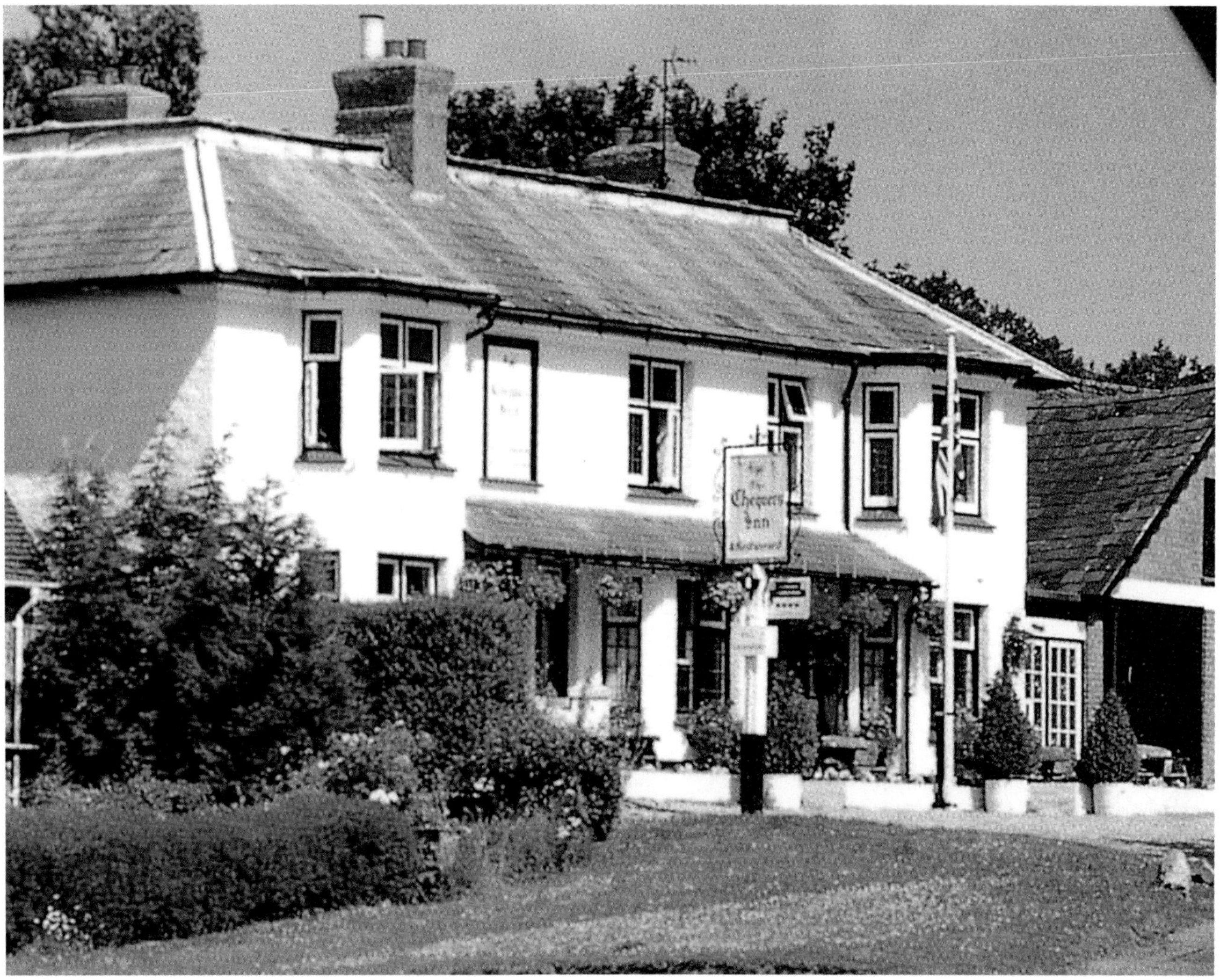

THE CHEQUERS AT SLAUGHAM

SLAUGHAM, NR HANDCROSS, WEST SUSSEX RH17 6AQ
TEL: 01444 400239/400996 FAX: 01444 400400

Situated in the 1996 award-winning Best Kept Village in Sussex, The Chequers at Slaugham is a delightful hostelry offering a good welcome, superior accommodation and acclaimed cooking. All six of the de luxe guest rooms have four-poster beds and are appointed to a high standard, each with a host of amenities that include remote-control television, trouser press, radio alarm, hairdryer and refreshments. All have four poster beds and some have spa or double baths. The public rooms are given over mainly to dining areas, however, there is a comfortable residents' lounge. The Chequers' culinary reputation has gone from strength to strength. The menu caters for all tastes but it reflects a special emphasis on seafood dishes as proprietor Paul Graham purchases fresh fish from the new Billingsgate Market. Depending upon availability, the menu may include wing of skate, halibut, monkfish, fresh crab, plaice, lemon sole, scollops, salmon and richly flavoured fish soups. Guests can also dine in the conservatory restaurant with outstanding views of the Sussex countryside. The Chequers is conveniently located just ten minutes from Gatwick and is easily accessible from London. It is also well placed for visiting the stately homes and gardens of Surrey and Sussex. **Directions**: From the main London- Gatwick-Brighton road (A23), exit 2 miles south of Handcross. Price guide: Single £55–£65; double £75–£80.

For hotel location, see maps on pages 212-218

THE BOAR'S HEAD HOTEL

RIPLEY, HARROGATE, NORTH YORKSHIRE HG3 3AY

TEL: 01423 771888 FAX: 01423 771509 E-MAIL: boarshead@ripleycastle.co.uk

Imagine relaxing in a four star hotel at the centre of a historic private country estate in England's incredibly beautiful North Country. The Ingilby family who have lived in Ripley Castle for 28 generations invite you to enjoy their hospitality at The Boar's Head Hotel. There are 25 luxury bedrooms, individually decorated and furnished, most with king-size beds. The restaurant menu is outstanding, presented by a creative and imaginative kitchen brigade and complemented by a wide selection of reasonably priced, good quality wines. There is a welcoming bar serving traditional ales straight from the wood and popular bar meal selections. When staying at The Boar's Head, guests can enjoy complimentary access to the delightful walled gardens and grounds of Ripley Castle, which include the lakes and a deer park. A conference at Ripley is a different experience – using the idyllic meeting facilities available in the castle, organisers and delegates alike will appreciate the peace and tranquillity of the location which offers opportunities for all types of leisure activity in the Deer Park. **Directions:** Ripley is very accessible, just 10 minutes from the conference town of Harrogate, 20 minutes from the motorway network, and Leeds/Bradford Airport, and 40 minutes from the City of York. Price guide: Single £95–£115; double £110–£130.

For hotel location, see maps on pages 212-218

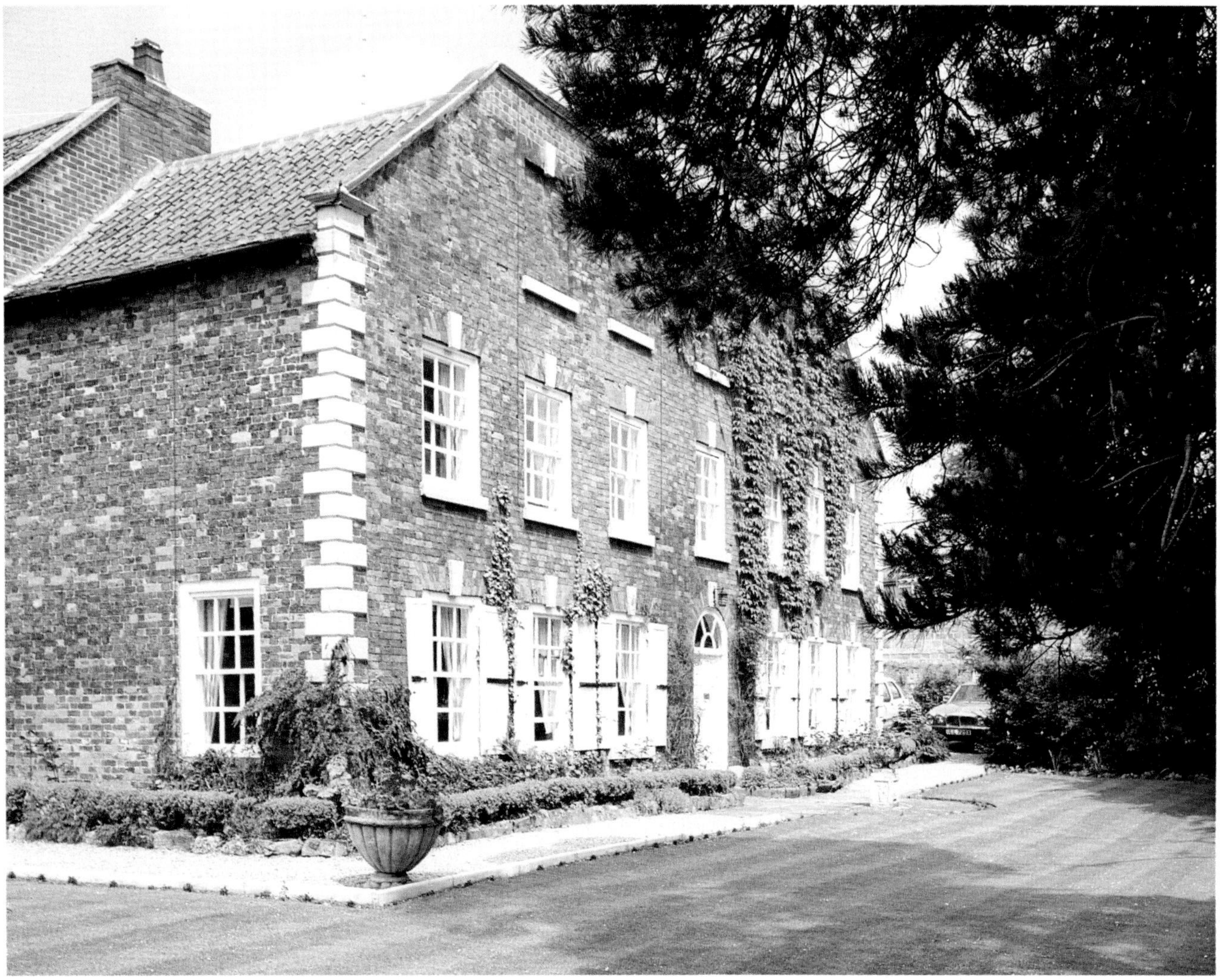

THE DOWER HOUSE

BOND END, KNARESBOROUGH, NR HARROGATE, NORTH YORKSHIRE HG5 9AL
TEL: 01423 863302 FAX: 01423 867665

The Dower House, set in the market town of Knaresborough, is a beautiful traditional hotel with features dating back to the Jacobean period. The interior, with its oak beams and comfortable furnishings, is beautifully appointed. The 32 bedrooms, in either the new wing or the main building, vary in size and offer en suite facilities, television, radio and many other amenities. Those seeking more spacious rooms will favour the older bedrooms in the original house. A truly convivial atmosphere is created in the cocktail bar, which serves all the favourite drinks alongside some more unusual combinations. The Terrace Restaurant, strictly non-smoking, has daily changing dishes and an inspired brasserie menu. Fitness enthusiasts may take advantage of the hotel's own leisure club, which may be accessed directly from the property. The Corniche Leisure Club has a swimming pool, spa pool, steam room, sauna, fully-equipped gymnasium and a poolside bar serving drinks, light refreshments and snacks. There is a wealth of historic properties within the area and these include Ripley Castle, Harewood House, Newby Hall and Castle Howard. **Directions:** From the A1(M), take the A59 into Knaresborough. Follow signs to Mother Shipton's Cave along the High Street and turn left at the traffic lights. The hotel is on the right. Price guide: Single £58–£87; double £85–£95; suite £100.

For hotel location, see maps on pages 212-218

The Low Hall Hotel

RIPON ROAD, KILLINGHALL, HARROGATE, NORTH YORKSHIRE HG3 2AY
TEL: 01423 508598 FAX: 01423 560848

The Low Hall is a lovely Grade II listed building circa 1672, personally owned and run by Richard and Maureen Stokes, with views of seven miles over beautiful Nidderdale. To the rear are lovely spacious gardens. Oak beams, stone walls and open fires all add to The Low Hall's character and cosy atmosphere. The seven bedrooms, created from the mainly Georgian part of this former family home are snug and comfortable, all en suite with modern facilities. A delightful, low ceiling bar/restaurant leads onto a patio and the gardens beyond. The hotel's original coach house is now an attractive, beamed dining area where the accent is on a high standard of cooking, quality and presentation that should please the most discerning palate. Floor-to-ceiling wine racks house a vast variety of choice for guests to consider before sitting down for dinner. The Barn Suite is a large room for parties and meetings for as many as 90 people. Harrogate is only 2 miles away, whilst Ripon is 9 miles. The historic city of York, Skipton and Leeds are within easy reach. There is trout and coarse fishing on the River Nidd, boating, horse-riding, shooting on the moors and several golf courses close by. **Directions:** The Low Hall Hotel is on the edge of the village of Killinghall, two miles north of Harrogate on the A61. Price guide: Single £50–£80; double £60–£90.

7 rms MasterCard VISA AMERICAN EXPRESS M 90

For hotel location, see maps on pages 212-218

The Hatchgate

BRAMSHILL, NR HOOK, HAMPSHIRE RG27 0JX
TEL: 01189 326666 FAX: 01189 326608

The Hatchgate is a delightful, white-fronted, traditional roadside inn that has been offering a warm welcome and serving fine beers and wine since the early years of this century. Surrounded by open countryside, it was formerly a cottage believed to have been used as a gate or toll house on the lane side between the great estates of Heckfield Park and Bramshill House, built by Lord Zouch and now the National Police College. The inn's comfortable bar, with its cosy fire and tasteful furnishings, has a relaxing atmosphere which tempts visitors to return again and again. It opens to a spacious dining area and out to a sun-catching patio and attractive garden which has a secluded and unobtrusive children's play area. A varied choice of good, substantial home cooked meals to satisfy the heartiest appetites are served. Visitors can enjoy a pre or post drinks stroll through the nearby Bramshill Wood and within easy reach are historic Heckfield Church, Wellington Country Park and Stratfield Saye House, originally built in the reign of Charles I and given to the Duke of Wellington after his victory at Waterloo. No bedrooms are available for guests. **Directions:** Exit the M3 at junctions 4 or 5. Take the A30 to Hartley Wintney and then the B3011. Bramshill is clearly signposted.

For hotel location, see maps on pages 212-218

THE PLOUGH INN

LEADMILL BRIDGE, HATHERSAGE, DERBYSHIRE S30 1BA
TEL: 01433 650319 FAX: 01433 651049

Situated in nine acres of grounds, the 16th century Plough Inn has recently been restored to give visitors every modern facility and comfort. It is in an idyllic position, close to the meandering River Derwent and surrounded by magnificent countryside which is home to many species of wildlife. Cosy and tastefully decorated, The Plough Inn provides an ideal environment in which to unwind and is an ideal base from which to explore the heritage of the Peak District. The adjoining spacious bedrooms, which are reached by an external staircase, are decorated in an attractive and welcoming cottage style and have satellite television, hairdryer and tea and coffee making facilities. All have countryside views. The inn is closed on Christmas Day. The owners have created a welcoming ambience complemented by attentive service. A good value menu offers a splendid choice of dishes. Castleton with its caves and caverns and the ruins of Pevril Castle, Bakewell's 700 -year-old arched bridge and 17th century Bath House built for the Duke of Rutland, Haddon Hall and 18th century Chatsworth House, one of the great stately homes of England, the Blue John Mine, Speedwell Cavern and Treak Cliff are all nearby. Potholing, riding, climbing, para-gliding and golf can be enjoyed locally. **Directions:** From M1 exit 29 take A617 west and then via A619 and A623. Shortly after Baslow turn north onto B6001 toward Hathersage. Price guide: Single From £40–£55; double From £60–£75.

For hotel location, see maps on pages 212-218

THE WHITE HORSE INN

HOLLOW HILL, WITHERSFIELD, HAVERHILL, SUFFOLK CB9 7SH
TEL: 01440 706081

The White Horse Inn is the ideal choice of venue for both pleasure and business. Set in the beautiful Suffolk countryside, it is only a short drive from East Anglia's many attractions and business centres. Guests are assured of a warm, personal welcome from Bernard and Cherry Lee and their excellent staff. The original character of this charming inn has been carefully retained and with its intimate corners and open fires, there is always somewhere cosy to escape to and relax with a magazine or book. The bedrooms are situated in the renovated Suffolk Cart Lodge, fronted by a pretty garden. The style is light and airy, with country pine furnishings lending a modern but homely feel to the surroundings. One ground floor room, with its romantic four-poster bed, opens out onto its own private garden. A growing reputation for superb food means that it is normally essential for guests to book a table for dinner. The excellent wine list offered here is renowned and the ales are similarly applauded. Small meetings and private functions can be held at The White Horse during the daytime. Among the many places of interest nearby are the university town of Cambridge, Newmarket and Saffron Walden. **Directions:** From the M11, junction 9, take A11 in direction of Newmarket and turn onto A1037. Withersfield is signed after Horse Heath. Price guide: Single £38.50; double £55; four poster £59.95.

4 rms MasterCard VISA M 20

For hotel location, see maps on pages 212-218

OLD WHITE LION HOTEL

HAWORTH, KEIGHLEY, WEST YORKSHIRE BD22 8DU
TEL: 01535 642313 FAX: 01535 646222

Situated on the cobbled main street in the village of Haworth, famous for being the home of the Brontë family, The Old White Lion is a 300 year old inn. Resident owners, Paul and Chris, extend a warm and friendly welcome to guests. Relax in the oak-panelled residents' lounge or enjoy a drink in one of the two cocktail bars, which also serve a wide range of home-made hot and cold bar snacks, as well as an extensive range of real ales. There are 14 comfortable bedrooms with en suite facilities, including some family rooms. Most have magnificent views over the surrounding countryside. There is a self-contained function room which seats up to 100 people, with private bar and dance area. Price on application. Featured in many of the food guides, the candle-lit restaurant offers an extensive à la carte menu as well as a good value table d'hôte. All meals are freshly cooked to order. Scenes of Jane Eyre and Wuthering Heights, Brontë Museum, Parsonage and Church; Keighley and Worth Valley Railway, Bradford, National Museum of Film, Photography and Television are all nearby. Ideal for exploring the Yorkshire Moors and Dales, the medieval city of York and the beautiful English Lake District, ten golf courses within 10 miles. Special offers and weekend breaks are available. **Directions:** Leave M62 at junction 24, then take A629 through Halifax towards Keighley. Follow signs to Haworth. Price guide: Single £60–£70; double £85–£95.

14 rms MasterCard VISA AMERICAN EXPRESS M 100

For hotel location, see maps on pages 212-218

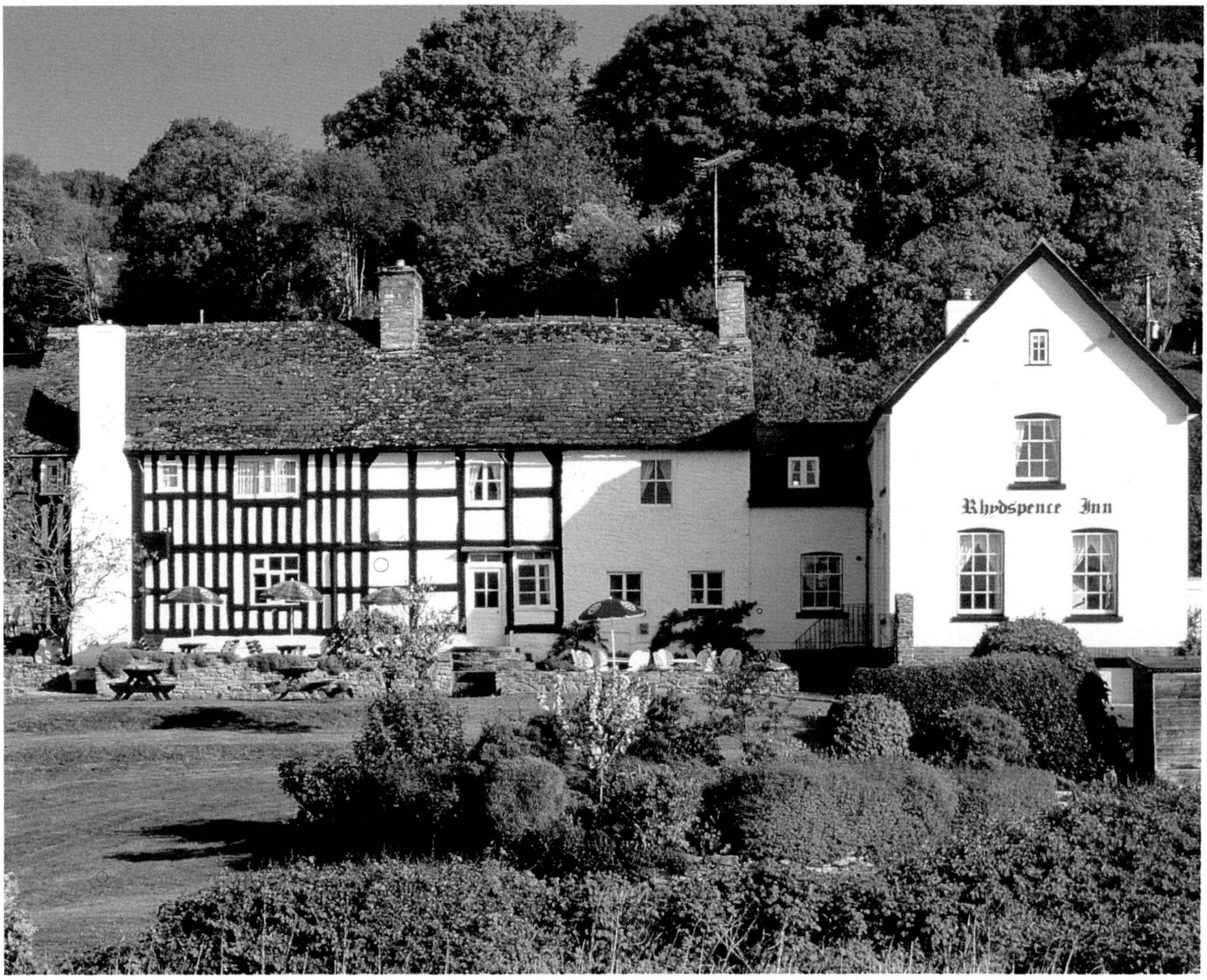

RHYDSPENCE INN

WHITNEY-ON-WYE, NR HAY-ON-WYE, HEREFORDSHIRE HR3 6EU
TEL: 01497 831262 FAX: 01497 831751

This 14th century manor house is set in the heart of Kilvert country and features several times in the works of the celebrated diarist. A striking half-timbered building, it has been tastefully extended to create an attractive dining room overlooking a well-kept garden. The bedrooms are individually furnished in time honoured style and all afford scenic views of the Wye Valley and the Black Mountains. The two welcoming bars have exposed beams and open fires typical of traditional inns and both serve draught ale and cider on tap. Closed for two weeks in January. An exceptionally well-balanced à la carte menu offers the best of country fare and international cuisine. Advantage is taken of the abundance of fresh local produce – Hereford beef, Welsh lamb, fresh fish and seasonally available game are among the choices on the frequently changing menu. The sweet trolley offers a delicious array of puddings. Snacks, both the traditional and more unusual, are served in the bar. Private parties can be catered for. The area is a paradise for nature lovers. Riding, pony-trekking, caving, wind-surfing and canoeing on the River Wye are all available and Hay-on-Wye, famous for its second-hand bookshops, is close by. For walkers Offa's Dyke Path passes near to the inn. **Directions:** The Rhydspence stands above and is well protected from the A438 Brecon-Hereford road. OS map reference 243472. Price Guide: Single £27.50–£35; double £65–£75.

6 rms MasterCard VISA AMERICAN EXPRESS M 14

THE WALTZING WEASEL

NEW MILLS ROAD, BIRCH VALE HIGH PEAK, HAYFIELD, DERBYSHIRE SK22 1BT
TEL: 01663 743402 FAX: 01663 743402

The Waltzing Weasel is a traditional country inn which, as its distinctive name suggests, offers a welcome alternative to the anonymous urban hotel. It is set within the heart of the Peak District, yet is only 40 minutes from Manchester and its international airport, Sheffield and Stockport. With its log fires, relaxed rustic character and country antiques, this is a civilised retreat for those looking for a restful break, be they tired executives, hardy walkers or confirmed slouches. They are guaranteed no jukeboxes nor fruit-machines here. Individually styled bedrooms offer comfortable accommodation and most of the rooms enjoy lovely views over the surrounding countryside. Acclaimed chef George Benham provides good, honest food in the intimate restaurant which overlooks the garden towards the dramatic landscape of Kinder Scout. Starters such as seafood pancakes, fresh asparagus and gravadlax promise good things to come. Main courses may include poached Scotch salmon, roast duck in tangy orange sauce and chicken cooked to order in white wine, tomatoes, mushrooms and crevettes. Excellent bar meals are served at lunchtime. Shooting, fishing and golfing facilities are within easy reach, as are Chatsworth, Haddon Hall, Castleton, Bakewell and Buxton with its opera house. **Directions:** The Waltzing Weasel is near A624 on the A6015 New Mills-Hayfield road, ½ mile from Hayfield. Price guide: Single £38–£78; double £65–£95.

8 rms MasterCard VISA AMERICAN EXPRESS M 12 8

For hotel location, see maps on pages 212-218

The Feathers Hotel

MARKET PLACE, HELMSLEY, NORTH YORKSHIRE YO6 5BH

TEL: 01439 770275 FAX: 01439 771101

This 15th century inn is set in the centre of Helmsley, a beautiful market town lying on the edge of the North Yorkshire Moors National Park. There are three bars: the Pickwick bar with its low beamed ceiling and open fire, the cosy Feversham lounge bar where bar meals are served and the Stables Restaurant cocktail bar. Local Thompson 'Mouse Man' furniture is featured throughout the hotel. Its 14 bedrooms have been recently refurbished and redecorated to a high standard. The hotel has an excellent local reputation for good food and fine ales. The restaurant has an à la carte menu and a carvery and bar meals are served at both lunch-time and in the evening. Delicious main courses include roulade of chicken filled with black pudding and Stilton cheese; pork fillet with a whisky and green peppercorn sauce; poached supreme of salmon set in a pool of lemon and chive butter sauce and home-made steak pie. Leisure activities in the area include golf at the Kirkbymoorside Golf Club, pony-trekking and racing at York. The East Coast resorts, Rievaulx Abbey, Byland Abbey, Duncombe Park and the historic city of York are all within easy reach. **Directions**: The Feathers is in the centre of Helmsley overlooking the Market Place. There is a private car park at the rear of the hotel. Price guide: Single £35–£40; double £60–£70.

For hotel location, see maps on pages 212-218

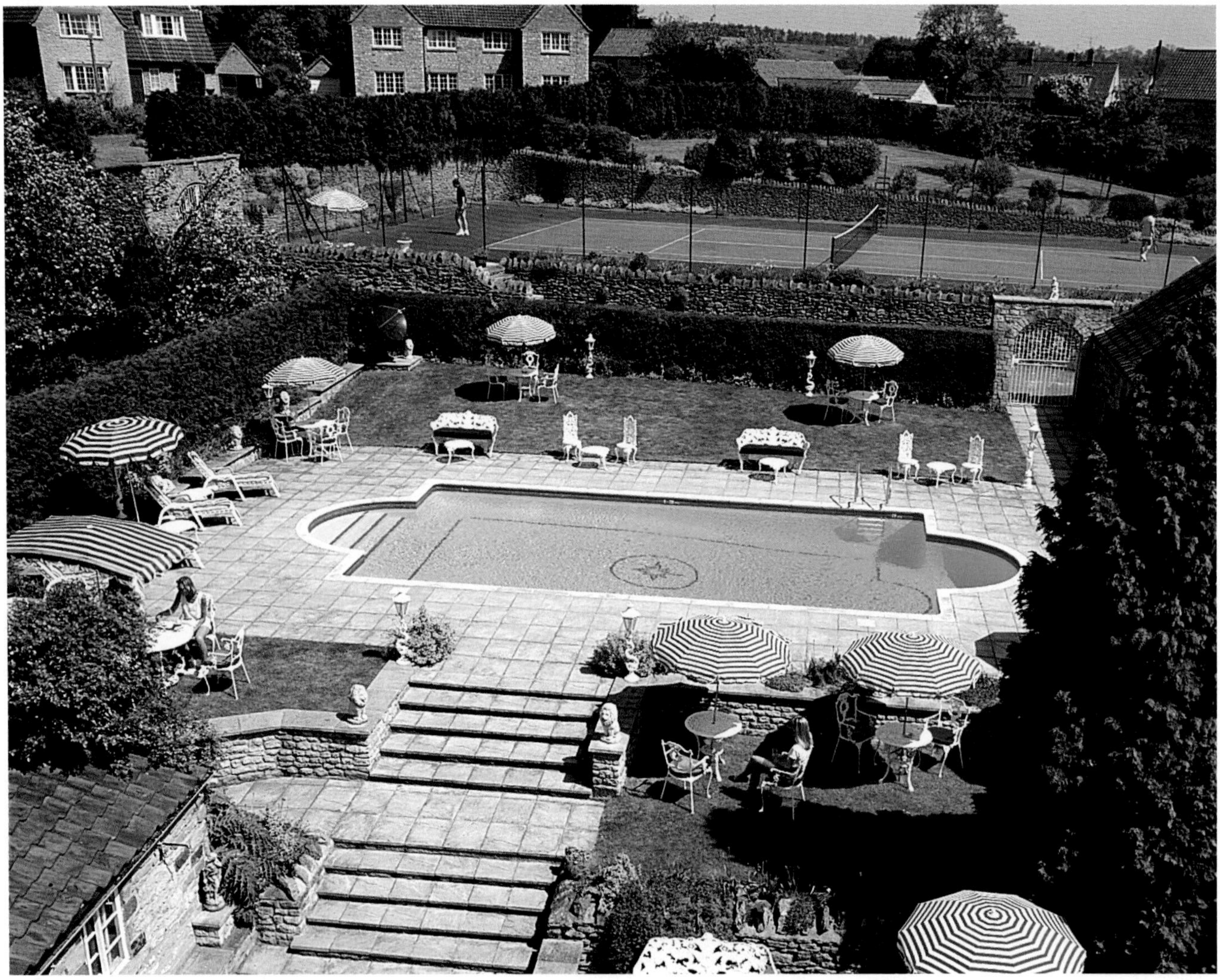

The Feversham Arms Hotel

HELMSLEY , NORTH YORKSHIRE YO6 5AG
TEL: 01439 770766 FAX: 01439 770346

This historic coaching inn, rebuilt in 1855 of mellow Yorkshire stone by the Earl of Feversham, has been owned and managed by the Aragues family since 1967. Set in two acres of walled gardens, The Feversham Arms has been updated to a high standard to offer every modern amenity, while special care has been taken to preserve the character and charm of the older parts of the hostelry. The bedrooms are individually furnished and some have special features such as four-poster beds and de luxe bathrooms. Open fires blaze in the winter months. Dogs can be accommodated by arrangement. The attractive candle-lit Goya Restaurant serves English, French and Spanish cuisine and by relying on fresh local produce, offers seasonal variety. There is a delicious fish and seafood menu. To accompany dinner, an extensive wine list includes a wide selection of Spanish wines and clarets. Situated in the North York Moors National Park and close to many golf courses, this comfortable and welcoming hotel is ideal for sporting pursuits as well as for touring the moors, dales, east coast and the medieval city of York. The ruins of Rievaulx Abbey in Ryedale (2½ miles) should not be missed. Special Bonanza Breaks available. **Directions:** From the A1 take the A64, then take the York north bypass (A1237) and then the B1363. Alternatively, from A1, take A168 signposted Thirsk, then A170. Price guide: Single £55–£65; double £80–£90.

For hotel location, see maps on pages 212-218

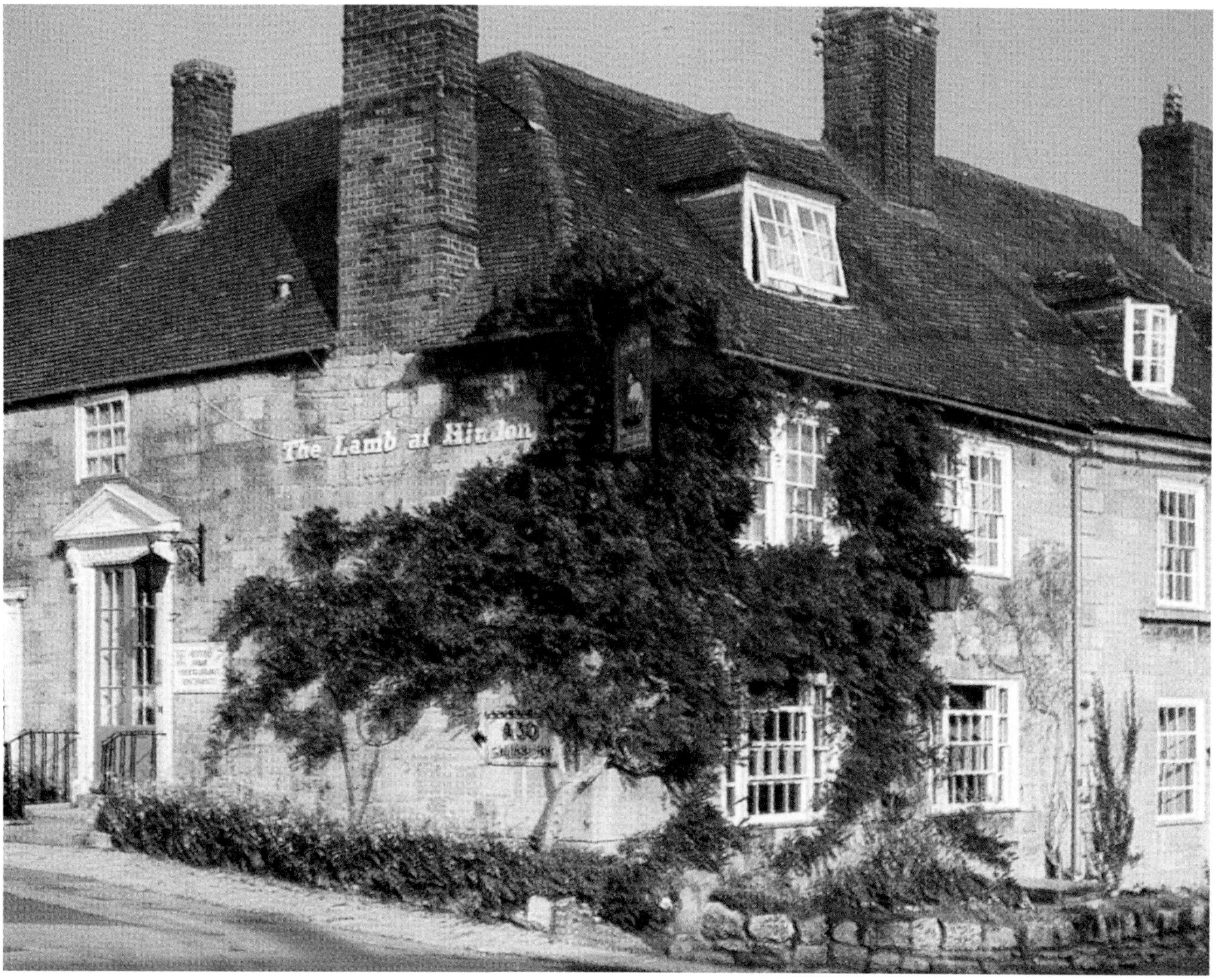

THE LAMB AT HINDON

HIGH STREET, HINDON, SALISBURY, WILTS SP3 6DP
TEL: 01747 820573 FAX: 01747 820605 E-MAIL: the-lamb.demon.co.uk

The Lamb at Hindon is a fine 17th century inn, set in the picturesque Wiltshire village, offering both comfortable accommodation and superb cuisine. The well-appointed, traditionally decorated bedrooms have en suite facilities. Popular with shooting parties and the local villagers, Cora Scott and John Croft have had a long association with the Inn and have recently acquired the freehold. The restaurant prides itself on its use of local produce and game, with seafood from Cornish ports dropped off on its way to the London markets. The friendly staff are both welcoming and professional and ensure an excellent standard of service. The Bar, with its enchanting log fires, has a relaxing ambience and guests may indulge in a variety of drinks including real ales brewed locally or choose from the extensive wine list. Trout fishing, shooting, riding and other outdoor pursuits can be organised locally. Other distractions close by include the superb cathedral at Salisbury and the breath-taking Stonehenge. Historic houses such as Stourhead, Longleat, Old Wardour Castle and Wilton are located nearby. **Directions:** From the A350 Warminster to Shaftsbury road, turn on to the B3089. Price guide: Single £43; double £65.

For hotel location, see maps on pages 212-218

Home Farm Hotel

WILMINGTON, NR HONITON, DEVON EX14 9JR

TEL: 01404 831278 FAX: 01404 831411

Home Farm is an attractive thatched farmhouse, set in four acres of beautiful grounds. A small hotel since 1950, which the owners have tastefully restored to create a charming and relaxing ambience. The staff are friendly and children are made welcome. The public rooms have big bowls of flowers in summer and enchanting log fires in the winter. Value for money is an important criterion. The Residents' Lounge is comfortable and there is a cosy, well-stocked bar serving light meals, draught beer and lager. The restaurant, oak-beamed and with an inglenook fireplace, offers a marvellous à la carte choice as well as a good 'home cooked' table d'hôte menu using local produce. The wine list is extensive. Bedrooms are in the main building or across a cobbled courtyard. All have private bathroom, telephone, colour television, hairdryer, radio alarm and tea/coffee making facilities. Wilmington is in the heart of 25 National Trust properties and there are six golf courses within 15 miles. Riding, water sports and fishing can be arranged. Honiton is known for its lace, as is Axminster for its carpets. **Directions:** Take the A303 to Honiton, join the A35 signposted to Axminster. Wilmington is three miles further on and Home Farm is set back off the main road on the right. Price Guide: Single from £35; double from £65.

10 rms

For hotel location, see maps on pages 212-218

THE ROSE & CROWN

OLD CHURCH ROAD, SNETTISHAM, NORFOLK PE31 7LX
TEL: 01485 541382 FAX: 01485 543172

Dating from the 14th century, this lovely little whitewashed inn is a favourite with visitors to North Norfolk. Tucked away in the delightful village of Snettisham it is an ideal base for bird-watching at the famous reserves of Snettisham, Holme and Titchwell, walking on the wonderful sandy beaches or on the ancient Peddars Way, golf at Hunstanton and Brancaster or visiting the area's many attractions including Sandringham, Houghton Hall and Holkham Hall. The inn has immense charm with its cosy bars, oak beams and log fires and offers excellent food, a wide range of real ales and friendly service. Each of the bedrooms has its own different character and all are decorated in rich glowing colours and fabrics and fully fitted with telephone, television, radio and tea and coffee making facilities as well as having bright and spacious bathrooms. Head chef Martin Lyon uses, wherever possible, fresh local produce to prepare a weekly changing menu of delicious modern British food. Meals may be taken in either the elegant restaurant, bustling bars or, in summer, in the lovely walled garden with its shady willow trees and herbaceous border. **Directions**: From King's Lynn take the A149 towards Hunstanton.Price guide: Single £40; double/twin £55.

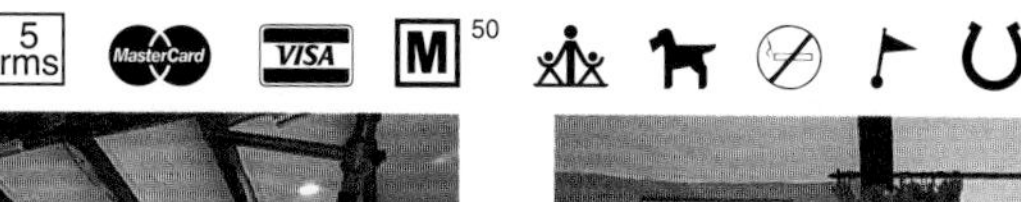

For hotel location, see maps on pages 212-218

THE KINGS ARMS HOTEL

FORE STREET, KINGSBRIDGE, SOUTH DEVON TQ7 1AB
TEL: 01548 852071 FAX: 01548 852977

Reputedly the first coaching inn in the South Hams, and with a history stretching back more than 200 years the Kings Arms Hotel offers a warm and hospitable welcome to all its guests. Located in the centre of Kingsbridge, old beams, pictures and interesting memorabilia add character to the public rooms. The peaceful Residents Lounge is the essence of comfort and is ideal for reclining and relaxing. All with en suite facilities and beautifully appointed, the 10 bedrooms feature many modern amenities and either a four-poster or half-tester bed. Imaginative cuisine is served in the restaurant and the à la carte menu comprises English and Continental dishes using local seasonal products. Excellent conference facilities are available and include the Huntsman Suite, accommodating up to 150 delegates and the Cookworthy Room, ideal for private meetings and seminars. An unexpected luxury is a superb indoor swimming pool. Guests may enjoy beautiful and scenic walks along the coast side or try their hand at sailing, golf and riding nearby. Fishing enthusiasts will be pleased with the opportunities for sea and fresh water fishing. Places of interest nearby include Dartmouth, Salcombe and the Elizabethan market town of Totnes. **Directions:** From the A38, follow signs for Kingsbridge.

10 rms MasterCard VISA AMERICAN EXPRESS M 200

For hotel location, see maps on pages 212-218

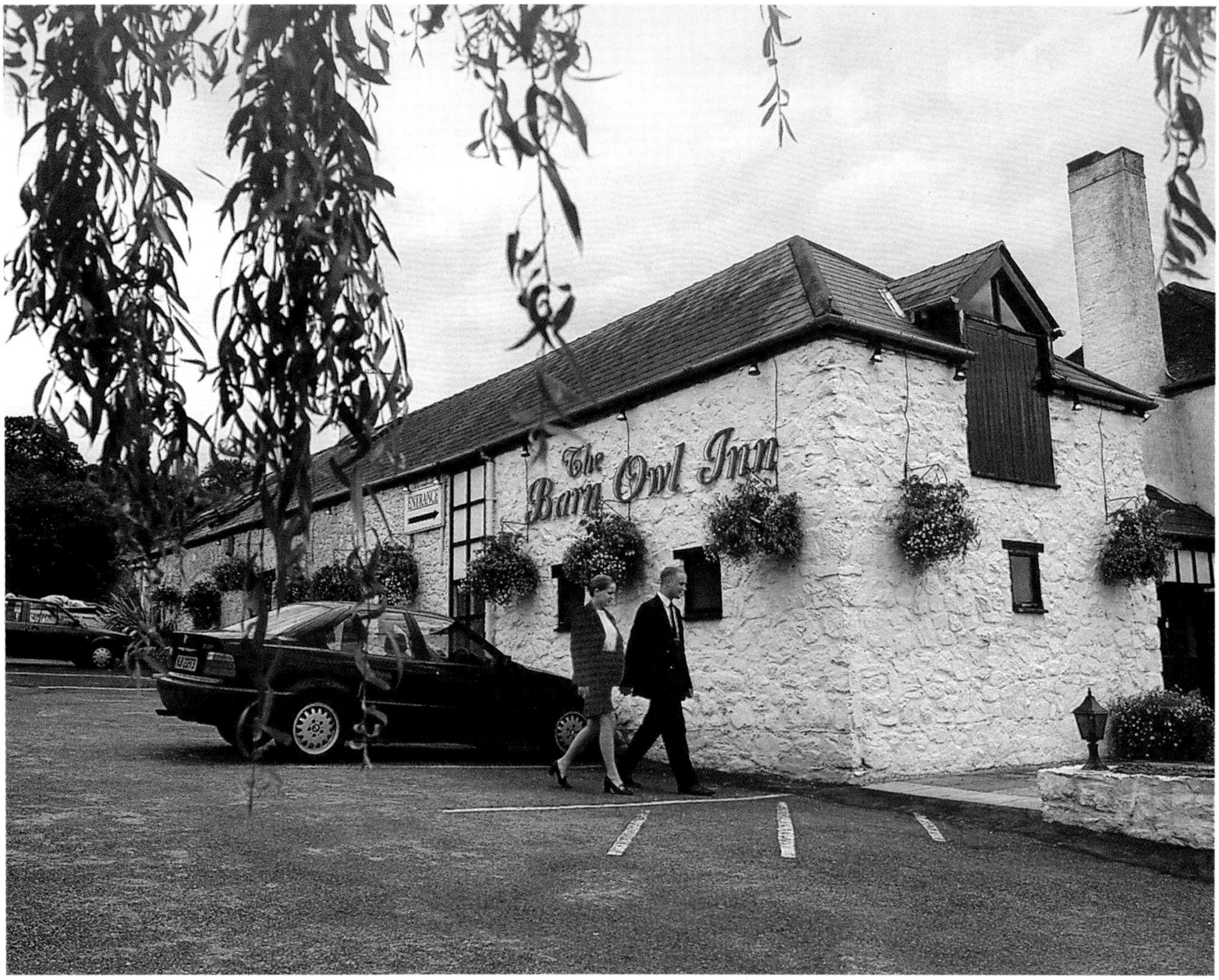

THE BARN OWL INN

ALLER MILLS, KINGSKERSWELL, DEVON TQ12 5AN
TEL: 01803 872130 FAX: 01803 875279

The Barn Owl Inn has been converted from a farmhouse into a very good value inn. Although the building dates back to the 16th century, it has modern facilities and services, while retaining many original features, including inglenook fireplaces, an ornate plaster ceiling in the largest bar and a sizeable black-leaded range. Handcrafted furniture can be found in the cottage-style bedrooms, where there are complimentary bottles of spring water and toiletries. Selecting ones meal from the fascinating menu is a challenge and the excellent but modestly priced wine list complements the superb dishes. Service is immaculate and the ambience is perfect. There is also a very good bar that serves real ale and excellent food. Torquay is a holiday town par excellence and the neighbouring seaside towns of Paignton and Brixham are in easy reach. Local places of interest include Compton Castle, once the home of Sir Walter Raleigh, Dartmoor and the underground caves in Kent's Cavern. Tennis and riding can be enjoyed locally. **Directions**: Take the M5 to Exeter, then follow the A380 signposted Torquay. Drive one mile past the Penn Inn traffic lights and the inn is on the right, signposted Aller Mills. Price guide: Single from £45; double from £60.

      35

For hotel location, see maps on pages 212-218

LONGVIEW HOTEL AND RESTAURANT

51/55 MANCHESTER ROAD, KNUTSFORD, CHESHIRE WA16 0LX
TEL: 01565 632119 FAX: 01565 652402 E-MAIL: longview_hotel@compuserve.com

This delightful house, once the home of a Victorian merchant, has been thoughtfully restored by Stephen and Pauline West to create an elegant, small, friendly hotel a few minutes walk from the centre of this little market town, so accessible from Manchester and the airport. The house has been furnished to reflect its era, with well polished antiques, fresh flowers and pleasant chintzes. The pretty bedrooms are decorated in floral cottons and benefit from hairdryers, television and a hot drinks tray, as well as Victorian pin cushions! Ten bedrooms are in the modernised 19th century house next door. There are also six luxury service apartments in a house nearby and all overlook 'The Heath'. There is a well stocked cosy cellar bar where you can relax before being seated in the comfortable period restaurant. Noted for its cuisine throughout the area, guests enjoy delights as roast beef and Cheshire puddings made with a home-made horseradish mixture, Tatton Estate venison fillet and superb vegetarian dishes. After dinner treats include lovely desserts and delicious home-made ice cream. The wine list is international with very reasonable house wines. Beautiful country house gardens and Tatton Park are nearby whilst Chester is within reasonable driving distance. **Directions:** Leave M6 at Jct19 on A556 westbound towards Chester. Left at lights, left at roundabout in Knutsford and hotel is 300 yards on the right. Price Guide: Single £40–£73; double £60–£85. Special breaks available.

For hotel location, see maps on pages 212-218

FEATHERS HOTEL

HIGH STREET, LEDBURY, HEREFORDSHIRE HR8 1DS
TEL: 01531 635266 FAX: 01531 638955 E-MAIL: feathers@ledbury.kc3ltd.co.uk

The black and white timbered exterior of The Feathers Hotel stands out very clearly in Ledbury's main street. This traditional coaching inn, which dates back to the 1560s, is impressive even by the high standards of the area. The bedrooms retain their quaint character, with beamed walls and ceilings, yet are comfortably appointed. There are two bars and a comfortable lounge area in which to relax, all with log fires. Up to 120 delegates can be seated in the excellent, first floor conference suite which also doubles as an ideal venue for social occasions. The new leisure suite comprises pool with adjacent spa, fitness gym, solarium and steam room. The Feathers' cooking has earned an AA Rosette and a great reputation in the area. The main restaurant offers an à la carte menu with appetising dishes, many of which are prepared simply, to maximise the flavour of the ingredients. More informal meals are served in Fuggles, a bistro-style bar where hops hang from the rafters. A wide range of ales and over 60 international wines are offered, to accompany dishes such as sautéd pork tenderloin with sage and calvados cream sauce. Ledbury, with its narrow lanes and cobblestone streets, is ideally placed for the Malvern Hills, Hereford, Worcester and Gloucester. Eastnor Castle and the Falconry Centre at Newent lie nearby. **Directions:** Leave M50 at Jct2 and take A417 towards Hereford. The Feathers Hotel is in Ledbury High Street. Price guide: Single £69.50–£77.50; double £89.50–£145.

24 rms MasterCard VISA AMERICAN EXPRESS M 120

For hotel location, see maps on pages 212-218

The Three Horseshoes Inn & Restaurant

BUXTON ROAD, BLACKSHAW MOOR, NR LEEK, STAFFORDSHIRE ST13 8TW
TEL: 01538 300296 FAX: 01538 300320

A homely family run hostelry situated in the beautiful Staffordshire Moorlands on the edge of the Peak District National Park, the Three Horseshoes is a traditional farmhouse style inn providing comfortable accommodation and excellent food. It stands in its own large and beautiful garden, with patios, terraces and a children's play area. The six en suite cottage style bedrooms have been recently redecorated and furnished. Affording superb views, the restaurant serves fine food, fresh vegetables and a choice of over 200 wines. In the evening, candlelight and romantic music combine to create a peaceful and relaxing atmosphere. A Bar Carvery provides home-cooked traditional dishes, as well as a roast of the day, accompanied by fresh market vegetables. On Saturday nights, there is a dinner and dance with a cabaret and à la carte menu offering an extensive choice of food. The inn is closed from Christmas through to the New Year. The area around the inn includes Rudyard Lake for sailing and walks (from which Kipling took his name),Tittesworth Reservoir for fishing, walking and bird watching and the Roaches for climbing and rambling. About 15 minutes away are the Manifold Valley, Dovedale, Berrisford Dale, Hartington, Alstonefield and Butterton. Alton Towers and Chatsworth are just 20 minutes away. **Directions:** Inn is on the A53 road to Buxton, easily reached by M6 via the Potteries and M1 via Derby. Price guide: Single £45; double £55–£65.

6 rms

For hotel location, see maps on pages 212-218

THE HARE & HOUNDS COUNTRY INN

THE GREEN, FULBECK, LINCOLNSHIRE NG32 3SS
TEL: 01400 272090 FAX: 01400 273663

The Hare and Hounds is a delightful 17th century Coaching Inn centrally located as the ideal base from which to tour the areas around Lincoln, Newark, Stamford, Grantham, Sleaford and Boston. Only 12 minutes drive from the A1 it is the perfect overnight stop when travelling north or south. Alison and David Nicholas the new owners have carried out an extensive re-furbishment programme, including central heating, new showers, carpets and decor in the 8 en-suite rooms and a revamp of the restaurant. This inn offers real olde worlde charm, the traditional pine panelled bar with log fire stocks several real ales. There is an excellent wine list to compliment the now extensive range of steaks, fish and continental dishes available on the restaurant menu. A function room with full video/conference facilities is also available, along with the 8 double/twin bedrooms makes it a superb small conference venue. The inn has 3 Crowns Commended ETB. Places of interest nearby are Lincoln Cathedral, Belton House, Fulbeck Hall, Rutland Water, Harlaxton Manor and many historic and modern airfields for the air enthusiast. **Directions:** On the A607 between Grantham and Lincoln, near the point where it crosses A17 between Newark and Sleaford. Price guide: Single £35; double £45; family £55.

For hotel location, see maps on pages 212-218

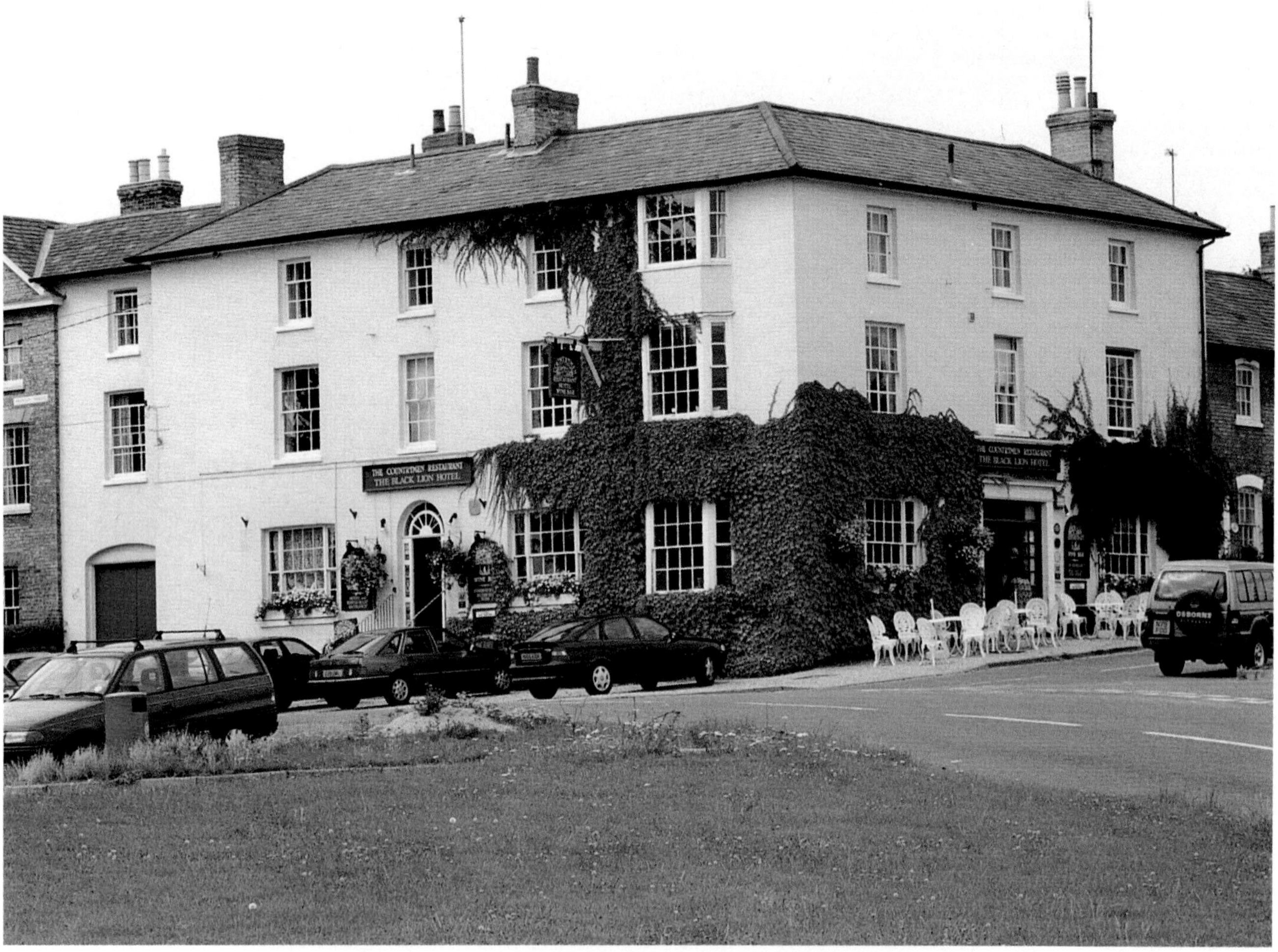

THE COUNTRYMEN

THE GREEN, LONG MELFORD, SUFFOLK CO10 9DN
TEL: 01787 312356 FAX: 01787 374557

Overlooking Melford's magnificent green, the Countrymen has received wide acclaim for its superb food and splendid accommodation. Recognised by all major guides, the Countrymen is enjoyed by visitors and locals alike. Stephen and Janet have earned much praise for their enthusiastic and generous hospitality. The bedrooms, individually furnished with country antiques, offer every modern amenity. If you are lucky or ask in advance you could be sleeping in one of the four-posters or in an antique brass bedstead in a room with panoramic views over Melford. The comfortable lounge offers scope to enjoy the many books and games; whilst the attractive restaurant leads out to a picturesque walled courtyard garden, where you can dine alfresco on warm summer nights. Stephen who learned his skills at the Dorchester creates dishes to tempt even the most jaded palate. The Countrymen Dinner menu is complemented by a unique Gastronomic menu with different wine, selected by Janet, to accompany each course. Today the Countrymen also offers a Bistro Wine Bar where Stephen's specialities, particularly his own pasta, can be enjoyed in relaxed informality. Melford Hall, Kentwell Hall and a plethora of antique shops; Constable country, Gainsborough's birthplace, historic Bury St Edmunds, Lavenham, Newmarket and Cambridge are all close by. **Directions**: On the village green on the A1092 and the A134. Price guide: Single £45–£65; double £65–£95.

For hotel location, see maps on pages 212-218

THE DEVONSHIRE ARMS HOTEL

LONG SUTTON, NR LANGPORT, SOMERSET TA10 9LP
TEL: 01458 241271 FAX: 01458 241037

Located in an idyllic Somerset village, overlooking the green, The Devonshire Arms Hotel was originally constructed as a hunting lodge in 1787 and is now a stylish small hotel. The hotel is renowned for its friendly service and has maintained the warm and inviting atmosphere of its former years. Comfort is an important criterion and the bedrooms, all of which are en suite, are decorated with soft fabrics and plush furnishings. Located across the courtyard or in the main house, the bedrooms feature modern conveniences such as colour television and tea/coffee making facilities. Popular with the local residents as well as guests, the superb restaurant serves traditional home-cooked cuisine. Those seeking a more informal atmosphere may enjoy a light snack in the cosy lounge bar. There are many beautiful walks nearby and the magnificent Somerset landscape must be explored. Historic properties abound and popular excursions include trips to Muchelney Abbey with its Abbots House, Wells Cathedral, Yeovilton Fleet Air Arm Museum and the interesting market-place in Somerton. **Directions:** Follow A303 towards Yeovilton branching off at Podimore roundabout onto the A372, Long Sutton is 3 miles along. Price guide: Single £50; double £60.

9 rms MasterCard VISA AMERICAN EXPRESS

For hotel location, see maps on pages 212-218

MR UNDERHILL'S

DINHAM WEIR, LUDLOW, SHROPSHIRE SY5 1EH
TEL: 01584 874431

Below the castle ramparts on the banks of the River Teme, Mr Underhill's is the new venture of experienced restaurateurs Chris and Judy Bradley. Having built a reputation for combining good food with caring, attentive service they now have the opportunity to provide comfortable accommodation. The bedrooms are cosy and furnished in a cottage-style, with en suite bathrooms and many thoughtful extras to add to their comfort. Views across the river to the wooded walks of Whitcliffe Common add their own touch of serenity. Chris Bradley established his reputation at his similarly-named restaurant in Suffolk, where he earned stars from Michelin and Egon Ronay. The same style and quality go into the daily-changing menu here, which presents first-rate ingredients in an essentially modern British idiom. The wine list is varied and informative with plenty of tasting notes and a good selection of half bottles. Ludlow is central to the Wye valley and Welsh Marches and stages annual arts and food and drink festivals. Nearby places of interest include the historic castle, church and market, and the popular racecourse. **Directions:** From the main A49 Hereford to Shrewsbury road head for the town centre. Proceed past the market square and castle to Dinham Weir: Mr Underhill's is on the right by the river bridge. Price guide: Single £55–£75; double/twin £65–£95.

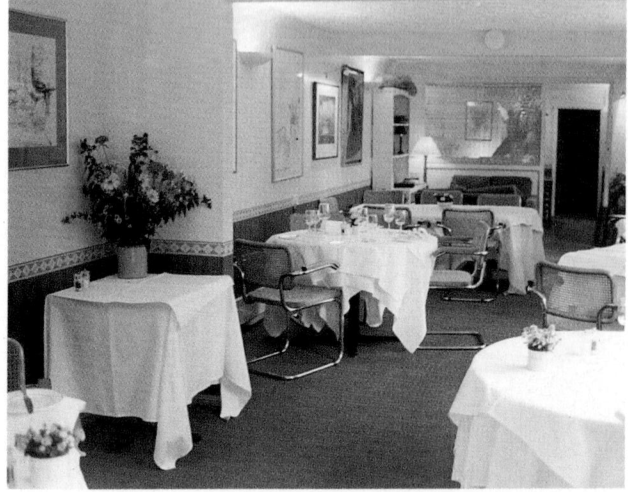

For hotel location, see maps on pages 212-218

HOTEL GORDLETON MILL

SILVER STREET, HORDLE, NR LYMINGTON, NEW FOREST, HAMPSHIRE SO41 6DJ
TEL: 01590 682219 FAX: 01590 683073

Hidden in the countryside between the New Forest National Park and the sea lies an ivy-clad 17th century Water Mill, now privately owned and sympathetically renovated to make a most luxurious hotel. It is set in 5½ acres of landscaped, natural garden, with woods, fields, millpond, sluice gates, rustic bridges and a lily pond creating a perfect riverside retreat. Gordleton Mill is renowned too for the gastronomique delights of Stephen Smith's nationally acclaimed 'Provence Restaurant', which has won a star from Egon Ronay, two Red Stars and four Rosettes from the AA for its excellent food. Also rated 'Restaurant of the Year' in the Good Food Guide 1997. This idyllic hotel boasts nine exquisitely furnished bedrooms all en suite including whirlpool baths and showers along with luxury towelling robes, flowers, bottled water, fruit and a half bottle of Joseph Perrier champagne to greet guests on their arrival. Five of the bedrooms are exclusively reserved for non-smokers. Prices include a full English or continental breakfast, and unlimited tea and coffee throughout a guest's stay. Places of interest nearby include Beaulieu. Bucklers Hard, Exbury Gardens, Romsey and Broadlands. **Directions:** M27, junction 1. A337 south for 11 miles near Lymington after the railway bridge and mini roundabout turn sharp right before Toll House Inn, head towards Hordle and hotel is on right in about 1½ miles. Price guide: Single £97; double £134–£160; millers suite £219.

For hotel location, see maps on pages 212-218

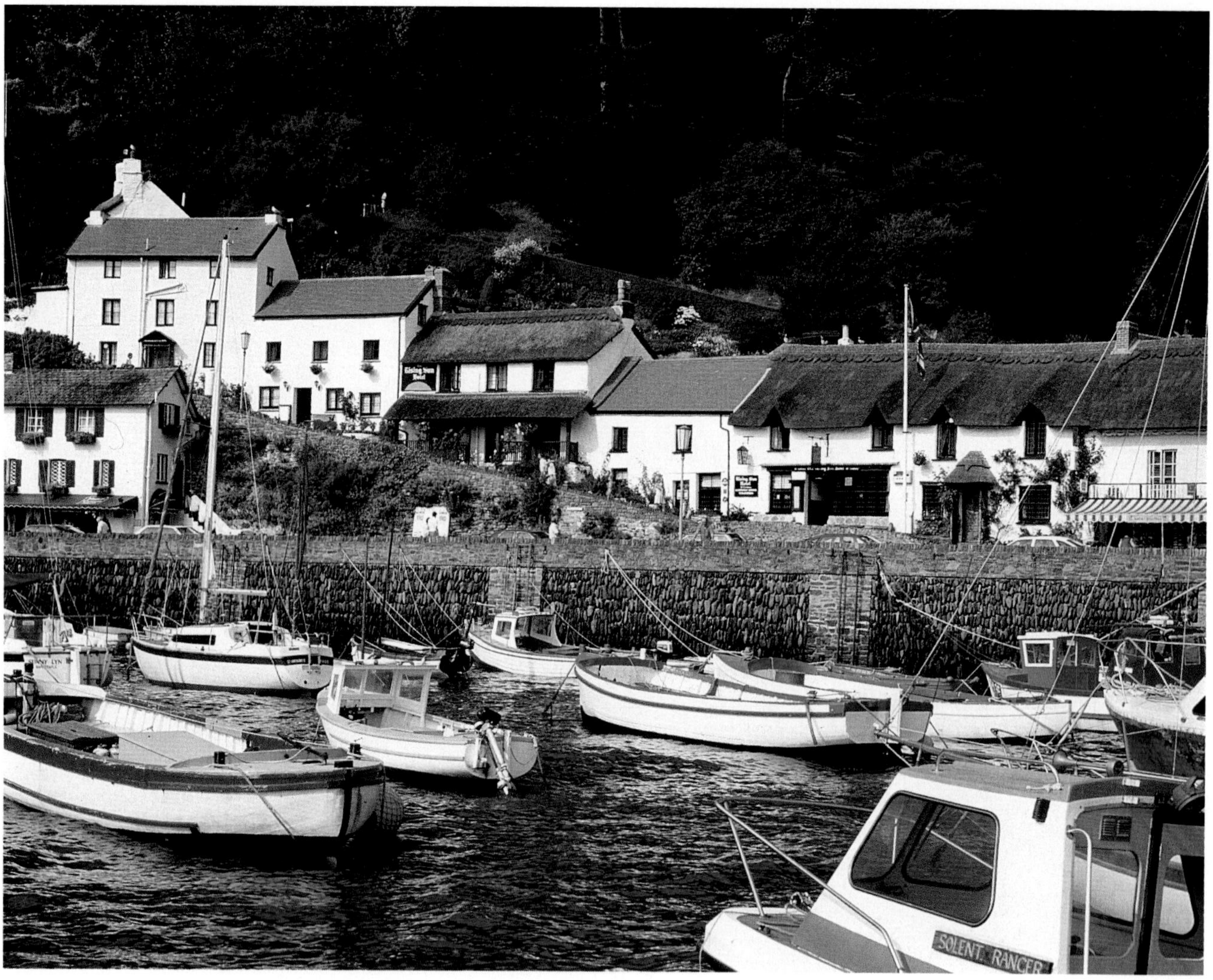

THE RISING SUN

HARBOURSIDE, LYNMOUTH, DEVON EX35 6EQ
TEL: 01598 753223 FAX: 01598 753480

Recommended in every way, this award-winning 14th century thatched smugglers' inn is perfectly positioned on the picturesque harbour overlooking East Lyn River. The building is steeped in history: Lorna Doone was partly written here and the inn's adjacent cottage – now luxuriously equipped for guests' use and pictured below – was once the honeymoon retreat for the poet Shelley. The best of the inn's medieval character has been preserved: oak panelling, uneven floors, open fires and crooked ceilings, all enhanced by tasteful furnishings and modern comforts. The bedrooms lack nothing and like the terraced gardens, have splendid views. Parking in Lynmouth can be difficult at the height of the season. The food served in the oak-panelled restaurant is of excellent quality. Classic modern English and French cuisine is provided on an à la carte menu, which also features local specialities such as fresh lobster and salmon. All this is accompanied by a superb wine list. Good value bar meals are also available. The inn owns a ½ mile stretch of river for salmon fishing and there are opportunities for sea angling. Exmoor National Park, the North Devon coastline and Doone Valley are also near. **Directions:** Leave M5 at Jct23 (signed Minehead) and follow A39 to Lynmouth. Or take A361, exit 27 (Tiverton) to South Molton, then B3226 in the direction of Ilfracombe and then A39 at Blackmoor Gate to Lynmouth. Price guide: Single £60; double £99–£150.

For hotel location, see maps on pages 212-218

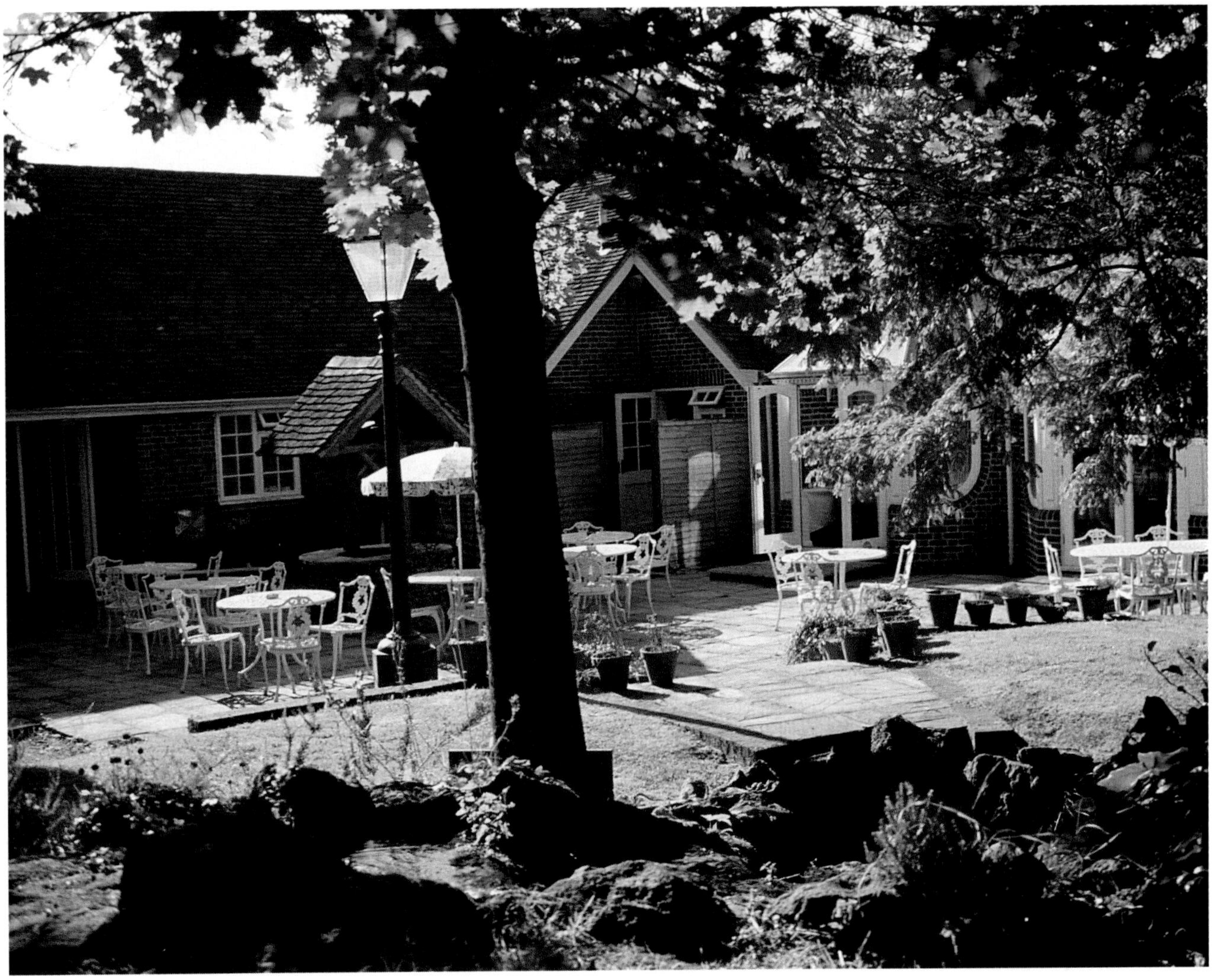

The Harrow At Warren Street

WARREN STREET, NR LENHAM, KENT ME17 2ED
TEL: 01622 858727 FAX: 01622 850026

High on the North Downs of Kent stands this attractive hostelry, amid rolling farmland in the hamlet of Warren Street. Once the forge and rest house for travellers en route to Canterbury via the nearby Pilgrims' Way, it has now been converted into a comfortable country inn. Refurbishments have ensured that all the guest accommodation is designed to a high standard. For guests who wish to enjoy a leisurely lie-in, a Continental breakfast can be brought to the bedroom. The traditional character and atmosphere of the public rooms are enhanced by open log fires in the winter and exposed oak beams. The Harrow enjoys a reputation locally for its good cooking. There is a superb conservatory restaurant with views over a delightful floodlit water garden and patio. The à la carte menu features a delicious choice of seasonal dishes. For an appetiser perhaps try the terrine de poireaux – a terrine of leeks and langoustines served with tarragon vinaigrette, followed by pot-roasted guinea fowl with Madeira sauce. An excellent range of meals is also presented on the bar menus. The inn's facilities can be tailored to accommodate special functions. Convenient for Canterbury, Maidstone and the Cinque Port of Rye. Leeds Castle is just a 10 minutes' drive away. **Directions:** Leave the M20 at junction 8 or 9. Warren Street is signed from the A20 between Harrietsham and Charing. Price guide: Single £39.50; double £49.50.

For hotel location, see maps on pages 212-218

Ringlestone Inn

'TWIXT HARRIETSHAM AND WORMSHILL, NR MAIDSTONE, KENT ME17 1NX
TEL: 01622 859900 FAX: 01622 859966 E-MAIL: michelle@ringlestone.com

Truly traditional is the welcome that awaits visitors as they step back in time into this delightfully unspoilt, medieval, lamplit tavern. Built in 1533 as a hospice for monks, the Ringlestone became one of the early Ale Houses around 1615 and little has changed since. Its delights include original brick and flint walls and floors, massive oak beams, inglenooks, old English furniture and eight acres of idyllic gardens. Recent additions are three en suite bedrooms in a charming farmhouse just a few steps opposite the inn. They are furnished in style and totally in keeping with expectations for a stay in this beautiful escapists' spot. The spacious farmhouse dining and reception rooms are also available for private and corporate functions. Full of character and candlelight ambience with sturdy, highly polished tables made from the timbers of an 18th century Thames barge, The Ringlestone has a reputation for excellent English cooking and features in many food guides. A help yourself 'hot and cold' buffet lunch offers a seasonal variety of traditional country recipes. The varied evening menu includes unusual and interesting pies and local trout, complemented by their exclusive house wines imported directly from France and a wide range of English country fruit wines. Leeds Castle is nearby. **Directions:** Leave M20 at Jct8. Head north off A20 through Hollingbourne, turn right at water tower crossroads towards Doddington. Price guide: Single from £69; double/twin from £79.

3 rms MasterCard VISA AMERICAN EXPRESS M 14

For hotel location, see maps on pages 212-218

THE HORSE AND GROOM INN

CHARLTON, NEAR MALMESBURY, WILTSHIRE SN16 9DL
TEL: 01666 823904 FAX: 01666 823390

In the small village of Charlton in the heart of Cotswold country, the Horse & Groom Inn possesses a unique rustic charm. Inside, this 16th century coaching inn has been sensitively reinterpreted, with no loss of its period atmosphere; careful thought and attention has been invested in each of the three bedrooms, resulting in peaceful, relaxing rooms with all modern conveniences (plus extra touches like mineral water, fresh fruit, flowers and bathrobes). Décor is muted, in elegant shades like sage green, jasmine and peach; windows look out over the beautiful Cotswold countryside. A full English breakfast is included in the tariff. Awarded an AA Rosette, The Horse & Groom has a fine reputation for its cuisine, which has attracted the attention (and recommendation) of food connoisseurs. There are simple bar snacks including ploughman's lunches and jacket potatoes, or more elaborate meals such as oven-baked sea bass with vegetable julienne and a light Pernod and cream sauce, pork tenderloin layered with Wiltshire ham and gruyère cheese and roasted vegetable basket. The Horse & Groom is a free house serving real ales from Wiltshire breweries. In summer, drinks and meals may be enjoyed in the private garden. In winter, guests choose to relax by log fires crackling in the grates. Bath, the Cotswolds and Malmesbury are nearby. **Directions:** Exit M4 junction 17. The inn is 2 miles east of Malmesbury on B4040. Price guide: Single from £60; double from £75.

12

For hotel location, see maps on pages 212-218

The Londesborough

HIGH STREET, MARKET WEIGHTON, NEAR YORK, EAST YORKSHIRE
TEL: 01430 872214 FAX: 01430 872219 E-MAIL: londesborough@obelus.co.uk

This charming 18th century coaching inn is set in the centre of Market Weighton – a town most famous for being the birthplace of William Bradley, the tallest man in Britain! The Londesborough's owners pride themselves on creating a friendly, personal atmosphere for their guests. In recent years the accomodation has been completely upgraded, refurbishing it in an elegant, traditional style with a fine collection of antique furniture, oil paintings and prints. A full range of modern comforts and amenities are provided in the luxury bedrooms and there is a beautiful bridal suite available for newly-weds. The restaurant offers both à la carte and table d'hôte menus with the impressive, although not expensive, cuisine complemented by a very carefully chosen wine list. For those who prefer a more casual setting, the Devonshire Bar provides country-style bar meals, while the Bistro offers excellent lunch, afternoon tea and dinner menus. Local leisure activities which can be enjoyed include fishing, golfing, walking and gliding. York, Hull and the North Yorkshire coast are all within around 30 minutes drive so this is an ideal touring base. With access to the M62, M18 and A1(M) within easy reach, the inn is also well placed for business users. **Directions**: The Londesborough is in the centre of Market Weighton, midway between Hull and York off the A1079. Price guide: Single £35–£79; double/twin £59–£89.

18 rms MasterCard VISA AMERICAN EXPRESS M 150

For hotel location, see maps on pages 212-218

THE TALBOT INN AT MELLS

HIGH STREET, MELLS, NR BATH, SOMERSET BA11 3PN
TEL: 01373 812254 FAX: 01373 813599

This beautiful coaching inn is set in the picturesque village of Mells on the edge of the Mendips. Parts of the building date back to the 15th century and the bedrooms have been individually furnished and decorated in keeping with an old 'traditional style' inn. However, character and charm are combined with every modern amenity to ensure that guests can relax in total comfort. The cobbled courtyard and pretty cottage garden are ideal places to sit and enjoy an early evening drink on a warm summer day or to take an alfresco meal. In the oak-beamed Oxford and Snug bar restaurant guests can enjoy a quick snack or a superb à la carte meal. Freshly prepared dishes include game from the local shoot and fresh fish which is delivered daily. Sample the poached fillet of salmon with linguini pasta, vermouth and fresh herb sauce; oven baked breast of chicken with a fresh sage mousse and port wine sauce; or oven roasted breast of guinea fowl with potato rosti, oyster mushrooms and rosemary cream sauce. An excellent wine list is also available. Nearby are the historic cities and towns of Bath, Wells, Cheddar, Glastonbury and Longleat. **Directions:** Exit M4 at junction 18 to Bath and then take A36 towards Warminster. Turn right onto A361 into Frome and then take A362 towards Radstock. Within ½ mile turn left to Mells and follow signposts. Price guide: Single £45 (including dinner £65); double £65 (including dinner £95).

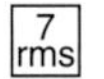

For hotel location, see maps on pages 212-218

THE DIFFERENT DRUMMER HOTEL

94 HIGH STREET, STONY STRATFORD, BUCKINGHAMSHIRE MK11 1AH
TEL: 01908 564733 FAX: 01908 260646

This charming hostelry dates back to 1470. During its long and interesting history, it passed through the hands of Bradwell Abbey and the de Longueville family before being leased to Lord Grey of Wilton by Queen Elizabeth 1. Following damage during the Great Fire of 1742, the present Georgian façade was added. In 1982 a programme of refurbishment was completed, bring this ancient coaching inn up to a superb standard of comfort. Elegant antique furniture sits comfortably alongside every modern accoutrement. Several en suite bedrooms are set in the seclusion of The Courtyard - including one with a four-poster bed for that special occasion. Original ideas, top-class ingredients, generous portions and a real enthusiasm for classic Italian food are all much in evidence in the Different Drummer's beautiful 'Al Tamborista' oak-panelled restaurant. As well as a profusion of pasta dishes, accompanied by imaginative sauces, chicken, veal, steak, lamb, beef and venison are all well represented on the menu. The dessert trolley offers a selection of deliciously tempting sweets, while a modestly-priced wine list is available to complement any meal. The historic town of Stony Stratford is just 10 minutes' drive from central Milton Keynes. Bletchley and Newport Pagnell are also within easy reach. **Directions**: From M1 junction 15A follow A421 to Stony Stratford. The hotel is in the High Street. Price guide: Single £45–£67; double £55–£87.

For hotel location, see maps on pages 212-218

THE KING'S ARMS INN & RESTAURANT

MONTACUTE, SOMERSET TA16 6UU
TEL: 01935 822513 FAX: 01935 826549

Set in the picturesque village of Montacute, this charming inn dates back to the 16th century. The discreet modernisation has preserved the mullioned windows and stone walls. The bedrooms recently decorated and comfortably furnished provide every amenity for the discerning traveller. All rooms are en suite and include a four-poster and a half tester room. ETB 4 crowns highly commended and AA 2 stars. The traditional Pickwick Bar welcomes guests, with real ales and an interesting selection of snacks and light meals; the popular cold buffet is available at lunchtimes. The Abbey Restaurant has established a fine reputation for its modern English cuisine with 2 AA Rosettes and commendations from Michelin and Egon Ronay. Salmon mousse is studded with truffles and pistachio nuts, while pork fillet is served with a cumin and coriander potato timbale. Asparagus, goats' cheese and mushroom strudel with a red and green pepper sauce will appeals to non-vegetarians as well. The wine list has been chosen carefully, to please all tastes. Special mini-breaks and room upgrades are usually available. Montacute House, of 'Sense and Sensibility' fame a magnificent Elizabethan mansion with superb gardens, Sherborne Castle and Abbey, Cricket St Thomas Wildlife Park and Dorset beaches are all nearby. **Directions:** Just off A303, take A3088. Montacute is clearly marked, the inn is in the centre of the village by the church. Price guide: Single £53–£62; double £69–£105.

15 rms 

For hotel location, see maps on pages 212-218

THE SWAN INN

NEWBURY ROAD, GREAT SHEFFORD, HUNGERFORD, BERKSHIRE RG17 7DS
TEL / FAX: 01488 648271

This charming inn standing on the banks of the River Lambourne is steeped in history dating back to the early 1800's when it was a welcoming stop for coach travellers on the busy routes of the Cotswolds and Thames Valley. Some of its history is depicted in the many prints around the walls, with the low-ceiling lounge bar displaying old photographs of the village as well as those illustrating The Swan's links with horse-racing. The Lambourne Valley is a historic horse-racing area and many of the country's leading trainers have their stables here. Several open their yards for public viewing during summer. The name of the inn was inspired by its beautiful riverside setting while Great Shefford derived from the words "Old Sheep Ford". The ford was adjacent to The Swan and provided access to an old track leading to the market town of Hungerford. The Swan has character, a very warm, friendly atmosphere and is beautifully and traditionally furnished. The congenial, welcoming bars are well stocked with fine beers and wines, complemented by delicious snacks and an interesting selection of more substantial meals. Dotted throughout the well-known area are numerous ancient burial mounds, some dating back to prehistoric times. **Directions:** Great Shefford is on the A338, a short distance north of junction 14 of the M4.

For hotel location, see maps on pages 212-218

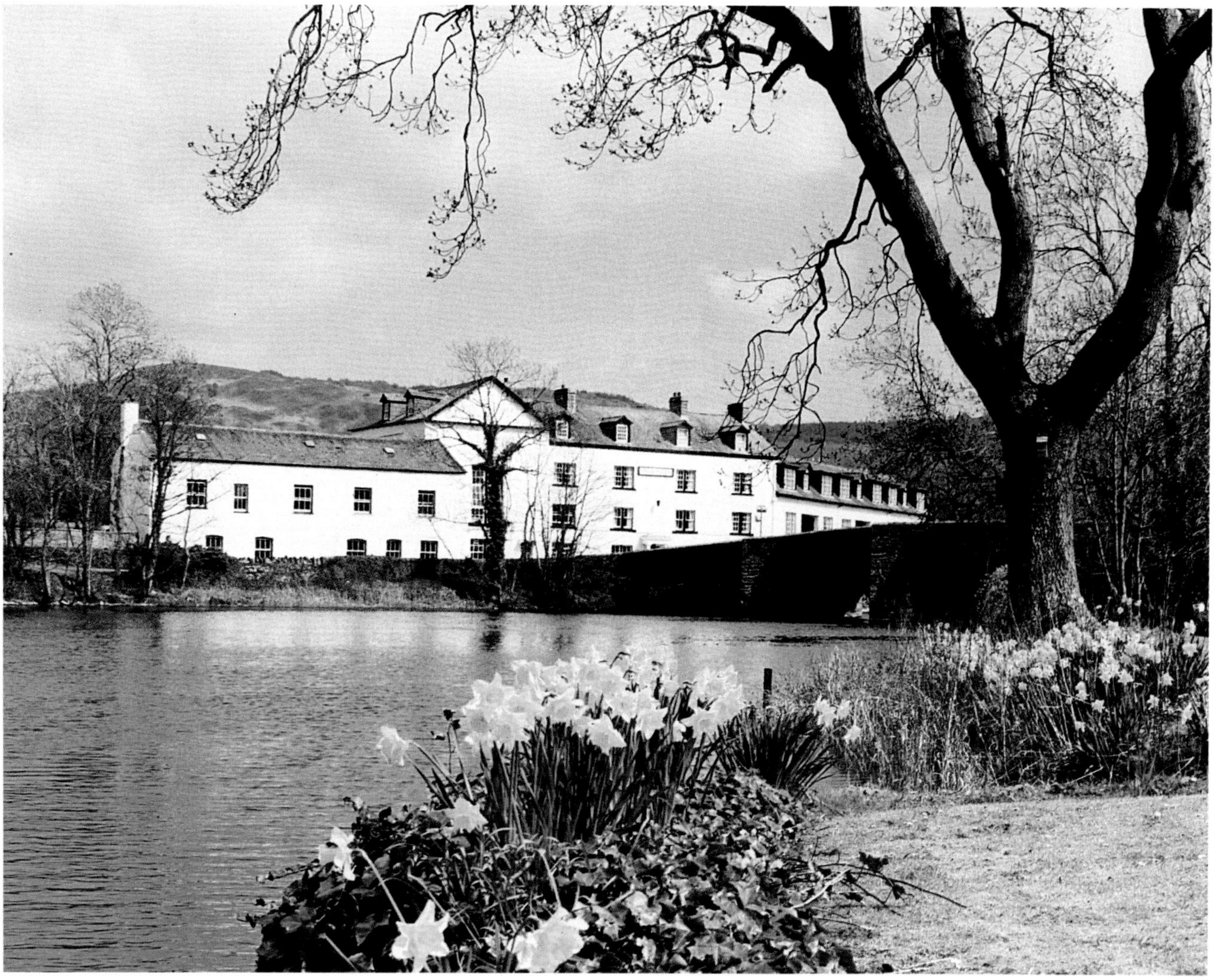

THE SWAN HOTEL

NEWBY BRIDGE, NR ULVERSTON, CUMBRIA LA12 8NB
TEL: 015395 31681 FAX: 015395 31917

At the southern end of Lake Windermere, The Swan Hotel undoubtedly has one of the most picturesque locations in the whole of the Lake District, with superb views over the water and surrounding countryside. Comfort is the declared first priority of the management. The 36 en suite bedrooms, ranging from suites and de luxe doubles to high standard doubles and singles, are traditional in character yet offer every modern amenity. The public rooms are attractively decorated, with comfortable bars as well as an elegant lounge which adjoins the restaurant. Choose from the traditional Tithe Barn (non-smoking) or less formal Mailcoach. Imaginative menus are complemented by a carefully compiled wine list. Local produce such as potted Morecambe Bay shrimps, Lakeland char, venison and Esthwaite trout are freshly cooked to order. Special diets can be catered for. A special children's menu is available. Smaller conferences may be accommodated and special breaks are available. ETB 4 Crowns Commended and AA 3 stars. The Lake District National Park, Holker Hall and Stott Park are all close by. There are facilities for many sports close by and the hotel has its own fishing rights and boat moorings. **Directions:** Newby Bridge is on the A590. Leave the M6 at junction 36 and follow the A590 to Barrow. The Swan is just across the bridge at Newby Bridge. Price guide: Single £60–£85; double £96–£135; suite £140.

For hotel location, see maps on pages 212-218

ELDERTON LODGE

GUNTON PARK, THORPE MARKET, NR NORTH WALSHAM, NORFOLK NR11 8TZ
TEL: 01263 833547 FAX: 01263 834673 E-MAIL: elderton@mistral.co.uk

Quietly grazing red deer, proudly strutting pheasants and cooing wood pigeons provide memorable awakening viewing to guests gazing from their bedroom windows over the vast and tranquil Gunton Park that is the scene of this 18th century, Grade II listed hotel. Standing in the heart of unspoiled countryside yet only four miles from the coast, the impressive Elderton Lodge Hotel and Restaurant, with its own six acres of mature gardens, was once the Shooting Lodge and Dower House to Gunton Hall Estate. Gunton Hall, home of the Barons of Suffield, was a favoured retreat for Lillie Langtry, the celebrated Victorian beauty, who according to legend entertained Edward VII here when he was Prince of Wales. Owners Christine and Martin Worby are restoring the hotel to its original country house splendour, complete with gun cupboards and elegant panelling. Bedrooms are attractive and comfortable, the bar informal and welcoming and the excellent cuisine featuring local game and seafood specialities – fit for a King, not only the Prince of Wales. This is an ideal venue for small meetings and conferences. The cathedral city of Norwich, National Trust properties including Blickling Hall, Felbrigg Hall, Sheringham Park and the Norfolk Broads National Park are nearby. **Directions**: Leave Norwich on A1151. Join A149 towards Cromer and the hotel is on the left prior to entering Thorpe Market. Price guide: Single £55; double £90.

For hotel location, see maps on pages 212-218

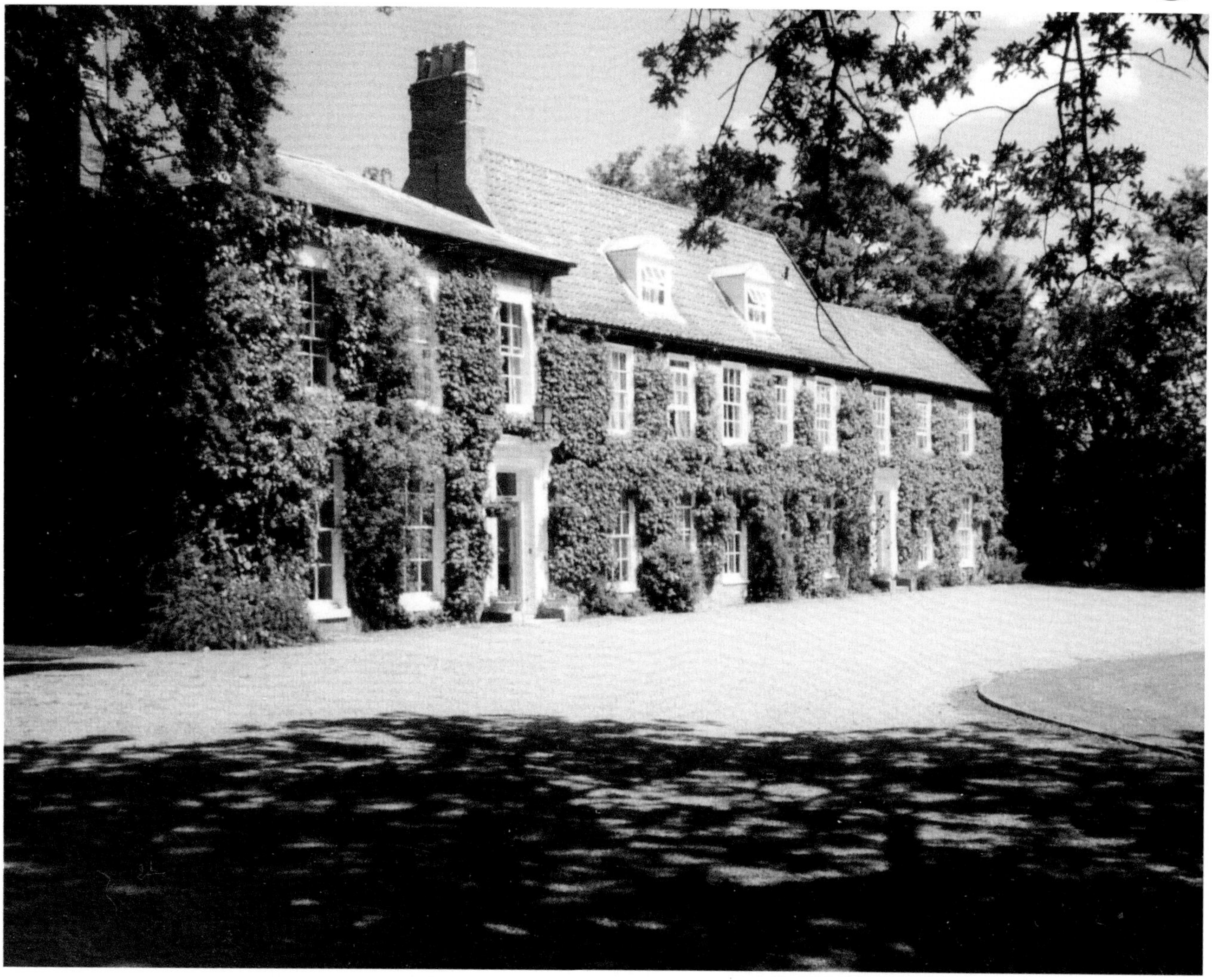

The Stower Grange

SCHOOL ROAD, DRAYTON, NORFOLK NR8 6EF
TEL: 01603 860210 FAX: 01603 860464

The Stower Grange, built of mellow Norfolk bricks under Dutch pantiles, dates back to the 17th century. In former times it was a gracious rectory. Today it offers travellers a peaceful retreat – the gardens have fine lawns with inviting shade provided by the mature trees – yet the property is only 4½ miles from the commercial and historic centre of Norwich. Stower is owned by the McCoy family; the atmosphere is friendly and informal. In cooler months open fires add to the welcome. There are eight spacious individually-decorated bedrooms with en suite facilities, including one with a pine four-poster bed for those in a romantic mood. The Blue Restaurant, locally renowned as a 'special place' to dine, is supervised by the owners' daughter Kate and looks directly on to the gardens. The imaginative cooking of their son-in-law Mark ensures good eating from the individually priced menus. The restaurant closes on Sunday evenings, however, residents can enjoy a steak and salad in the Lounge Bar. Norwich, Norfolk Broads, Holkham Hall, Houghton Hall, Blickling Hall, Sandringham and the Norfolk Coast are all nearby. **Directions:** From A11, turn left on to inner ring road and proceed to the ASDA junction with A1067 Norwich–Fakenham Road. Approximately two miles to Drayton turn right at the Red Lion public house. After 80 yards bear left. The Stower Grange is on the right. Price guide (incl. English breakfast): Single £50; double £67.50; four-poster £85.

For hotel location, see maps on pages 212-218

HOTEL DES CLOS

OLD LENTON LANE, NOTTINGHAM, NOTTINGHAMSHIRE NG7 2SA
TEL: 01159 866566 FAX: 01159 860343

An attractive conversion of Victorian farm buildings, this quiet privately run hotel retains the atmosphere of its origins while offering guests every modern comfort. The hotel benefits from its location on the banks of the River Trent, yet its close proximity to Nottingham and the motorway network ensures its convenient suitability for the traveller. Each designed around an individual theme, the en suite bedrooms and suites are well-equipped with colour TV, trouser press and refreshment facilities. Conference amenities enable executives to stage small meetings and a wide choice of weekend breaks is also on offer. Since the opening of the French restaurant in 1990, chef-proprietor John Abbey has established a reputation for cuisine and fine wines and has been rewarded this year with his 2nd AA Rosette. A choice of lunch and evening menus is presented and during the summer, guests may dine in the courtyard garden. An admirable list of French wines includes over 50 half-bottles and 60 Chablis labels. The city of Nottingham is home to the National Watersports Centre, Trent Bridge Cricket Ground and a large market. Other notable landmarks are Nottingham Castle, Sherwood Forest and Southwell Minster. **Directions:** Take exit 24 from M1 and take A453 signposted Nottingham (10 miles). Cross River Trent and follow signs to Lenton. Turn left at roundabout and immediately left again, down the lane to the river. Price guide: double £75–£90; suite £100–£125.

9 rms MasterCard VISA AMERICAN EXPRESS M 25

For hotel location, see maps on pages 212-218

THE WHEATSHEAF INN AT ONNELEY AND LA PUERTA DEL SOL RESTAURANTE ESPAÑOL

BARHILL ROAD, ONNELEY, STAFFORDSHIRE CW3 9QF
TEL: 01782 751581 FAX: 01782 751499

Since purchasing The Wheatsheaf Inn at Onneley more than 12 years ago, Mark and Milagros Bittner have turned this sleeping giant into one of the area's most popular venues. Well-stocked and comfortable bars offer a wide selection of cask beers, imported lagers, nearly 200 whiskies and an award-winning wine list. Indeed, The Wheatsheaf Inn won North Staffordshire's "Evening Sentinel's" first "Country Pub of the Year" award just over a year ago. The inn's bedrooms are all individually designed, decorated and furnished. All are en suite and offer direct dial telephone, hospitality tray, colour television, trouser press and many other amenities. Special touches such as a small basket of fruit and mineral water on arrival and a complimentary morning paper add to the welcome. Diners may choose from the informal lounge where Spanish tapas dishes and traditional "pub fayre" including grills and fresh fish are available or the candlelit restaurant " La Puerta del Sol" where Spanish cuisine and popular English dishes are available. The Wheatsheaf Inn is just a short drive from "The Potteries" whilst both Alton Towers and Chester can be reached in just over ½ hour. The inn is located on A525 between the villages of Madeley and Woore just 6½ miles west of Newcastle-under-Lyme and 4½ miles from Keele University. Crewe, Nantwich, Stoke-on-Trent and Market Drayton are all just 15 minutes away as are junction 15 and 16 on M6. Price guide: Single £50; double £55–£66.

5 rms M 50

For hotel location, see maps on pages 212-218

The Talbot

NEW STREET, OUNDLE, NR PETERBOROUGH, NORTHAMPTONSHIRE PE8 4EA
TEL: 01832 273621 FAX: 01832 274545

The Talbot is an impressive, historic hotel situated in the small country town of Oundle, which is surrounded on three sides by the River Nene. The building originates from 638AD when a group of monks founded it as a hostel giving food, drink and shelter to pilgrims and wayfarers. Stones and an oak staircase from nearby Fotheringhay Castle, where Mary, Queen of Scots, was imprisoned and executed, were used when The Talbot was rebuilt in the reign of Charles I. Beautifully renovated and refurbished over the centuries, The Talbot retains many of its original and added features. Heavy beams, antiques and fine furnishings abound throughout the hotel, including in the bedrooms, several of which are dedicated non-smoking. These are all en suite, extremely comfortable and have every 20th century facility. A lounge bar is open at mealtimes. The Talbot has a reputation for good food and Head Chef Paul Chance provides extensive menus of international and traditional English dishes in the no smoking Restaurant. The inn is within walking distance of Oundle School. There are facilities for meetings and small conferences. **Directions:** From the A1 join the A605 west of Peterborough to Oundle. Price guide: Single £70; double/twin £85; suite £100.

For hotel location, see maps on pages 212-218

HOLCOMBE HOTEL

HIGH STREET, DEDDINGTON, NR WOODSTOCK, OXFORDSHIRE OX15 0SL
TEL: 01869 338274 FAX: 01869 337167

Conveniently located a few miles north of the university city of Oxford, this delightful 17th century high quality hotel is family run and set in a pretty Cotswold village. It offers personalised attention and traditional hospitality and has a relaxed and friendly atmosphere. Each of the 17 bedrooms is tastefully appointed and has its own distinctive character. Every amenity, including ionisers, is provided for the comfort of guests. Holcombe Hotel is known locally for its superb French, classical and traditional English cuisine. It is highly recommended and is recognised with an AA Red Rosette and RAC awards. Great care is taken in creating original and beautifully presented food. Real ale and excellent bar meals are served in the oak-beamed cottage bar. The Holcombe has been in the resident ownership of Chedley and Carol Mahfoudh since 1988, during which time they have received 5 awards, including the AA Courtesy and Care Award 1993, one of only 15 hotels out of 4,000. The Cotswolds, Stratford, Woodstock and Oxford and Bicester Shopping Village "Bond Street at a 50% discount" and many National Trust properties are nearby. Golfing arranged at two excellent, 18-hole golf courses. **Directions:** Deddington is on A4260, 6 miles south of Banbury M40 J11. Follow A4260 to Adderbury; hotel is on the right at traffic light. M40 J10: follow A43, then B4100 to Aynho, then B4031 to Deddington Price guide: Single £65–£78; double £75–£98.

17 rms MasterCard VISA AMERICAN EXPRESS M 20

For hotel location, see maps on pages 212-218

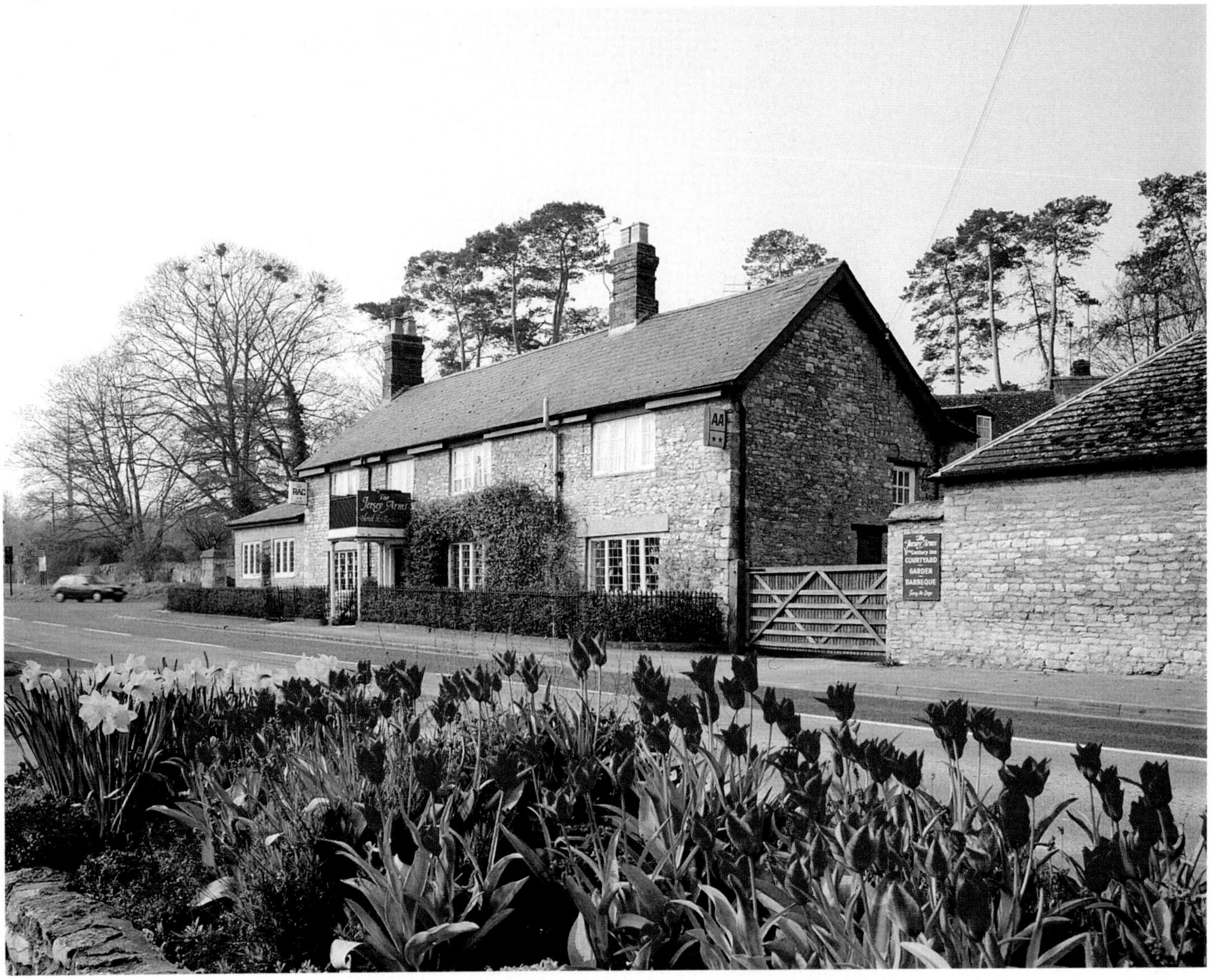

THE JERSEY ARMS

MIDDLETON STONEY, OXFORDSHIRE OX6 8SE
TEL: 01869 343234 FAX: 01869 343565

Near Oxford, the city of dreaming spires, in the country of sparkling streams and gentle green pastures, The Jersey Arms occupies a site rich in history. As far back as 1241, the inn was listed as providing William Longsword 'for 25 men of Middleton, necessaries as food and drink'. It thrived in the days of coach-and-horse long-distance travel and in 1823 was a key posting house for cross-country traffic. Today, The Jersey Arms has been honed into a retreat of comfort and peace. An informal air is created with old beams, antique flintlocks and simple, elegant furnishings. Bedrooms, all with private access, vary in size, while blending the charm of the past with modern décor. Facilities include hairdryers, colour TV and telephone. Cuisine of exceptional quality is prepared from the freshest local ingredients and the menu is changed according to season. Diners can sit in the Bar or Restaurant or, in fine weather, in the secluded courtyard garden. Relax first with an apéritif in the elegant lounge. Oxford, Woodstock, Blenheim Palace with its gardens, Towcester and Cheltenham racecourses and Silverstone Racetrack. Heathrow airport is an hour away by car. **Directions:** Between junctions 9 & 10 of the M40 on the B430 10 miles north of Oxford. From junction 9 take the Oxford Road, Middleton Stoney is signposted 1 mile down. From junction 10 Middleton Stoney is signposted as you leave the slip road. Price guide: Single £75; double £89.

For hotel location, see maps on pages 212-218

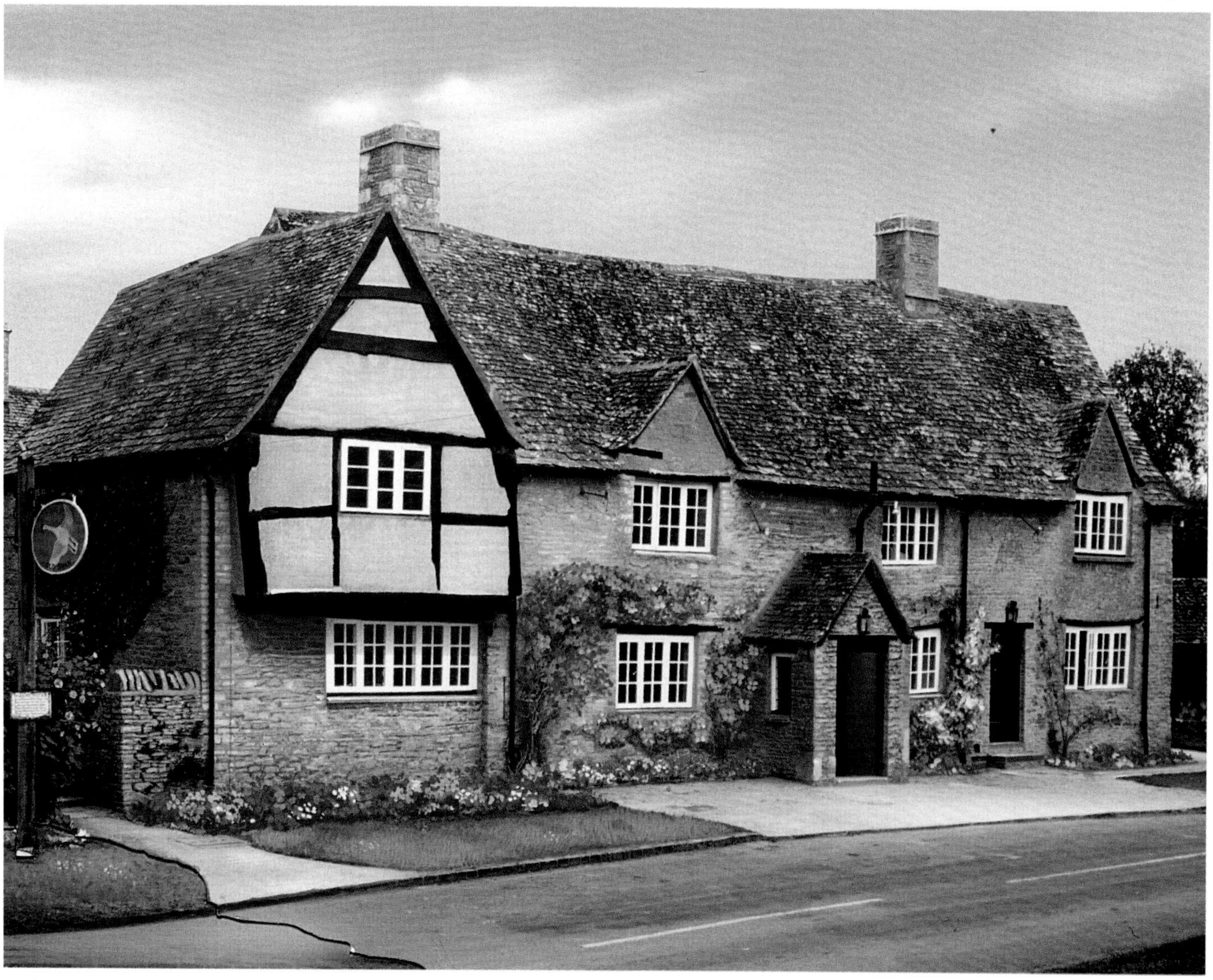

THE MILL & OLD SWAN

MINSTER LOVELL, BURFORD, OXFORDSHIRE OX8 5RN

TEL: 01993 774441 FAX: 01993 702002

The Old Swan stands in the historic village of Minster Lovell, a small Oxfordshire village lying in the valley of the River Windrush, on the edge of the Cotswolds. According to the Doomsday Book, three mills were at Minster Lovell, two of which existed on the present site and now constitute part of these historic properties. A wealth of oak beams, glowing fires, four-poster beds and antique furnishings welcome you to The Old Swan, which has been carefully restored to luxury standards. King Richard III was a regular guest at The Old Swan – his original crest 'The Sun in Splendour' can be found emblazoned on one of the bedroom walls. The Mill: Adjacent to The Old Swan is The Mill, a self-contained conference centre, set in a 60 acre estate by the River Windrush (which was the inspiration for Kenneth Grahame's children's book 'The Wind in the Willows'). It is a charming location for relaxing, walking through the gardens or enjoying a choice of sporting activities including tennis and fly-fishing. Fitness enthusiasts will be delighted with the gymnasium and sauna. The Mill was awarded the European Architecture Heritage Award for its design in bringing modern facilities into a historic building. **Directions:** From A40 (Oxford/Burford road), take B4047 signposted to Minster Lovell. Once in the village follow the signs for Minster Lovell Hall. Price guide: Single £50–£80; double £80–£140.

For hotel location, see maps on pages 212-218

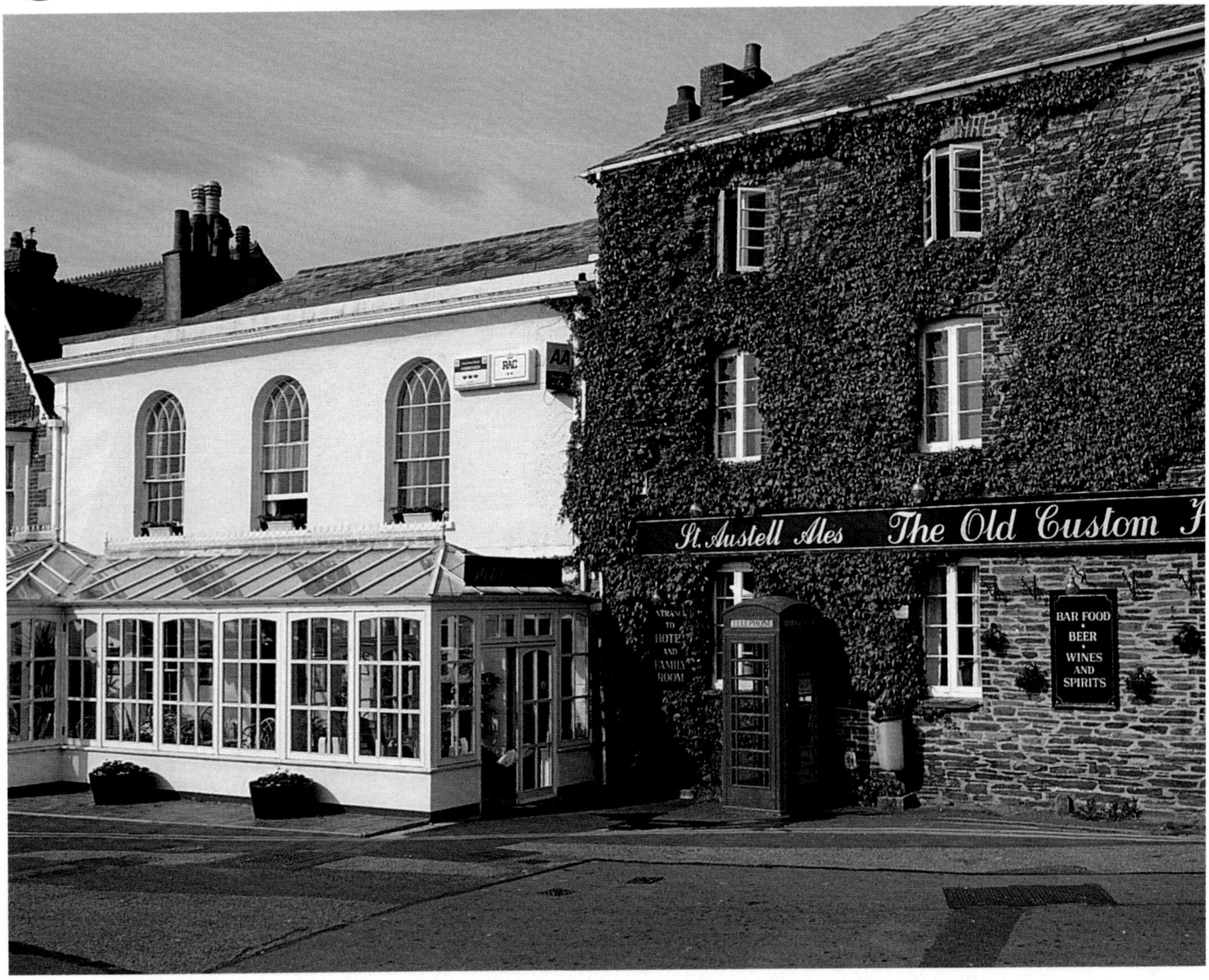

The Old Custom House Hotel

SOUTH QUAY, PADSTOW, CORNWALL PL28 8ED
TEL: 01841 532359 FAX: 01841 533372

Miles of golden sands, rugged cliffs topped with wild flowers and numerous old harbours make Cornwall's north coast one of Britain's most scenic areas. Padstow, a town of narrow, crooked streets lined with quaint inns and shops, is an ideal touring base. Originally built in the 1800s as the Customs and Excise building, this listed house occupies a fine position on Padstow's quayside. Most of the bedrooms overlook the harbour and the Camel estuary; all are decorated and equipped to a high standard. The bars are furnished in keeping with the building's character and there is also a pleasant conservatory lounge. Situated in the old grain warehouse, the dining room offers à la carte and table d'hôte menus, awarded an AA 3 Star and an RAC 3 Star. There is an extensive choice of fresh fish and seafood dishes as the hotel makes good use of the local produce available. Guests can walk the Coastal Path which passes through Padstow, discover the legend of King Arthur at Tintagel or visit the beautiful stately homes and gardens in the vicinity. Sports can be enjoyed locally including golf at Trevose and St Enodoc, surfing at Polzeath and sailing in the estuary. **Directions:** Entering Padstow, follow the signs for the quay. Price guide: Single £49–£73; double £60–£98.

For hotel location, see maps on pages 212-218

JUBILEE INN

PELYNT, NR LOOE, CORNWALL PL13 2JZ
TEL: 01503 220312 FAX: 01503 220920

The Jubilee has been an inn since the 16th century, changing its name from The Axe in 1887 to mark the 50th anniversary of Queen Victoria's accession. The low beamed ceilings, open hearths and old prints create an air of tradition and charm throughout. The bedrooms are tastefully furnished in a cottage style; three are for families and one is a bridal suite with a spiral staircase designed by the well-known artist, Stuart Armfield. With a residents' lounge, three bars, a beer garden plus a large garden with a children's play area and volley-ball net, there are plenty of places to relax. Barbecues are held in the summer. Special breaks arranged. An impressive à la carte menu and friendly, professional service are offered in the dining room. The inn's speciality is fish and shellfish, which come straight off the boats in nearby Looe. An extensive bar menu and traditional Sunday lunches are also on offer. The Duchy of Cornwall nurseries, several National Trust Properties and Dobwalls Adventure Park and Monley Sanctuary are a selection of the many interesting places to visit. Bodmin Moor, numerous picturesque villages and beautiful coastline are all to be explored. **Directions:** From Plymouth, cross Tamar Bridge and follow the main road to Looe. Leave Looe on the Polperro road and turn right for Pelynt. Price Guide: Single from £39.50; double from £65.

For hotel location, see maps on pages 212-218

THE FOUNTAIN INN & ROOMS

WELLTHORNE LANE, INGBIRCHWORTH, NR PENISTONE, SOUTH YORKSHIRE S36 7GJ
TEL: 01226 763125 FAX: 01226 761336

This attractive, historic inn stands peacefully in a quiet country lane just off the main A629 road, midway between Huddersfield and Sheffield. Built in the 17th century as a coaching inn it was bought by the present owner, David Broadbent, ten years ago and has been sympathetically renovated and restored. Over the past year additional bedrooms and a function room have been incorporated. The bedrooms are in an extension overlooking Ingbirchworth Reservoir and the South Yorkshire countryside. All are en suite, are beautifully and comfortably furnished and have a full range of facilities. These include CD players, welcoming decanters of sherry and home-made biscuits, and fluffy bathrobes. The atmosphere in the hotel is busy but friendly with the emphasis on informal eating in stylish surroundings. There is no restaurant but there are sections of the friendly bar for Diners Only, and an extensive menu is available.The Kirklees Light Railway, Holmfirth (Last of the Summer Wine country) and the Peak District are nearby. Barnsley, Huddersfield and Sheffield with its theatres, arena and Meadowhall Shopping Centre are approximately ten miles away. **Directions:** Exit the M1 at junction 37 and take the road to Manchester and Penistone. Then turn right onto the A629. In Ingbirchworth turn left into Wellthorne Lane. Price guide: Single £40–£65; double/twin £50–80.

For hotel location, see maps on pages 212-218

BADGERS

COULTERSHAW BRIDGE, PETWORTH, WEST SUSSEX GU28 OJF
TEL: 01798 342651 FAX: 01798 343649

This glorious Georgian inn, just outside Chichester in the beautiful countryside from which Turner derived so much inspiration, has a fascinating history. It was built in conjunction with the railway in 1860, with horse and carts from the inn transporting passengers and goods into Petworth. The bore hole dug to provide water is today a trout stream and pond. The interior of the inn is immaculate, the furnishings and decorations appropriate, and the ambience in the bar is wonderfully relaxing, enhanced by open fires in winter. The spacious bedrooms, each different, are exquisite. The beds are king-size, with attractive en suite bathrooms. The stylish restaurant has a fine reputation, the menu a Mediterranean influence. Zarzuela, a Spanish fish casserole, is a house speciality. It also includes delicious interpretations of classical English dishes. The wine list makes good reading. The Inn has a charming secluded sunny cobbled courtyard, perfect for alfresco apéritifs and summer dining. Sporting guests will enjoy golf at Cowdray Park and Goodwood. The former also is famous for polo and the latter for racing. Fly fishing, ballooning and speed festivals are alternatives. Petworth House and Arundel Castle should be visited and Chichester with its sailing harbour and theatre is a 'must'. **Directions:** Badgers is south of Petworth on the A285. Price guide: double £70.

3 rms MasterCard VISA M 30

For hotel location, see maps on pages 212-218

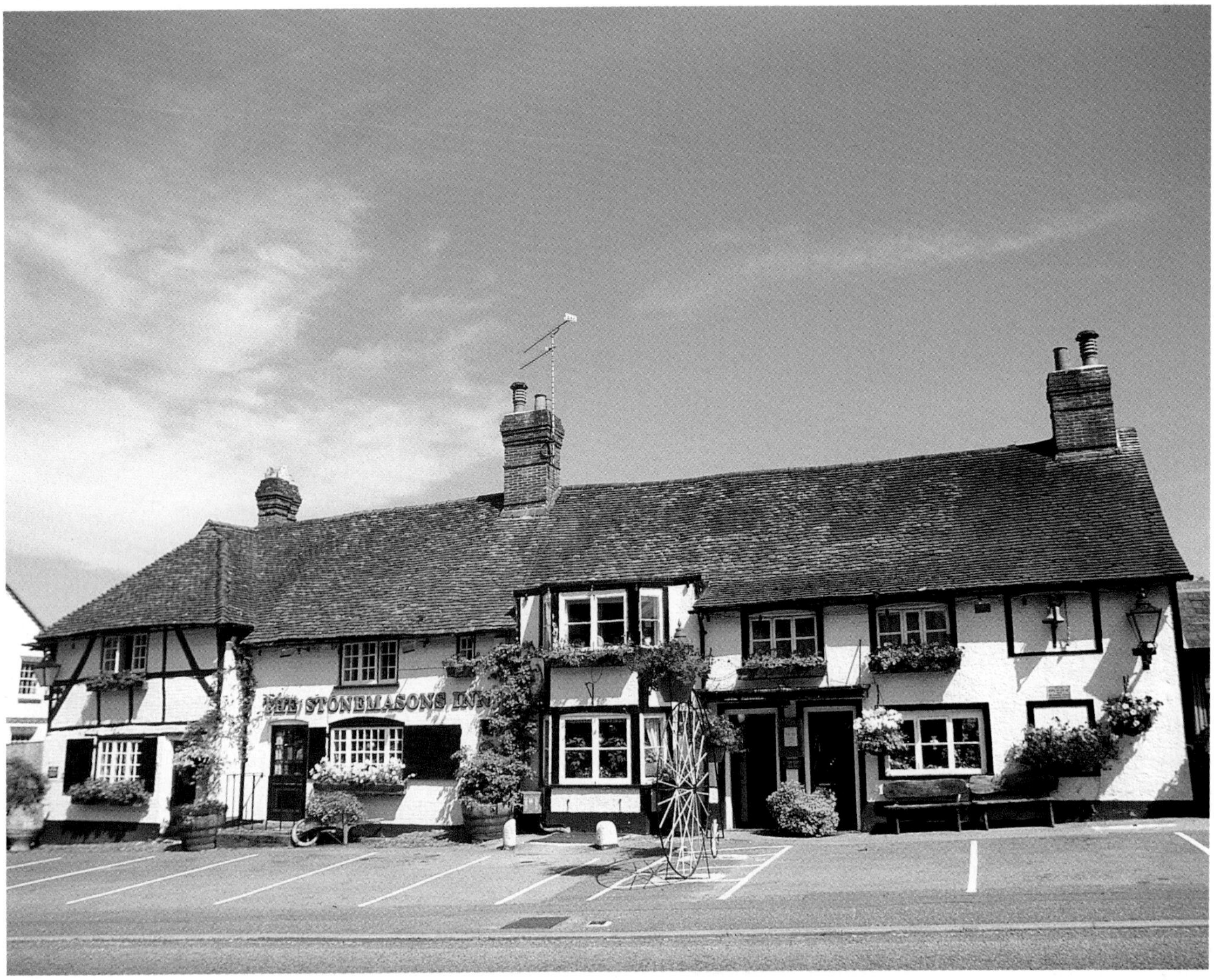

STONEMASON'S INN

NORTH STREET, PETWORTH, WEST SUSSEX GU28 9NL
TEL: 01798 342510 FAX: 01798 342510

Variously named The Vinson's, The Mason's and The Trap, The Stonemason's Inn can probably trace its origins to a row of 15th century cottages, while its present use as an inn of distinction certainly dates from at least 1780. Much effort has gone into preserving parts of its history, as evidenced by the quaintly-named Uncle Jed's Parlour and Mrs Smith's Cottage – both used now as dining areas – where fires glow in their open hearths in winter. Hosts Gwyn and Maggie Chivers proudly uphold the inn's fine traditions, providing excellent home-cooked food and stylish accommodation. The two cosy en suite bedrooms are comfortable and furnished to a very high standard. A welcoming atmosphere extends throughout the property to an enclosed rear patio that overlooks the colourful, award winning garden. In the Coach House Restaurant fare is both traditional and substantial. Home-made shortcrust pies, steak and kidney pudding and liver with bacon and onion gravy are supplemented on a daily basis by the freshest fish, seafood and other delights. A wide choice for vegetarians and a wine list including the landlord's selection of a dozen choices by the glass show commendable regard for guests' well-being. Nearby are Petworth Park, the town of Petworth, a haven for antique hunters and Goodwood racecourse. **Directions:** Leave Petworth on A283 for Guildford. The Stonemason's Arms is at the junction with A272 east of the town. Price guide: Single £45; double/twin £58.

30

For hotel location, see maps on pages 212-218

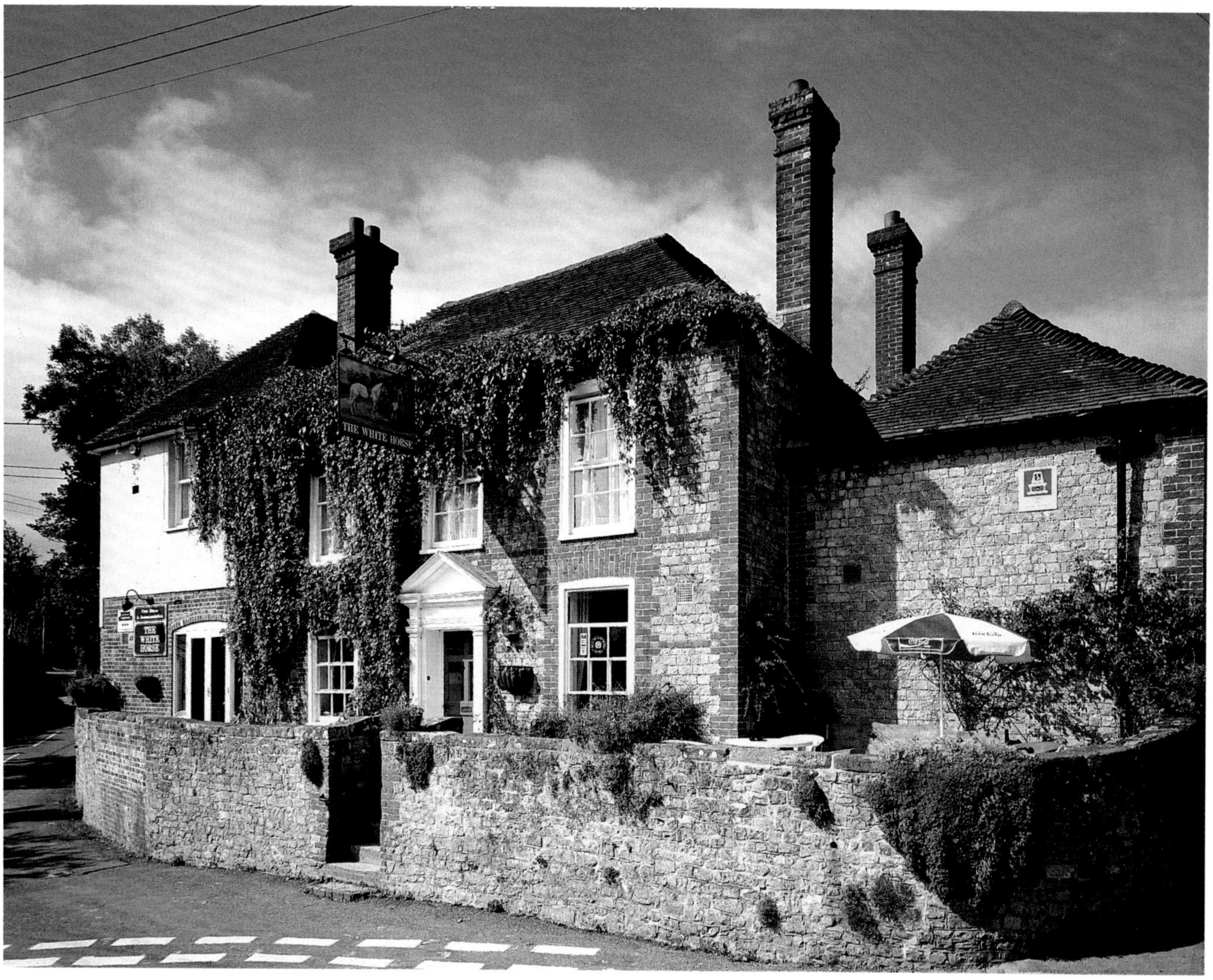

WHITE HORSE INN

SUTTON, NR PULBOROUGH, WEST SUSSEX RH20 1PS
TEL: 01798 869 221 FAX: 01798 869 291

This privately owned inn has offered rest and comfort to both travellers and locals since 1746. Howard and Susie Macnamara have restored the traditions of the inn by making available six pretty rooms which are comfortably furnished and appointed with modern amenities. The double-bedded rooms have king-size beds and all rooms have well-kept en suite bathrooms. All bedrooms are 'non-smoking' – all have tea and coffee facilities and colour television. There is also an attractive garden cottage; however, unlike the other bedrooms, this does not have a direct-dial telephone. Joss and Val Maude are always on hand to offer a friendly welcome. The White Horse is a popular place to eat, both with locals and patrons from further afield. Fresh wholesome food is always featured on the menu. The three-course table d'hôte dinner with coffee is very reasonably priced. Amberley Chalk Pits, horse-racing at Goodwood, the harbour town of Chichester, Arundel Castle, Petworth House, Parham House and Gardens and the Roman Villa at Bignor are nearby. **Directions:** Sutton is a little hamlet situated between A29 (Pulborough to Arundel road) and A285 (Petworth to Chichester road). Look for brown sign to Roman Villa at Bignor – Sutton is a mile further west. Price guide: Single £48; double £58–£68.

For hotel location, see maps on pages 212-218

The Port Gaverne Hotel

NR PORT ISACC, NORTH CORNWALL PL29 3SQ
TEL: 01208 880244 FAX: 01208 880151

Port Gaverne Hotel is situated on the North Cornwall Coastal Path in a secluded cove half a mile from the old fishing village of Port Isaac. Much of the surrounding area is supervised by the National Trust. The 350-year-old hotel is owned and managed by Midge Ross and its character owes as much to the skills and materials of local tradesmen as it does to the dedication of its proprietress. Bedrooms are cosy and well-appointed with direct dial telephone and TV. The residents' lounge never fails to woo guests with its old-world personality. At Port Gaverne Hotel chef Ian Brodey and his staff have built up an international reputation for fine cuisine with delicious seafood dishes and a vegetarian menu. It was recently awarded an AA Rosette. The hotel is also noted for its 'Breather' weekends in autumn and winter and its self-contained 18th century cottages and 2 flats overlooking the sea. Walk the coastal path in either direction for National Trust countryside in abundance. There is safe, sheltered swimming within seconds of the hotel door. Delabole Slate Quarry and Tintagel Castle (King Arthur's birthplace) are nearby. **Directions:** Port Gaverne is signposted from the B3314 south of Delabole and is reached along the B3267. Follow the signs for Port Gaverne only (not Port Isaac). Price guide: Single £51–£53; double £102–£106.

For hotel location, see maps on pages 212-218

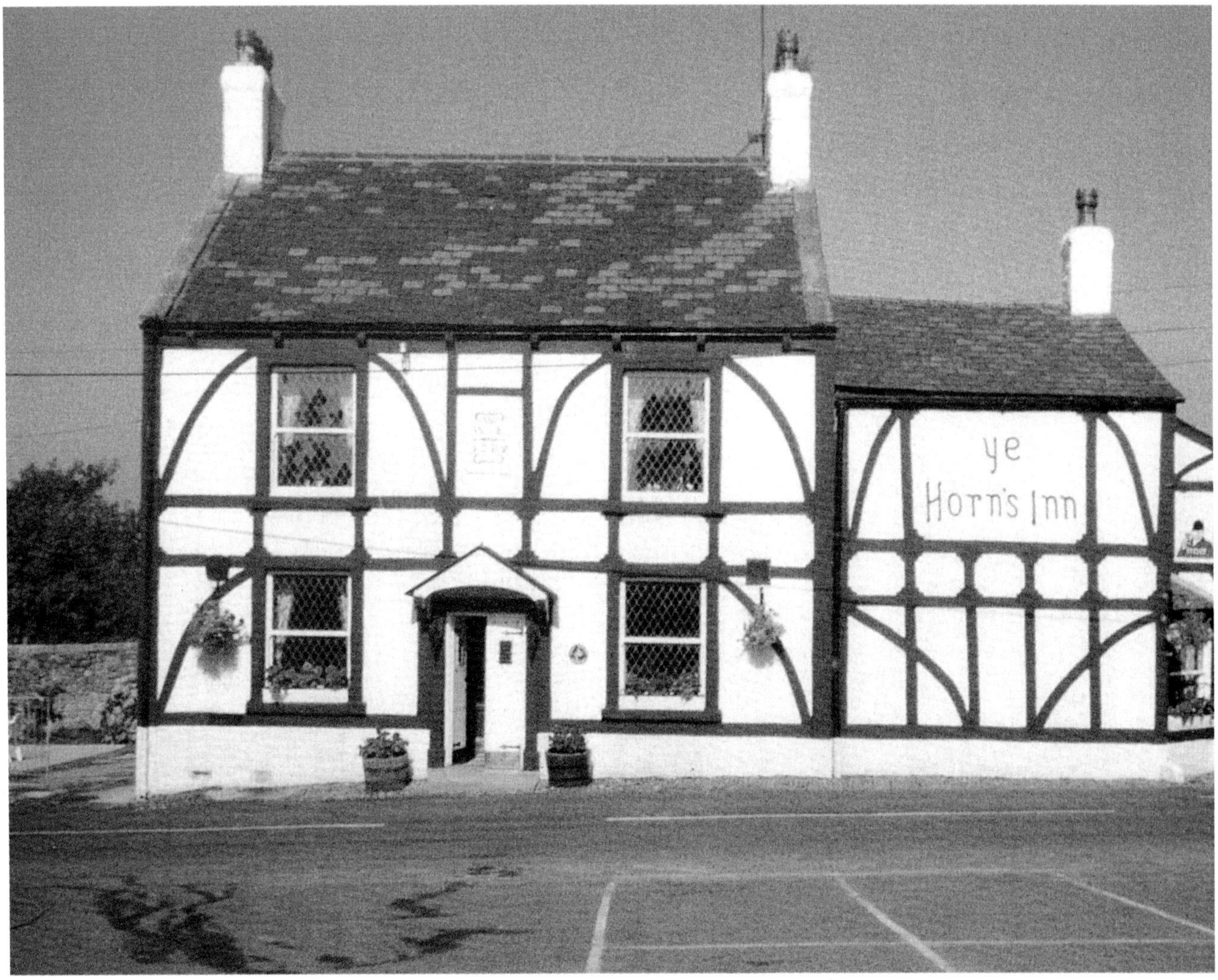

Ye Horn's Inn

HORN'S LANE, GOOSNARGH, NR PRESTON, LANCASHIRE PR3 2FJ
TEL: 01772 865230 FAX: 01772 864299 E-MAIL: yehornsinn@msn.com

A striking black-and-white timbered building standing at a crossroads in lovely rolling countryside, Ye Horn's radiates charm and atmosphere. Built in 1782 as a coaching inn, the hotel has been run by the Woods family for 40 years. Today it is expertly managed by Elizabeth Jones, her brother Mark Woods and his wife Denise, offering first-rate accommodation for both business visitors and the holiday-maker. The 6 spacious bedrooms, all en suite, are in the adjoining barn – a recent conversion – and are stylishly furnished. All offer tea and coffee-making facilities, trouser press and hairdryer. Oak beams, sumptuous carpets and in winter, open fires, combine to create a mood of cosy, relaxed hospitality throughout. The restaurant has earned a fine reputation for its delicious traditional cuisine, prepared wherever possible from fresh, local produce and served in the main dining room or the 'snug' next to it. Specialities include home-made soup, roast duckling, roast pheasant and a truly addictive sticky toffee pudding. Full English or Continental breakfasts are available. Chingle Hall, a haunted house, the Ribble Valley, the Forest of Bowland and Blackpool are all nearby. **Directions:** Exit M6 Jct32, take A6 north to first traffic lights. Turn right onto B5269 signposted Longridge, to just past Goosnargh village shop. Where the road veers sharply right, continue straight ahead into Camforth Hall Lane: the hotel is signed after a few minutes. Price guide: Single £49; double £75.

For hotel location, see maps on pages 212-218

The Bull At Streatley

STREATLEY ON THAMES, READING, BERKSHIRE RG8 9JJ
TEL: 01491 872392 FAX: 01491 875231

The Bull is situated in a beautiful setting on the west bank of one of the loveliest stretches of the River Thames. It is overlooked by Streatley Hill from where visitors who complete a 10 minutes climb to the summit can enjoy one of the best upstream views of the Thames Valley. Streatley is an unspoilt town with many fine Georgian houses and a 19th century malt house now used as a village hall. Tasteful and sympathetic refurbishment has complemented the ambience of The Bull whose history dates back to the 15th century. All the bedrooms have been individually designed to a high standard. They have every comfort to make guests feel at home, including colour television, trouser press, hairdryer, alarm clock and tea and coffee-making facilities. Two of the rooms have four-poster beds. The traditional character and atmosphere of the extensive bar and dining area is enhanced by open fires in the winter. The Bull enjoys a reputation locally for its good cooking which is modern English with seasonal and seafood dishes. There is also a vegetarian menu. Reading is within easy reach and events in the locality include Henley Regatta, Ascot and Newbury races. Windsor Castle, Blenheim Palace, Oxford and Reading are easily accessible. **Directions:** The Bull is on the A340, eight miles from junction 12 of the M4. Price guide: Single £60; double/twin £60.

For hotel location, see maps on pages 212-218

DUKE'S HEAD

GREATBRIDGE, NR ROMSEY, HAMPSHIRE SO51 0HB
TEL: 01794 514450 FAX: 01794 830192

This is a beautiful, fascinating old inn situated close to the ancient market town of Romsey. It is an absolute delight, offering great warmth, hospitality, style and outstanding food. Witty remarks from the great American comic W.C.Fields plus quotations and thought provoking texts from Oscar Wilde adorn the walls. There are a variety of rooms on different levels, all individually themed around dukes, local history, fishing and similar subjects. There has been an inn on the site since 1530 and a peculiar sense of history pervades the Duke's Head. The décor is relaxing and the furniture heavy and extremely comfortable. There are numerous original features and a superb collection of antiques. A notice by the entrance says the food is served with style. It is, and Chef Nigel Collins' dishes are delicious and cooked to perfection. They will satisfy the most discerning palate. Local produce and fresh vegetables are served in abundance, including old English favourites such as rabbit, pheasant and venison. To digest a memorable inn meal visitors may care to stroll around Romsey and take in its 10th century abbey, explore the early 13th century King John's Lodge or visit Broadlands and its beautiful park. **Directions:** Exit the M27 at junctions 2 or 3 and travel north through Romsey. Greatbridge is at the junction of the B3057 and B3084.

MasterCard VISA AMERICAN EXPRESS M 12

For hotel location, see maps on pages 212-218

COTTAGE OF CONTENT

CAREY, HEREFORD, HEREFORDSHIRE HR2 6NG
TEL: 01432 840242 FAX: 01432 840208

The hamlet of Carey stands alongside the River Wye and at its heart lies this rambling, picturesque hostelry beside a wooden bridge that separates the inn from its car park. The Cottage of Content is aptly named, with a long tradition of hospitality that dates back to the 15th century. Inside, its medieval appearance has been carefully preserved with original timbers, panelled walls and slate floors. An open staircase to the upper floor separates the lounge bar from the dining area. The three en suite bedrooms are much in keeping with their simple, modern comforts and attractive décor. Though there is no formal dining room, food of exceptional quality and value is provided by celebrated local chef Kevin Powles throughout the inn, whose two bars are informally congenial. Fresh fish, including Wye salmon, is a speciality alongside Hereford beef and Welsh salt-marsh lamb, with locally grown vegetables and strawberries in season. All meals are cooked to order and a choice of vegetarian dishes is always on offer. There is an interesting wine list and a good choice of real ales and Herefordshire ciders. In the chef's absence on Mondays and Tuesdays, main meals are not available. With the Wye Valley and Black Mountains to the south, the area surrounding the Cottage is ideal for anglers, horse-riders and walkers. **Directions:** Turn off the main A49 Ross-on-Wye to Hereford road following signs to Hoarwithy and then go on to Carey. Price guide: Single £35; double/twin £48.

3 rms

For hotel location, see maps on pages 212-218

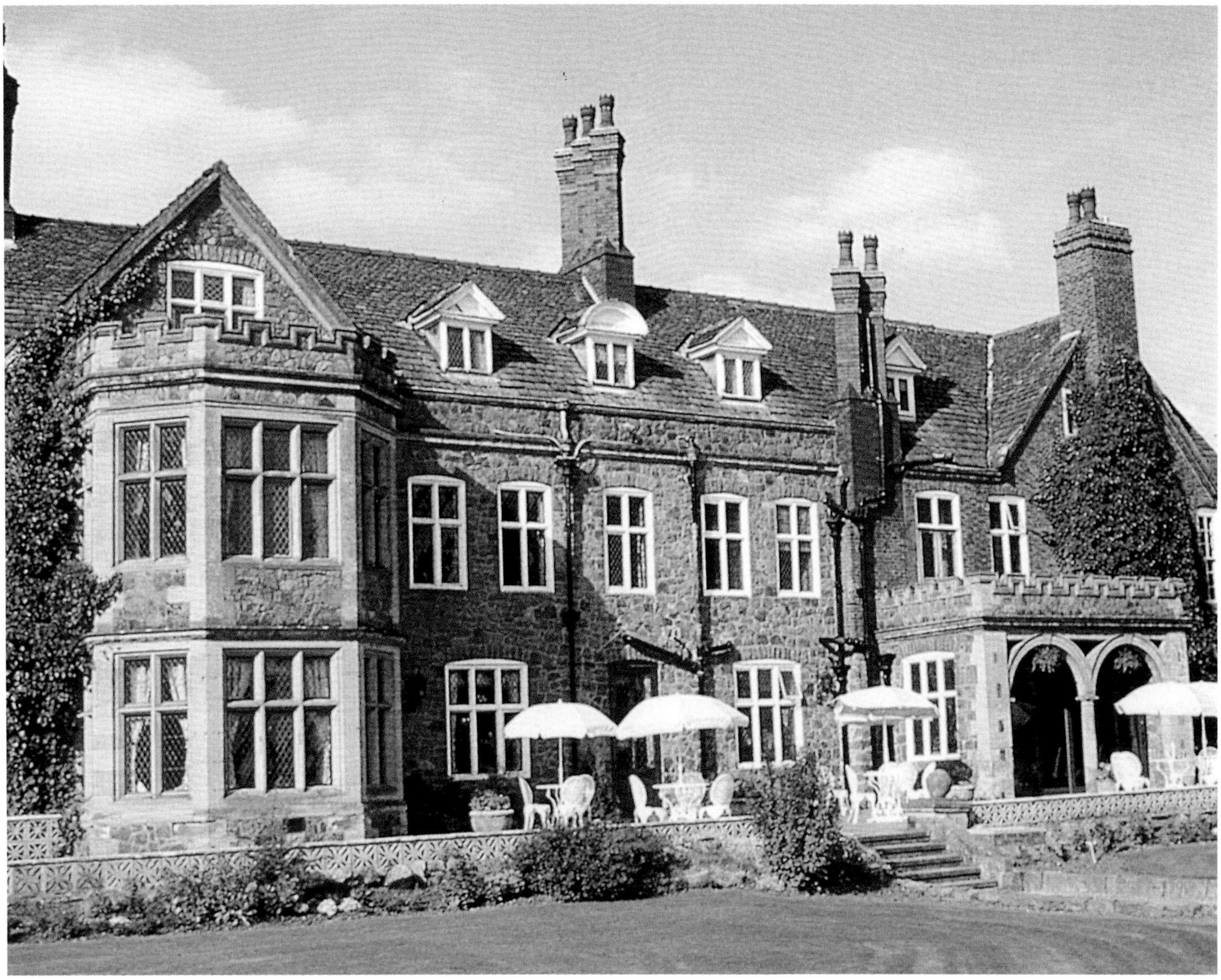

ROTHLEY COURT HOTEL

ROTHLEY COURT, WESTFIELD LANE, ROTHLEY, LEICESTER, LEICESTERSHIRE LE7 7LG
TEL: 0116 237 4141 FAX: 0116 237 4483

With its solid stone, ivy-clad walls, tall impressive chimneys, leaded windows and six acres of superb grounds, Rothley Court is the personification of a centuries old manor house. Situated on the edge of Charnwood Forest between Leicester and Loughborough it is a haven of peace and quiet. Home of the Holy Order of the Knights Templar in the 13th century, Rothley Court has its own perfectly preserved 11th century chapel. Throughout the hotel splendid furnishings, stone pillared arches, rich panelling and décor create an atmosphere of relaxed elegance. The 34 bedrooms are luxurious, en suite and equipped to the highest standard. Many overlook the magnificent gardens whose views can also be enjoyed from a sun terrace stretching the length of the building. Deep leather armchairs add to the enjoyment of taking morning coffee or afternoon tea in the delightful lounge where an open fire burns in winter months. Apéritifs can be sipped in a charming bar before sampling the restaurant's excellent table d'hôte and à la carte cuisine. Rothley has a restored Victorian railway station and close by is Bradgate Country Park and Leicester. **Directions:** Leave the M1 at junction 21A and follow the A6 towards Loughborough. Take the first exit at the roundabout and follow signs for Rothley, Anstey, Crossington and Steam Railway. Price guide: Single £90; double/twin £100.

For hotel location, see maps on pages 212-218

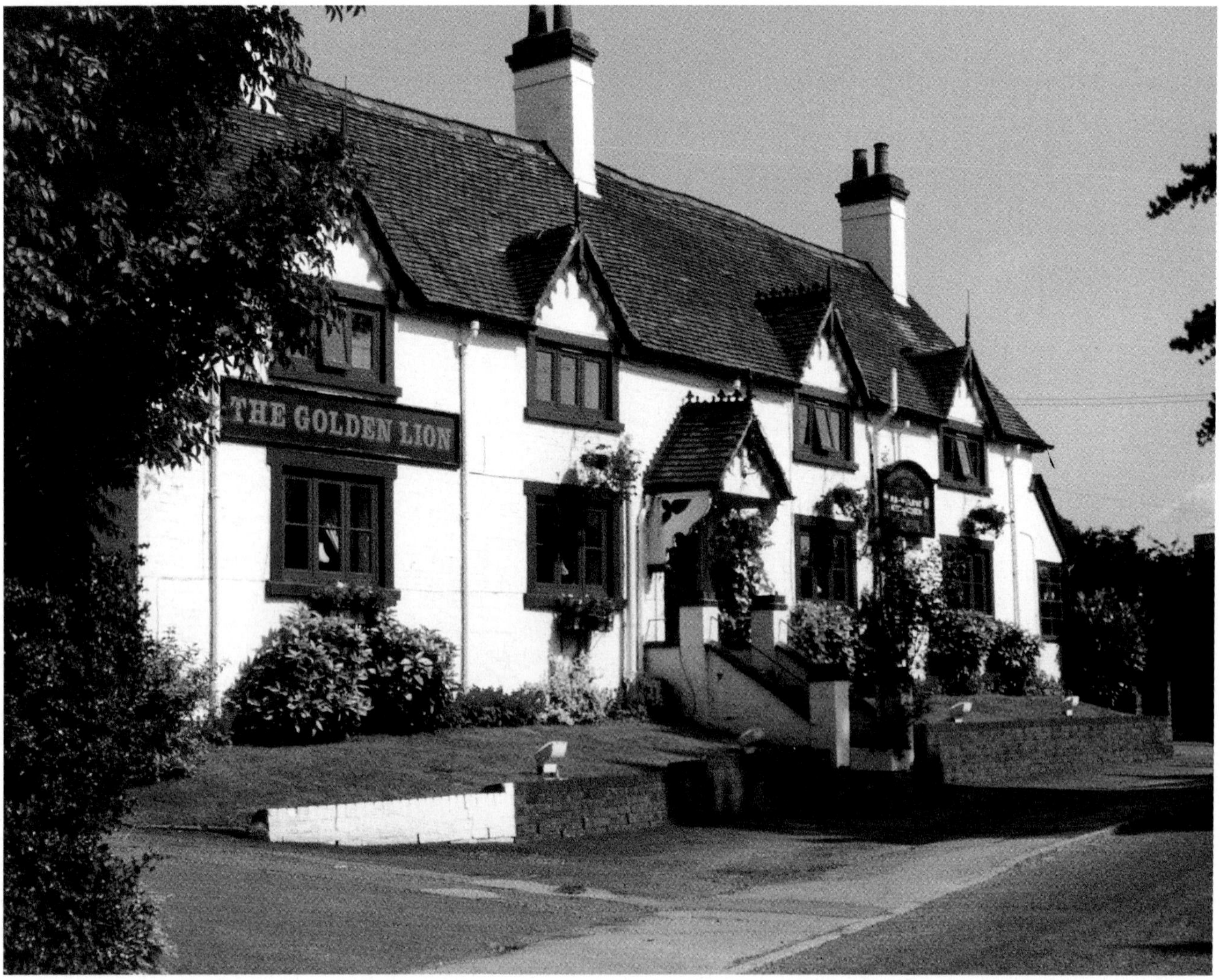

The Golden Lion Inn of Easenhall

EASENHALL, NR RUGBY, WARWICKSHIRE CV23 0JA
TEL: 01788 832265 FAX: 01788 832878 E-MAIL: James.Austin@btinternet.com

The Golden Lion, dating back to the 16th century, is set back from the main road through Easenhall, a delightful English village not far from Rugby and ideal for parents visiting the celebrated boarding school. It has low oak beamed ceilings, narrow doorways and uneven floors which all add to its charm and guests receive a traditional warm welcome. The small bar is proud of its best ales, fine wines and wide range of spirits. Delicious snacks are available both at lunchtime and in the evening. The bedrooms are extremely comfortable and quite spacious, with attractive cottage furniture. The restaurant is divided into two rooms and specialises in country cooking. In summer guests can eat alfresco in the garden and patio, where barbecues are often held, sometimes joined by the pet donkey. Guests can enjoy village cricket or go further afield to Coventry Cathedral, Coombe Abbey or Warwick Castle. The NEC Birmingham and Stoneleigh Agricultural Centre are also in easy reach. There are excellent golf courses in the neighbourhood. **Directions:** Easenhall is reached from the M6 junctions 1/2, taking the B4112 off the A426 for Rugby or the B4027 from the Coventry by-pass. Price guide: Single £42; double £62.

For hotel location, see maps on pages 212-218

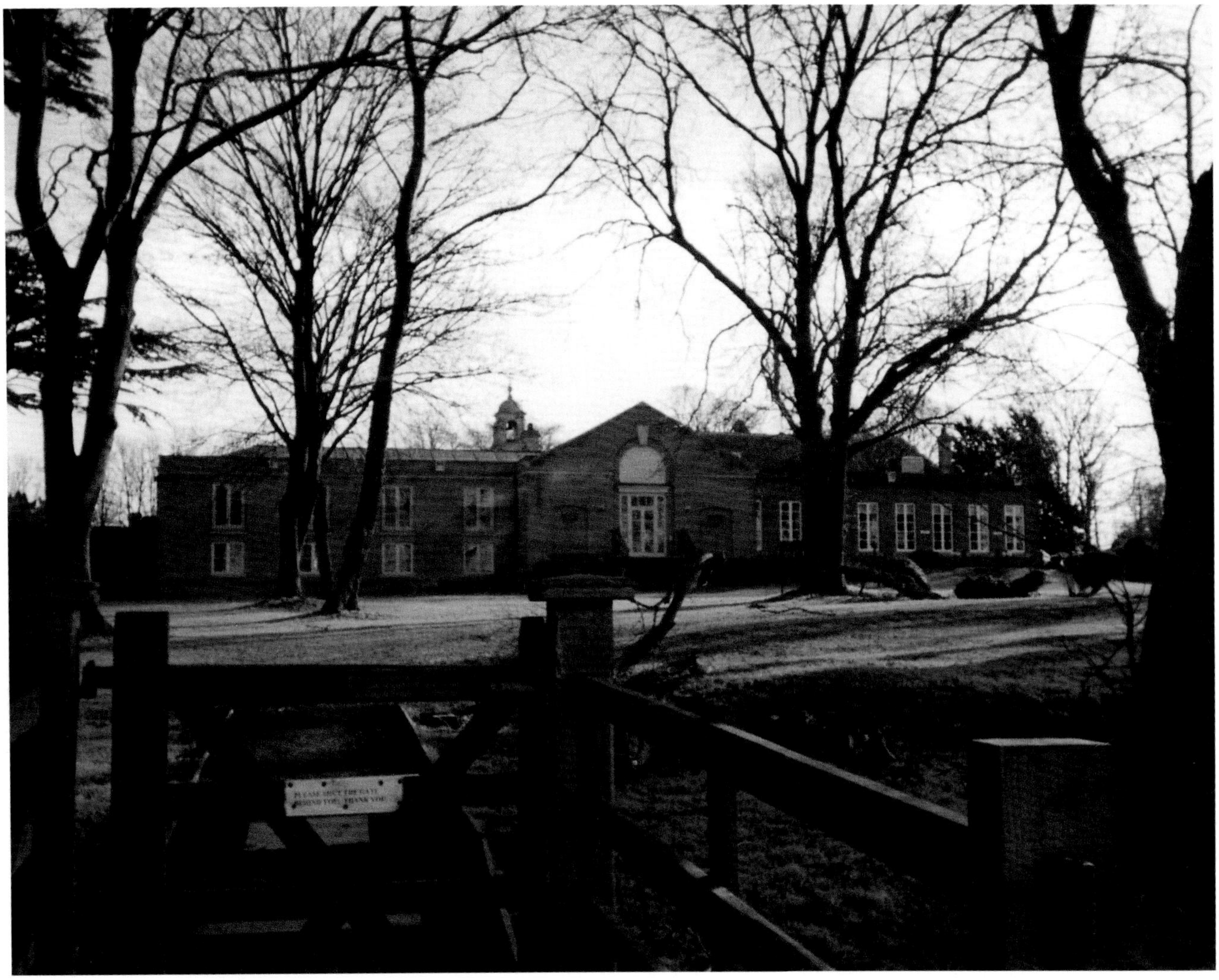

NORMANTON PARK HOTEL

NORMANTON PARK, RUTLAND WATER SOUTH SHORE, RUTLAND, LEICESTERSHIRE LE15 8RP
TEL: 01780 720315 FAX: 01780 721086

Situated alongside the famous 'submerged' church overlooking England's largest man-made reservoir, Normanton Park Hotel has been meticulously restored from its origins as the coach house to Normanton Park Hall. The Grade II listed hotel is set in four acres of grounds, which were landscaped in the 18th century and have one of the country's oldest Cedar of Lebanon trees. Many of the bedrooms overlook the lake, which provides fly and coarse fishing, boat hire, windsurfing, kite-flying, cycling, walking and bird-watching. The Sailing Bar offers a warm welcome and a good variety of meals, snacks and drinks is served throughout the day. Designed on an orangery theme, the delightful restaurant offers a gourmet's choice of both à la carte and reasonably priced Sunday lunch table d'hôte menus. The cocktail bar, decorated with ancient bellows and a blazing log fire in cooler months, makes a relaxing lounge area for guests. Many stately homes and National Trust properties are nearby and the A1 is easily accessible. Helicopters can land by prior arrangement. **Directions:** From the A1, take the A606 at Stamford towards Oakham; turn along the south shore road towards Edith Weston. Price guide: Single £60–£70; double/twin £75; suite/lake view £85.

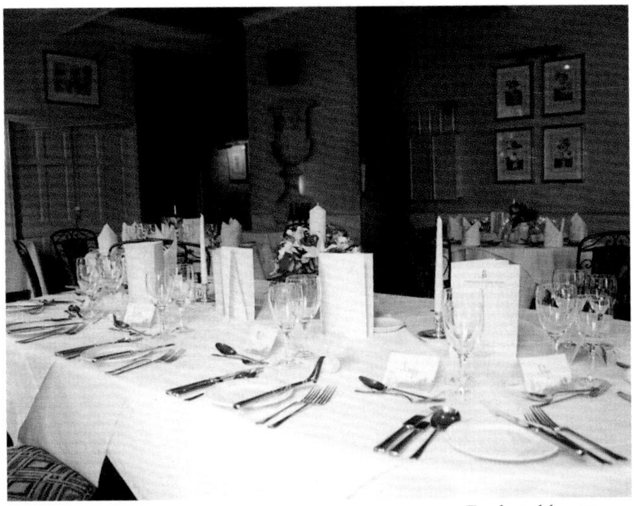

23 rms

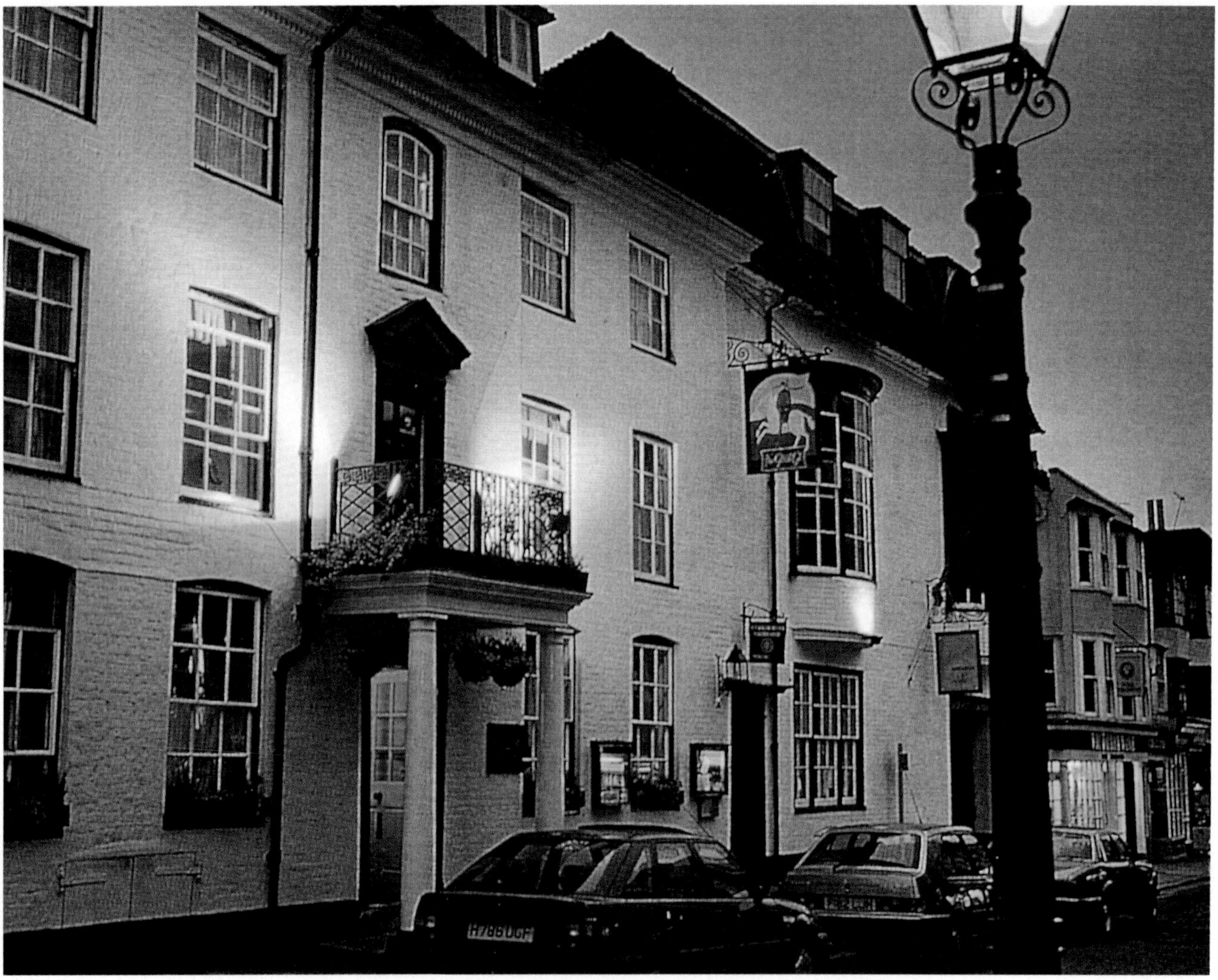

THE GEORGE HOTEL

HIGH STREET, RYE, EAST SUSSEX TN31 7JP
TEL: 01797 222114 FAX: 01797 224065

An imposing pillared entrance way and attractive black and white period façade greet visitors to this 16th century hotel situated at the centre of Rye's picturesque high street. The George was built in 1575 and over the years has been sympathetically and carefully modernised. However, the hotel retains many original features, including oak beams reputedly taken from a galleon which was part of the Spanish Armada. Surrounded by cobbled streets and numerous ancient houses and buildings it has a charming, unique character and offers a comfortable standard of accommodation. The atmosphere is friendly and inviting with the emphasis on total relaxation, cheerful service and value for money. All 22 individually styled bedrooms are equipped with en suite facilities and well provided with modern amenities. The Meryons Restaurant specialises in classic English cuisine and a typical menu might include baked mushroom filled with Provençal sauce topped with cheddar cheese, then margert duck with black olives followed by sticky toffee pudding and custard. Light snacks can be enjoyed in the comfortable John Crouch Bar. Rye boasts many art galleries, antique shops and booksellers. Winchelsea, Romney Marsh and Battle Abbey are within easy reach. **Directions:** Take the A21 to Flimwell then take the A268 to Rye. Price guide: Single £55; double/twin £90–£110.

For hotel location, see maps on pages 212-218

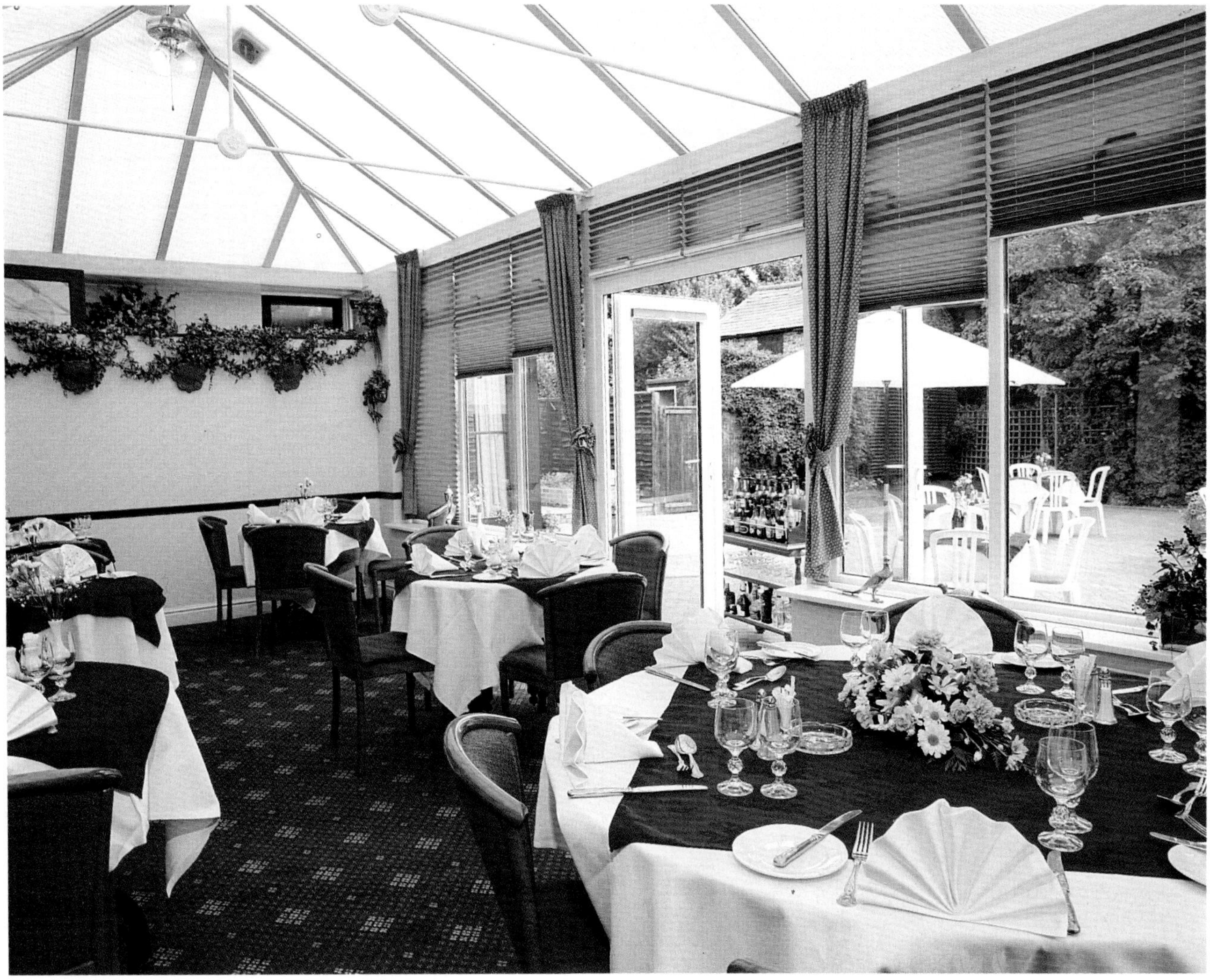

OLIVER'S LODGE HOTEL & RESTAURANT

NEEDINGWORTH ROAD, ST IVES, NR CAMBRIDGE, CAMBRIDGESHIRE PE17 4JP
TEL: 01480 463252 FAX: 01480 461150

Originally a Victorian building which has been sympathetically extended, Oliver's Lodge is centrally situated in a quiet residential area of the historic market town of St Ives. It is just a few minutes walk from the River Ouse, which for thousands of years was one of the main highways of Britain. Oliver Cromwell farmed here in the 1630's and his statue, in which he is booted and wearing an unpuritanically rakish hat, stands in the market-place. Privately owned and run, the hotel offers a warm, friendly welcome with the emphasis on individual attention and high quality food and service. Extensive à la carte and conservatory menus feature daily specials including salmon en croute with chive sauce, chateaubriand and other fish and game dishes in season. Alfresco diners enjoy the attractive patio garden. The bedrooms, some of which are on the ground floor, include three suites/family rooms. There are several function/conference rooms for 6 to 80 people. Special bargain two day breaks available. Cambridge, Huntingdon, Newmarket, the American Cemetery at Madingley, Burghley House Stamford, Imperial War Museum Duxford are all within easy reach. **Directions:** From Cambridge take A14 towards Huntingdon. Turn right onto A1096 for St Ives. Straight across first roundabout, left at next and first right. Price guide: Single £50–£65; double £75–£90.

For hotel location, see maps on pages 212-218

THE OLD BELL INN HOTEL

HUDDERSFIELD ROAD, DELPH, SADDLEWORTH, NR OLDHAM, LANCASHIRE OL3 5EG
TEL: 01457 870130 FAX: 01457 876597

Many famous figures from the past, including Queen Victoria and Charles Dickens, have visited this stone-built, 18th century inn, which acquired its current name under the tenancy of William Bell. Today's guests are offered attractive accommodation in furnished and well-equipped bedrooms. A number of rooms have four-poster beds – perfect for a romantic weekend. Old beams, open fires and lead lattice windows create a cosy atmosphere in the bar and comfortable residents' lounge. Private parties for up to 40 can be catered for. An imaginative menu is changed seasonally to offer plenty of choice and variety. Guests can try, for example, venison steak on a croûte topped with pâté coated in port wine sauce. A separate vegetarian menu is always provided. For less formal occasions, meals are also served in the bar. The village of Delph, with its weavers' cottages and cobbled side-streets still a reminder of its cloth-making history, lies on the edge of the Peak District National Park and Saddleworth Moor – an area of great natural beauty is also nearby. Places to visit include Castle Shaw Roman Fort, Huddersfield canal where boat trips can be taken, Dovestones Reservoir with its water sports and the art and craft centre at Uppermill. Various golf courses are close by. Special weekend rates are available on request. **Directions:** The Old Bell Inn is on A62 Oldham-Huddersfield road, in the village of Delph. Price guide: Single £35–£55; double £55–£75.

10 rms MasterCard VISA AMERICAN EXPRESS M 15

For hotel location, see maps on pages 212-218

THE OLD MILL HOTEL & RESTAURANT

TOWN PATH, HARNHAM, SALISBURY, WILTSHIRE SP2 8EU
TEL: 01722 327517 FAX: 01722 333367

Nestling peacefully at the edge of unspoilt water meadows this historic, Grade I listed hotel offers guests the same panoramic views of one of England's most beautiful cathedral cities as those captured on canvas by John Constable in the early 18th century. Built around 1135, the building became Wiltshire's first paper mill in 1550 when water from the River Nadder was diverted through its walls to drive three water wheels. Milling ceased in 1931 but the crystal clear water still cascades through the beamed restaurant to the enjoyment of the guests, dining upon the traditional English dishes. It is based on quality and simplicity with fresh produce from local farms used extensively. There are 11 tastefully decorated and furnished bedrooms. All are en suite, have individual character and offer every home comfort. Coffee, tea and pre-dinner drinks can be sipped in the relaxing lounge or in the delightful riverside gardens with their preponderance of wagtails, dippers, kingfishers, mallards and swans. Popular with locals and visitors alike, the pub bar has a superb range of real ales and malt whiskies. The medieval delights of Salisbury are close by and Stonehenge, Salisbury Plain and the New Forest are within easy each. **Directions:** Harnham is just west of Salisbury on the A3094. Price guide: Single £45–£55; double/twin £85.

11 rms · MasterCard · VISA · AMERICAN EXPRESS

For hotel location, see maps on pages 212-218

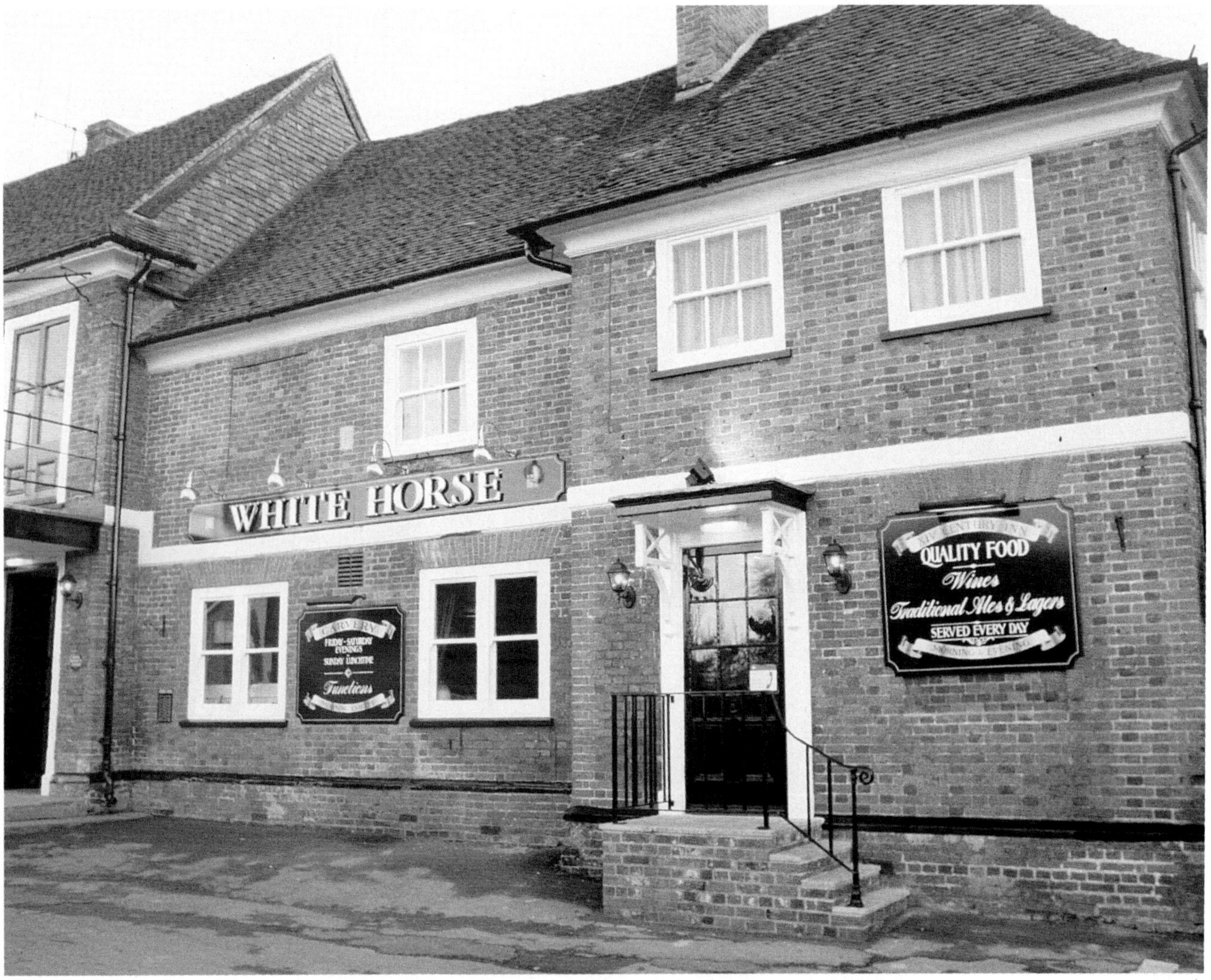

THE WHITE HORSE

DOWNTON, SALISBURY, WILTSHIRE SP5 3LY
TEL: 01725 510408 FAX: 01725 511954

Built in 1420 by and for the Bishop of Winchester for a country residence, The White Horse is beautifully situated close to the edge of the New Forest. It is a charming country inn, secluded and tranquil, an ideal spot in which to escape the modern world, take long peaceful walks, and enjoy the nearby River Avon and the delights of picturesque little villages. The hostess, Gilly Alexander, has invested a great deal of energy and enthusiasm into making The White Horse a welcoming haven of comfort, excellent food and attentive service. It is full of good humour, atmosphere and character. Gilly, herself is a cheerful personality with many interesting stories to tell of her days as a performer with the famous Black and White Minstrels Show. As well as an extensive bar menu of snacks and light meals, appetising and comprehensive à la carte cuisine tempts locals and visitors alike to the inn's restaurant. There is well- selected wine list featuring affordable vintages. Just a short drive away are Salisbury, one of Britain's most beautiful cathedral cities, 16th century Longford Castle with its notable collection of paintings and 18th century Trafalgar House at Alderbury, presented by a grateful nation to Lord Nelson's family in 1815. The inn is ideally placed for Salisbury race-goers. **Directions:** Downton is approximately six miles south of Salisbury just off the A338 road to Ringwood.

For hotel location, see maps on pages 212-218

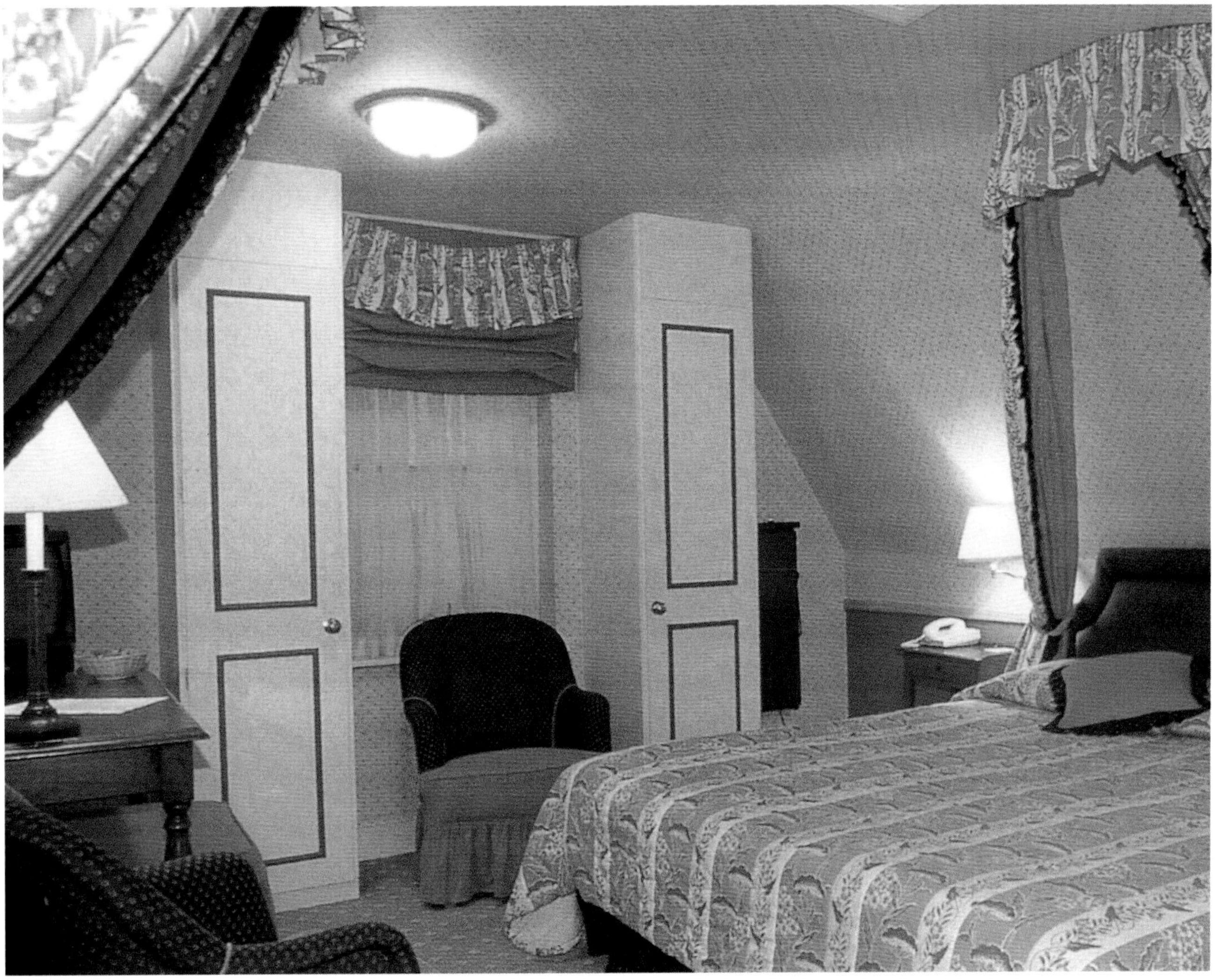

THE ROYAL OAK

HIGH STREET, SEVENOAKS, KENT TN14 5PG
TEL: 01732 451109 FAX: 01732 740187

The Royal Oak is located just a short walk from Sevenoaks town centre and its many shopping opportunities. Built in the 17th century, the hotel is an ideal base from which to explore the surrounding countryside of Kent, Surrey and Sussex and visit the area's many famous castles, houses, gardens and National Trust properties. The hotel has 37 comfortable en suite bedrooms, all attractively decorated and furnished and with 24-hour service. Guests may enjoy morning coffee or afternoon tea in the conservatory which opens out onto a delightful, paved patio with small tables and shady sun umbrellas. Two ground floor rooms are available for conferences, meetings and private functions. The light and airy Sycamore Restaurant plays an important role in the hotel. The head chef prepares a blend of modern English and French dishes making full use of Kent's abundance of natural produce. A good range of hot and cold dishes is also served in the bistro and bar. Leeds and Hever Castles, Chartwell, the 14th century manor house Igtham Mote, the Elizabethan village of Chiddingstone, Penshurst Place and Knole are all close by. Royal Tunbridge Wells and its excellent shops are within easy reach. **Directions:** Sevenoaks is only a short drive from junction 5 of the M25. Price guide: Single £55–85; double £80–£90.

For hotel location, see maps on pages 212-218

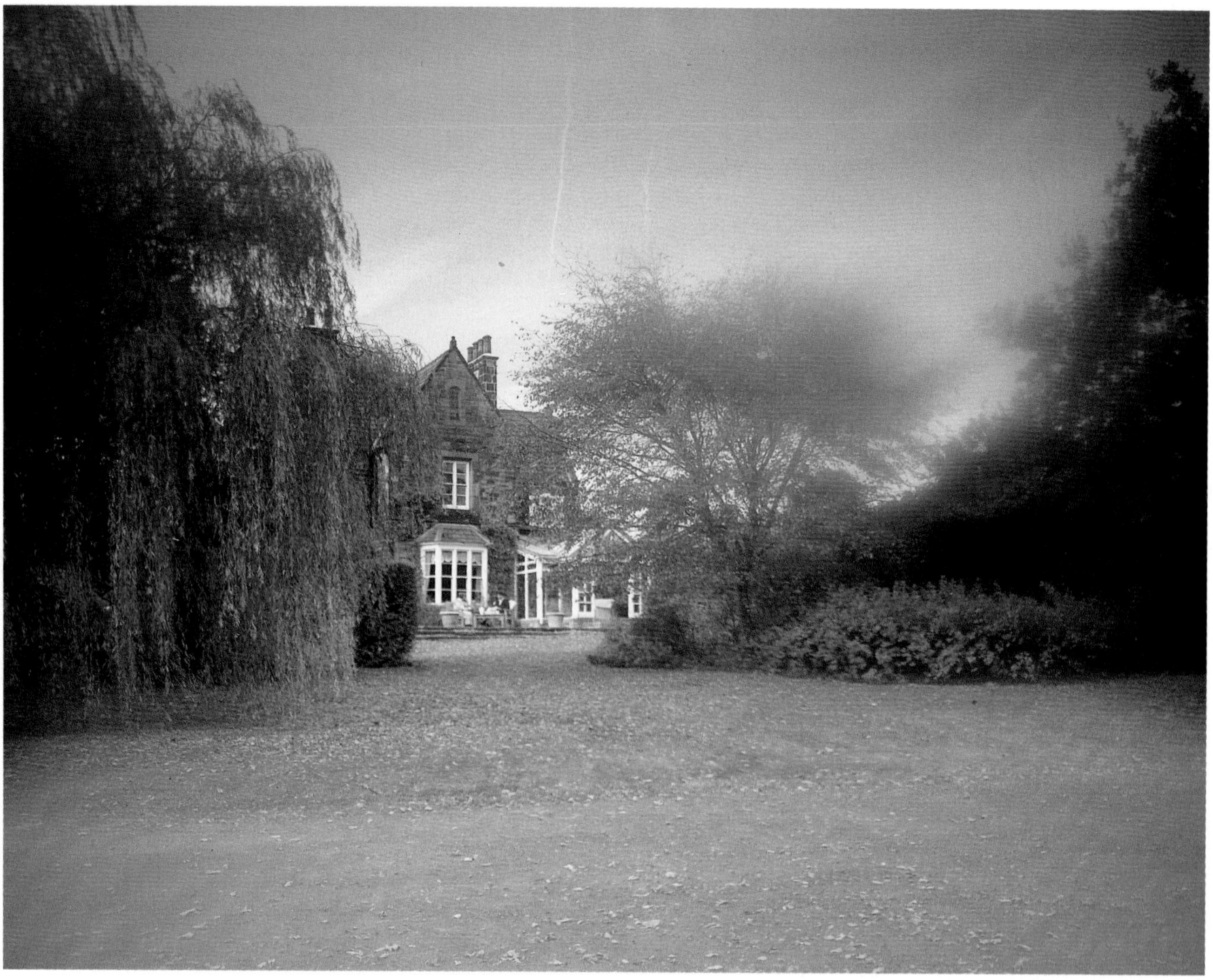

THE OLD VICARAGE

RIDGEWAY MOOR, RIDGEWAY, NEAR SHEFFIELD, DERBYSHIRE S12 3XW
TEL: 0114 247 5814 FAX: 0114 247 7079

Set in two acres of beautiful gardens, The Old Vicarage, a charming Victorian house, exudes style and character. The two dining rooms, one set in a conservatory, are beautifully appointed. The charming hostess and chef patron Tessa Bramley, author of a number of cookery books and a regular presenter on a popular television programme, is refreshingly modern in her approach to the cuisine. Created by the talented chef and her team, an inspired menu comprising an exciting fusion of British dishes, Oriental and Mediterranean flavours is served in the highly acclaimed restaurant, considered to be the best in the Sheffield area. Start with spatchcock quail on braised potato, bacon and fennel with shallots, followed by fillet of lamb on celeriac and cumin purée served with the livers on chilli corn fritters. The delicious selection of desserts includes praline parfait with banana crème brulée, caramelised fruits and a caramel sauce. Only the freshest locally sourced produce including vegetables and herbs from Mrs Bramley's kitchen garden is used. The Old Vicarage provides an ideal break for those touring The Peak District. There are many National Trust and other country houses within close proximity. **Directions:** Exit M1 at Jct30 and join A616, heading 5 miles to Masborough. Turn left at Ridgeway Arms and then left into Main Road. The Old Vicarage is ½ mile on the left.

For hotel location, see maps on pages 212-218

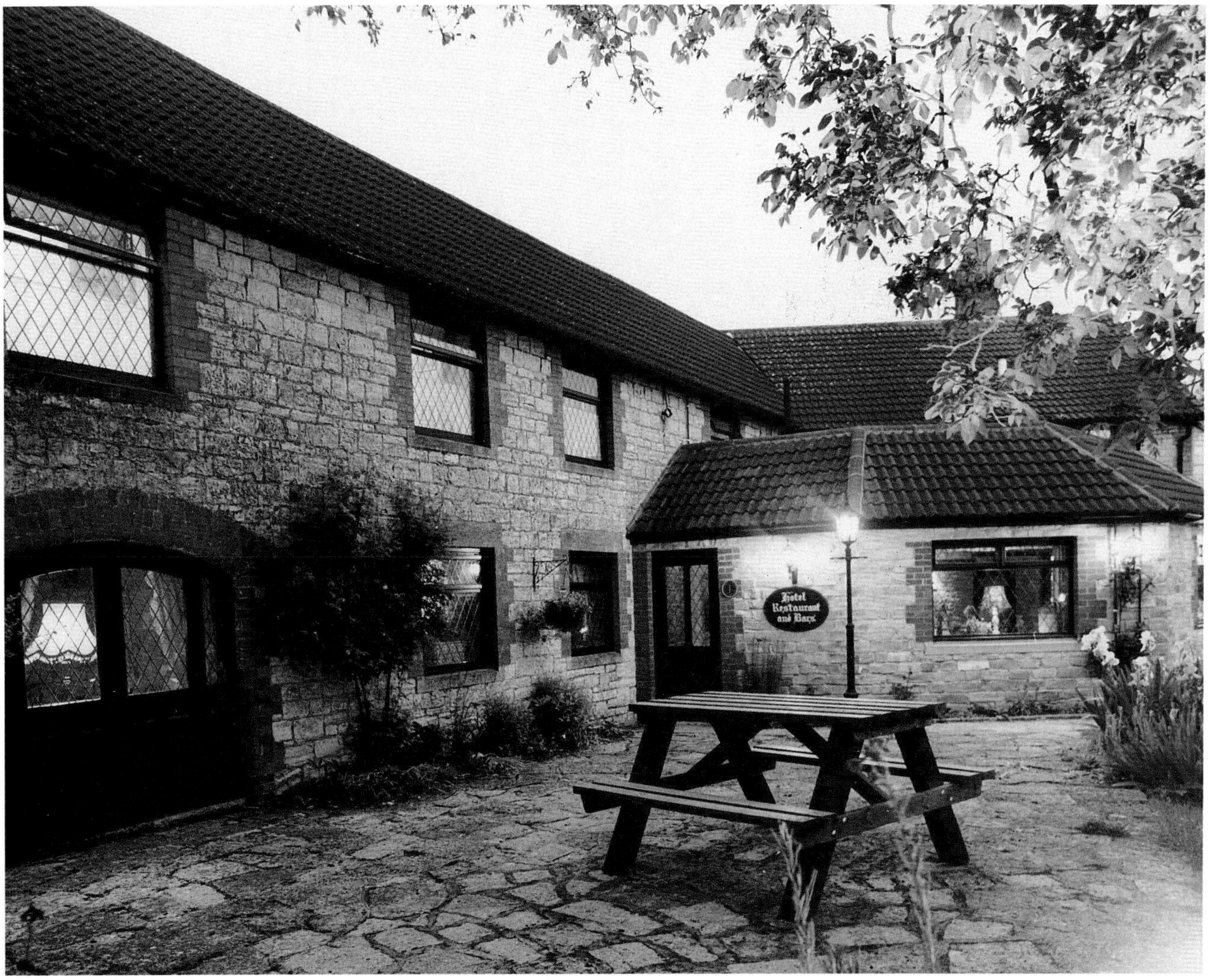

WALNUT TREE

WEST CAMEL, NR SHERBORNE, SOMERSET BA22 7QW
TEL: 01935 851292 FAX: 01935 851292

Just over the border from Dorset in a delightful Somerset village with its tranquil setting stands The Walnut Tree. The charming newly renovated en suite bedrooms will satisfy the demanding criteria of today's traveller, with finishing touches of toiletries, hairdryers, trouser-presses, colour television and telephones. Imaginative food is served in the charming candlelit dining room, which has a marvellous ambience. Alternatively, relax and eat in the delightful lounge bar. The Walnut Tree has a fine reputation for its cuisine and has been in the Egon Ronay guide for three successive years, also in the 'Which' guide for inns. For the discerning walker, the 'Leyland Trail' passes through the village of West Camel whilst for the golfer, there are six courses within the area. There are plenty of places to visit locally. The Fleet Air Arm Museum at Yeovilton, Haynes Motor Museum at Sparkford and historic the town of Sherborne and its Abbey Church are within easy reach. Cheddar Gorge, Wookey Hole, Longleat House Safari Park, Glastonbury, Stourhead Gardens, the ancient city of Wells, Montacute House, Stonehenge and Cricket St Thomas' Wildlife Park are also nearby. The Inn is also very convenient for visiting the old Dorset coastal towns of Weymouth and Lyme Regis. **Directions:** From Wincanton follow A303 westward. Cross A359 at Sparkford. West Camel is the next village you come to. Take the first turning left Price guide: Single £46; double £70–£80.

For hotel location, see maps on pages 212-218

NAUGHTY NELL'S

1 PARK STREET, SHIFNAL, SHROPSHIRE TF11 9BA
TEL: 01952 411412 FAX: 01952 463336

Naughty Nell's is a beautifully restored 16th century coaching inn at the heart of the historic market town of Shifnal, which was described by Charles Dickens in The Old Curiosity Shop. Grade II listed, the inn is surrounded by attractive half-timbered and Georgian houses and close to a Norman church which was one of the few buildings to escape a great fire in 1591 which destroyed most of the town. It was reputedly the home of Nell Gwynn and her legendary bedchamber is now the unique dining, meeting and functions room. Recent extensive and inspired conversions of the interior of the inn have created six low beamed, charming bedrooms which are all en suite and individually decorated and furnished to a very high standard. There is a traditional ale bar where guests may gather and converse over a pint of real ale. The inn has a genuine Mongolian Restaurant which is extremely popular. During most nights of the week there is live entertainment. There are several interesting towns and villages within close proximity and the attractions at Weston Park, the RAF Cosford Museum, Boscobel House and Ironbridge Gorge are close by. **Directions:** Exit the M54 at either junction 3 or 4. Naughty Nell's is situated in the town, on the A464. Price guide Single £55; double/twin £80; four-poster £95.

6 rms MasterCard VISA AMERICAN EXPRESS M 20

 For hotel location, see maps on pages 212-218

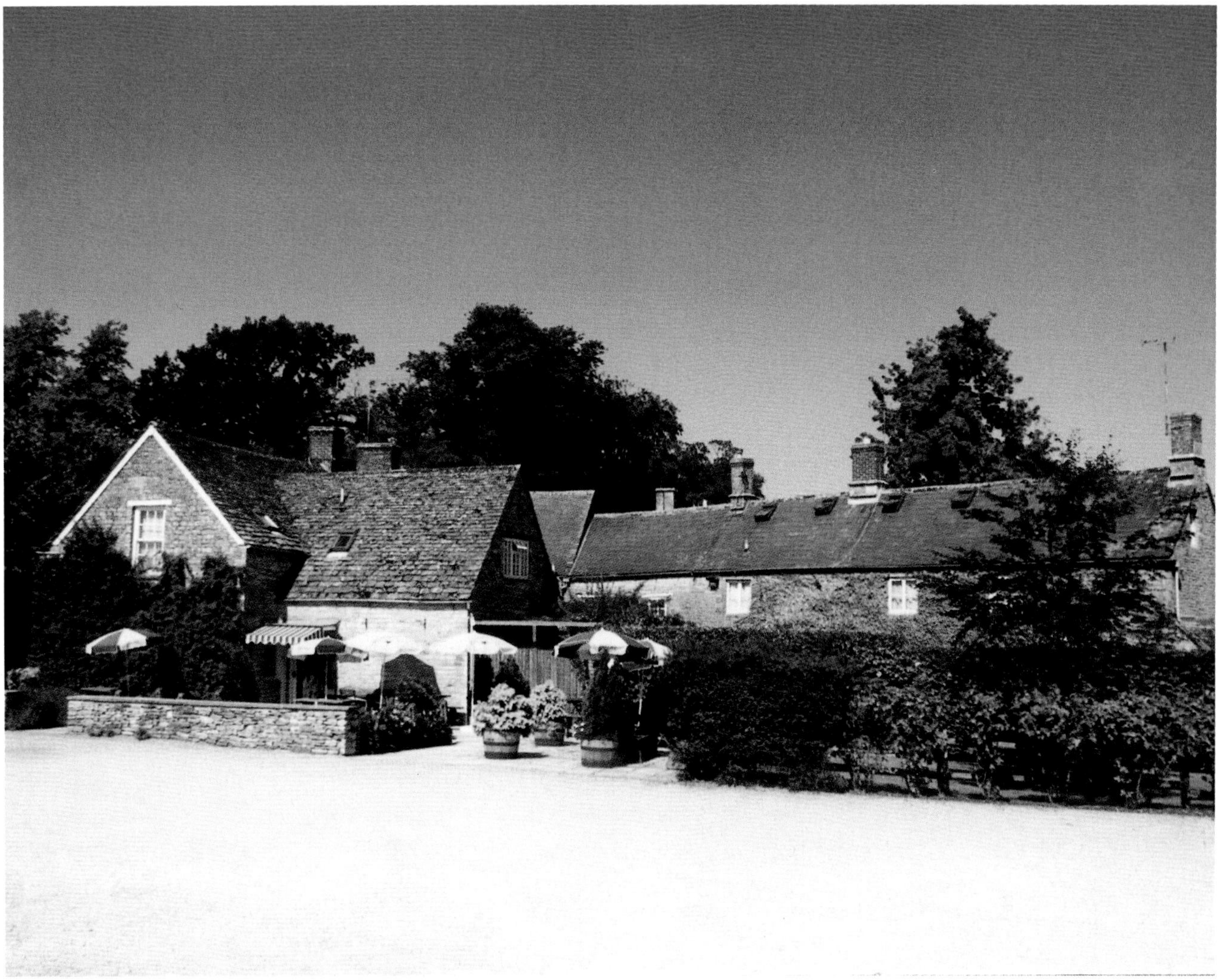

THE LAMB INN

SHIPTON-UNDER-WYCHWOOD, OXFORDSHIRE OX7 6DQ
TEL: 01993 830465 FAX: 01993 832025

Although it has been a hostelry for several hundred years, this inviting inn has lost none of its charm. It is situated on the outskirts of a delightful Cotswold village and has much to recommend it. The Lamb Bar has log fires and serves real ales, a carefully selected range of single malted whiskies, plus a choice of apéritifs and liqueurs. Bar meals are served during the day and evenings and there is a lunchtime buffet. The bedrooms, which offer every comfort, are tastefully furnished with character. The restaurant offers fresh fish from Cornwall, ducks from Minster Lovell, seasonally available game and carefully chosen beef, lamb and fresh vegetables. Specialities include Wychwood chicken – boned chicken stuffed with asparagus, sliced and served with tarragon mayonnaise. There is a wine list of over 30 bins. Private parties and receptions for up to 30 people can be accommodated. Open seven days a week all year. The Cotswolds, Blenheim Palace, Oxford and Cheltenham are just a few of the places to see locally. **Directions:** The Lamb is on the A361 near Shipton-under-Wychwood, between Burford and Chipping Norton. Price guide: Single £58; double £75–£95.

For hotel location, see maps on pages 212-218

THE SHAVEN CROWN HOTEL

HIGH STREET, SHIPTON UNDER WYCHWOOD, OXFORDSHIRE OX7 6BA
TEL: 01993 830330 FAX: 01993 832136

Built of honey-coloured stone around an attractive central courtyard, The Shaven Crown Hotel dates back to the 14th century, when it served as a monks' hospice. The proprietors have preserved the inn's many historic features, such as the medieval hall with its ancient timbered roof. This is now the residents' lounge. Each of the bedrooms has en suite facilities and has been sympathetically furnished in a style befitting its own unique character. Rooms of various style and sizes are available, including a huge family room and ground-floor accommodation. Dining in the intimate, candlelit room is an enjoyable experience, with meals served at the tables, beautifully laid with fine accessories. The best ingredients are combined to create original dishes with a cosmopolitan flair. The table d'hôte menu offers a wide and eclectic choice with a daily vegetarian dish among the specialities. An imaginative selection of dishes is offered every lunchtime and evening in the Monk bar. The Shaven Crown is ideal for day trips to the Cotswolds, Oxford, Stratford-upon-Avon and Bath. There are three golf courses and tennis courts close by. Trout fishing and antiques hunting are popular activities in the area. **Directions:** Take the A40 Oxford-Cheltenham road. At Burford follow the A361 towards Chipping Norton. The inn is situated directly opposite the village green in Shipton-under-Wychwood. Price guide: Single £55; double £75–£110.

For hotel location, see maps on pages 212-218

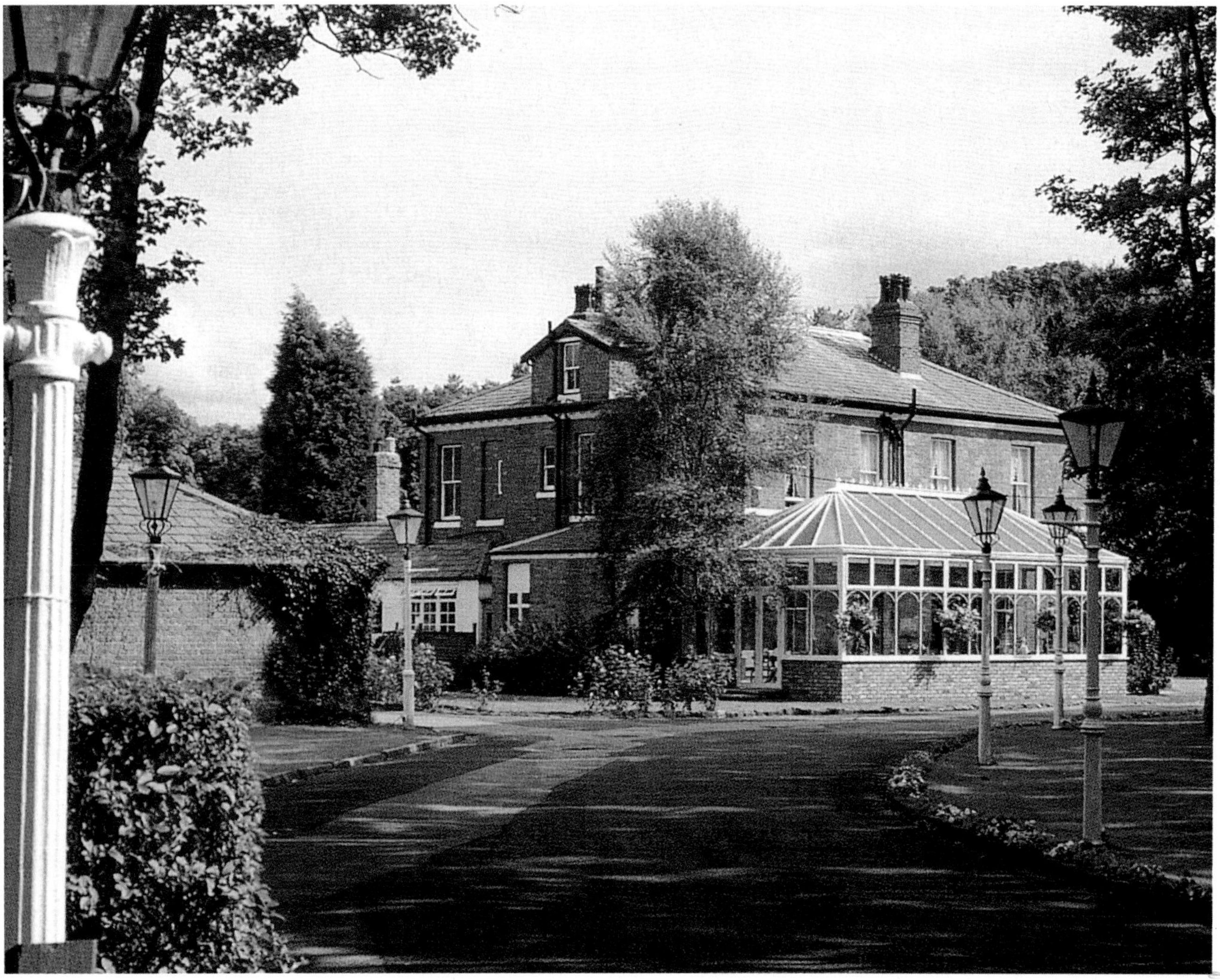

TREE TOPS COUNTRY HOUSE RESTAURANT & HOTEL

SOUTHPORT OLD ROAD, FORMBY, NR SOUTHPORT, LANCASHIRE L37 0AB
TEL: 01704 879651 FAX: 01704 879651

The Former Dower House of Formby Hall, Tree Tops, still retains all the elegance of a bygone age, set in five acres of lawns and woods. Over the last 16 years, the Winsland family have restored the house to its true glory and have installed all the modern conveniences sought after by today's visitor. Spacious accommodation is available in well-appointed en suite chalets with all the facilities a discerning guest would expect. An outdoor-heated swimming pool has direct access to the sumptuously decorated Cocktail Lounge. Rich, dark leather seating, oynx-and-gilt tables and subtle lighting all contribute to the overall ambience, complemented by a truly welcoming and friendly staff. Highly polished Regency furnishings, silver tableware and crystal chandeliers set the scene for culinary delights involving only the finest fresh ingredients. The new conservatory restaurant has a totally relaxed atmosphere with a superb new à la carte menu serving modern and interesting dishes together with a special snack selection. Tree Tops is only 7 minutes' drive from Southport with its sweeping sands and 20 minutes from Liverpool. 10 golf courses can be found within a 5 mile radius, including 6 championship courses. **Directions:** From M6 take M58 to Southport to the end of motorway. Follow signs to Southport on A565. Bypass Formby on dual carriageway and as it changes to single carriageway, turn right at traffic lights to Tree Tops. Price guide: Single £48–£68; double £85–£105.

For hotel location, see maps on pages 212-218

THE DOWER HOUSE

INGESTRE PARK, GREAT HAYWOOD, STAFFORDSHIRE ST18 0RE
TEL: 01889 270707 FAX: 01889 270707

A homely, family-run little hotel surrounded by mature, colourful gardens in the beautiful Royal parkland of Ingestre, The Dower House was formerly owned by the Earl of Shrewsbury and in the 17th century was used as a hunting lodge. It was converted into a Dower House during the 18th century with no expense being spared on the lavish pitch pine staircase and interior woodwork. After generations of farming, the Froggatt family have combined their talents to restore the house to its former Victorian glory and to introduce every modern comfort. There are open fires in the lounge and bar and the beautifully styled bedrooms include a honeymoon suite with four-poster bed. The restaurant, a large, pleasant dining room, serves traditional country food using fresh local produce in season. This is augmented by a good selection of wines. A Sunday lunch with a minimum choice of three roasts is offered and there is an extensive bar menu. Afternoon cream teas and light lunches are available on the garden terrace. Stafford, a charming county town, the old town of Stone with ruins of an ancient priory, 17th century Shugborough Hall and gardens and Cannock Chase, remnant of the vast hunting ground which covered much of Staffordshire in Norman times are all nearby. **Directions:** M6, exit at Jct14 and join A34 north from Stafford. Ingestre Park if off the Great Haywood to Milford Road. Price guide: Single £40–£60; double £75–£140.

4 rms MasterCard VISA AMERICAN EXPRESS M 16

For hotel location, see maps on pages 212-218

THE HORSE AND GROOM INN & RESTAURANT

UPPER ODDINGTON, MORETON-IN-MARSH, GLOUCESTERSHIRE GL56 0XH
TEL: 01451 830584 FAX: 01451 870494

This delightful, heavy stoned 16th century village inn stands serenely in the heart of the Cotswolds surrounded by honey coloured cottages, lush greenery and meandering rivers. Charming, traditional bars with old oak beams, Cotswold stone walling and a large inglenook fireplace, combined with tasteful furnishings, create a relaxing atmosphere which tempts guests to return again and again. The Horse and Groom is excellent value for money and offers every convenience, ensuring that your stay is comfortable. On warm days and evenings there is nothing more enjoyable than lounging in the hotel's large garden with its tinkling stream and fish ponds. Activities in the kitchen are supervised by the head chef whose talents have enhanced the inn's reputation for superbly prepared and presented cuisine backed up by a selection of fine wines. The Horse and Groom is ideally situated for exploring picturesque Cotswold villages such as Broadway, Bourton-on-the Water, Upper and Lower Slaughter, Broadwell and Chipping Campden. Blenheim Palace, Berkeley Castle, the Cotswold Wildlife Park, Oxford, Cheltenham and Gloucester are within easy reach. **Directions:** From A40, exit to Burford and take A424 to Stow-on-the Wold. Then join the A436 towards Chipping Norton. Upper Oddington is on the right 2½ miles east of Stow-on-the-Wold. Price guide: Single £45; double £59–£69.

7 rms

For hotel location, see maps on pages 212-218

THE KINGS HEAD INN & RESTAURANT

THE GREEN, BLEDINGTON, NR KINGHAM, OXFORDSHIRE OX7 6XQ
TEL: 01608 658365 FAX: 01608 658902 E-MAIL: kingshead@btinternet.com

The award-winning Kings Head Inn and Restaurant is peacefully located beside a traditional village green, complete with a babbling brook inhabited by friendly ducks. During the summer months Morris dancers and musicians can regularly be seen in action on the green performing the Bledington Dances. The building has always served as a hostelry and much of its medieval character remains. With its exposed stone walls, original beams, inglenook fireplace and old settles, the Kings Head fulfils everyone's anticipations of a traditional English inn. The attractive timbered bedrooms, are all furnished to complement with full facilities. Activities in the kitchen are supervised by Annette Royce, who has earned the reputation for superbly prepared English and Continental dishes with the 'personal' touch. The carefully compiled à la carte menu is changed daily and is backed up by a selection of fine wines. Excellent inventive bar food is served at lunchtimes and in the evenings together with a changing selection of real ales. The Kings Head Inn is situated in the heart of the Cotswolds, within easy reach of Oxford, Stratford-upon-Avon, Cheltenham and Blenheim. **Directions:** Take the A44 Oxford–Woodstock road to Chipping Norton, then the B4450 to Bledington; or take the Oxford–Burford road to Stow-on-the-Wold and join the B4450. Nearest motorway M40 junction 11. Price guide: Single £45; double £60–£75.

12 rms

For hotel location, see maps on pages 212-218

THE UNICORN HOTEL AND RESTAURANT

SHEEP STREET, STOW-ON-THE-WOLD, GLOUCESTERSHIRE GL54 1HQ
TEL: 01451 830257 FAX: 01451 831090

Low oak-beamed ceilings and large stone fireplaces pay tribute to The Unicorn's lengthy past. Over the last 300 years, the inn has changed its standards of accommodation, incorporating the latest modern facilities, yet many vestiges of the former centuries remain. The recently refurbished interior is decorated in a stylish manner featuring Jacobean furniture and antique artefacts whilst log fires abound. Enhanced by floral quilts and comfortable armchairs, the 20 en suite bedrooms are simple yet charming. Fine paintings adorn the walls of the public rooms and the cosy bar offers hand-carved wooden chairs and rich carpets. Modern British cooking is served in the elegant surroundings of the Georgian restaurant from an imaginative à la carte menu. The inn is well-frequented on Sundays by guests wishing to indulge in the delicious lunchtime roast. Local leisure facilities include horse-riding and the golf course. Shooting and fishing are popular outdoor pursuits. Many historic buildings and castles are within easy reach including the magnificent Blenheim Palace and Warwick Castle. Nature enthusiasts will be delighted with the splendid gardens at Sudeley Castle. **Directions:** The nearest motorway is the M40 junction 10. Then take the A44 or the A436 in the direction of Stow-on-the-Wold. Price guide: Single £50–£60; double/twin £99–£120.

For hotel location, see maps on pages 212-218

THE COACH HOUSE HOTEL & CELLAR RESTAURANT

16/17 WARWICK ROAD, STRATFORD-UPON-AVON, WARWICKSHIRE CV37 6YW
TEL: 01789 204109 / 299468 FAX: 01789 415916 E-MAIL: kiwiavon@aol.com.uk

For lovers of Shakespeare country the Coach House Hotel is an ideal base from which to explore the Bard's birthplace and the beautiful surrounding countryside. Consisting of two splendid adjacent buildings, one Georgian style dated 1843 and the other Victorian dating from 1857, the Coach House is just a five minutes walk from Stratford town centre and seven minutes from the Royal Shakespeare Theatre. Family owned and run it has a relaxed, friendly atmosphere. Careful thought and attention have been invested in the décor and furnishings of all the rooms. Guests may stay in a beautiful Victorian suite, a luxury Regency four-poster room with whirlpool bath or one of the well-appointed single, double or family rooms, situated either on ground or first floor level. All have a good range of facilities. Guests have complimentary use of the sports and leisure centre nearby. Golf enthusiasts have the choice of four local courses. Special breaks are available throughout the year. The Chef creates superb Continental and English dishes to tempt even the most jaded palate in the intimate Cellar Restaurant beneath the Victorian building. There are two dining areas and a cosy bar. The Royal Shakespeare Theatre and the delights of Stratford-upon-Avon, Warwick Castle, Ragley Hall, Blenheim Palace and the Cotswolds are close by. **Directions:** Five miles from exit 15 of M40, on A439. Price guide: Single £50–£60; double £68–£80; suite £90–£105.

21 rms MasterCard VISA AMERICAN EXPRESS M 12

For hotel location, see maps on pages 212-218

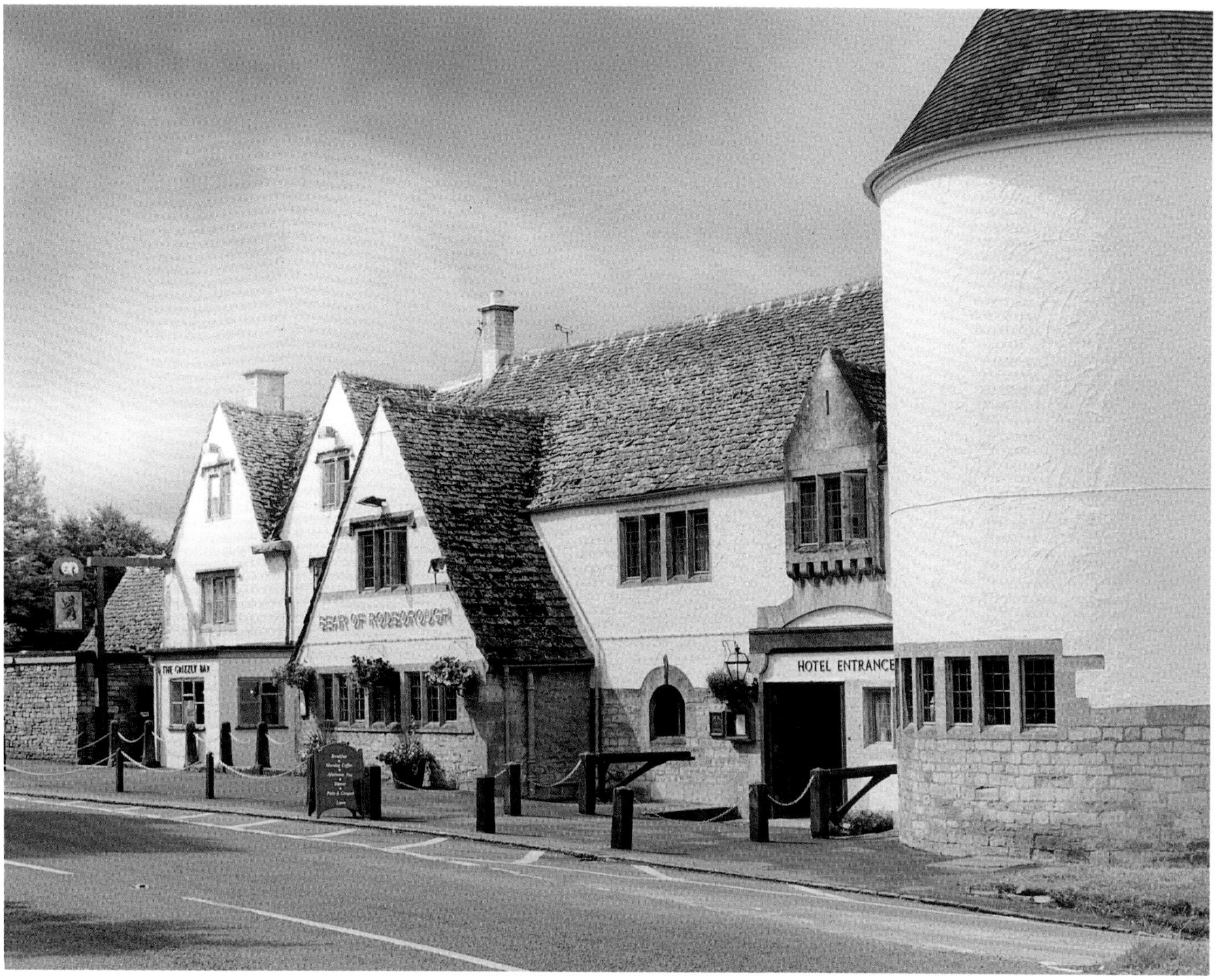

THE BEAR OF RODBOROUGH HOTEL & RESTAURANT

RODBOROUGH COMMON, STROUD, GLOUCESTERSHIRE GL5 5DE
TEL: 01453 878522 FAX: 01453 872523

This 17th century former Ale House offers comfortable accommodation in an area of outstanding beauty. Nestling on the top of a steep hill, The Bear of Rodborough is situated in the verdant landscape of the western Cotswolds, described by the author, Laurie Lee, as "vegetative virginity". The inn has recently undergone a careful and precise restoration, at the request of the new owners, yet many of its past features such as the original archway entrance have been retained. The refurbished bedrooms are exquisite, adorned with plush carpets and beautiful fabrics. All have en suite facilities and several thoughtful extras. The superb bar, popular with the locals, is renowned for its large selection of traditional beers. Elegantly furnished, the restaurant is enhanced by the ceiling beams with a 'running bear' design. Specialities include the full English breakfast, made with fresh local produce, whilst the light luncheons and sumptuous dinners must also be savoured. Special breaks include the charming two day 'Cider with Rosie' breaks, based on the famous novel by Laurie Lee. Badger breaks designed for those with a passion for wildlife give an insight into the behavioural patterns of these fascinating creatures. **Directions:** The nearest motorway is the M5, junction 13. Price guide: Single £55–£60; double/twin £99–£110; suite £120.

For hotel location, see maps on pages 212-218

THE BULL HOTEL

HALL STREET, LONG MELFORD, SUDBURY, SUFFOLK CO10 9JG
TEL: 01787 378494 FAX: 01787 880307

Elegance, style and service are the hallmarks of this 15th century hotel standing in the heart of one of Suffolk's prettiest villages and the antiques capital of East Anglia. This is "Lovejoy" country and behind the Bull's magnificent half-timbered façade there is a wealth of ancient delights to please the most ardent enthusiast and collector. From beams, inglenooks and carvings to highly polished brasses, pots and breastplates. There is even an impressive Elizabethan fireplace for lounge guests to relax around. Built in 1450 and an inn since 1570, The Bull has retained much of its original architectural character but has been carefully modernised to cater for today's visitors. Idle relaxation over morning coffee and afternoon tea while reading the newspapers is definitely encouraged. The 25 beautifully furnished, en suite bedrooms have every 20th century facility. Classic English cuisine is served in an intimate, warm restaurant that features open brickwork and solid, heavy furniture, and light snacks can be enjoyed over a drink in the Reeves Bar. Nearby are Melford and Kentwell Halls, Lavenham and Constable country, where Flatford Mill and East Bergholt are still recognisable from the artist's paintings. **Directions:** Exit the M11/A11 at junction 9. Take the A604 then the A1092 following the signs for Long Melford. Price guide: Single £65; double/twin £90–130.

25 rms MasterCard VISA AMERICAN EXPRESS M 70

For hotel location, see maps on pages 212-218

THE HUNDRED HOUSE HOTEL

BRIDGNORTH ROAD,NORTON, NR SHIFNAL, TELFORD, SHROPSHIRE TF11 9EE
TEL: 01952 730353 FAX: 01952 730355 E-MAIL: hundredhouse@compuserve.com

Character, charm and a warm, friendly atmosphere are guaranteed at this family-run, award-winning inn, situated only 45 minutes' drive from Birmingham International Airport. The bedrooms are attractively furnished with antiques and feature country-style patchwork bed linen and drapes; all guest rooms are fully equipped. There are pretty gardens with a pond, gazebo and herb garden. A special tariff is offered for mid-week and weekend breaks. The inn enjoys a growing reputation for its varied, interesting à la carte and table d'hôte menus. Home-made English fare such as steak pies and game is offered alongside continental dishes and sweets range from delicate sorbets to traditional favourites like treacle tart. Bar meals are served daily, alongside a number of real ales. Early booking is recommended as the restaurant is very popular locally. Severn Valley Railway, Midland Motor Museum, Weston Park, Ironbridge Gorge and Telford are within easy reach. Shifnal's cottages inspired Charles Dickens' Old Curiosity Shop. **Directions:** Norton is on the A442 Bridgnorth-Telford road. Price guide: Single £69; double £89–£110.

9 rms MasterCard VISA AMERICAN EXPRESS M 20

For hotel location, see maps on pages 212-218

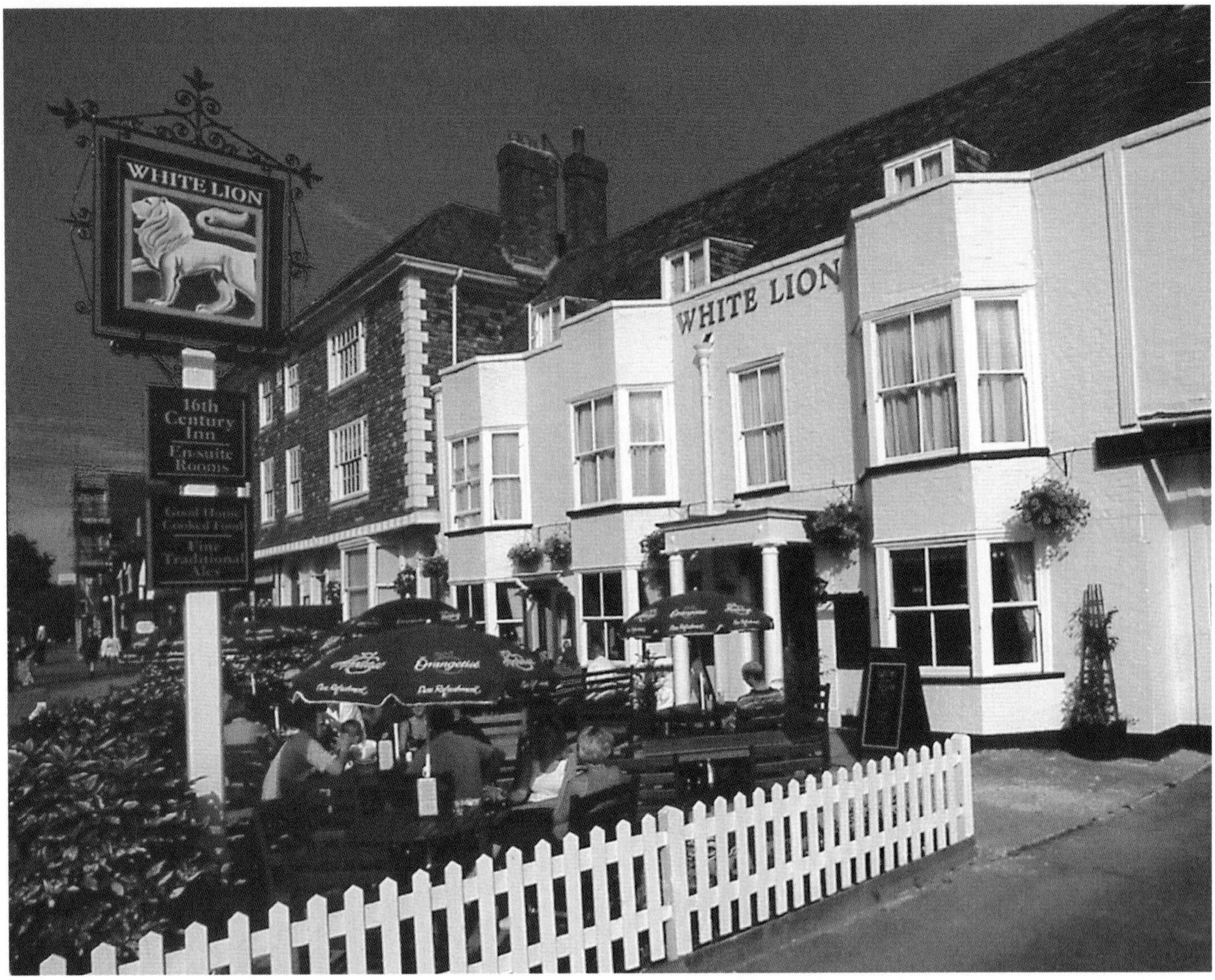

THE WHITE LION HOTEL

THE HIGH STREET, TENTERDEN, KENT TN30 6BD
TEL: 01580 765077 FAX: 01580 764157

The White Lion is a traditional old inn situated at the heart of the wide, green-fringed High Street in the historic market town of Tenterden, an important wool trading centre in medieval times. The inn is surrounded by many attractive, late 15th century buildings and was first mentioned in ancient documents in 1623 as an "Inn near the Market Place". The White Lion offers a warm, friendly welcome and the relaxing atmosphere of a past age. All 15 newly refurbished bedrooms have en suite facilities, are spacious and comfortable. The bar is proud of its best ales, fine wines and wide range of spirits. Delicious meals are available both at lunch time and in the evening and it is well worth looking out for the inn's "signature dishes". Some of these traditional delights include Brewers' Pie, Bangers and Mash, Spatchcock Chicken and Cloutie, Fruit and Ginger Pudding. Tenterden is reputed to be the birthplace of William Caxton, the father of English printing and it is an excellent base for touring the Kent countryside, travelling on the Kent and East Sussex railway and visiting the National Trust properties of Smallhythe Place and Lamb House. Rye and Canterbury are within easy reach. **Directions:** From the M20, exit at junction 9 and take the A28 to Tenterden. Price guide: Single from £49; double/twin £69–£79.

For hotel location, see maps on pages 212-218

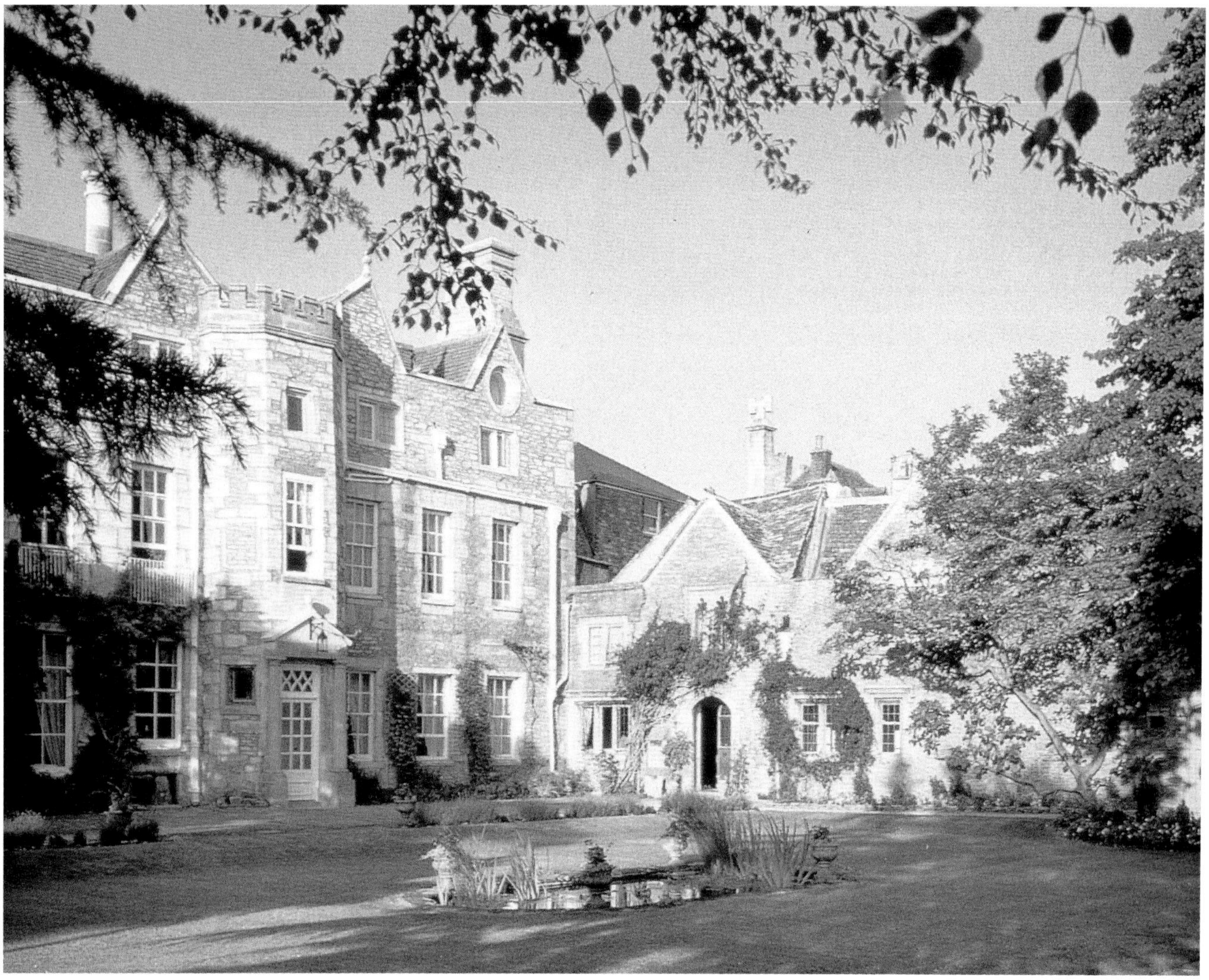

THE CLOSE HOTEL

LONG STREET, TETBURY, GLOUCESTERSHIRE GL8 8AQ
TEL: 01666 502272 FAX: 01666 504401 E-MAIL: hotel.reservations@virgin.co.uk

This distinctive town house, built over 400 years ago as a successful wool merchant's home, has been turned into a delightful hotel. It retains great character while boasting the facilities expected of a first class hotel. The Close is renowned for luxurious accommodation – individually styled bedrooms that are truly elegant, with hand-painted bathrooms and antique furniture. The award winning cuisine, served in the stylish restaurant with its Adam style ceilings, is delicious, imaginative and well complemented by an outstanding wine list, including some excellent vintages. The restaurant overlooks a traditional Cotswold walled garden and in fine weather, you can take drinks or even dinner on the terrace. The Close offers a variety of rooms for conferences accommodating up to 24 guests. The hotel is extremely popular for wedding receptions and ceremonies and can be booked for exclusive use. Many famous sporting venues are close by, including Cheltenham Racecourse and Badminton House. Tetbury itself is a must for shoppers and antique lovers, while the Cotswolds are just on the doorstep. **Directions:** The Close is on Long Street, the main street of Tetbury which can be found on the A433 – minutes from the M4 and M5. Private parking is at the rear of the hotel in Close Gardens. Price guide: Single £75; double/twin £130.

For hotel location, see maps on pages 212-218

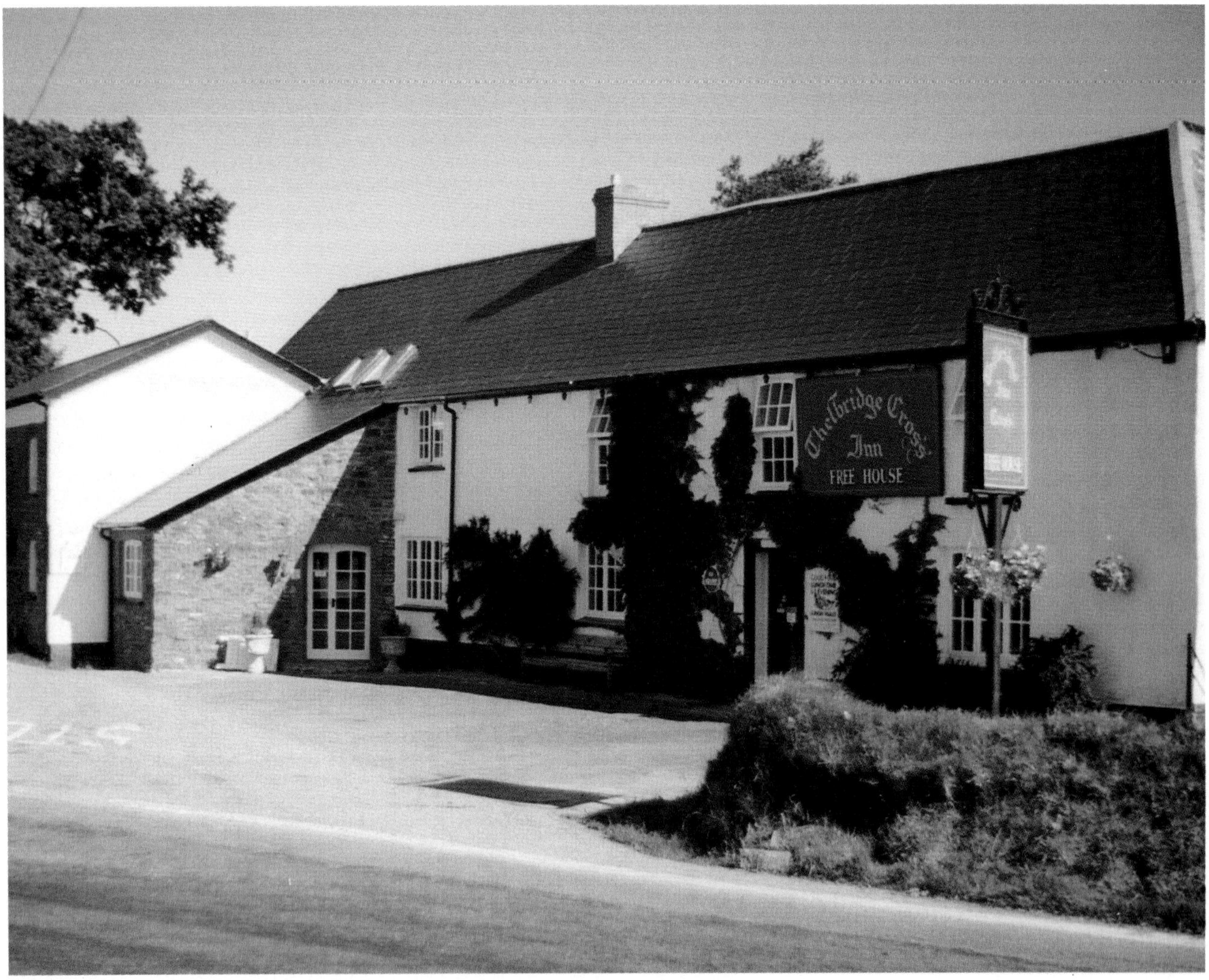

THELBRIDGE CROSS INN

THELBRIDGE, NR WITHERIDGE, DEVON EX17 4SQ
TEL: 01884 860316 FAX: 01884 861318

An attractive, picturesque family run, country inn situated in glorious mid-Devon. Built of stone and cob with oak beams and log fires it is the perfect base for exploring the Devonshire countryside. Exmoor and Dartmoor are only a short drive away. For those of you who are unashamedly romantic, this inn will definitely appeal. Legend relates it that Lorna Doone passed through Thelbridge in her carriage after being shipwrecked at Porlock. As a former coaching inn, it still fulfils that role today, for it is the only inn left where the original Lorna Doone stage coach still calls, with passengers who stop off to savour the Chefs outstanding cuisine. The accommodation is in eight en suite bedrooms all of which are extremely clean and comfortable. The inn boasts wonderful views over both Exmoor and Dartmoor and for walkers is only a short distance away from the famous Two Moors Way. First-time diners soon recognise the reason for the restaurant's popularity and why it is recommended by Egon Ronay. From the front of the inn there are views towards Dartmoor while from the rear Exmoor can be seen in the distance. Many outdoor activities can be arranged locally. **Directions:** Thelbridge Cross Inn is two miles west of Witheridge on the B3042, reached from M5 junction 27 via A361 and B3137. Price guide: Single £35; double £50–£70.

For hotel location, see maps on pages 212-218

THE LIFEBOAT INN

SHIP LANE, THORNHAM, NORFOLK PE36 6LT
TEL: 01485 512236 FAX: 01485 512323

The Lifeboat Inn has been a welcome sight for travellers for centuries, offering roaring open fires on a frosty night, real ales and hearty meals. The summer brings its own charm with scenic views over open meadows to the harbour and rolling white horses breaking on Thornham's sandy beach. The original character of this former 16th century smugglers' ale house has been sympathetically restored and modernised. Sitting in the cosy Smugglers' Bar under the warm glow of the hanging paraffin lamps it is easy to drift back through the years. The old English game of "Pennies" is still played here regularly. A vine-hung conservatory backs onto a delightful walled patio garden which is a perfect suntrap. All bedrooms are en suite and have tea and coffee-making facilities, television, telephone and hairdryer. Most of them have sea views. Chef Michael Sherman offers a splendid choice of innovative and traditional country dishes using local produce, game, fish and meat. The bar menu is enhanced by daily specials to bring the best from each catch or shoot. Several stately homes are in the area, including Holkham Hall, Sandringham House and Nelson's birthplace at Burnham Thorpe. There are six nature reserves, beach, clifftop and woodland walks, excellent sailing and windsurfing. Golf enthusiasts have the choice of five courses. **Directions:** Thornham is approx. 4m north east of Hunstanton on the A149 coast road to Wells-next-the-Sea. Price guide: Single from £48; double from £68.

For hotel location, see maps on pages 212-218

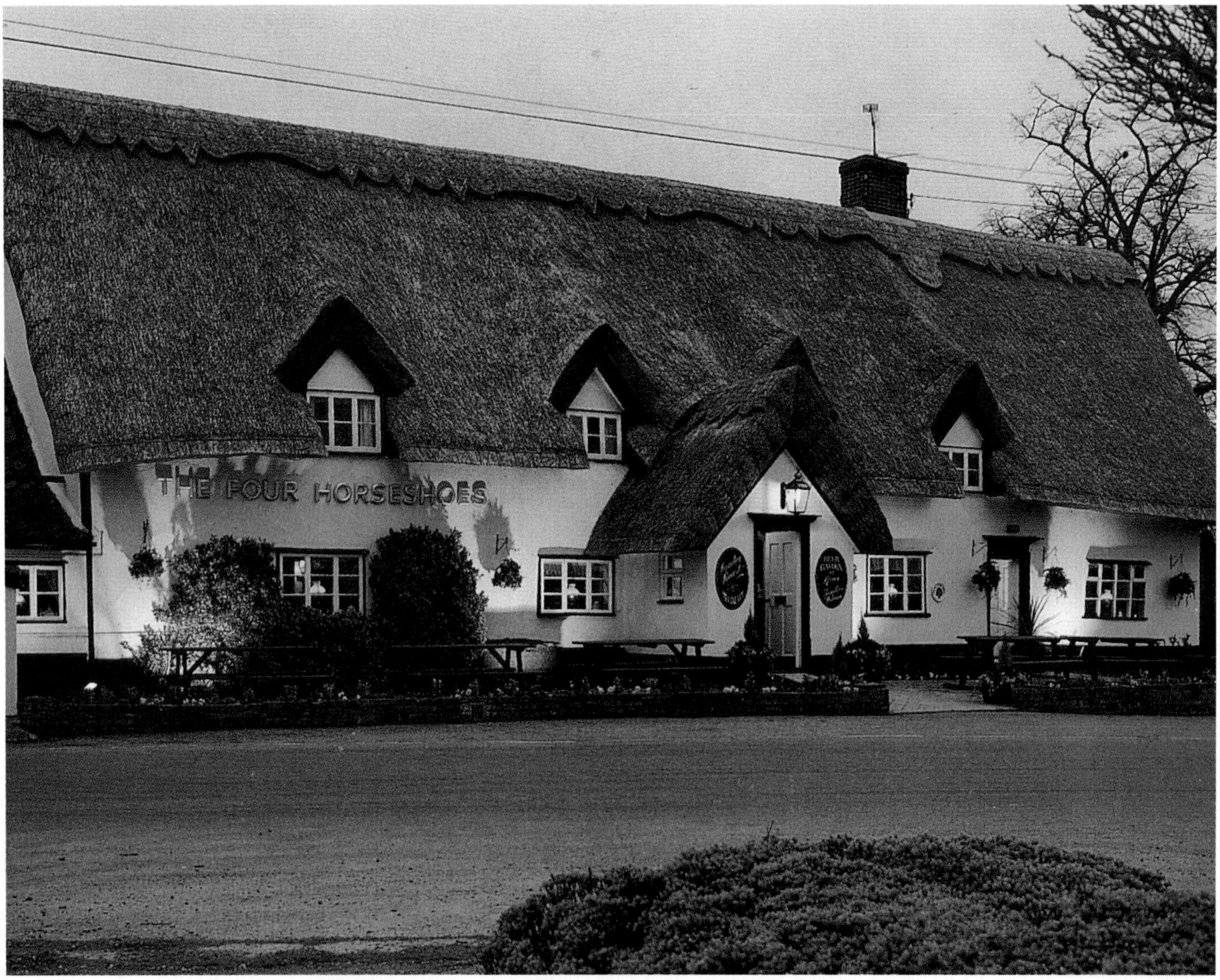

FOUR HORSESHOES

THORNHAM MAGNA, NR EYE, SUFFOLK IP23 8HD
TEL: 01379 678777 FAX: 01379 678134

This compact, cosy inn with its gleaming white façade and warm, attractive thatched roof is a historic reflection of the mid 12th century. It abounds with original features, including delightful open stone walls and heavy beams. There is even a wishing well in the comfortable main lounge. Seven of the eight bedrooms, one a four-poster and another a family room, are en suite. All have every home comfort and many offer lovely panoramic views over the surrounding countryside. The Four Horseshoes cuisine will please the most experienced palate. There is an extensive bar food menu and the head chef produces appetising English and international à la carte cuisine in the pleasant, comfortably furnished restaurant where full English breakfasts are served. The lounge bar has a range of traditional ales and there is a small garden at the rear in which to relax over a drink or snack on warm summer days. The inn is an ideal base from which to tour the Suffolk countryside. Immediately adjacent is the Thornham estate and Thornham Magna conservation area. A short drive away there are the Bressingham Gardens, plant centre and steam museum. **Directions:** The Four Horseshoes is situated between Bury St Edmunds and Ipswich. Take the main A140 road in the direction of Norwich. Price guide: Single £45; double £55–£65.

For hotel location, see maps on pages 212-218

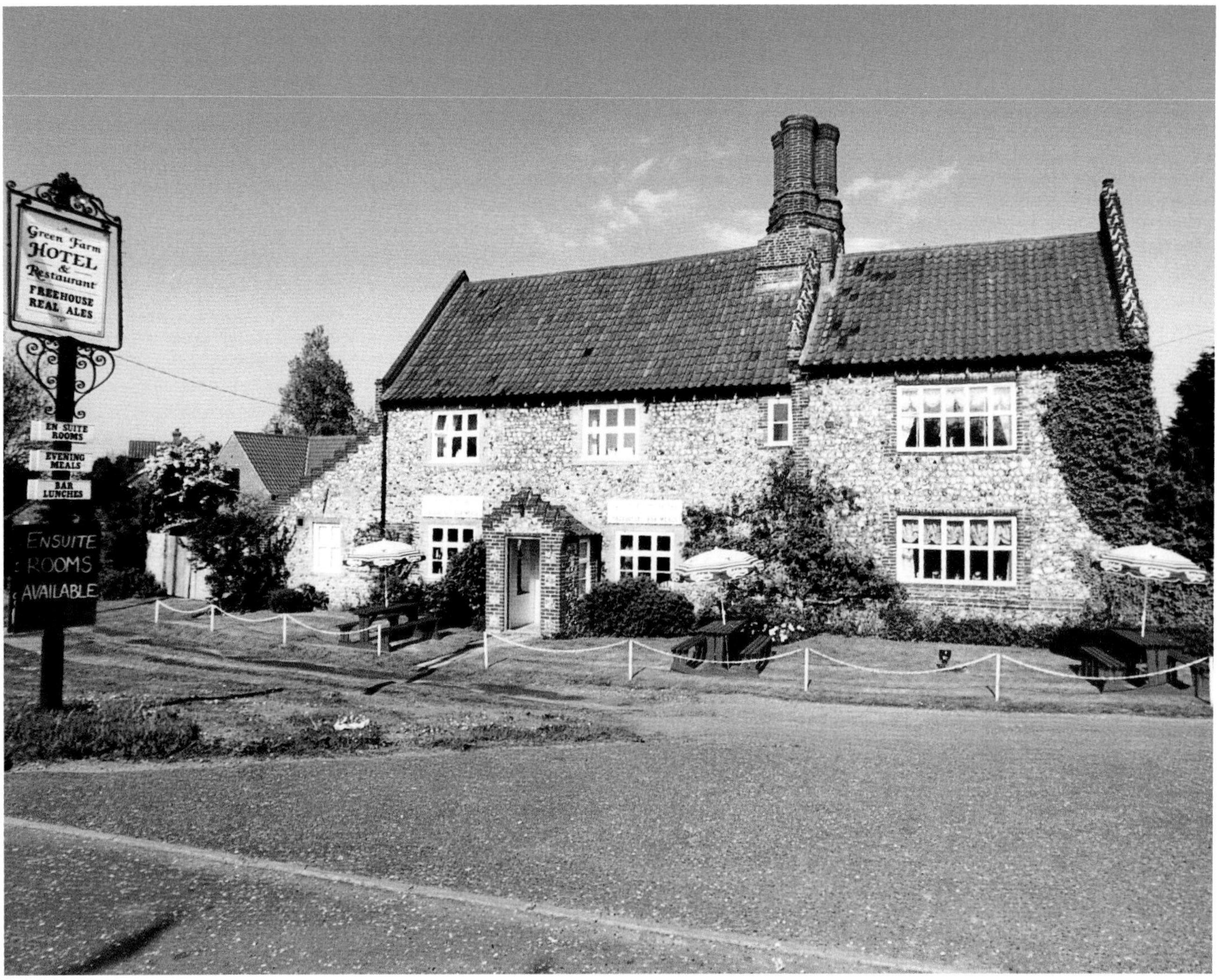

GREEN FARM RESTAURANT AND HOTEL

NORTH WALSHAM ROAD, THORPE MARKET, NORFOLK NR11 8TH
TEL: 01263 833602 FAX: 01263 833163 E-MAIL: grfarmh@aol.com

Green Farm is a delightful 16th Century Farmhouse Inn. A warm, friendly welcome awaits all guests, be it business or pleasure, from proprietors Philip and Dee Dee Lomax and their staff. All rooms are fully en suite with television, tea and coffee facilities, fresh fruit, flowers and home-made chocolates. Some of the rooms are on ground floor level and are ideal for elderly and less able bodied guests. The Restaurant and Bar are open 7 days a week and the Chef-patron has built up an excellent reputation for the food which is all home-made, and uses local produce such as Cromer crab, shellfish, sea trout and Holkham venison when in season. Many of the dishes are unique to Green Farm; subtle variations on well-loved themes. Try the brie wrapped in filo pastry, served with apple and peppercorn sauce, the Norfolk duckling with rhubarb compote followed by the Pillow of pear on a raspberry coulis. The terraced Marquee offers an ideal location for a wedding or family function. Midweek and weekend breaks are available and special rates for Winter House parties available on request. Green Farm is an excellent base for the Coast, Broads National Trust Properties and Historical Norwich. Ideal for those interested in walking, cycling, golf and bird-watching. **Directions:** On the A149, 4 miles from Cromer and North Walsham. Price guide: Single £52.50–£55; double £60–£85.

For hotel location, see maps on pages 212-218

The Port William

TREBARWITH STRAND, NR TINTAGEL, CORNWALL PL34 0HB
TEL: 01840 770230 FAX: 01840 770936 E-MAIL: william@eurobell.co.uk

The Port William is a delightful old inn, romantically situated 50 yards from the sea overlooking the beach and cliffs at Trebarwith Strand. The small but charming bedrooms have recently been refurbished and offer every modern amenity, including baths with showers, colour TVs, hair dryers and hospitality trays. Each bedroom is positioned so that guests can enjoy spectacular views during the day and dramatic sunsets over the sea in the evening. Well behaved children and dogs are welcome! All the bedrooms are non-smoking. Restaurant: The Inn enjoys an excellent local reputation for the quality of its food. An extensive breakfast menu and lunches and dinners are prepared using only the freshest produce, with home-cooked dishes and a range of superb fish courses and seafood among the specialities. A good selection of vegetarian food is always available. Service is friendly and informal. Proprietory brands and local Cornish ales are available. The unique and stunning display of seahorses and other marine species are guaranteed to relax the most stressed of travellers. In this area, noted for its outstanding beauty, there is no shortage of leisure activities. Apart from magnificent walks, there are plenty of opportunities for surfing, sea-fishing and golf. Nearby: Tintagel Castle, King Arthur's Great Halls and a host of National Trust properties. **Directions:** Follow B3263 from Camelford to Tintagel, then south to Trebarwith via Treknow. Price guide: Single £42.50–£60; double £55–£83.

For hotel location, see maps on pages 212-218

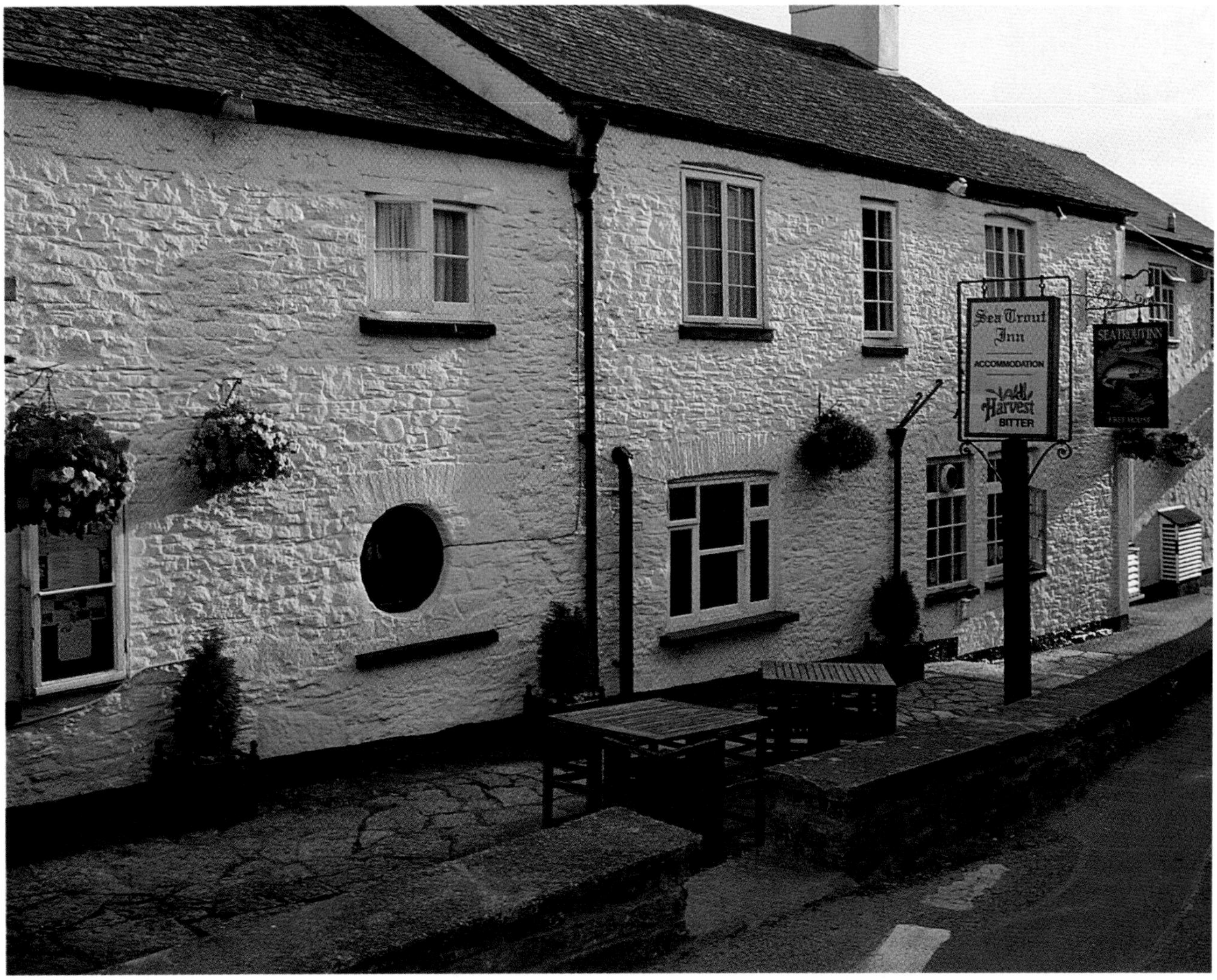

THE SEA TROUT INN

STAVERTON, NR TOTNES, DEVON TQ9 6PA
TEL: 01803 762274 FAX: 01803 762506

Runner-up for Johansens Most Excellent Service Award 1996, The Sea Trout Inn dates from the 15th century. It was named by a previous landlord who caught such a fish in the nearby River Dart. Several specimens of the prize fish now adorn the inn in showcases. The two bars retain much of their period charm, with uneven floors, exposed oak beams, brass fittings and log fires. The bedrooms are decorated in an attractive cottage style, while the public rooms are cosy and inviting. Angling permits for trout, sea trout and salmon are available and the inn offers special fishing breaks with tuition. The inn's restaurant is highly acclaimed locally and has been mentioned in several guides. Chef John Hughes finely balanced menus are based on the best seasonal produce from local suppliers. Both table d'hôte (£18.50 for three courses including coffee) and à la carte menus are available. Dartmoor is excellent for walking, fishing and pony-trekking. Local attractions include the Devon coast, the Dart Valley Railway, Buckfast Abbey and Dartington Hall. **Directions:** Turn off the A38 on to the A384 at Buckfastleigh (Dartbridge) and follow the signs to Staverton. Price guide: Single £42.50–£45; double £60–£70.

For hotel location, see maps on pages 212-218

THE WATERMAN'S ARMS

BOW BRIDGE, ASHPRINGTON, NR TOTNES, SOUTH DEVON TQ9 7EG
TEL: 01803 732214 FAX: 01803 732314

The Waterman's Arms boasts an idyllic setting on the bank of the River Harbourne, just two miles from the Elizabethan town of Totnes. The warm and welcoming atmosphere of today's inn is a far cry from Napoleon's era, when it was a prison and a favourite haunt of the feared press gangs! The nicely-appointed bedrooms, which vary in size, all offer the comfort and luxury associated with a first class hostelry. Tastefully decorated and featuring fine hand-crafted furniture, they include every modern convenience. The bar, with its natural stone walls and wealth of beams, is the perfect place to enjoy a quiet drink before moving on to the candlelit restaurant. Here guests are offered an excellent choice of cuisine, complemented by a good wine list. Bar meals – available at lunchtime and in the evenings – can be eaten by log fires or in the inn's lovely gardens, according to the season. Bow Bridge and its surrounding area offers a host of leisure activities. Bird lovers, in particular, will find this an ideal location – a Kingfisher with its young is one sight that spring visitors can hope to glimpse. Totnes is packed with interesting and unusual shops and places to visit, while Dartmoor with its ponies and fabulous walks, is only a short drive away. **Directions:** From A38 follow signs to Totnes. Join the A381 towards Dartmouth and pick up Ashprington to Bow Bridge signs. Price guide: Single from £44; double/twin from £64.

15 rms

For hotel location, see maps on pages 212-218

THE MORTAL MAN HOTEL

TROUTBECK, NR WINDERMERE, CUMBRIA LA23 1PL

TEL: 015394 33193 FAX: 015394 31261 E-MAIL: the–mortalman@btinternet.com

Few country inns can match the spectacular Lakeland position of this 300 year old hostelry. Lake Windermere is in view at the foot of the Troutbeck Valley, while Grasmere, the home of Wordsworth, and Coniston, where Ruskin lived, are just slightly further away. The inn is an ideal retreat, offering old-fashioned, friendly service in highly traditional surroundings. The interiors have an abundance of beautiful oak beams, panelling, open fires and solid furniture. All of the bedrooms have stunning views of the surrounding countryside and are equipped with every convenience, including hairdryers and trouser presses. An à la carte menu is presented in the inn's dining room, with its wonderful views of the valley. The dishes are all freshly prepared, accompanied by a variety of sauces and garnishes. The menu is supported by a well-chosen wine list. Bar snacks available all day in the bar, which has a warm, inviting atmosphere. The area is a paradise for country lovers, with fells and mountains to explore. Guests have complimentary use of a nearby leisure complex, while sailing and pony-trekking facilities are available close by. **Directions:** Take the A592 Windermere-Ullswater road. From the roundabout drive for 2½ miles, then turn left to Troutbeck and right at the T-junction. The hotel is on the right. Price guide: (including dinner) Single £60–£70; double £110–£130.

For hotel location, see maps on pages 212-218

THE WHITE LION HOTEL

HIGH STREET, UPTON-UPON-SEVERN, NR MALVERN, WORCESTERSHIRE WR8 0HJ
TEL: 01684 592551 FAX: 01684 593333

Henry Fielding wrote part of his novel "The History of Tom Jones" way back in 1749 where he described the Hotel as "the fairest Inn on the street" and "a house of exceedingly good repute". The new owners Jon & Chris Lear have committed themselves to upholding this tradition with good old fashioned hospitality along with examples of the finest cuisine in the area cooked for the popular Pepperpot Brasserie. Using only the finest ingredients Jon and his team produce an imaginative menu served with flair – and home-made breads – which have attracted the attention of a discriminating local clientele and the AA who awarded a Rosette in under one year of ownership. A lunch time menu with lighter meals can be enjoyed in The Pepperpot Café, the lounge or in the congenial bar. All ten bedrooms are from varying periods dating from 1510, the Rose Room and the Wild Goose Room at the White Lion are named in Fielding book. The White Lion is central for visiting The Malvern Hills, The Three Counties Show Ground, the market town of Ledbury, Tewksbury's Norman Abbey, Worcester, Cheltenham and Gloucester. The Cotswolds, Black mountains and Shakespeare's Stratford-Upon-Avon are all within an easy drive from this popular town. **Directions:** From M5 Jct8 follow M50. Exit at Jct1 on to A38 north. After 3 miles turn left on to A4104. Go over the bridge, turn left, then right. Parking is at the rear of the hotel. Price guide: Single £49.50; double £72.50.

10 rms · MasterCard · VISA · AMERICAN EXPRESS · M 25

For hotel location, see maps on pages 212-218

THE BELL INN

WALBERSWICK, SUFFOLK
TEL: 01502 723109 FAX: 01502 722728

Walberswick, renowned for its artists community and lovely village green, is home to this 600 year old inn. Its lengthy past is clearly evident in the original building, where the floor has been worn down by those who once frequented the property. Oak beams, glowing log fires and quaint 'snugs' add character to The Bell Inn and create a most welcoming atmosphere. The floral arrangements are indicative of the constant care that is lavished upon the residence on a daily basis. The six en suite bedrooms are individually decorated with fresh flowers chosen specifically to complement each colour scheme. Furnished with a quirky nautical theme, the family room at the top of the building affords fine views of the sea. The food served in the bars is typically English and comprises generous portions of traditional pub fare and more unusual dishes such as deep fried Halloumi cheese with Greek salad. The seafood is excellent, using freshly caught local fish. Many sports may be played on site or nearby and include boules, riding and shooting. Blythburgh and its famous 'Cathedral of the Marshes' and the concerts and crafts at Snape are worth a visit whilst nature enthusiasts must visit the bird sanctuary at Minsmere. The regency town of Southwold is easily accessible by either foot or ferry. **Directions:** The hotel is 4 miles off the A12, just south of the exit for Southwold. Price guide: Single £40; double/twin £60–£100.

6 rms MasterCard VISA M 50

For hotel location, see maps on pages 212-218

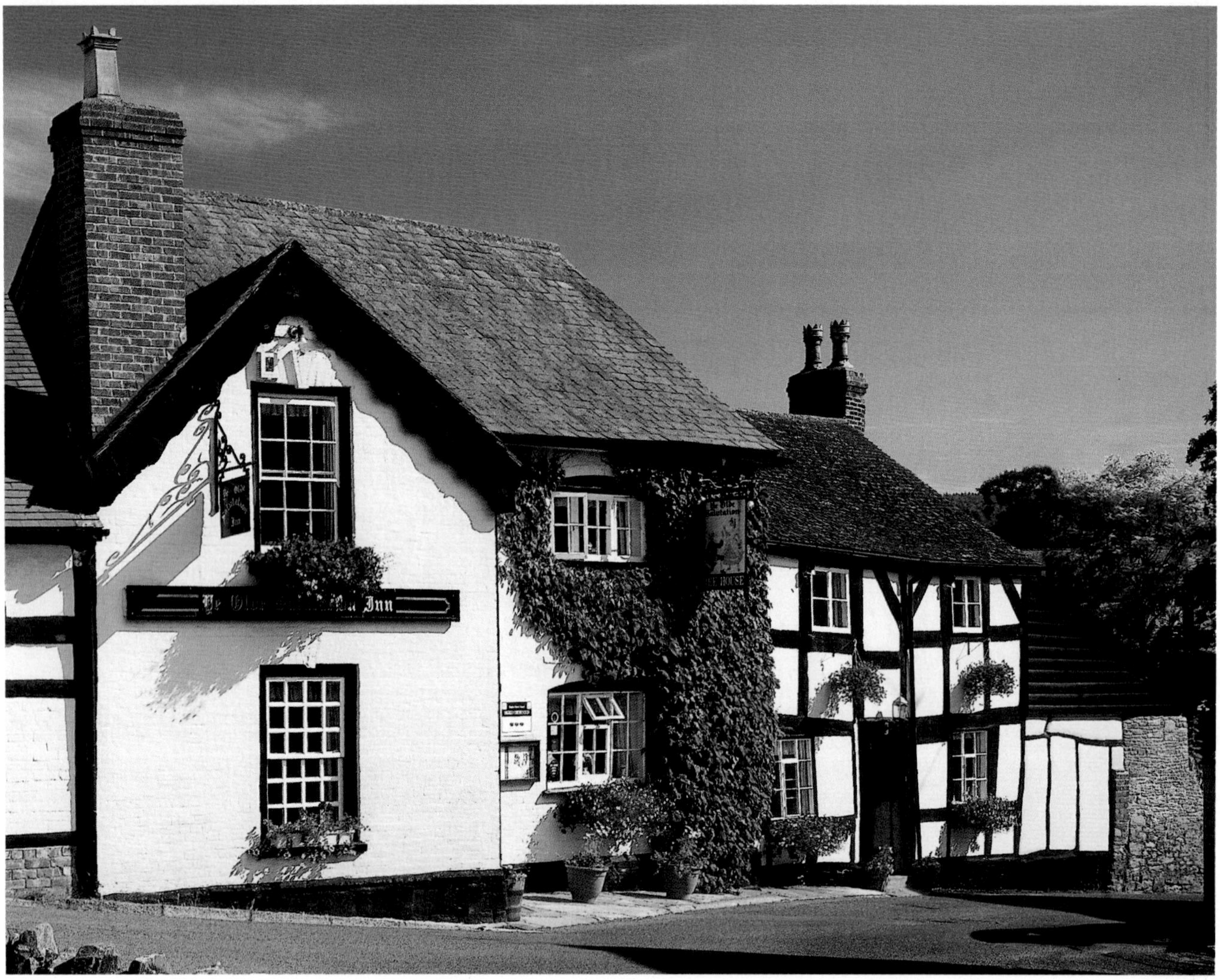

Ye Olde Salutation Inn

MARKET PITCH, WEOBLEY, HEREFORDSHIRE HR4 8SJ
TEL: 01544 318443 FAX: 01544 318216

This black and white timbered inn, an inspired conversion of an ale and cider house and a cottage, over 500 years old, is in the centre of Weobley village. The spire of the 900 year old church is a landmark in the green Herefordshire countryside, as yet undiscovered by tourists. The bedrooms are so individual, with delightful chintz or patchwork quilts, that returning guests demand their favourite, perhaps one with traditional brass bedsteads or a four-poster. Smoking is not allowed in the bedrooms, but is forgiven in the elegant residents' lounge, with its antiques and big, comfortable furniture. Guests will enjoy the well-equipped fitness room. The owners have achieved many accolades in their ten years here. A non-smoking room, the Oak Room restaurant plays an important role in the inn and has been awarded 2 AA Rosettes. Talented chefs prepare sophisticated and aromatic dishes to order, ensuring they arrive fresh at the table. English with a continental accent describes the menu, which refers to puddings as 'the finishing touch'. There is a very well stocked cellar from which to select fine wines. Informal meals are served in the traditional bar. Nearby attractions include Hereford Cathedral, Hay-on-Wye with its antique books, open air Shakespeare at Ludlow Castle, pony-trekking in the Black Mountains and golf. **Directions:** Leave Hereford on A438 Brecon, taking A480 signed Weobley/Credenhill. Price guide: Single £40–£45; double £65–£70.

For hotel location, see maps on pages 212-218

THE WENSLEYDALE HEIFER INN

WEST WITTON, WENSLEYDALE, NORTH YORKSHIRE DL8 4LS
TEL: 01969 622322 FAX: 01969 624183 E-MAIL: heifer@daelnet.co.uk

Few inns can claim such a beautiful setting as that of The Wensleydale Heifer. This typical Dales inn, dating from 1631, is situated in the tranquil village of West Witton, in the heart of Wensleydale and set against the backdrop of the Yorkshire Dales National Park. The oak-beamed rooms are furnished in chintz, with antiques and log fires to retain the ancient charm of the building. The quaint bedrooms are located in the inn itself and across the road in The Old Reading Room – they have all been recently refurbished, upgraded to 4 crowns highly commended standard and 3 have ground floor access. There are 3 with four-poster beds. A private room can be hired for small meetings of up to 14 people. Both the informal bistro and the beamed restaurant offer rustic country cooking. Extensive menus include fresh fish, shellfish and seafood from the North-East Coast and Scotland, complemented by a good selection of wines. Local produce appears frequently including Dales lamb, Aberdeen Angus beef, game and fresh herbs from their own garden. Recent awards include AA Red Rosette, and RAC Merit Award. The Heifer is situated in the Yorkshire Dales National Park and is ideally placed for undiscovered country walks, Yorkshire abbeys, castles, gardens and racecourses. **Directions:** The inn is on A684 trans-Pennine road between Leyburn and Hawes. Price guide: Single £55; double £70–£95.

For hotel location, see maps on pages 212-218

THE INN AT WHITEWELL

FOREST OF BOWLAND, CLITHEROE, LANCASHIRE BB7 3AT
TEL: 01200 448222 FAX: 01200 448298

An art gallery and wine merchant all share the premises of this friendly, welcoming inn, the earliest parts of which date back to the 14th century. It was at one time inhabited by the Keeper of the 'Forêt' – the Royal hunting ground and nowadays it is not uncommon for distinguished shooting parties to drop in for lunch. Set within grounds of 3 acres, the inn has a splendid outlook across the dramatically undulating Trough of Bowland. Each bedroom has been attractively furnished with antiques and quality fabrics. All rooms have videos and hi-tech stereo systems. Head chef Breda Murphy from Ballymalde creates cooking of a consistently high quality. The à la carte menu features predominately English country recipes such as seasonal roast game with traditional accompaniments: grilled red snapper on a savoury confit, home-made puddings and farmhouse cheeses. Good bar meals and garden lunches are also offered. 8 miles of water is available to residents only from the banks of the River Hodder, where brown trout, sea trout, salmon and grayling can be caught. Other country sports can be arranged locally. Browsholme Hall and Clitheroe Castle are close by and across the river there are neolithic cave dwellings. **Directions:** From M6 take Jct32; follow A6 towards Garstang for ¼ mile. Turn right at first traffic lights towards Longridge, then left at roundabout, then follow signs to Whitewell and Trough of Bowland. Price guide: Single £52–£65; double £73–£88; suite £110.

For hotel location, see maps on pages 212-218

THE TANKERVILLE ARMS HOTEL

WOOLER, NORTHUMBERLAND NE71 6AD
TEL: 01668 281581 FAX: 01668 281387

Set in the beautiful village of Wooler, Tankerville Arms Hotel has been frequented by travellers to Northumbria since the 17th century and is no less popular today. Comfort and convenience are key qualities of the en suite bedrooms, which are equipped with colour television, hairdryer, direct-dial telephone and several modern facilities. The Cheviot Restaurant affords pleasant views across the attractive gardens and is enveloped by a tranquil ambience, making it the perfect place to enjoy the very best of local fayre. An excellent menu includes over a dozen main courses, including several vegetarian options. There is a variety of wines available to complement any meal. Delicious sweets, such as sticky toffee pudding, banoffee roulade and english trifle can be walked off in the surrounding countryside. The finest of local beer and real ales is served in The Copper Bar, dominated by an imposing log fire. This 17th century coaching inn has been awarded many accolades and is 4 Crown Highly Commended. The area offers visitors the chance to play golf, fish or go horse-riding, as well as enjoying coastal walks and admiring the superb scenery. There are also many magnificent castles within easy reach. The hotel is located in the charming town of Wooler, within easy driving distance of Newcastle and Edinburgh. **Directions:** In the village of Wooler on A697 between Coldstream and Morpeth. Price guide: Single £45; double £76.

For hotel location, see maps on pages 212-218

THE OLD SCHOOLHOUSE

SEVERN STOKE, WORCESTER, WORCESTERSHIRE WR8 9JA
TEL: 01905 371368 FAX: 01905 371591

An old-fashioned welcome awaits guests of the Old Schoolhouse, a delightful hotel overlooking the Severn Valley and offering superb views of the Malvern Hills. The building is an interesting combination of 17th century farmhouse and an old Victorian school, with cosy rooms of all shapes and sizes. The bedrooms are decorated in individual styles, most feature beamed ceilings and all offer a range of modern facilities. A hearty appetite is the major requirement for guests sampling the very best of British cooking in the award winning but informal Restaurant. Here many regional specialities are incorporated into the menu and dishes are created using fresh local produce wherever possible. The eclectic dishes on the menu reflect the range of interesting tastes and flavours to suit every palate. There is always a vegetarian selection and the chef is happy to cater for special requirements. Lighter lunchtime snacks are served in the Headmaster's Study. A short drive away are the Cotswolds and the lovely towns of Worcester, Tewkesbury and Cheltenham. The villages of Herefordshire, with their oast houses, hops fields and unusual churches, are also within easy reach. **Directions:** The Old Schoolhouse is midway between junction 7 of the M5 and junction 1 of the M50 on the A38. Price Guide: Single £50; double £60–£80.

For hotel location, see maps on pages 212-218

THE OLD TOLLGATE RESTAURANT AND HOTEL

THE STREET, BRAMBER, STEYNING, WEST SUSSEX BN44 3WE
TEL: 01903 879494 FAX: 01903 813399

An original Tollhouse centuries ago, travellers now look forward to stopping here and paying their dues for wonderful hospitality. Part of the old building is still in evidence with newer additions attractively blending. There are some splendid suites, even a four-poster, which are excellent value and delightful bedrooms, some of which are reached across the courtyard. The hotel is a popular meeting place for visitors and locals alike, with friendly staff adding to the welcoming ambience. The restaurant has built up a fine reputation, extending far beyond Sussex. It has a magnificent award-winning carvery and sumptuous cold table. Breakfast, lunch and dinner are all catered for at various price structures according to the number of courses consumed. Soups and broths, fresh and smoked fish, roasts and casseroles, pies and puddings and vegetarian dishes are in abundance. Bramber is famous for its Norman Castle and spectacular views over the South Downs. Brighton, with its shops, beach and Pavilion is an easy drive away, as is Worthing. Sporting activities nearby include riding, golf and fishing. **Directions:** Bramber is off the A283 between Brighton and Worthing, easily accessed from the A24 or A27. Price guide: Single £61; double £61–£83; suite £83.

31 rms MasterCard VISA AMERICAN EXPRESS M 60

For hotel location, see maps on pages 212-218

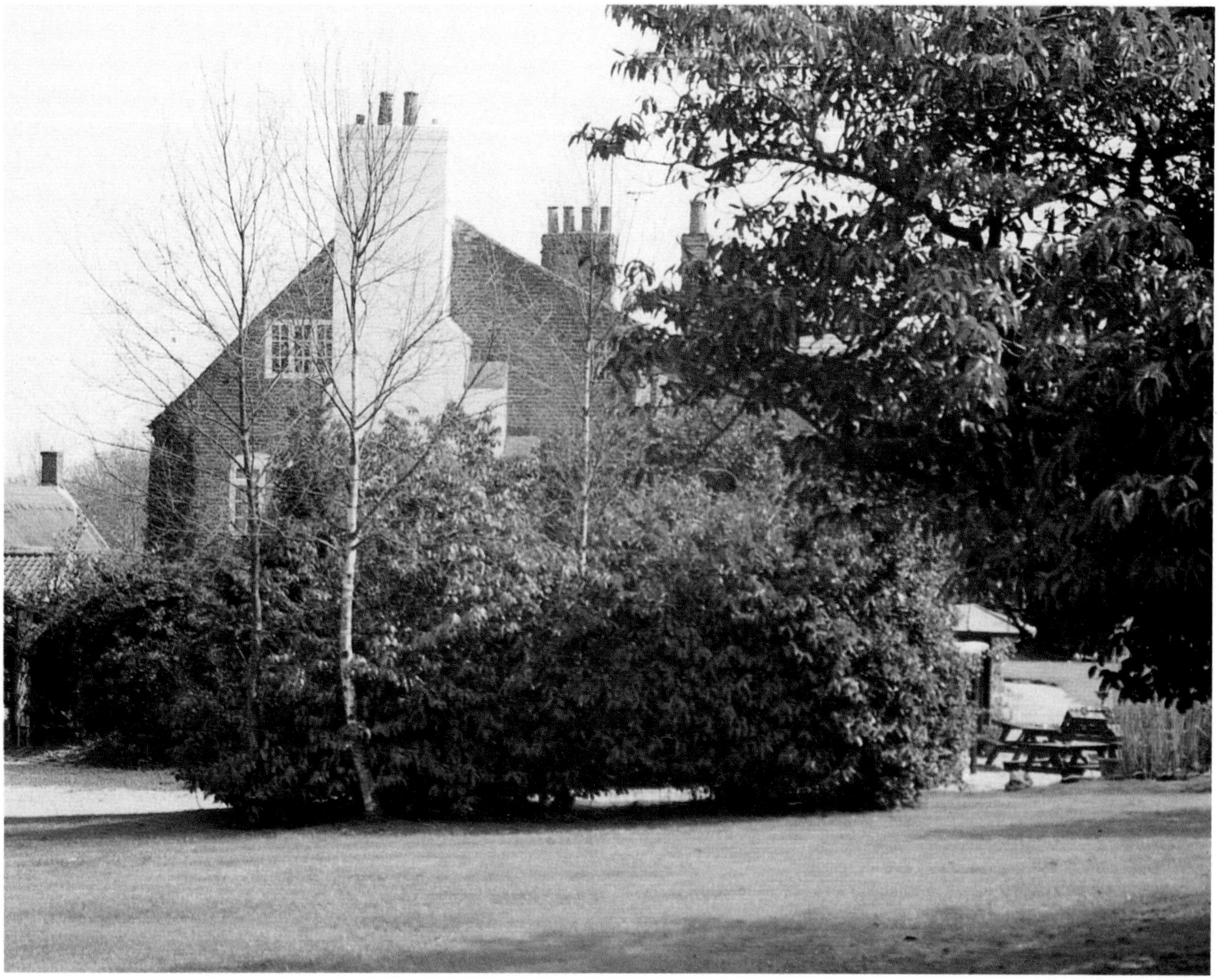

THE BARTON ANGLER COUNTRY INN

IRSTEAD ROAD, NEATISHEAD, NR WROXHAM, NORFOLK NR12 8XP
TEL: 01692 630740 FAX: 01692 631122

While learning to sail on the Norfolk Broads, the young Lord Nelson stayed at this unspoiled hostelry that dates back some 450 years. Set in large gardens, it previously catered exclusively for fishing clubs; but now provides excellent accommodation for anyone wishing to explore North Norfolk. The individually styled bedrooms are pleasantly furnished and some have fine locally crafted four-poster beds. Open fires, exposed beams and antiques feature in the reception rooms all add to the interesting character of this attractive building. Special week or weekend breaks are available during winter months. The kitchens are under the supervision of the chef, Jenwyn and all meals are prepared in the hotel. Bar meals are provided on a first come first served basis. In the Restaurant tables can be reserved – at popular times of the year it is essential to book in advance. Barbecues are a regular summer event on Saturday evenings. Owned by English Heritage, Barton Broad, which is now within Broadlands National Park, offers plenty of opportunities for bird-watching, fishing, sailing and cruising. Boats can be hired for guests. The coast and many historic churches and houses are nearby. **Directions:** A1151 north from Norwich, turn right one mile beyond Wroxham. The inn lies midway between the villages of Neatishead and Irstead. Price guide: Single £35; double £58–£80.

7 rms MasterCard VISA AMERICAN EXPRESS M 30

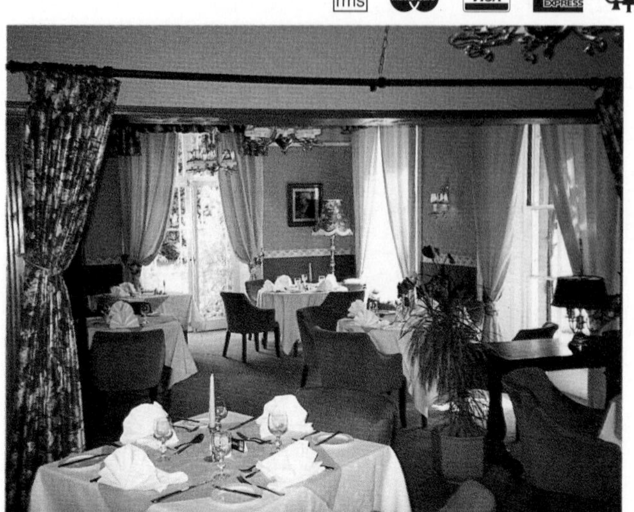

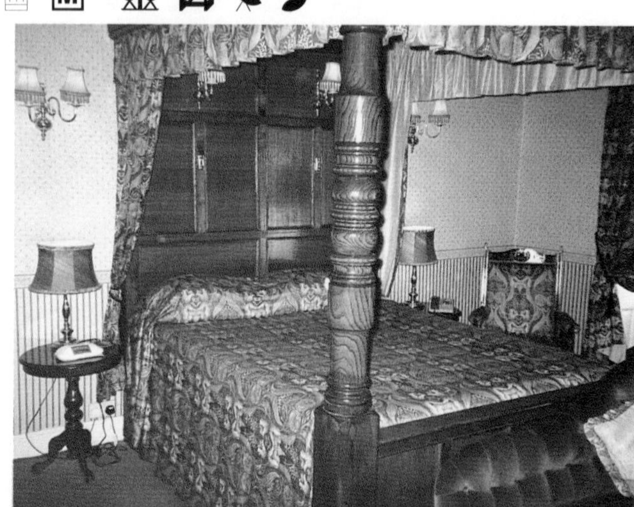

For hotel location, see maps on pages 212-218

THE GEORGE AT EASINGWOLD

MARKET PLACE, EASINGWOLD, YORK, NORTH YORKSHIRE YO6 3AD
TEL: 01347 821698 FAX: 01347 823448

The George at Easingwold is an 18th century coaching inn standing in the old cobbled square of the pretty Georgian market town of Easingwold. Open fires, a wealth of beams and horse brasses all add to its character and cosy atmosphere. The bedrooms vary in style - some are traditionally furnished while others are more modern - but all have a high level of comfort in common. A large inter-connected bar serves a fine selection of real cask ales, including locally brewed beers pulled straight from the cask and coffee is provided in the relaxing atmosphere of the lounge. The inn's original open courtyard is now an attractive candlelit area where a wide selection of freshly prepared bar meals are served. The 'chef's specials' board changes daily. A choice of à la carte or table d'hôte menus is provided in the cosy oak-beamed lamplit restaurant which overlooks the market square, while on Sundays a traditional two or three course Sunday lunch is offered. The historic city of York is just 10 miles away and Castle Howard and the Howardian hills are also close by. The George is an ideal base for touring the North York Moors and the National Park. **Directions:** The George is in the centre of the town of Easingwold which is off the A19 midway between York and Thirsk. Price guide: Single £38–£50; double £53–£72.

30

For hotel location, see maps on pages 212-218

MOËT
BRUT IMPÉRIAL
BRUT IMPÉRIAL
MOËT & CHANDON
CHAMPAGNE
BRUT
ÉPERNAY FRANCE
75cl
FONDE EN 1743
The first choice at
every Johansens
Recommended Hotel

Tenby Harbour

Johansens Recommended Traditional Inns, Hotels and Restaurants in Wales

Magnificent scenery, a rich variety of natural, cultural and modern leisure attractions, and the very best accommodation awaits the Johansens visitor to Wales.

Wales is sometimes referred to as one of Britain's best kept secrets. An air of mystery surrounds the purple-headed mountains of Wales, the green round hills rolling away to infinity, and the beguiling Celtic character of this country on the Western shores of Britain.

With a population of just 2.9 million people, almost two thirds of which is concentrated in the south-east and north-east, this compact country – no more than 198 miles in length – offers an escape from the pressures of modern living to some of Britain's most beautiful surroundings.

In this small area you will find 176 golf courses to please the eye and test the handicap – major links like Royal Porthcawl, the green swards of the Vale of Llangollen and the stunning panorama offered by Nefyn on the Llyn Peninsula.

Wales boasts three National Parks; Snowdonia, the Brecon Beacons and the Pembrokeshire Coast National Park – Britain's only coastal National Park; five Areas of Outstanding Natural Beauty – the Wye Valley, Isle of Anglesey Coast, Llyn Peninsula, Gower Peninsula and the Clwydian Hills – not to mention eight cathedrals and 12 islands full of rare wildlife.

Wales is full of surprises. And the biggest surprise of all is Cardiff, Wales's stylish, European capital city which has a colourful and rich history, dating back almost 2,000 years to the time when the Romans built a camp here. However, its centre has a vast tract of natural parkland donated by the Bute family alongside which is set its civic centre – a modest version built in white Portland stone of Lutyen's design for New Delhi. And its shopping centre is regularly rated one of the best in the UK – a compact pedestrianised zone in the heart of the city comprising a mix of Victorian and Edwardian Arcades with modern malls.

Wales has one of the highest concentrations of castles in Europe. The castles of Wales are a history lesson carved in stone – from the imperial grandeur of Caernarfon and Conwy in the north, built by an English King to intimidate the Welsh, to the romantic ruins of mountain-locked Castell-y-Bere in Mid Wales, stronghold of the Welsh native princes.

The Brecon Beacons National Park in South Wales offers 519 square miles of swooping mountains, exhilarating landscapes, deep green forests and river valleys and breath-taking waterfalls. Further West, the incredible landscape of The Pembrokeshire Coast National Park in the south-west corner of Wales is not only a haven for wildlife but also golden beaches, remote coves, sleepy harbours and magnificent walks. But to offer a thrilling change for the children, a day out at Oakwood Leisure Park near Narberth, will provide a few white-knuckle rides as well as some more gentle amusements.

Mid-Wales is an area of great beauty and variety – farmlands and forests, vales and hills, mountains and moors and, of course, rivers, canals and lakes. Within its boundaries – which stretch at least 150 miles from the spectacular Brecon Beacons National Park in the South to Snowdonia in the North – you'll find the heart of Wales and all the sport you could wish for. Its rivers and lakes offer fine fishing and all manner of water sports. Its uplands and forests are host to motor sports enthusiasts and mountain-bikers. Its varied landscape is a joy for walkers and pony-trekkers and the wide sweep of Cardigan Bay attracts beach-lovers, sailors, surfers and scuba-divers alike.

Going North, the Snowdonia National Park forms a huge, alpine landscape, stretching southwards from Snowdon as far as Machynlleth, and eastwards to Bala. Although mountains dominate the landscape, Snowdonia has its gentler side. The lush Vale of Conwy is green and fertile – a paradise for walkers and nature lovers. For a change of pace, the North Wales resorts of Prestatyn, Rhyl and Colwyn Bay offer a wide range of conventional seaside leisure facilities.

Wales is full of wonderful surprises. Wherever you choose to go in Wales, there will be something new and exciting to see and do. There will also be a warm Welsh welcome – Croeso i Gymru, Welcome to Wales.

For more information on Wales, please contact

Wales Tourist Board
Brunel House, 2 Fitzalan Road
Cardiff, Wales
CF2 1UY
Tel: 01222 475226

THE CASTLE VIEW HOTEL

16 BRIDGE STREET, CHEPSTOW, MONMOUTHSHIRE NP6 5EZ
TEL: 01291 620349 FAX: 01291 627397 E-MAIL: mart@castview.demon.co.uk

This historic 17th century, ivy-clad hotel is set in a prime location opposite Britain's oldest stone castle, begun in the reign of William the Conqueror. It is a friendly, family-owned hostelry, which offers good value accommodation, with Sky television. All rooms have recently been refurbished and many still have original features. There is a hand-turned oak staircase leading to comfortable bedrooms. Some of these have 200-year-old wall paintings and many have views of the castle. There is also a secluded garden which is ablaze with colour during the summer. The kitchen is Michelin 'Fork and Pitcher' Commended and serves imaginative home-cooked meals. Wye salmon and Welsh lamb often appear on the seasonally changing menu, which always offers fresh vegetables, plus many delicious home-made puddings. There is also an interesting range of bar snacks, real ales, a varied wine list and a few good malts. Chepstow is on the edge of the Wye Valley and Forest of Dean. It is well situated for international rugby in Cardiff, racing at Chepstow, golf at St Pierre and visits to Tintern Abbey. **Directions:** Leave M48 at junction 2, follow signs to Chepstow (A48), then follow signs to the Castle. Price guide: Single £46–£51; double £64–£71; suite £76.

12 rms MasterCard VISA AMERICAN EXPRESS

For hotel location, see maps on pages 212-218

The West Arms Hotel

LLANARMON D C, NR LLANGOLLEN, DENBIGHSHIRE LL20 7LD
TEL: 01691 600665 FAX: 01691 600622

Originally a 16th century farmhouse, the character of this charming old inn is evident throughout, with log fires, inglenooks, beams and flagstone floors. Its cosy lounges, furnished with chintz-covered sofas and armchairs, are an invitation to relaxation, aided by the warm and unpretentious hospitality of Rod and Margaret Evans. All of the bedrooms are furnished to a high standard, spacious yet cosy with impressive brass bedsteads: all share a view of the surrounding hills. With formal rose gardens and lawns running down to the river, the setting is idyllic. Dogs by prior arrangement. Cooking of high quality makes the best use of local ingredients – locally reared lamb, venison and game in season and Ceiriog trout. Imaginative vegetables and delicious desserts display equal care in cooking and presentation. Dinner served in the beamed, candlelit dining room is complemented by a well chosen list of classic and New World wines and the hearty Welsh breakfast is a perfect start to the day. The inn can offer free private fishing on a 2 mile stretch of the Ceiriog river. The unspoiled hills and valleys of the Berwyn Mountains give plenty of opportunities for walking and pony-trekking. Local attractions include Chirk Castle, the house of the 'Ladies of Llangollen', Erddig Hall and the Roman city of Chester. **Directions:** Take A5 to Chirk, then B4500 for 11 miles to Llanarmon DC. Once over the bridge, the inn is on the right. Price guide: Single £40–£55; double £70–£100; suite £80–£110.

For hotel location, see maps on pages 212-218

The Plough Inn

RHOSMAEN, LLANDEILO, CARMARTHENSHIRE SA19 6NP
TEL: 01558 823431 FAX: 01558 823969 E-MAIL: theploughinn@rhosmaen.demon.co.uk

Originally a farmhouse, The Plough Inn has been elegantly converted and extended to provide good food and accommodation in the rural market town of Llandeilo. In the older part of the building guests will find a public bar, adjoining which is the cosy and intimate Towy Lounge. The 12 en suite bedrooms enjoy glorious views over surrounding countryside and are all well appointed for your comfort. A gym and sauna provide an added dimension to your stay – why not start the day with an invigorating work-out in the gym or unwind in the sauna before a comfortable night's sleep? A conference suite can cater for business meetings: a comprehensive range of audio-visual aids is available for hire. Closed Christmas. Guests may dine in style and comfort in the à la carte restaurant. Local salmon and sewin, venison, Welsh lamb and beef, cooked simply or in continental recipes, all feature on the menus. An extensive choice of hot and cold bar meals can be enjoyed in the Towy Lounge. One of the inn's specialities is its tradition for Welsh afternoon teas. These are served in the elegant, chandeliered Penlan Lounge. The Plough Inn is an ideal point of departure for touring the beautiful Towy Valley and surrounding Dinefwr countryside, including the Brecon Beacons National Park. **Directions:** A mile from Llandeilo on the A40, towards Llandovery. The inn is 14 miles from exit 49 at the end of the M4. Price guide: Single £47.50; double £65–£70.

12 rms MasterCard VISA AMERICAN EXPRESS M 45

For hotel location, see maps on pages 212-218

THE LION HOTEL AND RESTAURANT

BERRIEW, NR WELSHPOOL, MONTGOMERYSHIRE SY21 8PQ
TEL: 01686 640452 FAX: 01686 640604

Standing next to the church in one of mid-Wales' prettiest villages, The Lion Hotel is a striking 17th century inn, situated on the Shropshire border. A more genuinely friendly welcome than that extended to guests by the Thomas family would be hard to find. The bedrooms, with dark beams, contrasting white walls and lovely views, are all decorated in an attractive cottage style. Real ales and delicious meals are served in the new style bistro. The restaurant has a graceful and intimate atmosphere and offers a good choice of Welsh dishes as well as a selection of English, continental meals and Far Eastern meals. Choices might include marinated shoulder of Welsh lamb, local game, Thai style chicken and fresh fish dishes. With the Cambrian Mountains, the River Severn and Shropshire so close, guests can enjoy a variety of beautiful landscapes. The Welshpool Museum contains interesting treasures and historical memorabilia. Powis Castle, just a few miles away, is just one of the many castles to visit in the area. There are three golf courses within 10 miles and pony-trekking nearby too. **Directions:** Welshpool is 18 miles west of Shrewsbury on A458. Berriew is signposted off A483 five miles south of Welshpool. Welshpool Airport is 4½ miles to the north. Price guide: Single £55–£60; double £80–£100.

6 rms MasterCard VISA AMERICAN EXPRESS M 20

For hotel location, see maps on pages 212-218

HIGHLAND.
An almost feminine charm and character all of its own. Light and aromatic, the Gentle Spirit is rich in body with a soft heather honey finish.

ISLE OF SKYE.
Assertive but not heavy. Fully flavoured with a pungent, peaty ruggedness. It explodes on the palate and lingers on. Well balanced. A sweetish seaweedy aroma.

SPEYSIDE.
Finely balanced with a dry, rather delicate aroma, good firm body and a smoky finish. A pleasantly austere malt of great distinction with a character all its own.

WEST HIGHLAND.
Oban is the West Highland malt. A singular, rich and complex malt with the merest suggestion of peat in the aroma, slightly smoky with a long smooth finish.

ISLE OF ISLAY.
Seaweed, peat, smoke and earth are all elements of the assertive Islay character. Pungent, an intensely dry 16 year old malt with a firm robust body and powerful aroma.

LOWLAND.
Typically soft, restrained and with a touch of sweetness. An exceptionally pale smooth malt which, experts agree, reaches perfection at 10 years maturity.

DALWHINNIE 15 YEARS OLD HIGHLAND | TALISKER 10 YEARS OLD SKYE | CRAGGANMORE 12 YEARS OLD SPEYSIDE | OBAN 14 YEARS OLD WEST HIGHLAND | LAGAVULIN 16 YEARS OLD ISLAY | GLENKINCHIE 10 YEARS OLD LOWLAND

Les grands crus de Scotland.

In the great wine-growing regions, there are certain growths from a single estate that are inevitably superior.

For the Scots, there are the single malts. Subtle variations in water, weather, peat and the distilling process itself lend each single malt its singular character. The Classic Malts are the finest examples of the main malt producing regions. To savour them, one by one, is a rare journey of discovery.

You'll also find that when your customers taste The Classic Malts, their appreciation will almost certainly increase your sales of malt whisky – in itself a discovery worth making.

To find out more, contact our Customer Services team on 0345 444 111, or contact your local wholesaler.

SIX OF SCOTLAND'S FINEST MALT WHISKIES

Johansens Recommended Traditional Inns, Hotels and Restaurants in Scotland

Myths and mountains, lochs and legends – Scotland's stunning scenic splendour acts as a magnet for visitors from all over the globe. Superb as it is, Scotland's charismatic charm is more than just visual.

There's little doubt that Scotland's stunning scenery is the most often cited reason for visiting Northern Britain, and it's easy to see why.

This is a domain laced with lochs and threaded with roaring rivers and bubbling burns. Mountains and glens form its waft and weft, while legends weave a note of mystery and romance into the landscape.

From the rolling Border hills to the highest Highland 'Munro', you'll find enticing views and vistas that will surely stay with you for ever.

Superlatives trip off the tongue, like malt from an open bottle, the minute you try to put into words the sheer emotional power and visual pleasure that this land inspires, but Scotland is a country with a lot more to offer.

Steeped in history and populated by a proud and hospitable people with a strong sense of their own identity and cultural heritage, Scotland repays those who look beyond the picture postcard countryside and experience city life too.

Scotland's cities certainly rival the best in the world. Edinburgh, its grand capital, is graceful and alluring. Scotland's Festival City, Edinburgh is world-famous for its International Festival and Fringe, which has caught the public's imagination as no other for more than 50 years.

Whatever time of year you visit, you'll find a festival to interest you. And if not, the city's wonderful array of child-friendly attractions, such as Edinburgh Castle and Edinburgh Zoo, will tempt you from the comfort of your recommended hotel, country house or inn.

The National Museum of Scotland, opening in November 1998, will join the city's extensive list of exhibitions, museums and art galleries, and in April 1999, a new permanent and innovative exhibition – Dynamic Earth – will open at the foot of Edinburgh's Royal Mile.

Situated next to the Palace of Holyroodhouse, where construction is already underway on Scotland's New Parliament, Dynamic Earth is the largest new visitor attraction in Scotland. The development cost of £34 million – a King's ransom – has been made possible with £15 million from the Millennium Commission Fund of the National Lottery.

Edinburgh's Royal connections ripple on in 1999 with the permanent berthing of the former Royal Yacht Britannia at her new home in Leith Docks. Coupled with Edinburgh's colourful heritage and wealth of historic landmarks, Edinburgh becomes a 'must' on anyone's Scottish itinerary, but if you're thinking of joining the city's huge Millennium Hogmanay celebrations, book early!

Across the country, Glasgow is also gearing up for an exciting year. Perhaps, not surprisingly for the city that boasts Charles Rennie MacIntosh's greatest buildings, Glasgow takes on the mantle of 'City of Architecture and Design 1999'. A fitting title for a city that has evolved from ecclesiastical and academic beginnings through a long and successful period of commerce and industry to its present reincarnation as Scotland's style capital – now a Mecca for shoppers and for those with an appetite for classy cosmopolitan culture.

And it's not just a 'tale of two cities' – Aberdeen, Dundee, Inverness, Perth and Stirling can also offer a superb short break holiday, conference venue or incentive destination.

The new Food Festival in Inverness coincides with the popular Highland Festival. Its programme of arts and crafts, music and dance celebrating the unique cultural tradition of the Highlands of Scotland, takes place throughout the region in village halls and rural schools as well as town and city locations.

Sporting events continue to pull in the crowds. Golf, one of Scotland's most popular exports, is high on the sporting calendar in 1999. The championship links course at Nairn (near Inverness) has the privilege of hosting the Walker Cup, while further down the coast between Dundee and Arbroath, The British Open returns to Carnoustie – the first time since 1975.

Scotland's hills and mountains are a natural magnet for walkers and climbers, and the fretted coastline and hundreds of islands create a maritime playground for sailors, fishermen, divers, surfers and anyone who simply loves messing around on or in the water. And, of course, wherever you go and whatever you do, it will be against a magnificent backdrop.

Getting around is easy and most of the islands are accessible by car-ferry. The problem will be deciding where to start, what to see and do and just how long to spend in this gloriously diverse country with its magical mix of rural wilderness and cosmopolitan charm!

For further information on Scotland, please contact:

The Scottish Tourist Board
23 Ravelston Terrace
Edinburgh EH4 3BU
Tel: 0131 332 2433

BIRSE LODGE HOTEL

CHARLSTON ROAD, ABOYNE, ROYAL DEESIDE, SCOTLAND, AB34 5EL
TEL: 01339 886253 FAX: 01339 887796 E-MAIL: birse-lodgehotel@compuserve.com

The Birse Lodge Hotel has recently come under new ownership and a thorough refurbishment is well underway to upgrade the accommodation offered to match the most exacting standards. The hotel is situated close to River Dee and is set in is own large garden. All bedrooms have en suite facilities and are equipped with a colour television, direct dial telephone, baby listening and tea/coffee making facilities. The hotel prides itself in providing a warm welcome to all of the family and children under 12 stay free if they share their parents bedrooms, although meals have to be paid for. Excellent Scottish food is served in the pleasant dining room, complemented by a good wine list. This scenic part of Scotland has much to offer everyone. Ideally situated for golf, there are six courses in the area – including one in Aboyne. There are also opportunities to fish for salmon on the River Dee and trout on other rivers and lochs within easy reach. Other leisure and sporting activities include walking, cycling, horse-riding and gliding. Aboyne is close to the famous Castle Trail with six impressive castles and three historic houses. **Directions:** From north or south take A93 in centre of Aboyne and turn into Charlston Road. Price guide: Single £33–£42; double £60–£74.

For hotel location, see maps on pages 212-218

THE LOFT RESTAURANT

GOLF COURSE ROAD, BLAIR ATHOLL, PERTHSHIRE PH18 5TE
TEL: 01796 481377 FAX: 01796 481511

As its name suggests, The Loft at Blair Atholl was originally a hay loft which formed part of the estate. It has been charmingly converted into an elegant yet informal restaurant, with great care having been taken to retain the original twisted old beams, stone walls and oak flooring. Open daily, the restaurant serves morning coffee, lunches, afternoon tea and pre-theatre supper and dinners. Only the freshest ingredients are used in the compilation of the imaginative menus and all meals are cooked to order. A vegetarian option is available. Menus include whole bream baked and served with its own juices; chargrilled rump steak with wild mushroom and onion marmalade and roast chump of local lamb with crushed garlic potato and shallot confit. Delicious desserts, made in The Loft's own patisserie, feature tempting delights such as hot bread and butter pudding with vanilla anglais; chocolate marquise with passion fruit sauce; and glazed lemon tart with orange confiture sauce. Taste of Scotland and 2 AA Rosettes. Accommodation is in 3 adjoining cottages sleeping from 2 to 6 people. The surrounding countryside is rich in attractions, including Blair Atholl Castle and the stunning scenery of Glen Tilt and the Forest of Atholl. Pitlochry, a major tourist centre with a large variety of shops and famous Festival Theatre, can be reached within 15 minutes by car. **Directions:** From A9, turn off to Blair Atholl, 4 miles north of Pitlochry. The restaurant is well signposted.

3 Cottages MasterCard AMERICAN EXPRESS M 20

For hotel location, see maps on pages 212-218

THE GLENISLA HOTEL

KIRKTON OF GLENISLA, BY ALYTH, PERTHSHIRE PH11 8PH
TEL: 01575 582223 FAX: 01575 582203 E-MAIL: glenislahotel@sol.co.uk

A coaching inn in the 17th century, hospitality has long been a tradition at this attractive hotel in the middle of the tiny village of Kirkton of Glenisla, close to the River Isla. The Drawing Room is filled with flowers, inviting sofas and chairs and the six bedrooms are charming. Some have a bath, others a shower. Locals and guests frequent the big, friendly bar with its log fire, wooden tables, cask ales and malt whiskies and they enjoy substantial bar lunches and suppers served at wooden tables. The Games Room, in the stable block, opens on to the Function Hall where Highland Dances are held. The elegant dining room serves the best of Scottish fare, winning several accolades including a recommendation from the Taste of Scotland. Orkney herrings, local venison, Aberdeen Angus beef, wild salmon and hill-reared lamb all feature on the menu. There are interesting starters and puddings! The wine list is impressive. The Glenisla is an ideal touring centre for Glamis, Scone, Braemar and Royal Deeside, while immediate activities include trout fishing, skiing, stalking, shooting, salmon fishing and golf. Hill walking, bird-watching and pony-trekking are also on the doorstep. **Directions:** From the M90 take the A93 to Blairgowrie, then A926 by-passing Alyth to next roundabout. Then follow signs to Glenisla for 12 miles, hotel is on the right. Price guide: Single £40–£50; double £65–£85.

6 rms MasterCard VISA M 60

For hotel location, see maps on pages 212-218

THE SEAFIELD ARMS HOTEL

19 SEAFIELD STREET, CULLEN, BANFFSHIRE AB56 2SG
TEL: 01542 840791 FAX: 01542 840736 E-MAIL: @theseafieldarms.co.uk

Situated in the heart of Cullen, The Seafield Arms is an impressive former coaching inn offering classic comfort and style. It was built by the Earl of Seafield in 1822 and is recorded in the statistical account of Scotland of 1845 as having "no superior between Aberdeen and Inverness". The old character and friendly traditions have remained and are now combined with modern standards of quiet luxury. The staff are attentive and the accommodation comfortable and traditional. All 20 en suite bedrooms are attractively furnished and offer every required facility. The restaurant, which features a specially woven carpet of the Grant Tartan, has established a reputation for its excellent innovative treatment of traditional Scottish recipes. Fresh local produce is used in the preparation of dishes, which are always beautifully presented. After dinner, guests can relax in front of a magnificently carved fireplace in the Findlater Lounge and choose from 120 malt whiskies. Cullen is on the coast of Banffshire which is renowned for its beaches and the only malt whisky trail in the world. Games and gatherings are held in the area and there are many historical sites to explore. Golf courses abound, with Cullen's own course situated on the beach side. **Directions:** On the main A98 road close to the town square. Price guide: Single £38–45; double £60–£80.

For hotel location, see maps on pages 212-218

GROUSE AND TROUT

FLICHITY, BY FARR/LOCHNESS, INVERNESS, SCOTLAND IV1 2XE
TEL/FAX: 01808 521314

Original farm steading from 1860 forms part of the original Flichity Hotel, which has been carefully converted and refurbished whilst preserving much of the traditional features. The result is a charming hotel adorned with timber beams and stonework, set amidst the superb landscape of lochs and heather fields. The five bedrooms in house enjoy glorious views over the magnificent hills of Strathnairn and Loch Flichity adjacent to the famous nature reserve. Kept in simple country house style, they are all en suite with television and tea/coffee making facilities. The menu comprises hearty bar meals, prepared by the chef for lunch and dinner. A warm welcome is extended to all guests in the friendly Lounge and Restaurant, where the range of single malts and extensive wine list complement the convivial atmosphere. Loch fishing, grouse shooting, stalking and horse riding are some of the many outdoor activities available within the locality. The hotel itself offers a hard tennis court and bicycle hire for guests. Other pursuits include the many nearby golf courses, clay pigeon shooting, cruises on the Loch Ness or simply enjoying the beautiful countryside. Places of interest include Culloden Battlefield, Cawdor Castle and Fort Augustus Abbey. **Directions:** From the A9 South of Inverness, take the B851 (Fort Augustus) for 7 miles. Price guide: Single £45; double/twin £80.

For hotel location, see maps on pages 212-218

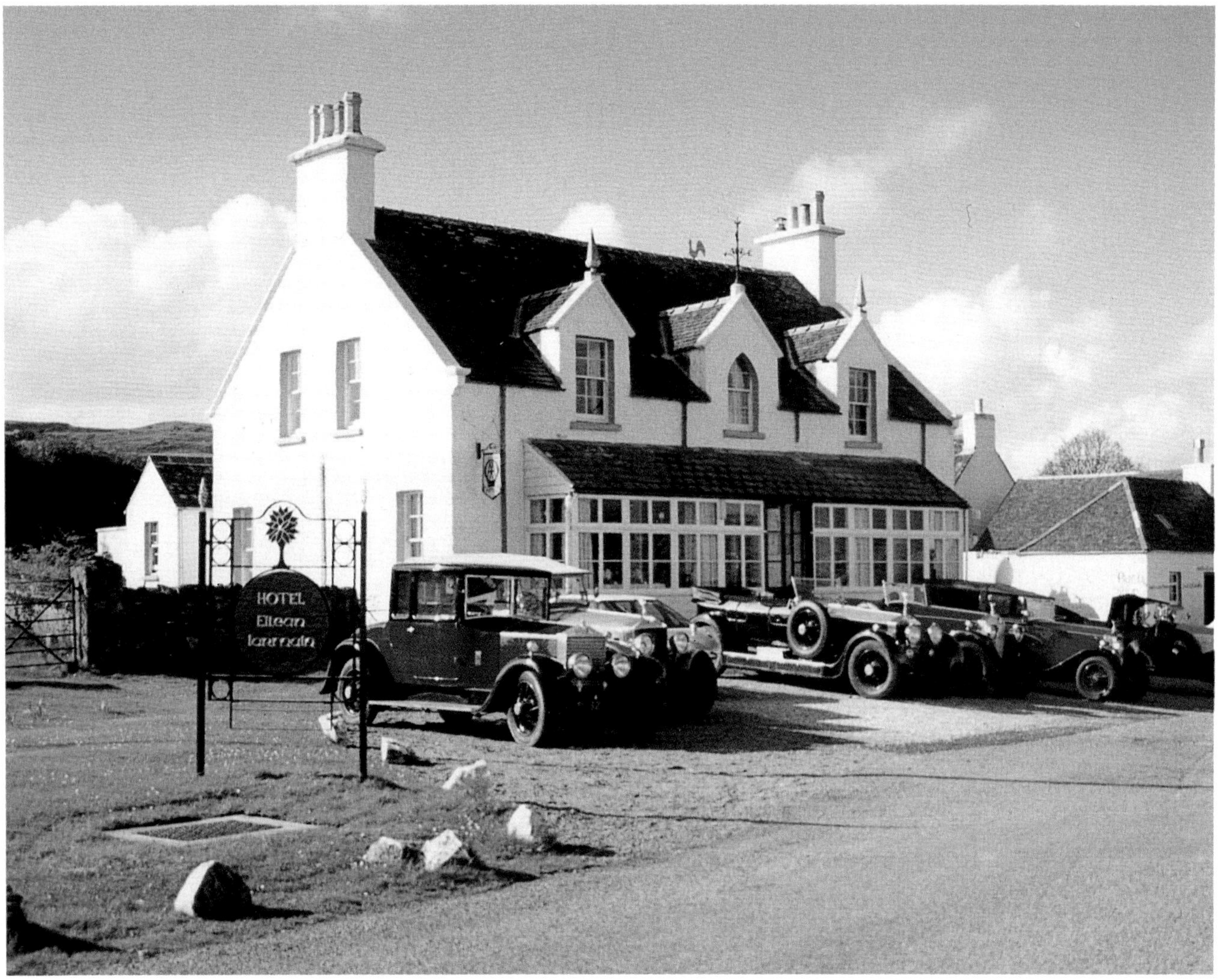

HOTEL EILEAN IARMAIN OR ISLE ORNSAY HOTEL

SLEAT, ISLE OF SKYE IV43 8QR
TEL: 01471 833332 FAX: 01471 833275

Hotel Eilean Iarmain stands on the small bay of Isle Ornsay in the South of Skye with expansive views over the Sound of Sleat and has always meant 'failte is furan' a warmth of welcomes. The hotel prides itself on its log fires, inventive cooking and friendly Gaelic-speaking staff. 1997/8 accolades include the RAC Restaurant Award, RAC Merit Award for Hospitality, Comfort and Restaurant, AA Rosette for Restaurant, AA Romantic Hotel of Great Britain and Ireland Award, Les Routiers Corps d'Elite Wine Award and Macallan Taste of Scotland, runner-up Hotel of the Year Award. The 12 bedrooms are all different, with 6 of them in the Garden House with special views of sea and hills. Original features, period furniture, pretty fabrics and pictures create a cosy atmosphere. Every evening the menu features game in season and guests enjoy fresh seafood landed at the pier. The extensive wine list includes premier cru clarets. A large selection of malt whiskies includes local Poit Dhubh and Talisker, highly regarded by connoisseurs. The bar offers lunchtime meals and in the evening is a haunt of yachtsmen, often the scene of ceilidhs. Clan MacDonald Centre, Armadale Castle and Talisker Distillery are close by. Sports include sea-fishing, stalking, shooting and walking. **Directions:** The hotel is in Sleat, between Broadford and Armadale on A851. 20 mins from Skye Bridge; 15 mins from Mallaig Armadale Ferry and Lochalsh railway station. Price guide: Single £80; double £105–£130.

For hotel location, see maps on pages 212-218

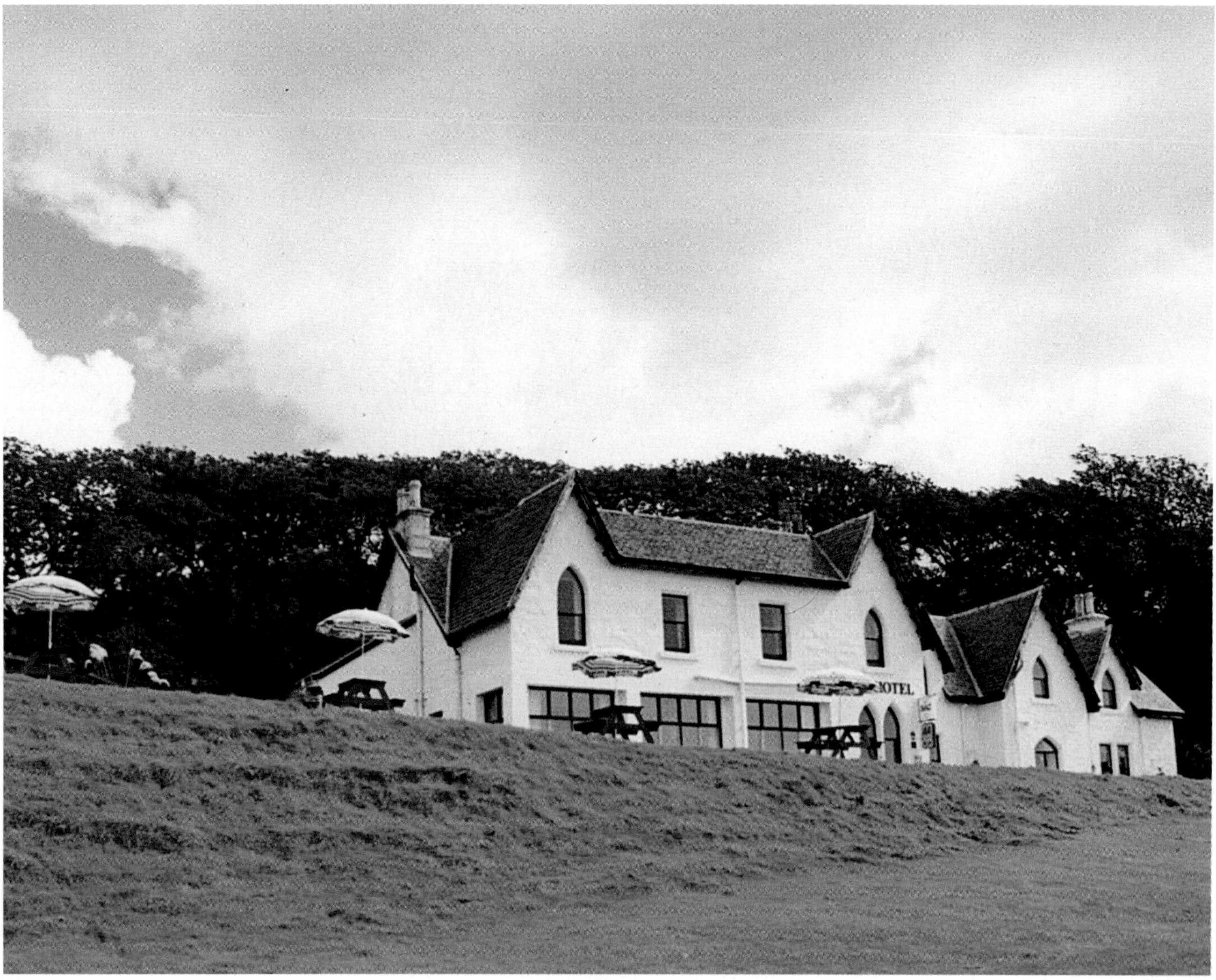

Uig Hotel

UIG, ISLE OF SKYE, ISLE OF SKYE IV51 9YE
TEL: 01470 542205 FAX: 01470 542308

Cool, gleaming white-faced walls and a warm Scottish welcome greet visitors to this delightful old coaching hostelry standing in three acres of hillside grounds overlooking beautiful Uig Bay and Loch Snizort. The hotel was awarded the 1998 Les Routiers hospitality award for a genuine welcome and warm friendly ambience. The en suite bedrooms have been individually decorated and offer all modern facilities. Pretty fabrics and well chosen water-colours create a cosy atmosphere and a relaxing sun lounge overlooks the bay. The restaurant is comfortable and welcoming with chef Steven Moffett providing a good choice of menus featuring fresh locally landed seafood and lamb from the hotel's own flock of Island Blackface sheep. Appetites are sure to be tempted by dishes such as a trellis of salmon and sole presented on a pool of ginger scented tomato sauce, or maybe pan seared breast of duck served on stir fried leeks. Guests enjoy pony trekking from the hotel's Native Pony Centre in magnificent coastal scenery, fishing, shooting and various excursions. The Trotternish Peninsula, Quiraing, Storr, Fairy Glen, Duntulm Castle and Museum of Island Life are all nearby. One mile from the ferry sailing to the Outer Hebridean Isles of Harris, Lewis and the Uists, day trips in summer. **Directions:** Skye is reached by road bridge via A87 or by ferry via A830. Approaching Uig from Portree, the hotel is on the right, beside a white church. Price guide: Single £37–£55; double £74–£140.

For hotel location, see maps on pages 212-218

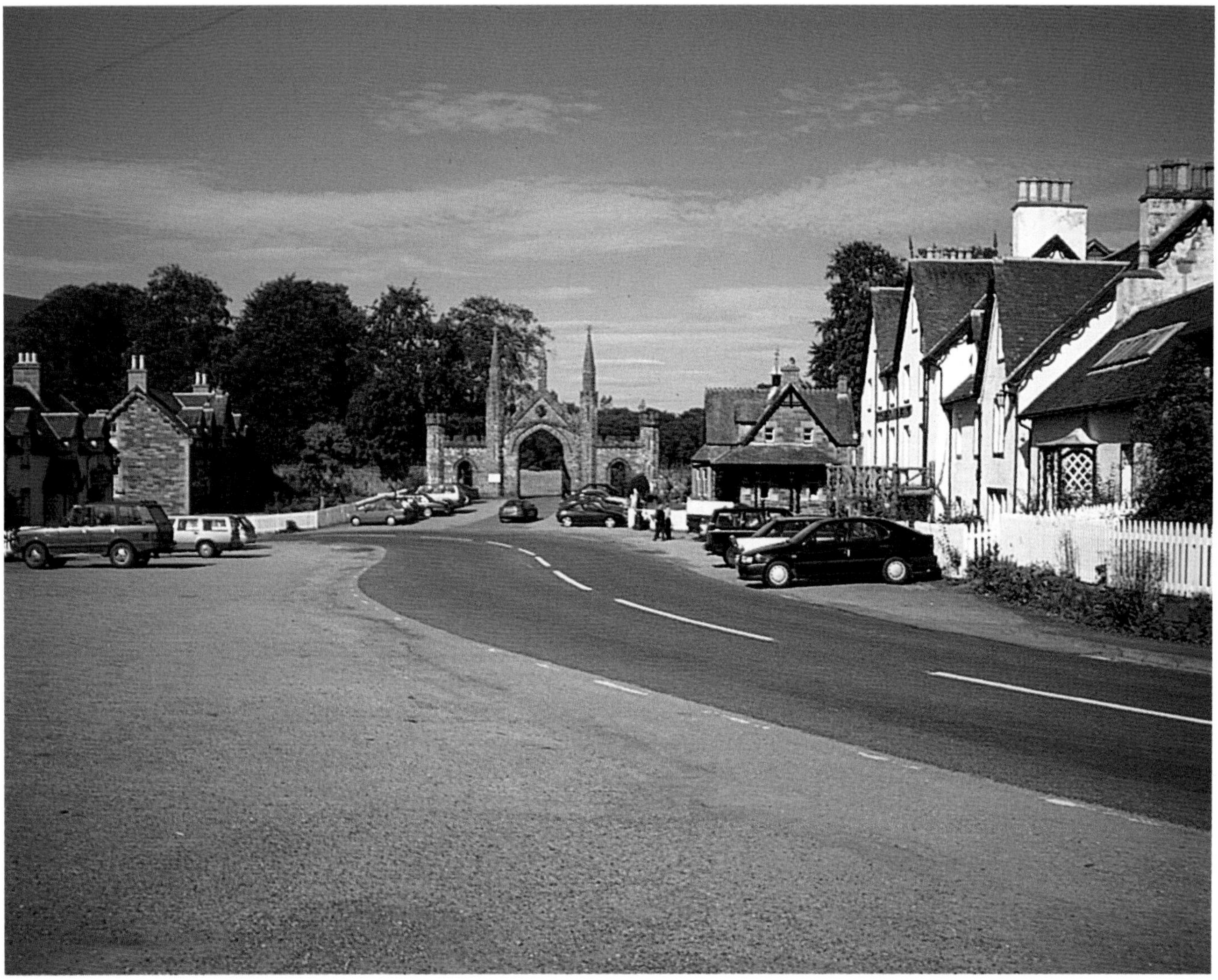

THE KENMORE HOTEL

PERTHSHIRE PH15 2NU
TEL: 01887 830205 FAX: 01887 830262

The Kenmore Hotel boasts the proud title of Scotland's oldest inn. Steeped in history, this charming inn dates back to 1572 and still retains the warmth and friendly hospitality enjoyed by guests over 400 years ago. Most of the 40 bedrooms have recently been refurbished and contain classic furnishings and comfortable décor. Offering many amenities such as en suite facilities and colour television, they are well-equipped for the modern traveller. A framed poem, penned by the famous poet Robert Burn, hangs above the fireplace in the cosy Poet's Parlour. Here, guests may choose to recline with a glass of Scottish malt whisky or venture into Archie's Bar and drink a beer whilst enjoying the fine surroundings. The River View restaurant, which affords panoramic views of the River Tay, serves a varied and seasonal menu created by the talented chef. The well-stocked cellars are filled with wine selected as a complement to the dishes. Traditional Highland breakfasts include many local delicacies such as Kenmore oatcakes, porridge oats, Scottish kippers and Arbroath Smokies. The hotel's golf course at Taymouth Castle has 18 holes and is both rough and challenging. Salmon fishing on the Tay is available and boats are provided for those wishing to fish on the loch. Other sports include riding, tennis, hill-walking and swimming at the nearby indoor pool. **Directions:** From the A9, take the A827(Aberfeldy) for 14 miles. Price guide: Single £43–£75; double/twin £85–£150.

For hotel location, see maps on pages 212-218

THE BLACK BULL

THE SQUARE, KILLEARN G63 9NG
TEL: 01360 550215 FAX: 01360 550143

The Black Bull, situated in the village of Killearn, dates back to the nineteenth century. During the last two years, this historic inn has undergone an extensive refurbishment resulting in a fine property with every modern facility. The eleven en suite bedrooms are beautifully appointed and are enhanced by the new carpets and comfortable furnishings. The sybaritic residents' lounge, with its attractive bay window, enjoys glorious views over the gardens. This calm and comfortable room, adorned with hand-carved Indian and Chinese ornaments, is complemented by a trust bar for the guests' use. The two restaurants are varied in style but both share the same high standard of service and fine cuisine. At lunchtime guests frequent the Brasserie, a bright, spacious room with a large double-sided fireplace and indulge in the à la carte dishes made with fresh local produce. Those wishing to dine in style must visit the Conservatory in the evening. Renowned for its oversized tables and elegant music, guests may feast upon the sumptuous food and excellent wines. **Directions:** Come off the A81 road to Aberfoyle, just past the Glengoyne Distillery. As the road forks, veer to the right and follow the A875 through Killearn village. Turn left at the top and the hotel is just in front. Price guide: Single £50; double/twin £70.

11 rms MasterCard VISA AMERICAN EXPRESS M 40

For hotel location, see maps on pages 212-218

THE FOYERS HOTEL

FOYERS, LOCH NESS, INVERNESS-SHIRE, SCOTLAND IV1 2XT
TEL: 01456 486216 FAX: 01456 486216

In the 1720s, whilst working on the military road between Inverness and Fort Augustus, General George Wade built himself a shelter at Foyers on the south side of the fabulous 25-mile long Loch Ness. It is on the same site that The Foyers Hotel now stands, looking down on Foyers Bay and over to the majestic Meall Fuar-mhonaidh peak soaring above the shores on the far side of the water. The landscape of the surrounding Highlands is as dramatic as its history. The hotel has been refurbished over the past two years to offer visitors modern comforts whilst retaining the building's unique character. Eight of the nine bedrooms are en suite, are spacious and have all the latest facilities. From the finest ingredients chef, Sue O'Neill, produces both traditional Scottish fare and her own selected dishes, gleaned from her worldwide travels. These delights can be accompanied by the spectacular views from the attractive restaurant or enjoyed in the more informal atmosphere of "The General's Hut" bar. The overall effect is one of attentive yet relaxed hospitality. Local places of interest include the Falls of Foyers, Loch Ness Visitors Centre, Fort Augustus, Culloden battlefield and many beautiful glens. Golf, fishing, shooting and riding are nearby. **Directions:** From Inverness take B862 towards Dores, then fork right onto B852. From Fort Augustus take B862 to just beyond the village of Whitebridge and then turn left onto B852. Price guide: Single £30–£40; double/twin: £60–£80.

For hotel location, see maps on pages 212-218

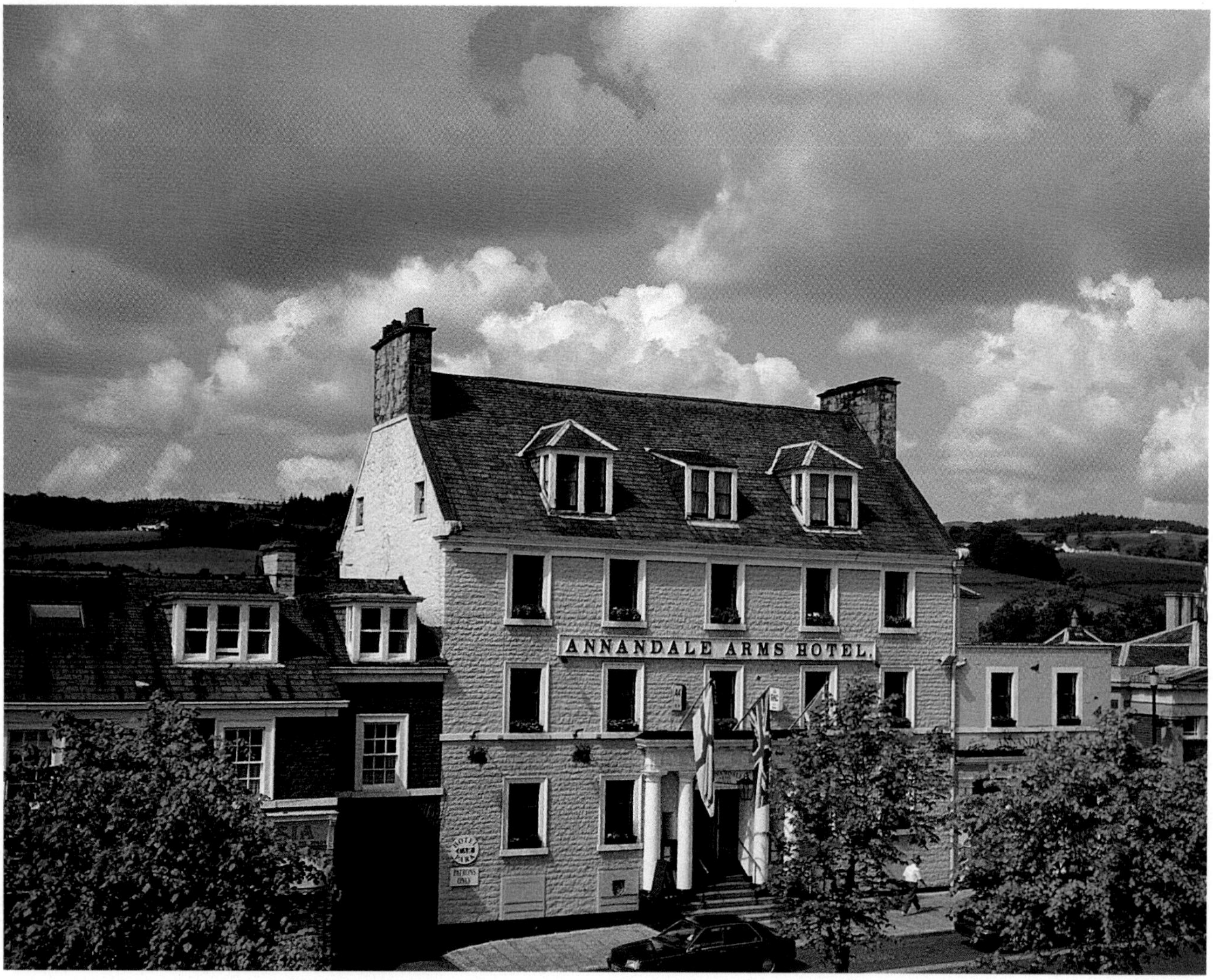

ANNANDALE ARMS HOTEL

HIGH STREET, MOFFATT, DUMFRIESSHIRE DG10 9HF
TEL: 01683 220013 FAX: 01683 221395

True Scottish hospitality can be enjoyed at this welcoming, 200-year-old coaching inn which offers attractive accommodation and excellent value for money. The Annandale Arms stands in the centre of the pretty Southern Upland Hill town of Moffat, where Robert Burns, Sir Walter Scott and John Buchanan found inspiration for many of their works. The area thrives as a sheep farming centre, symbolised by a statue of a ram in the wide High Street. The beautiful surrounding countryside, which looks much like the English Lake District, is steeped in history, making it popular with sightseers, sports enthusiasts and hill climbers. The panelled bar also draws locals and visitors as it serves a wide selection of malt whiskies. All 15 bedrooms are charming and provide full modern comforts. Some have panoramic views over the magnificent Border countryside. In addition to an extensive bar menu, there is sophisticated à la carte cuisine using local produce. The Annandale Arms is an ideal base for visiting many historic castles and National Trust properties. North of the town is the Devil's Beef Tub, a sheer-sided hollow in the hills, White Coomb (2,696ft) and Grey Mare's Tail, one of Scotland's highest waterfalls. Immediate activities include fishing, golf, shooting, sailing, riding and bird-watching. **Directions:** Moffat is 2 miles off A74M on A 701 road from Dumfries. Price Guide: Single £30–£40; double £40–£64.

For hotel location, see maps on pages 212-218

The Moulin Hotel

MOULIN, BY PITLOCHRY, PERTHSHIRE PH16 5EW
TEL: 01796 472196 FAX: 01796 474098 E-MAIL: hotel@moulin.u-net.com

The Moulin Hotel stands pristine white against a towering mountain backdrop of deep blues and greens capped by scudding clouds racing to and from the Highlands. Behind its attractive black framed windows is a welcoming world of peace, tranquillity and Scottish homeliness. Opened as an inn in 1695, The Moulin Hotel stands proudly in the village square just three-quarters of a mile from the bustling town of Pitlochry, gateway to the Highlands. All 15 bedrooms have been recently refurbished to include every modern amenity. The comfortable lounge and lounge bar overlook the hotel's garden and Moulin Burn, where the cooing of doves and water babbling over stones is calming music to the ears of visitors wearied by a day's walking, exploring or sightseeing. The chefs serve a varied choice of imaginatively prepared dishes in the spacious and charmingly furnished restaurant. Begin with haggis wrapped in filo pastry on an onion cream, followed by salmon wrapped in lemon sole on a prawn sauce and then a dessert of highland cranachan with local berries before enjoying an after-dinner coffee and malt. Many walks and gentle climbs are close by such as the 2,759 foot summit of Ben-y-Vrackie. Golf, fishing, riding, Pitlochry Theatre, Blair Castle, Scone Palace and numerous historical sites abound. Directions: From Perth, take A9 to Pitlochry then turn right onto A924 for Moulin. Price guide: Single £53–£63; double £58–£68 per room.

For hotel location, see maps on pages 212-218

THE PLOCKTON HOTEL AND GARDEN RESTAURANT

HARBOUR STREET, PLOCKTON, WESTER ROSS IV52 8TN
TEL: 01599 544274 FAX: 01599 544475

With its sheltered harbour fringed by tall palm trees the picturesque village of Plockton, at the mouth of Loch Carron, is a favourite with film makers. Over the years this 18th century waterside hotel has been host to a succession of actors and actresses attracted by its beamed charm, ambience, good food and the scenic splendour of the Applecross Mountains viewed from its windows. It is as far from city life as you can imagine and an ideal centre for visiting Skye or touring north to Applecross, Torridon or Ullapool. Tom and Dorothy Pearson offer a particularly friendly welcome to their antique-furnished hotel with its pretty little garden. They have recently invested in extensive refurbishment and additions which have increased the number of comfortable, en suite bedrooms and introduced a garden restaurant. The food produced by chefs Lorna Murray and Jane Stewart is superb and has earned a beer glass and fork symbol award in the prestigious 1998 Michelin Hotel and Restaurant Guide. Particularly renowned are their fresh fish and Plockton prawns dishes There are attractive gardens and National Trust properties nearby, sailing on the loch, swimming from small coral beaches, golf, sea and hill loch fishing. **Directions**: Take the A87 to Kyle of Lochalsh. Plockton is five miles north. Price guide: Single £30–£33; double/twin £60–£65.

For hotel location, see maps on pages 212-218

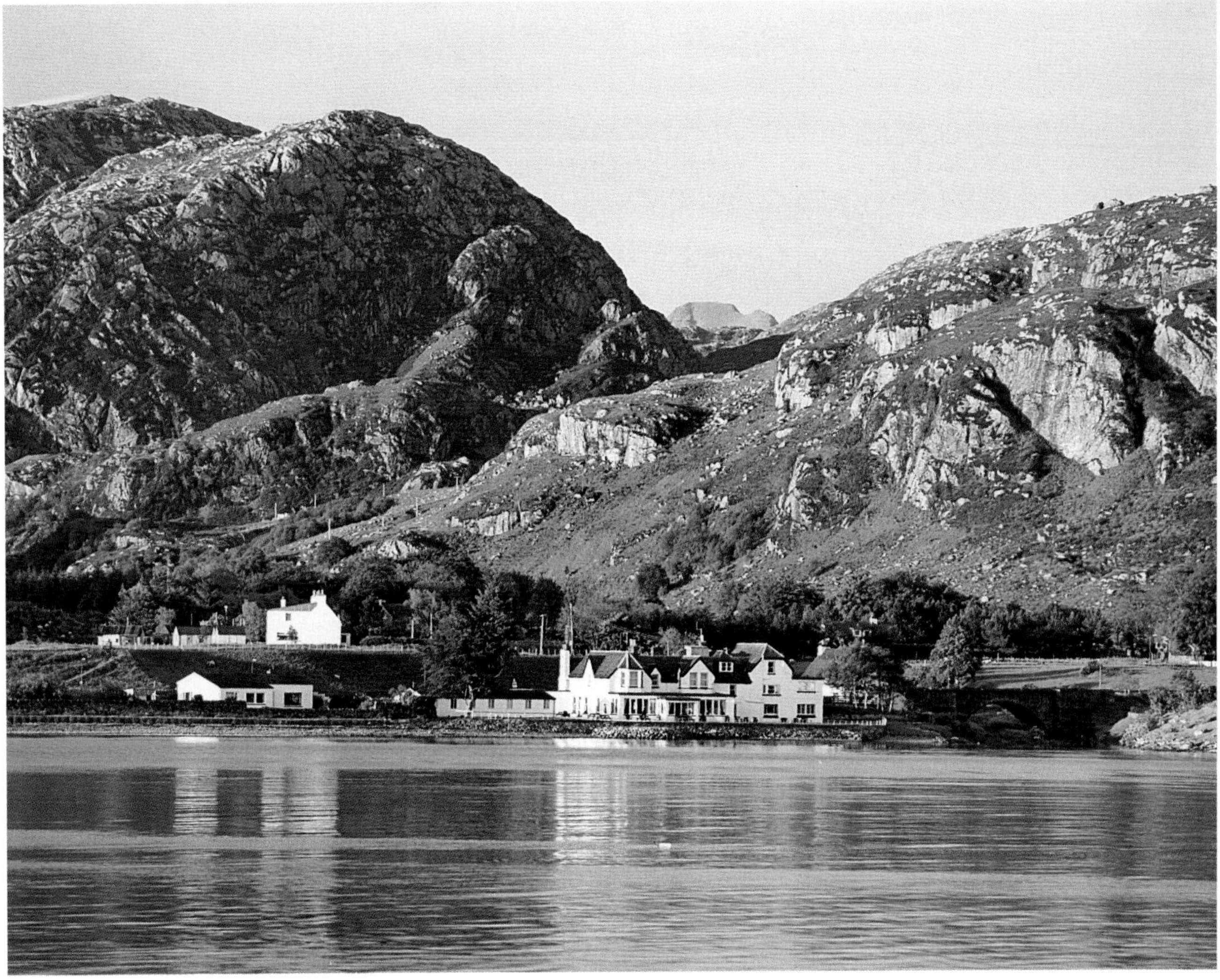

Pool House Hotel

POOLEWE, ACHNASHEEN, WESTER ROSS IV22 2LD

TEL: 01445 781272 FAX: 01445 781403 E-MAIL: Poolhouse@inverewe.co.uk

The scenic splendour of Wester Ross, with its majestic mountains and spectacular sunsets, makes a perfect backdrop for Pool House. The hotel stands on the shores of Loch Ewe, just across the bay from the world-famous, subtropical Inverewe Gardens. All the bedrooms are nicely decorated and furnished and most benefit from lovely views of the loch or river. They are also strictly non-smoking. On view from the ideally-situated lounge is an abundance of wildlife, including seals, cormorants, herons and even occasionally a family of otters. Excellent food and wine is a well-noted feature of the hotel, which has won several prestigious awards in recognition of this. Specialising in local seafood, the 'Lochside Restaurant' serves an extensive menu comprising Loch Ewe langoustine, lobster and scallops, while the wine list offers a choice to suit every palate and pocket. Some of the more unusual whiskies can be sampled in the Rowallan bar, which is also the place to enjoy an informal meal. Hill walkers, keen ornithologists and wildlife enthusiasts will all be delighted by the excellent opportunities to indulge their favourite pastimes. **Directions:** Pool House is on the A832 to Poolewe, 6 miles north-east of Gairloch. Price guide: Single £28–£44; double £56–£96.

For hotel location, see maps on pages 212-218

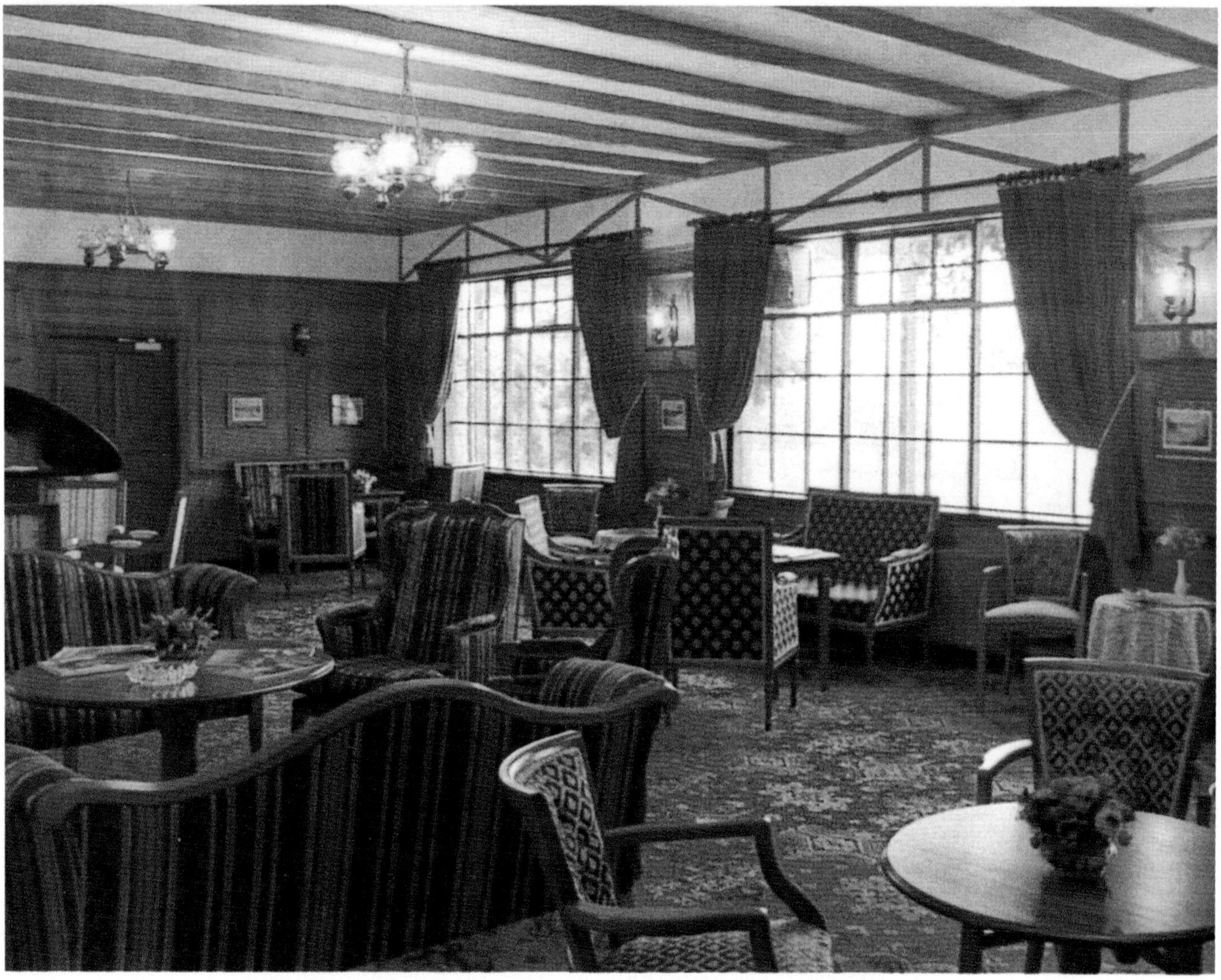

The Gartwhinzean

POWMILL, BY KINROSS, FK14 7NW
TEL: 01577 840595 FAX: 01577 840779

Experience Scottish inn-keeping hospitality at its best at The Gartwhinzean. Set in a charming location overlooking the Gairney Hills and the countryside all around, this inn combines excellent accommodation with mouth-watering cuisine. The spacious bedrooms are decorated and furnished to the highest standards and include every modern amenity. The delightful bistro-style restaurant has open fires and a special private dining area. From the lunch and snack menu why not try a hearty casserole of Boeuf Bourgignon or penne pasta enriched with a sauce of onion, mushroom, smoked ham, cream and a hint of nutmeg. The dinner menu will be equally tempting - roast breast of duck served on buttered leeks with a cassis sauce, or maybe pan fried fillet of trout coated in oatmeal and simply served with citrus fruit and parsley. An interesting wine list and real ales are available to complement this fine food. Fishing, golfing, shooting, falconry and car racing are just a few of the sporting activities than can be arranged for guests. The inn also has access to a number of estates. The scenic Scottish Perthshire countryside boasts many castles and monuments and Edinburgh and Glasgow are both about 30 miles away. **Directions:** From M90 turn off at Jct 6, Kinross Services, onto A977 for six miles. Price guide: Single £50–£55; double £65–£75.

For hotel location, see maps on pages 212-218

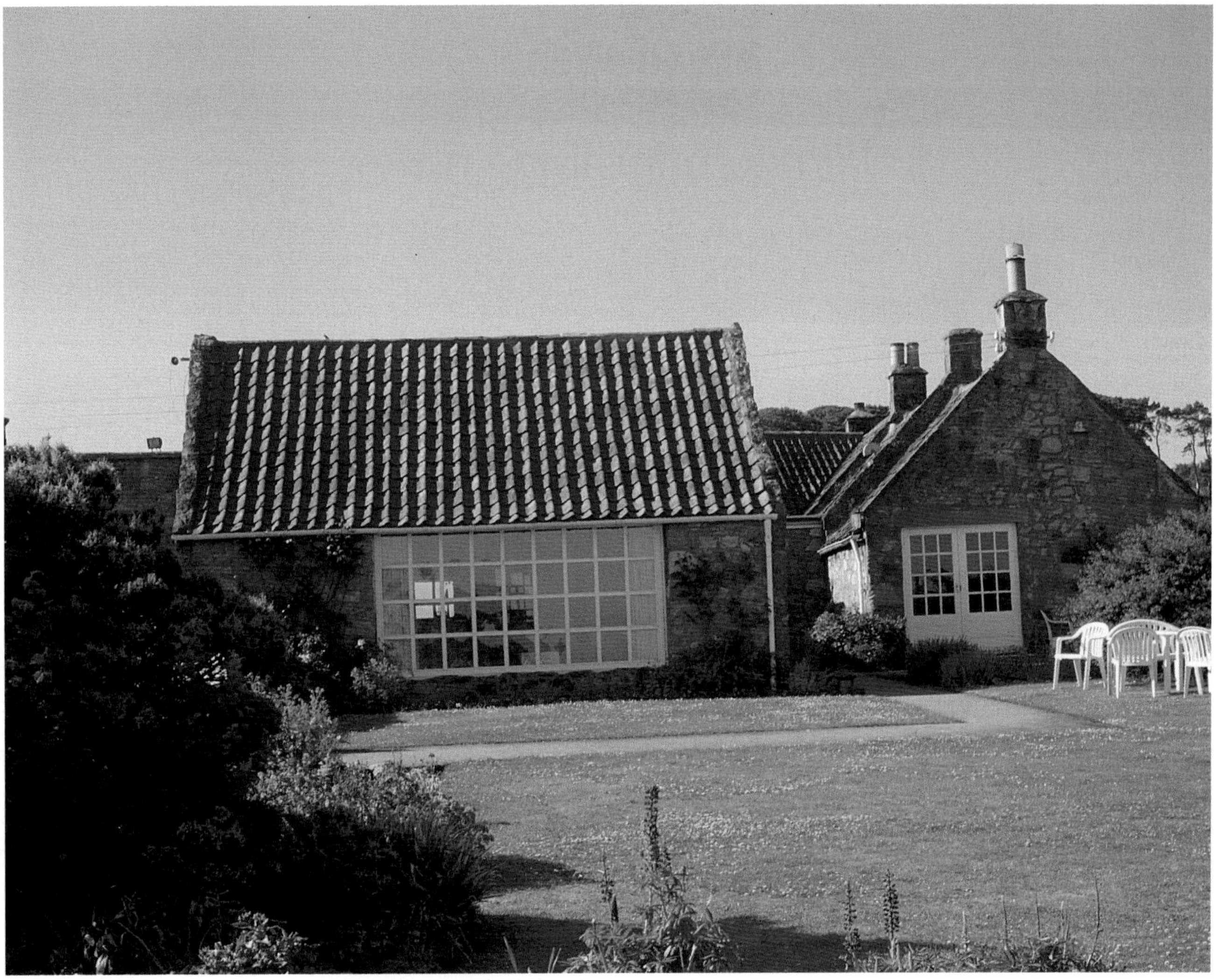

THE GRANGE INN

GRANGE ROAD, ST. ANDREWS, FIFE KY16 8LJ
TEL: 01334 472670 FAX: 01334 472604

Set in a beautiful hillside location, the Grange Inn affords panoramic views over St. Andrews Bay. Well-kept lawns and a small kitchen garden are clustered around the property, which dates back to the 17th century. The two bedrooms, one with a four-poster bed, are well-appointed and have en suite facilities. Amongst the other amenities offered are television and central heating. A welcoming atmosphere is created in all three of the dining areas, particularly during the winter seasons when open fires burn in the traditional fireplaces. An inspired menu comprises real Scottish fare and is enhanced by the fresh vegetables and herbs in the kitchen garden. Fresh fish such as halibut are caught by the local fishermen and the meat and poultry are largely bought from Scottish suppliers to provide the freshest of produce. The wine list includes a selection from both the Continent and the New World. Guests may indulge in one of the 35 single malt and grain whiskies displayed at the inn. There are several attractions within easy reach such as Falkland Palace, HMS 'Discovery' and the Sealife Centre. Sports enthusiasts may use the nearby leisure centre with pool or enjoy the many country pursuits. For golf players the five courses at St. Andrews are a must. Directions: ½ mile out of St. Andrews on A917 to Crail. At double mini roundabout take middle road signposted Grange for a further ½ mile. Price guide: Twin £60; Four-poster £80.

For hotel location, see maps on pages 212-218

St Peter Port, Guernsey

Johansens Recommended Traditional Inns, Hotels and Restaurants in the Channel Islands

With a wealth of wonderful scenery, magnificent coastlines, historic buildings, natural and man-made attractions plus mouthwatering local produce, the Channel Islands provide a memorable destination that's distinctly different.

All of the Johansens Recommended establishments in the Channel Islands are able to make favourable travel arrangements for you.

Jersey and Guernsey offer VAT free shopping, the official language is English, passports are not required and both islands can be reached by sea from Poole or any one of about 30 airports in Britain and Europe.

And don't forget the other islands. Herm has dazzling beaches, Sark lives in a rural timewarp without traffic and Alderney's cobbled streets, pretty cottages and Victorian forts are another world again.

JERSEY

The largest and most southerly of the Channel Islands, Jersey, measures only nine miles by five and is just fourteen miles from the French coast. The island slopes from north to south, creating dramatic differences between the high cliffs of the north and broad sandy bays of the south.

Jersey was originally part of Normandy. When William the Conqueror invaded England, it came under English rule until 1204, when King John lost Normandy to France.

The Islanders were given a choice – stay with Normandy or remain loyal to the English Crown. They chose England and gained rights and privileges which to this day are subject not to the British Parliament, but only to the reigning monarch.

The French influence is still strong however, and visitors are often surprised to find the names of streets and villages in French. The granite architecture of the farms and manor houses has a Continental feel too, and in rural areas, you may still hear farmworkers speaking in the local 'patois' or dialect.

Food is also something for which Jersey is renowned. Shellfish and fresh fish are the specialities of the island and lobster, crab, seafood platter, bass and Jersey plaice feature on many menus. The annual Good Food Festival, held in early summer, is a must for food lovers.

History enthusiasts can trace the island's development from prehistory to the present day through a variety of different sites. The Channel Islands were the only part of the British Isles to be occupied by the Germans during World War II and there are reminders all over Jersey.

For a small island, Jersey boasts more than its fair share of museums. The Maritime Museum, which opened in 1997, tells the story of Jersey people's ability to find new ways in which to adapt to the opportunities presented by the sea. Designed as an interactive, hands on museum, it has a strong family focus.

You're never far from Jersey's spectacular coastline – all 50 miles of it – but the interior of the Island is worth exploring too. The largely rural landscape is criss-crossed by a network of narrow country roads, some of which have been designated as 'Green Lanes', where priority is given to walkers, cyclists and horseriders.

But the cultural attractions of Jersey can never eclipse the Island's natural beauty. Every bend in the lane, every turn in the coast path reveals a new view to be savoured and enjoyed.

GUERNSEY

Guernsey, with a total area of only 25 square miles, lies at the centre of a group of even smaller islands which, together, comprise 'The Bailiwick of Guernsey'. Like Jersey, only 20 miles away, Guernsey has its own government – quite independent of that of the United Kingdom – at the head of which is the Bailiff, and within its jurisdiction are the islands of Sark, Alderney, Herm and Jethou. Guernsey, therefore, offers the visitor not only its own varied attractions, but also opportunities to discover these smaller islands, each with its own very distinctive character.

Getting there is easy, with regular flights from many UK and Continental airports, and departures by sea, for both passengers and cars, from the UK and nearby French ports. Arrival by sea at St Peter Port, Guernsey's little capital, provides a memorable introduction to the island as it is one of the prettiest ports in Europe, its distinctive buildings rising in tiers above the quays of the busy harbour where colourful banners of yachts of all nations flutter in the sunshine. It's a friendly town, whose narrow cobbled streets are lined with interesting shops, and where the choice of restaurants is quite outstanding.

Within its small size, Guernsey offers enormous variety. Roughly triangular in shape, the south coast – the base as it were – comprises high cliffs, covered in springtime with a profusion of colourful flowers, at the foot of which nestle lovely little sandy coves. A network of cliff paths provides superb walking all the way from St Peter Port to the extreme south-west corner of the island, a distance of some twenty five miles, one spectacular sea view succeeding another all the way. Inland, high-banked country lanes lead past old granite farmhouses and tiny fields where the world-famous Guernsey cows contentedly graze.

For those interested in the past, Guernsey offers a fascinating choice of subjects to investigate; prehistoric tombs and menhirs, medieval churches and chapels, the remarkable house where the great French writer Victor Hugo lived for fifteen years during his exile from France, elegant Regency architecture and fortifications dating from the 13th century up to the German occupation during World War II. Not to be missed is Castle Cornet, which dominates the entrance to St Peter Port harbour and contains galleries and museums which narrate the Castle's own turbulent history, as well as revealing the island's maritime past.

For further information, please contact:

Jersey Tourism
Liberation Square, St Helier, JE1 IBB
Tel: 01534 500 700

Guernsey Tourist Board
PO Box 23, St Peter Port, Guernsey GY1 3AN
Tel: 01481 723557 (24 hours); 01481 723552

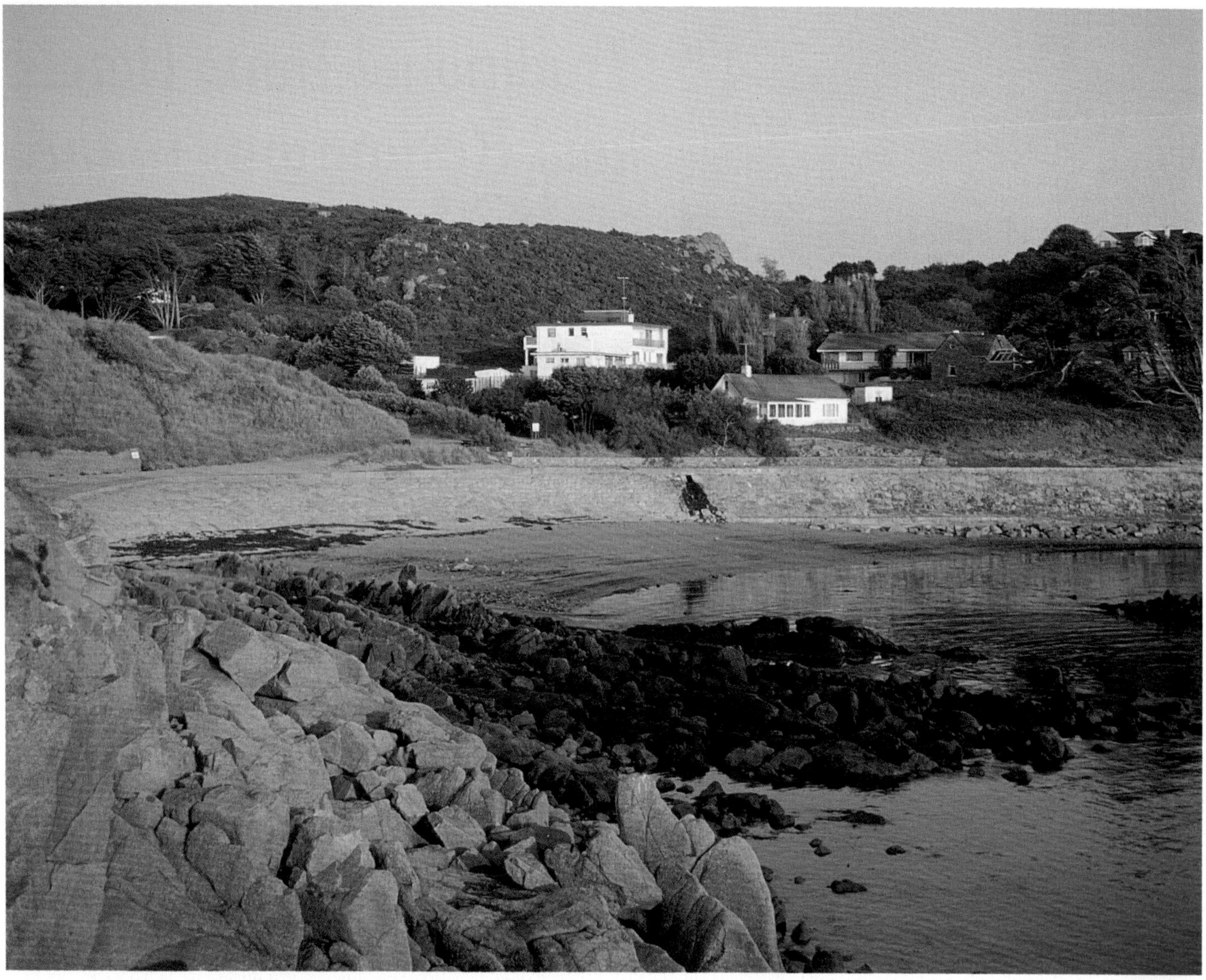

SEA CREST HOTEL AND RESTAURANT

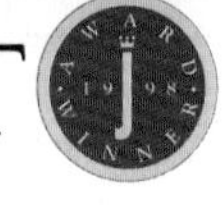

PETIT PORT, ST BRELADE JE3 8HH
TEL: 01534 46353 FAX: 01534 47316

The intimate Sea Crest Hotel and Restaurant stands serenely on the sunny south west coast of Jersey in the picturesque bay of Petit Port. It overlooks the beautiful conservation area of La Pulente Headland and is only a short walk from the five-mile stretch of St Ouen's Bay sands. Originally a traditional Jersey granite cottage, Sea Crest has been extended, sympathetically modernised and won a Jersey Tourism Gold Merit Award. All six bedrooms, most of them with their own balcony and sun loungers, have full facilities, handmade English furniture, pretty French soft furnishings and superb views of the bay. The cosy, beamed cocktail bar leads onto the Sun Lounge and terrace where, overlooking a tempting swimming pool and secluded gardens, guests can enjoy drinks and light meals throughout the day. Excellent value accommodation, service and friendliness are assured. Chef Roger White is continuing the enviable, award-winning reputation for excellent cuisine with delicious local seafood dishes and Jersey Fresh Produce. All meals are well presented and complemented by an extensive wine list. The air-conditioned restaurant displays its own distinctive collection of modern art. Walking along beaches and coastal paths, riding, fishing and golf at La Moye. Shopping at the Les Quennevais and Red Houses. **Directions:** The hotel is on the south west coast, only seven minutes drive from the airport and 20 minutes from St Helier. Price guide: Single £50–£65; double £75–£105.

For hotel location, see maps on pages 212-218

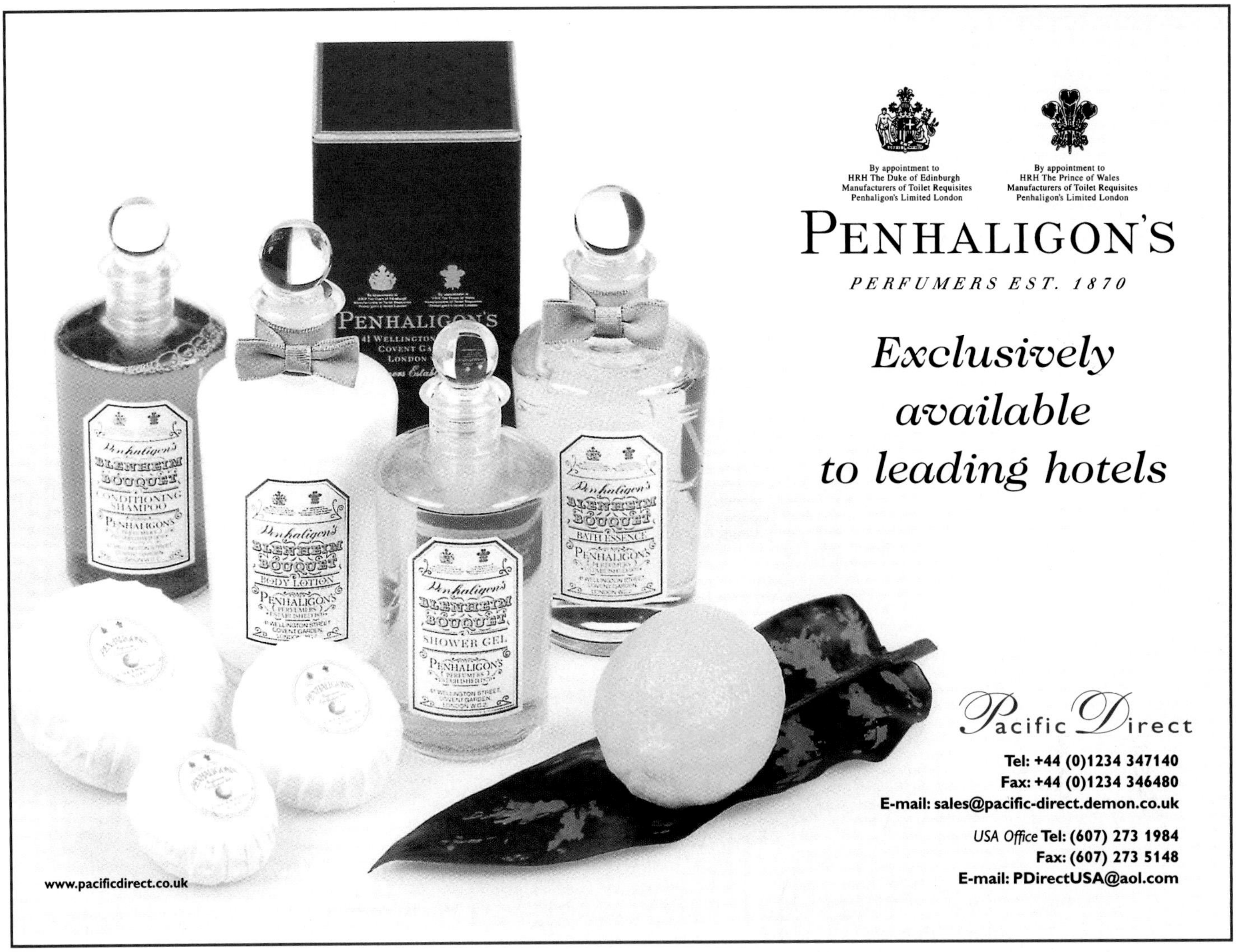
By appointment to HRH The Duke of Edinburgh Manufacturers of Toilet Requisites Penhaligon's Limited London
By appointment to HRH The Prince of Wales Manufacturers of Toilet Requisites Penhaligon's Limited London
PENHALIGON'S
PERFUMERS EST. 1870
Exclusively available to leading hotels
Pacific Direct
Tel: +44 (0)1234 347140
Fax: +44 (0)1234 346480
E-mail: sales@pacific-direct.demon.co.uk
USA Office Tel: (607) 273 1984
Fax: (607) 273 5148
E-mail: PDirectUSA@aol.com
www.pacificdirect.co.uk

Exquisite Toiletries
for Hotels of Distinction
Luxury packaging for that special finishing touch.
Exclusive brands from:
Pacific Direct
Johansens Preferred Toiletry Partner
UK Office Tel: +44 (0)1234 347140
Fax: +44 (0)1234 346480
E-mail: sales@pacific-direct.demon.co.uk
USA Office Tel: (607) 273 1984
Fax: (607) 273 5148
E-mail: pdirectusa@aol.com
www.pacificdirect.co.uk

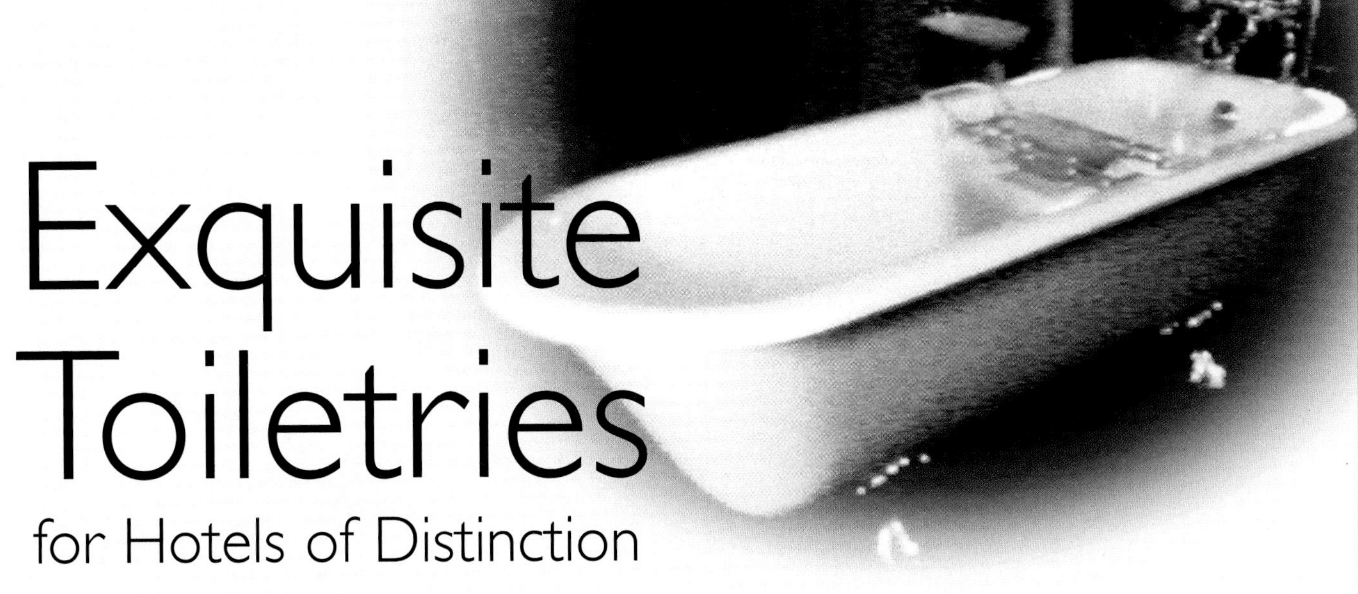

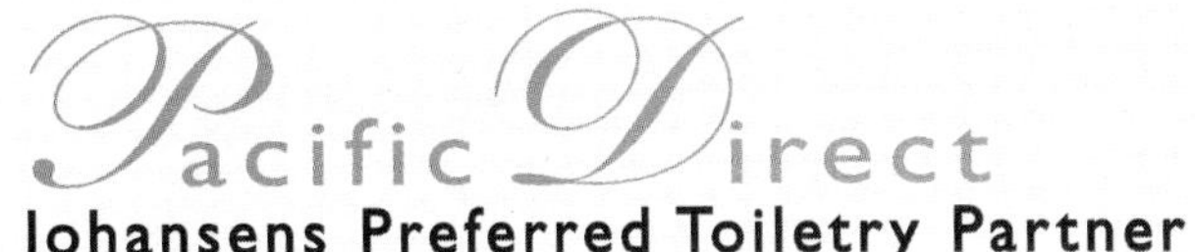

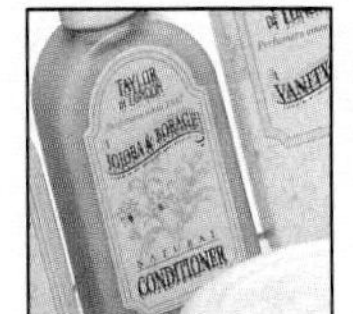

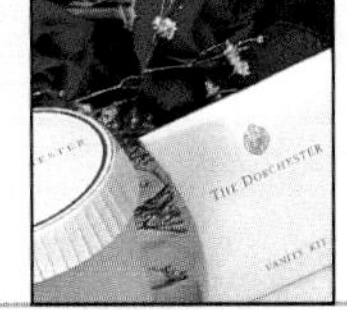

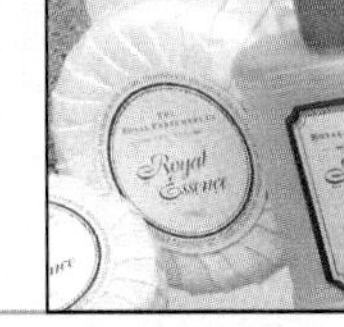

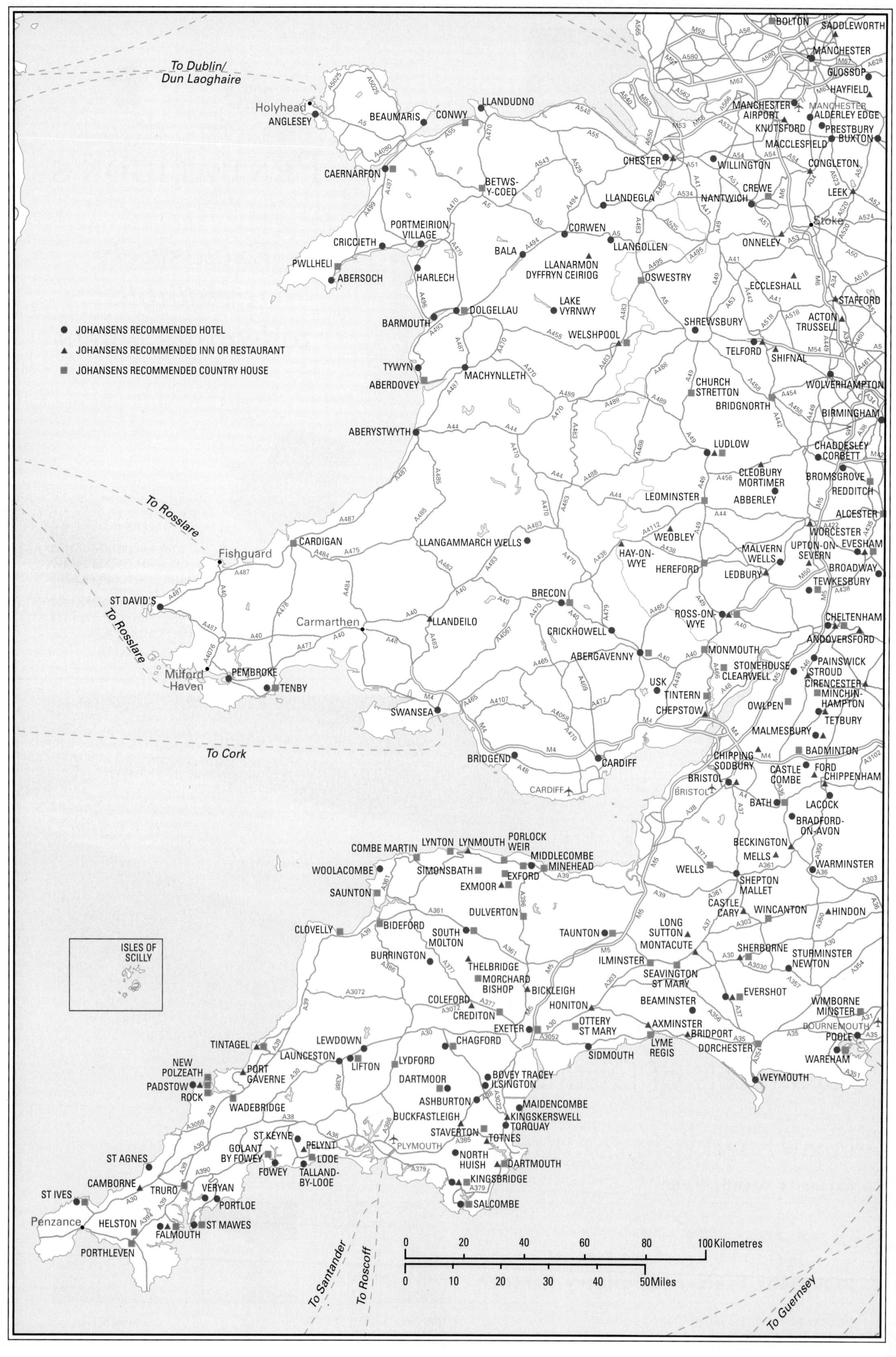

JOHANSENS RECOMMENDED HOTEL
JOHANSENS RECOMMENDED INN OR RESTAURANT
JOHANSENS RECOMMENDED COUNTRY HOUSE
To Dublin/
Dun Laoghaire
Holyhead
ANGLESEY
BEAUMARIS
CONWY
LLANDUDNO
CAERNARFON
BETWS-
Y-COED
PORTMEIRION
VILLAGE
CRICCIETH
PWLLHELI
ABERSOCH
HARLECH
BALA
CORWEN
LLANGOLLEN
LLANDEGLA
LLANARMON
DYFFRYN CEIRIOG
OSWESTRY
LAKE
VYRNWY
BARMOUTH
DOLGELLAU
WELSHPOOL
TYWYN
ABERDOVEY
MACHYNLLETH
ABERYSTWYTH
BOLTON
SADDLEWORTH
MANCHESTER
GLOSSOP
HAYFIELD
MANCHESTER
AIRPORT
ALDERLEY EDGE
KNUTSFORD
PRESTBURY
MACCLESFIELD
BUXTON
CHESTER
WILLINGTON
CONGLETON
CREWE
NANTWICH
LEEK
Stoke
ONNELEY
ECCLESHALL
STAFFORD
SHREWSBURY
ACTON
TRUSSELL
TELFORD
SHIFNAL
WOLVERHAMPTON
CHURCH
STRETTON
BRIDGNORTH
BIRMINGHAM
LUDLOW
CHADDESLEY
CORBETT
CLEOBURY
MORTIMER
BROMSGROVE
REDDITCH
LEOMINSTER
ABBERLEY
ALCESTER
WORCESTER
WEOBLEY
To Rosslare
Fishguard
CARDIGAN
LLANGAMMARCH WELLS
HAY-ON-
WYE
HEREFORD
MALVERN
WELLS
UPTON-ON-
SEVERN
EVESHAM
LEDBURY
BROADWAY
TEWKESBURY
ST DAVID'S
To Rosslare
Carmarthen
LLANDEILO
BRECON
CRICKHOWELL
ROSS-ON-
WYE
CHELTENHAM
ANDOVERSFORD
Milford
Haven
PEMBROKE
TENBY
ABERGAVENNY
MONMOUTH
PAINSWICK
STROUD
STONEHOUSE
CLEARWELL
CIRENCESTER
MINCHIN-
HAMPTON
USK
TINTERN
OWLPEN
SWANSEA
CHEPSTOW
TETBURY
MALMESBURY
To Cork
BRIDGEND
CARDIFF
CHIPPING
SODBURY
BADMINTON
CASTLE
COMBE
FORD
CHIPPENHAM
BRISTOL
CARDIFF
BRISTOL
BATH
LACOCK
BRADFORD-
ON-AVON
COMBE MARTIN
LYNTON
LYNMOUTH
PORLOCK
WEIR
MIDDLECOMBE
MINEHEAD
WOOLACOMBE
SIMONSBATH
EXFORD
EXMOOR
SAUNTON
BECKINGTON
MELLS
WARMINSTER
WELLS
SHEPTON
MALLET
DULVERTON
CASTLE
CARY
WINCANTON
HINDON
CLOVELLY
BIDEFORD
SOUTH
MOLTON
TAUNTON
LONG
SUTTON
MONTACUTE
ISLES OF
SCILLY
BURRINGTON
THELBRIDGE
MORCHARD
BISHOP
BICKLEIGH
ILMINSTER
SEAVINGTON
ST MARY
SHERBORNE
STURMINSTER
NEWTON
EVERSHOT
COLEFORD
CREDITON
HONITON
BEAMINSTER
WIMBORNE
MINSTER
BOURNEMOUTH
EXETER
OTTERY
ST MARY
AXMINSTER
BRIDPORT
POOLE
TINTAGEL
LEWDOWN
CHAGFORD
LYME
REGIS
DORCHESTER
WAREHAM
NEW
POLZEATH
LAUNCESTON
LIFTON
SIDMOUTH
PORT
GAVERNE
LYDFORD
BOVEY TRACEY
ILSINGTON
WEYMOUTH
PADSTOW
ROCK
DARTMOOR
WADEBRIDGE
ASHBURTON
MAIDENCOMBE
KINGSKERSWELL
BUCKFASTLEIGH
TORQUAY
STAVERTON
TOTNES
ST KEYNE
PELYNT
PLYMOUTH
GOLANT
BY FOWEY
LOOE
NORTH
HUISH
DARTMOUTH
ST AGNES
FOWEY
TALLAND-
BY-LOOE
CAMBORNE
TRURO
VERYAN
KINGSBRIDGE
ST IVES
PORTLOE
SALCOMBE
Penzance
HELSTON
FALMOUTH
ST MAWES
PORTHLEVEN
To Santander
To Roscoff
0 20 40 60 80 100 Kilometres
0 10 20 30 40 50 Miles
To Guernsey

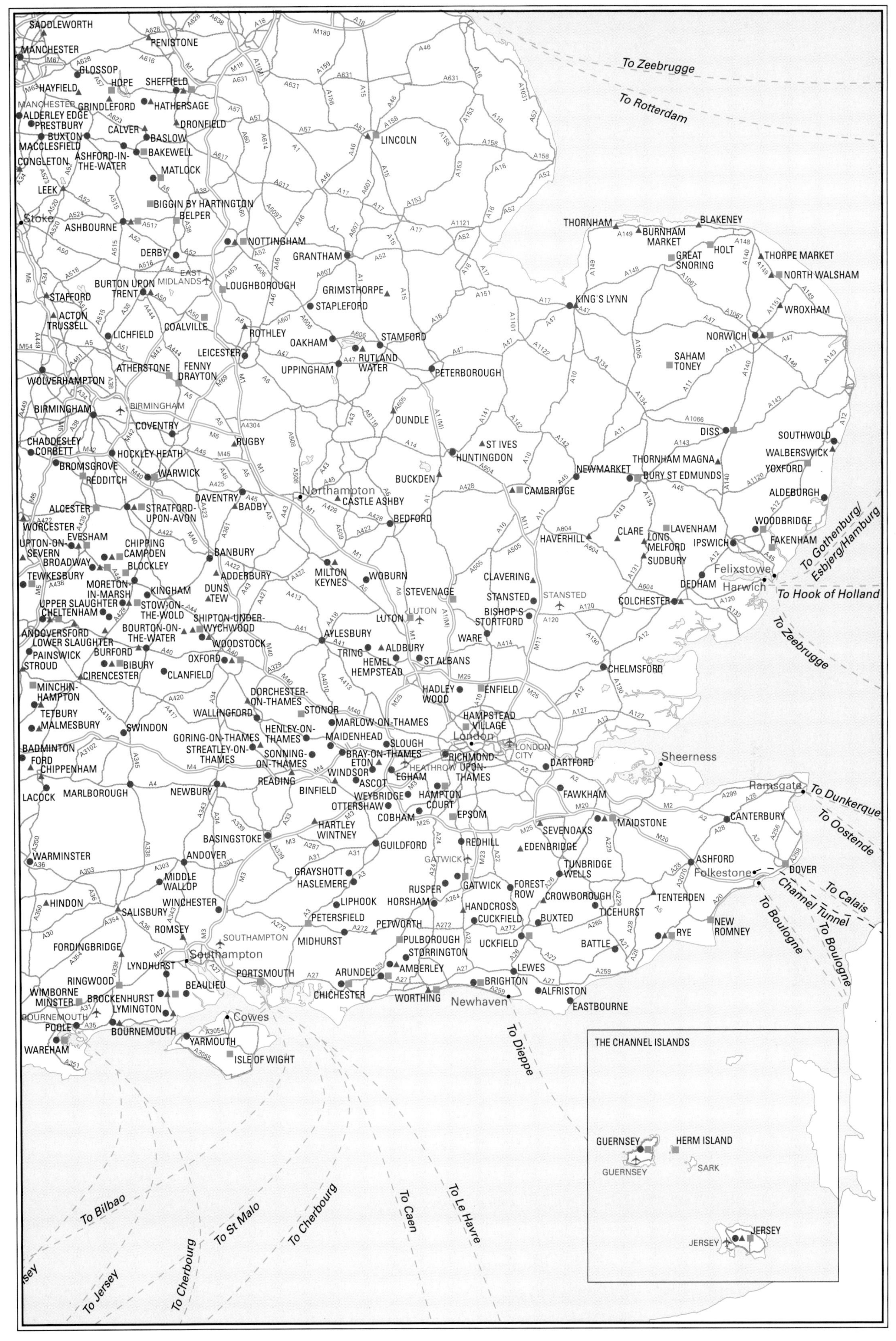

SADDLEWORTH
MANCHESTER
PENISTONE
GLOSSOP
HAYFIELD
HOPE
SHEFFIELD
MANCHESTER
GRINDLEFORD
HATHERSAGE
ALDERLEY EDGE
PRESTBURY
CALVER
DRONFIELD
BUXTON
BASLOW
MACCLESFIELD
ASHFORD-IN-THE-WATER
BAKEWELL
CONGLETON
MATLOCK
LEEK
BIGGIN BY HARTINGTON
BELPER
Stoke
ASHBOURNE
NOTTINGHAM
DERBY
EAST MIDLANDS
BURTON UPON TRENT
LOUGHBOROUGH
STAFFORD
ACTON TRUSSELL
LICHFIELD
COALVILLE
ROTHLEY
LEICESTER
ATHERSTONE
FENNY DRAYTON
WOLVERHAMPTON
BIRMINGHAM
BIRMINGHAM
COVENTRY
CHADDESLEY CORBETT
HOCKLEY HEATH
RUGBY
BROMSGROVE
REDDITCH
WARWICK
DAVENTRY
ALCESTER
STRATFORD-UPON-AVON
BADBY
WORCESTER
EVESHAM
UPTON-ON-SEVERN
CHIPPING CAMPDEN
BROADWAY
BLOCKLEY
BANBURY
TEWKESBURY
MORETON-IN-MARSH
ADDERBURY
KINGHAM
DUNS TEW
UPPER SLAUGHTER
STOW-ON-THE-WOLD
CHELTENHAM
SHIPTON-UNDER-WYCHWOOD
ANDOVERSFORD
BOURTON-ON-THE-WATER
LOWER SLAUGHTER
WOODSTOCK
PAINSWICK
BURFORD
OXFORD
STROUD
BIBURY
CIRENCESTER
CLANFIELD
MINCHIN-HAMPTON
TETBURY
MALMESBURY
SWINDON
BADMINTON
FORD
CHIPPENHAM
LACOCK
MARLBOROUGH
WARMINSTER
HINDON
SALISBURY
FORDINGBRIDGE
RINGWOOD
WIMBORNE MINSTER
BOURNEMOUTH
POOLE
WAREHAM
BOURNEMOUTH
LINCOLN
GRANTHAM
GRIMSTHORPE
STAPLEFORD
OAKHAM
STAMFORD
RUTLAND WATER
UPPINGHAM
PETERBOROUGH
OUNDLE
Northampton
CASTLE ASHBY
BEDFORD
MILTON KEYNES
WOBURN
STEVENAGE
LUTON
LUTON
AYLESBURY
TRING
ALDBURY
HEMEL HEMPSTEAD
ST ALBANS
DORCHESTER-ON-THAMES
STONOR
WALLINGFORD
HENLEY-ON-THAMES
MARLOW-ON-THAMES
GORING-ON-THAMES
STREATLEY-ON-THAMES
SONNING-ON-THAMES
MAIDENHEAD
SLOUGH
BRAY-ON-THAMES
ETON
WINDSOR
HEATHROW
EGHAM
NEWBURY
READING
ASCOT
BINFIELD
WEYBRIDGE
OTTERSHAW
HAMPTON COURT
COBHAM
EPSOM
BASINGSTOKE
HARTLEY WINTNEY
GUILDFORD
ANDOVER
MIDDLE WALLOP
WINCHESTER
GRAYSHOTT
HASLEMERE
LIPHOOK
PETERSFIELD
ROMSEY
SOUTHAMPTON
Southampton
LYNDHURST
BEAULIEU
BROCKENHURST
LYMINGTON
PORTSMOUTH
Cowes
YARMOUTH
ISLE OF WIGHT
CHICHESTER
MIDHURST
PETWORTH
PULBOROUGH
STORRINGTON
ARUNDEL
AMBERLEY
WORTHING
BRIGHTON
Newhaven
LEWES
ALFRISTON
EASTBOURNE
HORSHAM
RUSPER
GATWICK
GATWICK
REDHILL
CUCKFIELD
HANDCROSS
UCKFIELD
FOREST ROW
CROWBOROUGH
BUXTED
TICEHURST
BATTLE
RYE
NEW ROMNEY
TENTERDEN
ASHFORD
Folkestone
DOVER
CANTERBURY
Ramsgate
MAIDSTONE
SEVENOAKS
EDENBRIDGE
TUNBRIDGE WELLS
FAWKHAM
DARTFORD
Sheerness
London
LONDON CITY
RICHMOND-UPON-THAMES
HAMPSTEAD VILLAGE
HADLEY WOOD
ENFIELD
WARE
BISHOP'S STORTFORD
STANSTED
STANSTED
CLAVERING
CHELMSFORD
COLCHESTER
DEDHAM
Harwich
Felixstowe
IPSWICH
WOODBRIDGE
FAKENHAM
SUDBURY
LONG MELFORD
LAVENHAM
CLARE
HAVERHILL
CAMBRIDGE
NEWMARKET
BURY ST EDMUNDS
THORNHAM MAGNA
ALDEBURGH
YOXFORD
WALBERSWICK
SOUTHWOLD
DISS
HUNTINGDON
ST IVES
BUCKDEN
KING'S LYNN
THORNHAM
BURNHAM MARKET
BLAKENEY
HOLT
GREAT SNORING
THORPE MARKET
NORTH WALSHAM
WROXHAM
NORWICH
SAHAM TONEY
To Zeebrugge
To Rotterdam
To Gothenburg/Esbjerg/Hamburg
To Hook of Holland
To Zeebrugge
To Dunkerque
To Oostende
To Calais
Channel Tunnel
To Boulogne
To Boulogne
To Dieppe
To Le Havre
To Caen
To Cherbourg
To St Malo
To Cherbourg
To Bilbao
To Jersey
sey
THE CHANNEL ISLANDS
GUERNSEY
GUERNSEY
HERM ISLAND
SARK
JERSEY
JERSEY

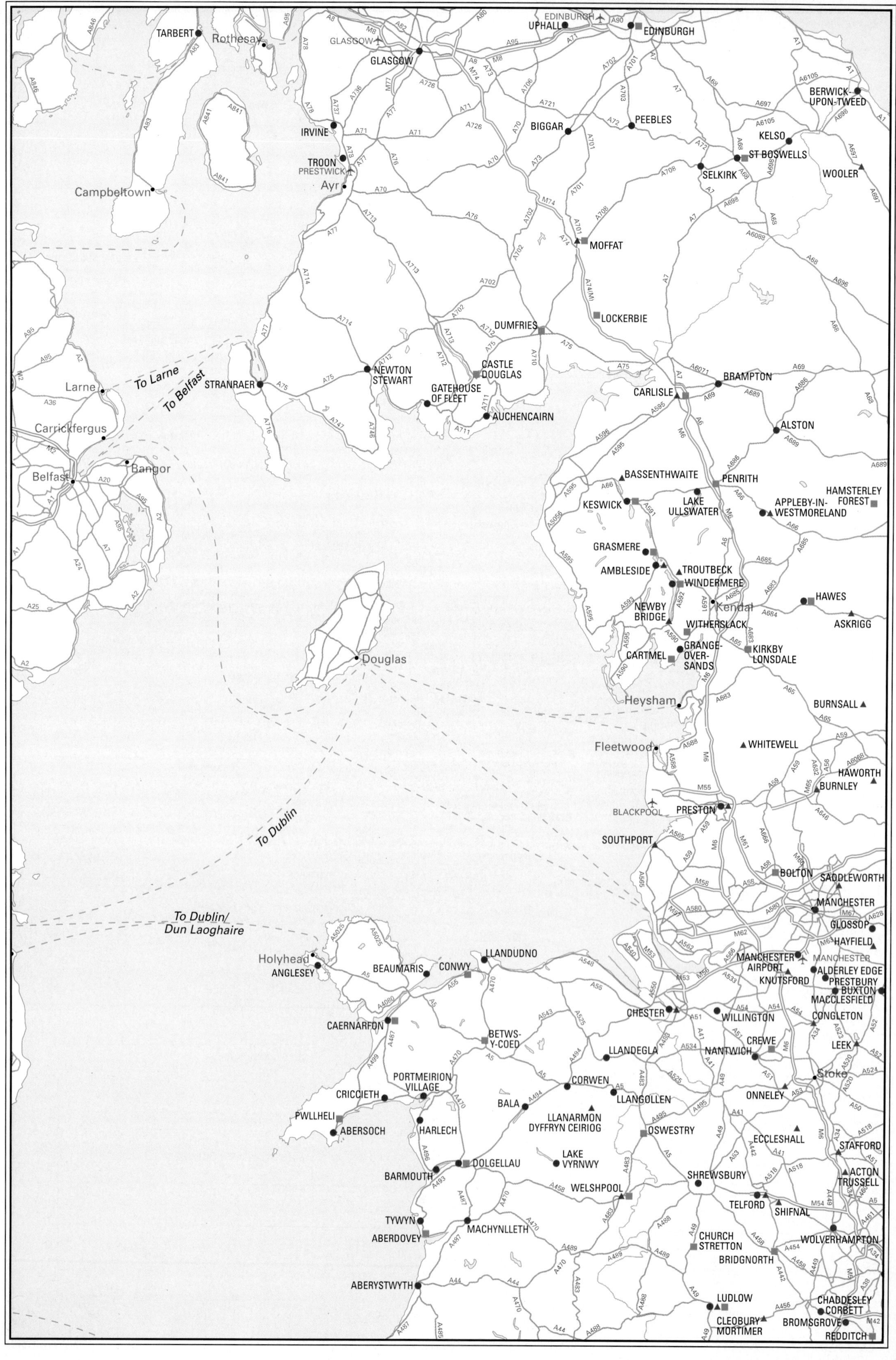

TARBERT
Rothesay
GLASGOW
EDINBURGH
UPHALL
EDINBURGH
GLASGOW
BERWICK-UPON-TWEED
IRVINE
BIGGAR
PEEBLES
KELSO
TROON
PRESTWICK
Ayr
ST BOSWELLS
SELKIRK
WOOLER
Campbeltown
MOFFAT
LOCKERBIE
DUMFRIES
To Larne
To Belfast
Larne
STRANRAER
NEWTON STEWART
CASTLE DOUGLAS
GATEHOUSE OF FLEET
AUCHENCAIRN
CARLISLE
BRAMPTON
Carrickfergus
ALSTON
Bangor
Belfast
BASSENTHWAITE
PENRITH
KESWICK
LAKE ULLSWATER
HAMSTERLEY FOREST
APPLEBY-IN-WESTMORELAND
GRASMERE
AMBLESIDE
TROUTBECK
WINDERMERE
HAWES
NEWBY BRIDGE
Kendal
ASKRIGG
WITHERSLACK
CARTMEL
GRANGE-OVER-SANDS
KIRKBY LONSDALE
Douglas
Heysham
BURNSALL
Fleetwood
WHITEWELL
HAWORTH
BURNLEY
BLACKPOOL
PRESTON
To Dublin
SOUTHPORT
BOLTON
SADDLEWORTH
MANCHESTER
GLOSSOP
To Dublin/ Dun Laoghaire
HAYFIELD
MANCHESTER AIRPORT
MANCHESTER
Holyhead
ANGLESEY
LLANDUDNO
BEAUMARIS
CONWY
ALDERLEY EDGE
KNUTSFORD
PRESTBURY
BUXTON
MACCLESFIELD
CHESTER
WILLINGTON
CONGLETON
CAERNARFON
BETWS-Y-COED
CREWE
LEEK
LLANDEGLA
NANTWICH
Stoke
PORTMEIRION VILLAGE
CORWEN
CRICCIETH
LLANGOLLEN
ONNELEY
BALA
LLANARMON DYFFRYN CEIRIOG
PWLLHELI
ABERSOCH
HARLECH
OSWESTRY
ECCLESHALL
STAFFORD
LAKE VYRNWY
BARMOUTH
DOLGELLAU
SHREWSBURY
ACTON TRUSSELL
WELSHPOOL
TELFORD
SHIFNAL
TYWYN
MACHYNLLETH
ABERDOVEY
CHURCH STRETTON
WOLVERHAMPTON
BRIDGNORTH
ABERYSTWYTH
LUDLOW
CHADDESLEY CORBETT
CLEOBURY MORTIMER
BROMSGROVE
REDDITCH

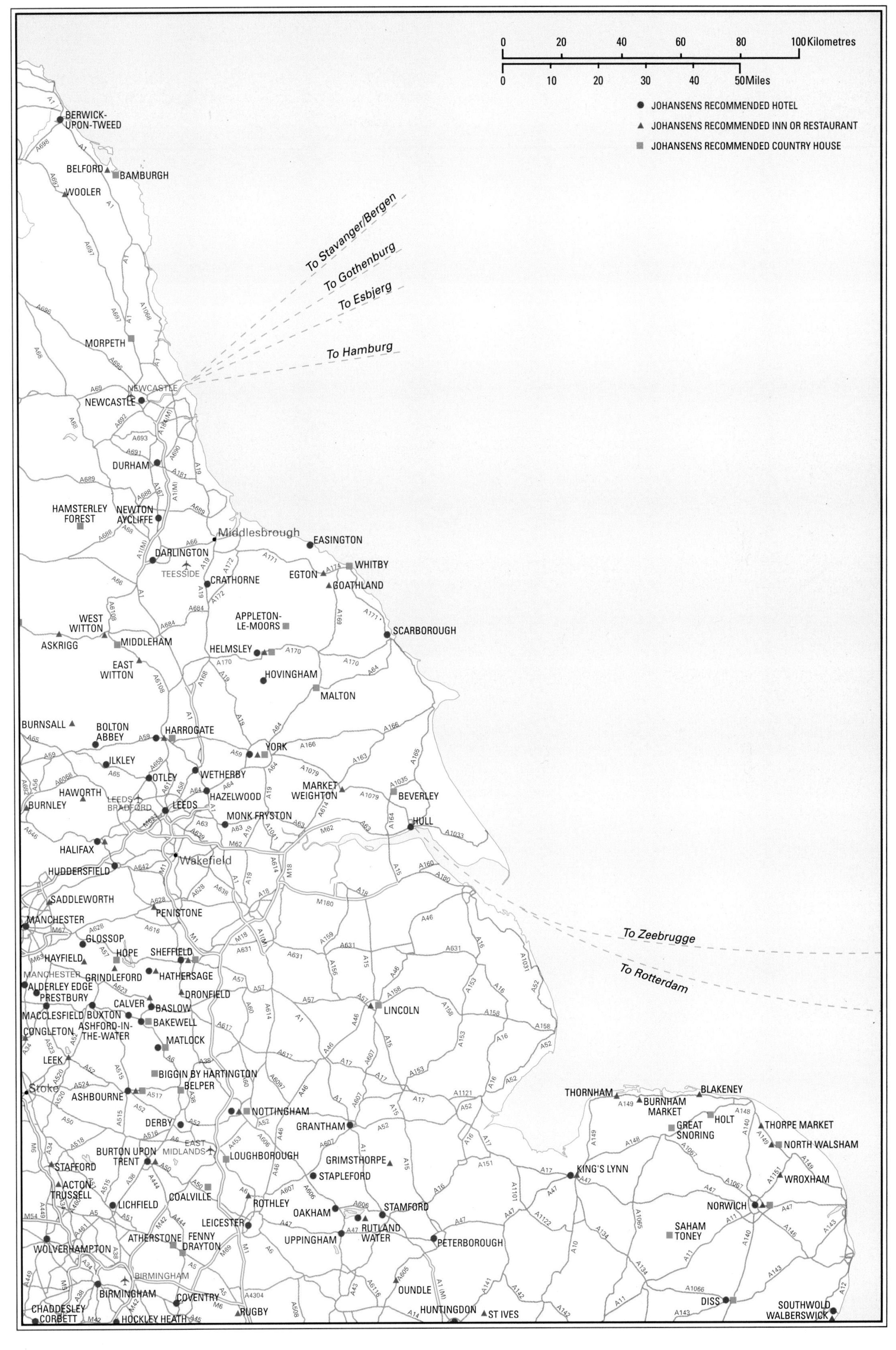
0 20 40 60 80 100 Kilometres
0 10 20 30 40 50 Miles
JOHANSENS RECOMMENDED HOTEL
JOHANSENS RECOMMENDED INN OR RESTAURANT
JOHANSENS RECOMMENDED COUNTRY HOUSE
To Stavanger/Bergen
To Gothenburg
To Esbjerg
To Hamburg
To Zeebrugge
To Rotterdam
BERWICK-UPON-TWEED
BELFORD
BAMBURGH
WOOLER
MORPETH
NEWCASTLE
DURHAM
HAMSTERLEY FOREST
NEWTON AYCLIFFE
Middlesbrough
EASINGTON
DARLINGTON
TEESSIDE
WHITBY
EGTON
GOATHLAND
CRATHORNE
APPLETON-LE-MOORS
WEST WITTON
ASKRIGG
MIDDLEHAM
SCARBOROUGH
HELMSLEY
EAST WITTON
HOVINGHAM
MALTON
BURNSALL
BOLTON ABBEY
HARROGATE
YORK
ILKLEY
WETHERBY
OTLEY
MARKET WEIGHTON
BEVERLEY
HAWORTH
HAZELWOOD
BURNLEY
LEEDS BRADFORD
LEEDS
MONK FRYSTON
HULL
HALIFAX
Wakefield
HUDDERSFIELD
SADDLEWORTH
PENISTONE
MANCHESTER
GLOSSOP
HAYFIELD
HOPE
SHEFFIELD
GRINDLEFORD
HATHERSAGE
ALDERLEY EDGE
DRONFIELD
PRESTBURY
CALVER
BASLOW
LINCOLN
MACCLESFIELD
BUXTON
ASHFORD-IN-THE-WATER
BAKEWELL
CONGLETON
MATLOCK
LEEK
BIGGIN BY HARTINGTON
Stoke
ASHBOURNE
BELPER
THORNHAM
BLAKENEY
BURNHAM MARKET
NOTTINGHAM
HOLT
DERBY
GRANTHAM
GREAT SNORING
THORPE MARKET
NORTH WALSHAM
EAST MIDLANDS
BURTON UPON TRENT
LOUGHBOROUGH
GRIMSTHORPE
STAFFORD
STAPLEFORD
KING'S LYNN
WROXHAM
ACTON TRUSSELL
COALVILLE
LICHFIELD
ROTHLEY
STAMFORD
NORWICH
OAKHAM
LEICESTER
RUTLAND WATER
SAHAM TONEY
ATHERSTONE
FENNY DRAYTON
UPPINGHAM
PETERBOROUGH
WOLVERHAMPTON
BIRMINGHAM
OUNDLE
COVENTRY
DISS
CHADDESLEY CORBETT
HOCKLEY HEATH
RUGBY
HUNTINGDON
ST IVES
SOUTHWOLD
WALBERSWICK

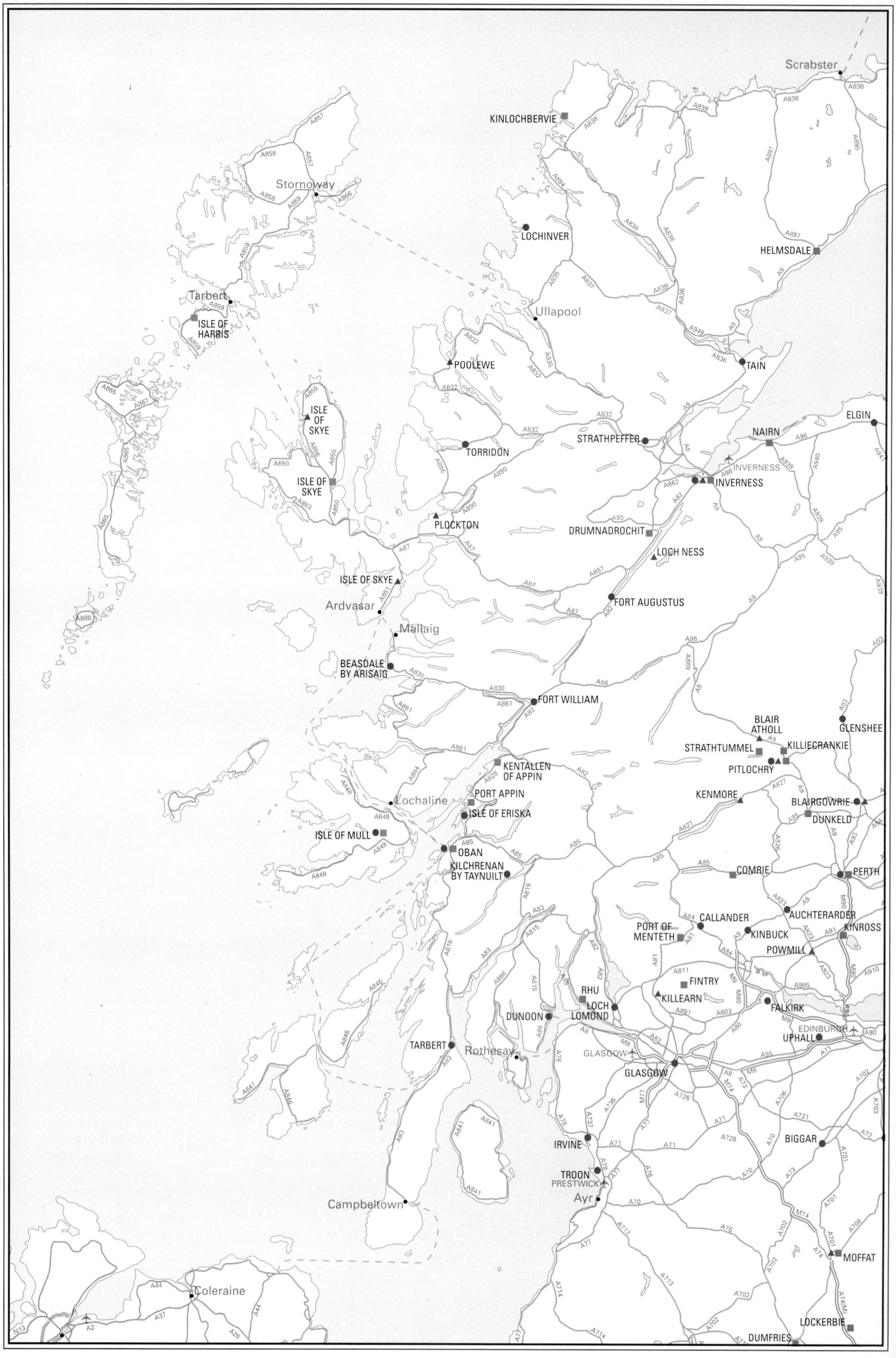

Scrabster
KINLOCHBERVIE
Stornoway
LOCHINVER
HELMSDALE
Tarbert
ISLE OF HARRIS
Ullapool
POOLEWE
TAIN
ISLE OF SKYE
ELGIN
NAIRN
STRATHPEFFER
TORRIDON
INVERNESS
INVERNESS
ISLE OF SKYE
DRUMNADROCHIT
PLOCKTON
LOCH NESS
ISLE OF SKYE
FORT AUGUSTUS
Ardvasar
Mallaig
BEASDALE BY ARISAIG
FORT WILLIAM
BLAIR ATHOLL
GLENSHEE
STRATHTUMMEL
KILLIECRANKIE
PITLOCHRY
KENTALLEN OF APPIN
PORT APPIN
KENMORE
Lochaline
BLAIRGOWRIE
ISLE OF ERISKA
DUNKELD
ISLE OF MULL
OBAN
KILCHRENAN BY TAYNUILT
COMRIE
PERTH
AUCHTERARDER
CALLANDER
PORT OF MENTETH
KINBUCK
KINROSS
POWMILL
FINTRY
KILLEARN
RHU
LOCH LOMOND
FALKIRK
DUNOON
EDINBURGH
UPHALL
TARBERT
Rothesay
GLASGOW
GLASGOW
BIGGAR
IRVINE
TROON
PRESTWICK
Ayr
Campbeltown
MOFFAT
Coleraine
LOCKERBIE
DUMFRIES

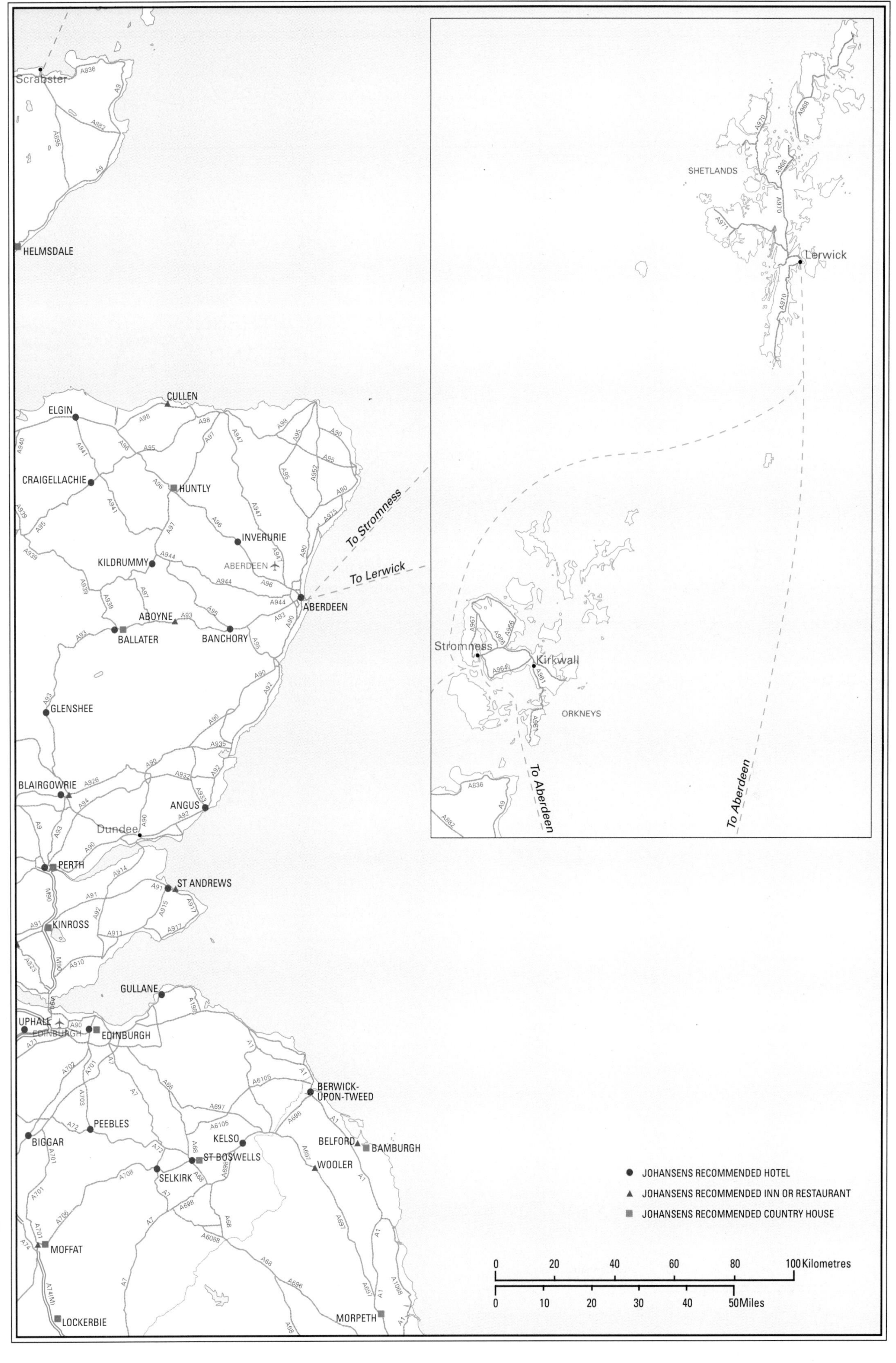

Scrabster
HELMSDALE
CULLEN
ELGIN
CRAIGELLACHIE
HUNTLY
INVERURIE
KILDRUMMY
ABERDEEN
ABOYNE
BALLATER
BANCHORY
GLENSHEE
BLAIRGOWRIE
ANGUS
Dundee
PERTH
ST ANDREWS
KINROSS
GULLANE
UPHALL
EDINBURGH
BERWICK-UPON-TWEED
PEEBLES
BIGGAR
KELSO
ST BOSWELLS
SELKIRK
BELFORD
BAMBURGH
WOOLER
MOFFAT
LOCKERBIE
MORPETH
To Stromness
To Lerwick
SHETLANDS
Lerwick
Stromness
Kirkwall
ORKNEYS
To Aberdeen
To Aberdeen
JOHANSENS RECOMMENDED HOTEL
JOHANSENS RECOMMENDED INN OR RESTAURANT
JOHANSENS RECOMMENDED COUNTRY HOUSE
0 20 40 60 80 100 Kilometres
0 10 20 30 40 50 Miles

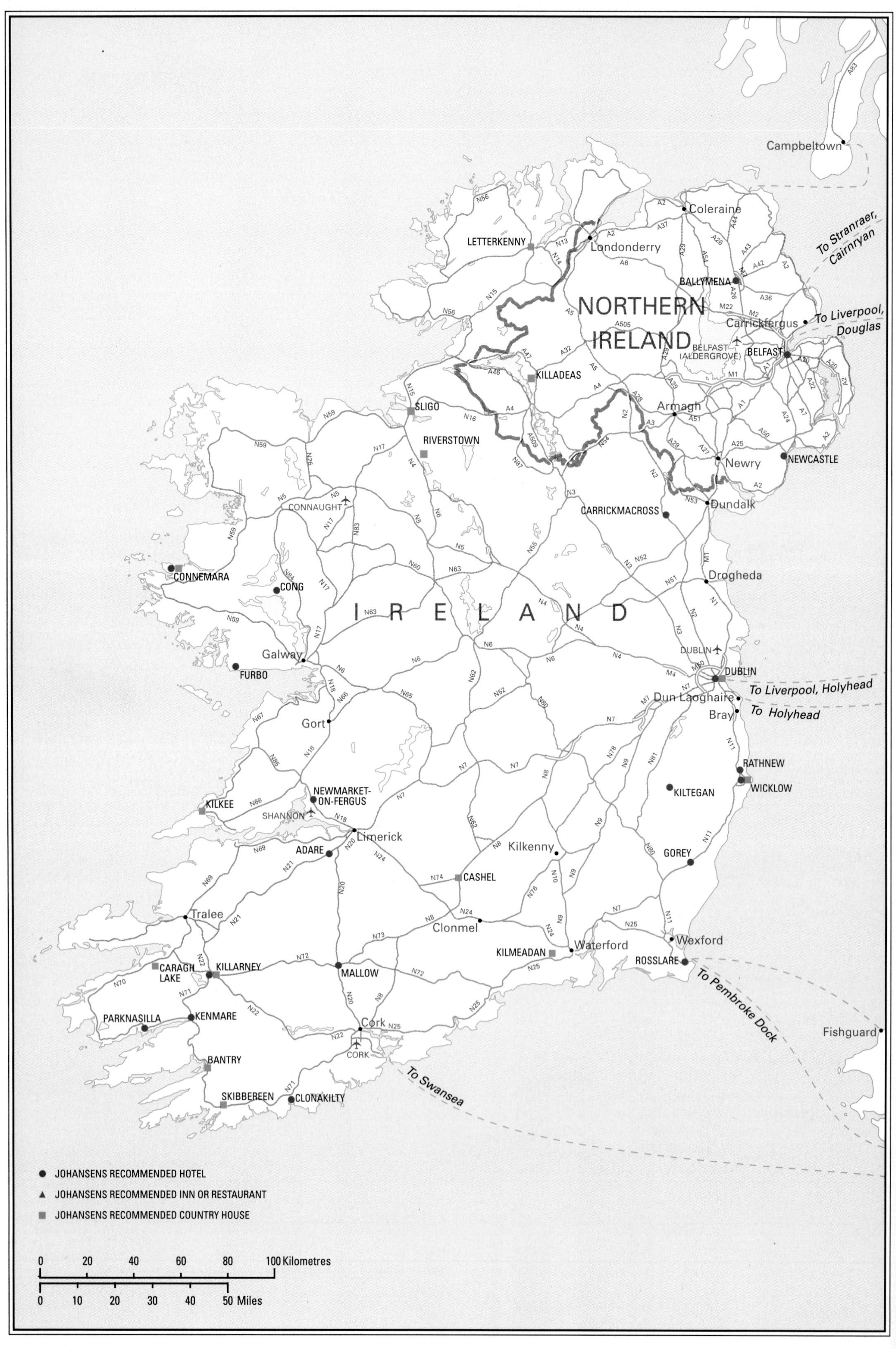

Campbeltown
To Stranraer, Cairnryan
Coleraine
Londonderry
LETTERKENNY
BALLYMENA
NORTHERN IRELAND
Carrickfergus
To Liverpool, Douglas
BELFAST (ALDERGROVE)
BELFAST
KILLADEAS
SLIGO
Armagh
RIVERSTOWN
Newry
NEWCASTLE
CONNAUGHT
CARRICKMACROSS
Dundalk
CONNEMARA
CONG
Drogheda
IRELAND
Galway
DUBLIN
FURBO
DUBLIN
To Liverpool, Holyhead
Dun Laoghaire
Bray
To Holyhead
Gort
RATHNEW
WICKLOW
KILTEGAN
KILKEE
NEWMARKET-ON-FERGUS
SHANNON
Limerick
ADARE
Kilkenny
GOREY
CASHEL
Tralee
Clonmel
Wexford
KILMEADAN
Waterford
ROSSLARE
CARAGH LAKE
KILLARNEY
MALLOW
To Pembroke Dock
PARKNASILLA
KENMARE
Cork
Fishguard
CORK
BANTRY
To Swansea
SKIBBEREEN
CLONAKILTY
JOHANSENS RECOMMENDED HOTEL
JOHANSENS RECOMMENDED INN OR RESTAURANT
JOHANSENS RECOMMENDED COUNTRY HOUSE
0 20 40 60 80 100 Kilometres
0 10 20 30 40 50 Miles

When we first set out to design the CR-V, we approached it with the same philosophy that Sochiro Honda, our founder, encouraged.

He insisted that everything done in his name be done for a reason, rather than developing technology for technology's sake. Everything has to have a purpose, a relevance, a benefit.

For example, with the CR-V, we bore in mind that the vast majority of journeys it would undertake would be on tarmac. So instead of giving it permanent 4-wheel drive, we developed a system that could detect when 4-wheel drive was needed and immediately engage it.

It's this kind of thinking that's evident across the Honda range, whether in major pieces of technology, or in the more considered placing of switchgear.

For dealers and details, phone **0345 159 159** and find out why we try to follow our founder's example.

Technology you can enjoy, from Honda.

Some places are more accessible than others.

Johansens Recommended Country Houses in Great Britain & Ireland

ENGLAND

Alcester (Arrow) – Arrow Mill Hotel And Restaurant, Arrow, Nr Alcester, Warwickshire B49 5NL. Tel: 01789 762419

Appleton-Le-Moors – Appleton Hall, Appleton-Le-Moors, North Yorkshire YO6 6TF. Tel: 01751 417227

Arundel (Burpham) – Burpham Country House Hotel, Old Down, Burpham, Nr Arundel, West Sussex BN18 9RV. Tel: 01903 882160

Ashbourne – The Beeches Farmhouse, Waldley, Doveridge, Nr Ashbourne, Derbyshire DE6 5LR. Tel: 01889 590288

Atherstone – Chapel House, Friars' Gate, Atherstone, Warwickshire CV9 1EY. Tel: 01827 718949

Badminton – Petty France, Dunkirk, Badminton, South Gloucestershire GL9 1AF. Tel: 01454 238361

Bakewell (Rowsley) – East Lodge Country House Hotel, Rowsley, Matlock, Derbyshire DE4 2EF. Tel: 01629 734474

Bakewell (Rowsley) – The Peacock Hotel at Rowsley, Rowsley, Near Matlock, Derbyshire DE4 2EB. Tel: 01629 733518

Bamburgh – Waren House Hotel, Waren Mill, Bamburgh, Northumberland NE70 7EE. Tel: 01668 214581

Bath – Apsley House, 141 Newbridge Hill, Bath, B & NE Somerset BA1 3PT. Tel: 01225 336966

Bath (Norton St Philip) – Bath Lodge Hotel, Norton St Philip, Bath, Somerset BA3 6NH. Tel: 01225 723040

Bath – Bloomfield House, 146 Bloomfield Road, Bath, Somerset BA2 2AS. Tel: 01225 420105

Bath – Duke's Hotel, Great Pulteney Street, Bath, Somerset BA2 4DN. Tel: 01225 463512

Bath – Eagle House, Church Street, Bathford, Somerset BA1 7RS. Tel: 01225 859946

Bath – Oldfields, 102 Wells Road, Bath, Somerset BA2 3AL. Tel: 01225 317984

Bath – Paradise House, Holloway, Bath, Somerset BA2 4PX. Tel: 01225 317723

Bath (Bradford-On-Avon) – Widbrook Grange, Trowbridge Road, Bradford-On-Avon, Wiltshire BA15 1UH. Tel: 01225 864750 / 863173

Bath (Woolverton) – Woolverton House, Nr Bath, Somerset BA3 6QS. Tel: 01373 830415

Belper (Shottle) – Dannah Farm Country Guest House, Bowman's Lane, Shottle, Nr Belper, Derbyshire DE56 2DR. Tel: 01773 550273 / 630

Beverley (Walkington) – The Manor House, Northlands, Walkington, East Yorkshire HU17 8RT. Tel: 01482 881645

Bibury – Bibury Court, Bibury, Gloucestershire GL7 5NT. Tel: 01285 740337

Bideford (Northam) – Yeoldon House Hotel, Durrant Lane, Northam, Nr Bideford, Devon EX39 2RL. Tel: 01237 474400

Biggin-By-Hartington – Biggin Hall, Biggin-By-Hartington, Buxton, Derbyshire SK17 0DH. Tel: 01298 84451

Blockley (Chipping Campden) – Lower Brook House, Blockley, Nr Moreton-In-Marsh, Gloucestershire GL56 9DS. Tel: 01386 700286

Bolton (Edgworth) – Quarlton Manor Farm, Plantation Road, Edgeworth,Turton, Bolton, Lancashire BL7 0DD. Tel: 01204 852277

Bridgnorth – Cross Lane House Hotel, Cross Lane Head, Bridgnorth, Shropshire WV16 4SJ. Tel: 01746 764887

Brighton – The Granville, 124 Kings Road, Brighton, East Sussex BN1 2FA. Tel: 01273 326302

Broadway – Collin House Hotel, Collin Lane, Broadway, Worcestershire WR12 7PB. Tel: 01386 858354

Broadway (Willersey) – The Old Rectory, Church Street, Willersey, Broadway, Gloucestershire WR12 7PN. Tel: 01386 853729

Brockenhurst – Thatched Cottage Hotel & Restaurant, 16 Brookley Road, Brockenhurst, New Forest, Hampshire SO42 7RR. Tel: 01590 623090

Brockenhurst – Whitley Ridge & Country House Hotel, Beaulieu Road, Brockenhurst, New Forest, Hampshire SO42 7QL. Tel: 01590 622354

Bury St. Edmunds – The Priory, Tollgate, Bury St. Edmunds, Suffolk IP32 6EH. Tel: 01284 766181

Cambridge (Melbourn) – Melbourn Bury, Melbourn, Cambridgeshire, Nr Royston, Cambridgeshire SG8 6DE. Tel: 01763 261151

Carlisle (Crosby-On-Eden) – Crosby Lodge Country House Hotel, High Crosby, Crosby-On-Eden, Carlisle, Cumbria CA6 4QZ. Tel: 01228 573618

Cartmel – Aynsome Manor Hotel, Cartmel, Grange-Over-Sands, Cumbria LA11 6HH. Tel: 015395 36653

Chagford – Easton Court Hotel, Easton Cross, Chagford, Devon TQ13 8JL. Tel: 01647 433469

Cheltenham (Charlton Kings) – Charlton Kings Hotel, Charlton Kings, Cheltenham, Gloucestershire GL52 6UU. Tel: 01242 231061

Cheltenham (Withington) – Halewell, Halewell Close, Withington, Nr Cheltenham, Gloucestershire GL54 4BN. Tel: 01242 890238

Chichester (Apuldram) – Crouchers Bottom Country Hotel, Birdham Road, Apuldram, Nr Chichester, West Sussex PO20 7EH. Tel: 01243 784995

Chichester (Charlton) – Woodstock House Hotel, Charlton, Nr Chichester, West Sussex PO18 0HU. Tel: 01243 811666

Chipping Campden (Broad Campden) – The Malt House, Broad Campden, Gloucestershire GL55 6UU. Tel: 01386 840295

Church Stretton (Little Stretton) – Mynd House Hotel & Restaurant, Little Stretton, Church Stretton, Nr Shrewsbury, Shropshire SY6 6RB. Tel: 01694 722212

Clearwell – Tudor Farmhouse Hotel & Restaurant, High Street, Clearwell, Nr Coleford, Gloucestershire GL16 8JS. Tel: 01594 833046

Clovelly (Horns Cross) – Foxdown Manor, Horns Cross, Clovelly, Devon EX39 5PJ. Tel: 01237 451325

Coalville (Greenhill) – Abbots Oak, Greenhill, Coalville, Leicestershire LE67 4UY. Tel: 01530 832 328

Combe Martin (East Down) – Ashelford, Ashelford, East Down, Nr Barnstaple, Devon EX31 4LU. Tel: 01271 850469

Crediton (Coleford) – Coombe House Country Hotel, Coleford, Crediton, Devon EX17 5BY. Tel: 01363 84487

Crewe (Balterley) – Pear Tree Lake Farms, Balterley, Nr Crewe, Cheshire CW2 5QE. Tel: 01270 820307

Dartmoor (Haytor Vale) – Bel Alp House, Haytor, Nr Bovey Tracey, Devon TQ13 9XX. Tel: 01364 661217

Dartmouth – Broome Court, Bromhill, Dartmouth, Devon TQ6 0LD. Tel: 01803 834275

Dartmouth (Kingswear) – Nonsuch House, Church Hill, Kingswear, Dartmouth, Devon TQ6 0BX. Tel: 01803 752829

Dartmoor (Nr Two Bridges) – Prince Hall Hotel, Two Bridges, Dartmoor, Devon PL20 6SA. Tel: 01822 890403

Diss (Fressingfield) – Chippenhall Hall, Fressingfield, Eye, Suffolk IP21 5TD. Tel: 01379 588180 / 586733

Dorchester (Lower Bockhampton) – Yalbury Cottage Hotel, Lower Bockhampton, Dorchester, Dorset DT2 8PZ. Tel: 01305 262382

Dover (West Cliffe) – Wallett's Court, West Cliffe, St. Margaret's-at-Cliffe, Nr Dover, Kent CT15 6EW. Tel: 01304 852424

Dover (Temple Ewell) – The Woodville Hall, Temple Ewell, Dover, Kent CT16 1DJ. Tel: 01304 825256

Dulverton – Ashwick Country House Hotel, Dulverton, Somerset TA22 9QD. Tel: 01398 323868

Enfield (London) – Oak Lodge Hotel, 80 Village Road, Bush Hill Park, Enfield, Middlesex EN1 2EU. Tel: 0181 360 7082

Epsom – Chalk Lane Hotel, Chalk Lane, Epsom, Surrey KT18 7BB. Tel: 01372 721179

Evershot – Rectory House, Fore Street, Evershot, Dorset DT2 0JW. Tel: 0193583 273

Evesham (Harvington) – The Mill At Harvington, Anchor Lane, Harvington, Evesham, Worcestershire WR11 5NR. Tel: 01386 870688

Exeter (Dunchideock) – The Lord Haldon Hotel, Dunchideock, Nr Exeter, Devon EX6 7YF. Tel: 01392 832483

Exford (Exmoor) – The Crown Hotel, Exford, Exmoor National Park, Somerset TA24 7PP. Tel: 01643 831554/5

Exmoor (Minehead) – The Beacon Country House Hotel, Beacon Road, Minehead, Somerset TA24 5SD. Tel: 01643 703476

Fakenham (*WEEKLY LET*) – Vere Lodge, South Raynham, Fakenham, Norfolk NR21 7HE. Tel: 01328 838261

Falmouth (Mawnan Smith) – Trelawne Hotel-The Hutches Restaurant, Mawnan Smith, Nr Falmouth, Cornwall TR11 5HS. Tel: 01326 250226

Fenny Drayton (Leicestershire) – White Wings, Quaker Close, Fenny Drayton, Nr Nuneaton, Leicestershire CV13 6BS. Tel: 01827 716100

Gatwick (Charlwood) – Stanhill Court Hotel, Stanhill, Charlwood, Nr Horley, Surrey RH6 0EP. Tel: 01293 862166

Golant by Fowey – The Cormorant Hotel, Golant, Fowey, Cornwall PL23 1LL. Tel: 01726 833426

Grasmere (Rydal Water) – White Moss House, Rydal Water, Grasmere, Cumbria LA22 9SE. Tel: 015394 35295

Great Snoring – The Old Rectory, Great Snoring, Fakenham, Norfolk NR12 0HP. Tel: 01328 820597

Hampstead Village (London) – Sandringham Hotel, 3 Holford Road, Hampstead Village, London, NW3 1AD. Tel: 0171 435 1569

Hampton Court (Hampton Wick) – Chase Lodge, 10 Park Road, Hampton Wick, Kingston Upon Thames, Surrey KT1 4AS. Tel: 0181 943 1862

Hamsterley Forest (Near Durham) – Grove House, Hamsterley Forest, Nr Bishop Auckland, Co.Durham DL13 3NL. Tel: 01388 488203

Harrogate – The White House, 10 Park Parade, Harrogate, North Yorkshire HG1 5AH. Tel: 01423 501388

Hawes (Wensleydale) – Rookhurst Georgian Country House Hotel, West End, Gayle, Hawes, North Yorkshire DL8 3RT. Tel: 01969 667454

Helmsley (Nunnington) – Ryedale Country Lodge, Nunnington, Nr Helmsley, York, North Yorkshire YO6 5XB. Tel: 01439 748246

Helston – Nansloe Manor, Meneage Road, Helston, Cornwall TR13 0SB. Tel: 01326 574691

Hereford (Fownhope) – The Bowens Country House, Fownhope, Herefordshire HR1 4PS. Tel: 01432 860430

Hereford (Ullingswick) – The Steppes, Ullingswick, Nr Hereford, Herefordshire HR1 3JG. Tel: 01432 820424

Holt (Felbrigg) – Felbrigg Lodge, Aylmerton, Norfolk NR11 8RA. Tel: 01263 837588

Hope (Castleton) – Underleigh House, Off Edale Road, Hope, Hope Valley, Derbyshire S33 6RF. Tel: 01433 621372

Ilminster (Cricket Malherbie) – The Old Rectory, Cricket Malherbie, Ilminster, Somerset TA19 0PW. Tel: 01460 54364

Isle of Wight (Shanklin) – Rylstone Manor, Rylstone Gardens, Shanklin, Isle of Wight PO37 6RE. Tel: 01983 862806

Keswick (LakeThirlmere) – Dale Head Hall Lakeside Hotel, Thirlmere, Keswick, Cumbria CA12 4TN. Tel: 017687 72478

Keswick (Newlands) – Swinside Lodge Hotel, Grange Road, Newlands, Keswick, Cumbria CA12 5UE. Tel: 017687 72948

Kingsbridge (Chillington) – The White House, Chillington, Kingsbridge, Devon TQ7 2JX. Tel: 01548 580580

Kirkby Lonsdale – Hipping Hall, Cowan Bridge, Kirkby Lonsdale, Cumbria LA6 2JJ. Tel: 015242 71187

Lavenham – Lavenham Priory, Water Street, Lavenham, Sudbury, Suffolk CO10 9RW. Tel: 01787 247404

Leominster – Lower Bache House, Kimbolton, Nr Leominster, Herefordshire HR6 0ER. Tel: 01568 750304

Lifton (Sprytown) – The Thatched Cottage Country Hotel And Restaurant, Sprytown, Lifton, Devon PL16 0AY. Tel: 01566 784224

Lincoln (Washingborough) – Washingborough Hall, Church Hill, Washingborough, Lincoln, Lincolnshire LN4 1BE. Tel: 01522 790340

Looe (Talland Bay) – Allhays Country House, Talland Bay, Looe, Cornwall PL13 2JB. Tel: 01503 272434

Looe (Widegates) – Coombe Farm, Widegates, Looe, Cornwall PL13 1QN. Tel: 01503 240223

Loughborough – The Old Manor Hotel, 11-14 Sparrow Hill, Loughborough, Leicestershire LE11 1BT. Tel: 01509 211228

Ludlow (Diddlebury) – Delbury Hall, Diddlebury, Craven Arms, Shropshire SY7 9DH. Tel: 01584 841267

Ludlow (Overton) – Overton Grange Hotel, Overton, Ludlow, Shropshire SY8 4AD. Tel: 01584 873500

Luton (Little Offley) – Little Offley, Hitchin, Hertfordshire SG5 3BU. Tel: 01462 768243

Lydford (Vale Down) – Moor View House, Vale Down, Lydford, Devon EX20 4BB. Tel: 01822 820220

Lyme Regis (Charmouth) – Thatch Lodge Hotel, The Street, Charmouth, Nr Lyme Regis, Dorset DT6 6PQ. Tel: 01297 560407

Lynton – Hewitt's Hotel, North Walk, Lynton, Devon EX35 6HJ. Tel: 01598 752293

Maidstone (Boughton Monchelsea) – Tanyard, Wierton Hill, Boughton Monchelsea, Nr Maidstone, Kent ME17 4JT. Tel: 01622 744705

Malton – Newstead Grange, Norton-On-Derwent, Malton, North Yorkshire YO17 9PJ. Tel: 01653 692502

Matlock (Dethick) – The Manor Farmhouse, Dethick, Matlock, Derbyshire DE4 5GG. Tel: 01629 534246

Matlock – Sheriff Lodge Hotel, The Dimple, Dimple Road, Matlock, Derbyshire DE4 3JX. Tel: 01629 760760

Middlecombe (Minehead) – Periton Park Hotel, Middlecombe, Nr Minehead, Somerset TA24 8SN. Tel: 01643 706885

Middleham (Wensleydale) – Millers House Hotel, Middleham, Wensleydale, North Yorkshire DL8 4NR. Tel: 01969 622630

Minchinhampton – Burleigh Court, Minchinhampton, Gloucestershire GL5 2PF. Tel: 01453 883804

Minehead – Channel House Hotel, Church Path, Minehead, Somerset TA24 5QG. Tel: 01643 703229

Morchard Bishop – Wigham, Morchard Bishop, Crediton, Devon EX17 6RJ. Tel: 01363 877350

Morpeth (Eshott) – Eshott Hall, Eshott, Morpeth, Nr Newcastle-upon-Tyne, Northumberland ME65 9EP. Tel: 01670 787777

New Polzeath – The Cornish Cottage Hotel & Gourmet Restaurant, New Polzeath, Rock, North Cornwall PL27 6US. Tel: 01208 862213

New Romney (Littlestone) – Romney Bay House, Coast Road, Littlestone, New Romney, Kent TN28 8QY. Tel: 01797 364747

North Walsham – Beechwood Hotel, Cromer Road, North Walsham, Norfolk NR28 0HD. Tel: 01692 403231

Norwich – The Beeches Hotel & Victorian Gardens, 4-6 Earlham Road, Norwich, Norfolk NR2 3DB. Tel: 01603 621167

Norwich (Old Catton) – Catton Old Hall, Lodge Lane, Catton, Norwich, Norfolk NR6 7HG. Tel: 01603 419379

Norwich (Coltishall) – Norfolk Mead Hotel, Coltishall, Norwich, Norfolk NR12 7DN. Tel: 01603 737531

Norwich (Thorpe St Andrew) – The Old Rectory, 103 Yarmouth Road, Thorpe St Andrew, Norwich, Norfolk NR7 0HF. Tel: 01603 700772

Nottingham (Ruddington) – The Cottage Country House Hotel, Ruddington, Nottingham, Nottinghamshire NG11 6LA. Tel: 01159 846882

Nottingham (Langar) – Langar Hall, Langar, Nottinghamshire NG13 9HG. Tel: 01949 860559

Oswestry – Pen-y-Dyffryn Country Hotel, Rhydycroesau, Nr Oswestry, Shropshire SY10 7JD. Tel: 01691 653700

Ottery St. Mary (Venn Ottery) – Venn Ottery Barton, Venn Ottery, Near Ottery St. Mary, Devon EX11 1RZ. Tel: 01404 812733

Owlpen – Owlpen Manor, Near Uley, Gloucestershire GL11 5BZ. Tel: 01453 860261

Oxford (Kingston Bagpuize) – Fallowfields, Kingston Bagpuize With Southmoor, Oxfordshire OX13 5BH. Tel: 01865 820416

Padstow – Cross House Hotel, Church Street, Padstow, Cornwall PL28 8BG. Tel: 01841 532391

Penrith (Temple Sowerby) – Temple Sowerby House Hotel, Temple Sowerby, Penrith, Cumbria CA10 1RZ. Tel: 017683 61578

Petersfield (Langrish) – Langrish House, Langrish, Nr Petersfield, Hampshire GU32 1RN. Tel: 01730 266941

Porlock Weir – The Cottage Hotel, Porlock Weir, Porlock, Somerset TA24 8PB. Tel: 01643 863300

Porthleven (Nr Helston) – Tye Rock Hotel, Loe Bar Road, Porthleven, Nr Helston, South Cornwall TR13 9EW. Tel: 01326 572695

Portsmouth – The Beaufort Hotel, 71 Festing Road, Portsmouth, Hampshire PO4 0NQ. Tel: 01705 823707

Pulborough – Chequers Hotel, Church Place, Pulborough, West Sussex RH20 1AD. Tel: 01798 872486

Redditch (Ipsley) – The Old Rectory, Ipsley Lane, Redditch, Worcestershire B98 0AP. Tel: 01527 523000

Ringwood – Moortown Lodge, 244 Christchurch Road, Ringwood, Hampshire BH24 3AS. Tel: 01425 471404

Rock (Nr Wadebridge) – The St Enodoc Hotel, Rock, Nr Wadebridge, Cornwall PL27 6LA. Tel: 01208 863394

Ross-On-Wye (Glewstone) – Glewstone Court, Nr Ross-On-Wye, Herefordshire HR6 6AW. Tel: 01989 770367

Rye – White Vine House, High Street, Rye, East Sussex TN31 7JF. Tel: 01797 224748

St. Ives (Cardis Bay) – Boskerris Hotel, Boskerris Raod, Cardis Bay, St Ives, Cornwall TR26 2NQ. Tel: 01736 795295

St Ives (Trink) – The Countryman At Trink Hotel & Restaurant, Old Coach Road, St Ives, Cornwall TR26 3JQ. Tel: 01736 797571

St Mawes (Ruan Highlanes) – The Hundred House Hotel, Ruan Highlanes, Truro, Cornwall TR2 5JR. Tel: 01872 501336

Saham Toney (Thetford) – Broom Hall, Richmond Road, Saham Toney, Thetford, Norfolk IP25 7EX. Tel: 01953 882125

Salcombe – The Lyndhurst Hotel, Bonaventure Road, Salcombe, Devon TQ8 8BG. Tel: 01548 842481

Saunton – Preston House Hotel, Saunton, Braunton, Devon EX33 1LG. Tel: 01271 890472

Seavington St Mary, Nr Ilminster – The Pheasant Hotel, Seavington St Mary, Nr Ilminster, Somerset TA19 0HQ. Tel: 01460 240502

Sheffield (Chapeltown) – Staindrop Hotel & Restaurant, Lane End, Chapeltown, Sheffield, South Yorkshire S35 3UH. Tel: 0114 284 6727

Sherborne – The Eastbury Hotel, Long Street, Sherborne, Dorset DT9 3BY. Tel: 01935 813131

Shipton-Under-Wychwood – The Shaven Crown Hotel, High Street, Shipton-Under-Wychwood, Oxfordshire OX7 6BA. Tel: 01993 830330

Simonsbath (Exmoor) – Simonsbath House Hotel, Simonsbath, Exmoor, Somerset TA24 7SH. Tel: 01643 831259

South Molton – Marsh Hall Country House Hotel, South Molton, Devon EX36 3HQ. Tel: 01769 572666

Staverton (Nr Totnes) – Kingston House, Staverton, Totnes, Devon TQ9 6AR. Tel: 01803 762 235

Stevenage (Hitchin) – Redcoats Farmhouse Hotel & Restaurant, Redcoats Green, Nr Hitchin, Hertfordshire SG4 7JR. Tel: 01438 729500

Stonor (Henley-on-Thames) – The Stonor Arms, Stonor, Nr Henley-on-Thames, Oxfordshire RG9 6HE. Tel: 01491 638866

Stow-On-The-Wold (Kingham) – Conygree Gate Hotel, Kingham, Oxfordshire OX7 6YA. Tel: 01608 658389

Stratford-upon-Avon (Loxley) – Glebe Farm House, Loxley, Warwickshire CV35 9JW. Tel: 01789 842501

Tewkesbury (Kemerton) – Upper Court, Kemerton, Tewkesbury, Gloucestershire GL20 7HY. Tel: 01386 725351

Tintagel (Trenale) – Trebrea Lodge, Trenale, Tintagel, Cornwall PL34 0HR. Tel: 01840 770410

Truro – The Royal Hotel, Lemon Street, Truro, Cornwall TR1 2QB. Tel: 01872 270345

Uckfield – Hooke Hall, High Street, Uckfield, East Sussex TN22 1EN. Tel: 01825 761578

Wadebridge (Washaway) – Trehellas House & Memories of Malaya Restaurant, Washaway, Bodmin, Cornwall PL30 3AD. Tel: 01208 72700

Wareham (East Stoke) – Kemps Country House Hotel & Restaurant, East Stoke, Wareham, Dorset BH20 6AL. Tel: 01929 462563

Warwick (Claverdon) – The Ardencote Manor Hotel & Country Club, Lye Green Road, Claverdon, Warwick CU35 8LS. Tel: 01926 843111

Wells – Beryl, Wells, Somerset BA5 3JP. Tel: 01749 678738

Wells (Coxley) – Coxley Vineyard, Coxley, Wells, Somerset BA5 1RQ. Tel: 01749 670285

Wells – Glencot House, Glencot Lane, Wookey Hole, Nr Wells, Somerset BA5 1BH. Tel: 01749 677160

Whitby – Dunsley Hall, Dunsley, Whitby, North Yorkshire YO21 3TL. Tel: 01947 893437

Wimborne Minster – Beechleas, 17 Poole Road, Wimborne Minster, Dorset BH21 1QA. Tel: 01202 841684

Wincanton (Holbrook) – Holbrook House Hotel, Wincanton, Somerset BA9 8BS. Tel: 01963 32377

Windermere (Bowness) – Fayrer Garden House Hotel, Lyth Valley Road, Bowness-On – Windermere, Cumbria LA23 3JP. Tel: 015394 88195

Windermere – Quarry Garth Country House Hotel, Windermere, Lake District, Cumbria LA23 1LF. Tel: 015394 88282

Windermere – Storrs Hall, Windermere, Cumbria LA23 3LG. Tel: 015394 47111

Witherslack – The Old Vicarage Country House Hotel, Church Road, Witherslack, Grange-Over-Sands, Cumbria LA11 6RS. Tel: 015395 52381

Woodbridge – Wood Hall Hotel & Country Club, Shottisham, Woodbridge, Suffolk IP12 3EG. Tel: 01394 411283

Worthing (Findon) – Findon Manor, High Street, Findon, Nr Worthing, West Sussex Tel: 01903 872733

York (Escrick) – The Parsonage Country House Hotel, Escrick, York, North Yorkshire YO19 6LF. Tel: 01904 728111

Yoxford – Hope House, High Street, Yoxford, Saxmundham, Suffolk IP17 3HP. Tel: 01728 668281

WALES

Aberdovey – Plas Penhelig Country House Hotel, Aberdovey, Gwynedd LL35 0NA. Tel: 01654 767676

Abergavenny (Glangrwyney) – Glangrwyney Court, Glangrwyney, Nr Abergavenny, Powys NP8 1ES. Tel: 01873 811288

Abergavenny (Govilon) – Llanwenarth House, Govilon, Abergavenny, Monmouthshire NP7 9SF. Tel: 01873 830289

Abergavenny (Llanfihangel Crucorney) – Penyclawdd Court, Llanfihangel Crucorney, Abergavenny, Monmouthshire NP7 7LB. Tel: 01873 890719

Betws-y-Coed – Tan-y-Foel, Capel Garmon, Nr Betws-y-Coed, Conwy LL26 0RE. Tel: 01690 710507

Brecon (Three Cocks) – Old Gwernyfed Country Manor, Felindre, Three Cocks, Brecon, Powys LD3 0SU. Tel: 01497 847376

Caernarfon – Ty'n Rhos Country House, Llanddeiniolen, Caernarfon, Gwynedd LL55 3AE. Tel: 01248 670489

Cardigan (Cilgerran) – The Pembrokeshire Retreat, Rhos-Y-Gilwen Mansion, Cilgerran, Nr Cardigan, Pembrokeshire SA43 2TW. Tel: 01239 841387

Conwy – Berthlwyd Hall Hotel, Llechwedd, Nr Conwy, Gwynedd LL32 8DQ. Tel: 01492 592409

Conwy – The Old Rectory, Llansanffried Glan Conwy, Nr Conwy, Colwyn Bay, Conwy LL28 5LF. Tel: 01492 580611

Dolgellau (Ganllwyd) – Plas Dolmelynllyn, Ganllwyd, Dolgellau, Gwynedd LL40 2HP. Tel: 01341 440273

Monmouth (Whitebrook) – The Crown At Whitebrook, Restaurant With Rooms, Whitebrook, Monmouth, Monmouthshire NP5 4TX. Tel: 01600 860254

Pwllheli – Plas Bodegroes, Nefyn Road, Pwllheli, Gwynedd LL53 5TH. Tel: 01758 612363

Tenby (Waterwynch Bay) – Waterwynch House Hotel, Waterwynch Bay, Tenby, Pembrokeshire SA70 8TJ. Tel: 01834 842464

Tintern – Parva Farmhouse and Restaurant, Tintern, Chepstow, Monmouthshire NP6 6SQ. Tel: 01291 689411

Welshpool (Buttington) – Buttington House, Buttington, Nr Welshpool, Powys SY21 8HD. Tel: 01938 553351

SCOTLAND

Ballater,Royal Deeside – Balgonie Country House, Braemar Place, Royal Deeside, Ballater, Aberdeenshire AB35 5NQ. Tel: 013397 55482

Castle Douglas – Longacre Manor, Ernespie Road, Castle Douglas, Dumfries & Galloway DG7 1LE. Tel: 01556 503576

Comrie (Perthshire) – The Royal Hotel, Melville Square, Comrie, Perthshire PH6 2DN. Tel: 01764 679200

Drumnadrochit (Loch Ness) – Polmaily House Hotel, Drumnadrochit, Loch Ness, Inverness-shire IV3 6XT. Tel: 01456 450343

Dunfries (Thornhill) – Trigony House Hotel, Closeburn, Thornhill, Dunfriesshire DG3 5RZ. Tel: 01848 331211

Dunkeld – The Pend, 5 Brae Street, Dunkeld, Perthshire PH8 0BA. Tel: 01350 727586

Edinburgh – No 22 Murrayfield Gardens, 22 Murrayfield Gardens, Edingburgh, Lothian EH12 6DF. Tel: 0131 337 3569

Fintry (Stirlingshire) – Culcreuch Castle Hotel & Country Park, Fintry, Loch Lomond, Stirling & Trossachs G63 0LW. Tel: 01360 860555

Helmsdale (Sutherland) – Navidale House Hotel, Helmsdale, Sutherland KW8 6JS. Tel: 01431 821 258

By Huntly (Bridge of Marnoch) – The Old Manse of Marnoch, Bridge of Marnoch, By Huntly, Aberdeenshire AB54 5RS. Tel: 01466 780873

Inverness – Culduthel Lodge, 14 Culduthel Road, Inverness, Inverness-shire IV2 4AG. Tel: 01463 240089

Isle Of Harris – Ardvourlie Castle, Aird A Mhulaidh, Isle Of Harris, Western Isles HS3 3AB. Tel: 01859 502307

Isle of Mull (Tobermory) – Highland Cottage, Breadalbane Street, Tobermory, Isle of Mull, Argyll PA75 6PD. Tel: 01688 302030

Isle Of Mull – Killiechronan, Killiechronan, Argyllshire PA72 6JU. Tel: 01680 300403

Isle of Skye (Portree) – Bosville Hotel & Chandlery Seafood Restaurant, Bosville Terrace, Portree, Isle of Skye IV51 9DG. Tel: 01478 612846

Kentallen Of Appin – Ardsheal House, Kentallen Of Appin, Argyll PA38 4BX. Tel: 01631 740227

Killiecrankie,By Pitlochry – The Killiecrankie Hotel, Killiecrankie, By Pitlochry, Perthshire PH16 5LG. Tel: 01796 473220

Kinlochbervie – The Kinlochbervie Hotel, Kinlochbervie, By Lairg, Sutherland IV27 4RP. Tel: 01971 521275

Kinross (Cleish) – Nivingston Country House, Cleish, By Kinross, Kinross-shire KY13 7LS. Tel: 01577 850216

Lockerbie – The Dryfesdale Hotel, Lockerbie, Dumfriesshire DG11 2SF. Tel: 01576 202427

Moffat – Well View Hotel, Ballplay Road, Moffat, Dumfriesshire DG10 9JU. Tel: 01683 220184

Nairn (Auldearn) – Boath House, Auldearn, Nairn, Inverness IV12 5TE. Tel: 01667 454896

Oban – Dungallen House Hotel, Gallanach Road, Oban, Argyllshire PA34 4PD. Tel: 01631 563799

Oban – The Manor House Hotel, Gallanch Road, Oban, Argyllshire PA34 4LS. Tel: 01631 562087

Perth (Guildtown) – Newmiln Country House, Newmiln Estate, Guildtown, Perth, Perthshire PH2 6AE. Tel: 01738 552364

Pitlochry – Dunfallandy House, Logierait Road, Pitlochry, Perthshire PH16 5NA. Tel: 01796 472648

Port Appin – Druimneil, Port Appin, Argyllshire PA38 4DQ. Tel: 01631 730228

Port Of Menteith – The Lake Hotel, Port Of Menteith, Perthshire FK8 3RA. Tel: 01877 385258

Rhu – Aldonaig, Rhu, Argyll & Bute G84 8NH. Tel: 01436 820863

St. Boswell – Clint Lodge, St. Boswells, Melrose, Roxburgshire TD6 0DZ. Tel: 01835 822027

Strathtummel (By Pitlochry) – Queen's View Hotel, Strathtummel, By Pitlochry, Perthshire PH16 5NR. Tel: 01796 473291

IRELAND

Bantry (Co Cork) – Ballylickey Manor House, Ballylickey, Bantry Bay, Co Cork Tel: 00 353 27 50071

Caragh Lake (Co Kerry) – Ard-na-Sidhe, Co Kerry Tel: 00 353 66 69105

Caragh Lake (Co Kerry) – Caragh Lodge, Caragh Lake, Co Kerry Tel: 00 353 66 69115

Cashel (Co Tipperary) – Cashel Palace Hotel, Cashel, Co Tipperary Tel: 00 353 62 62707

Connemara (Co Galway) – Ross Lake House Hotel, Rosscahill, Oughterard, Co Galway Tel: 00 353 91 550109

Dublin – Aberdeen Lodge, 53-55 Park Avenue, Ailesbury Road, Dublin 4 Tel: 00 353 1 2838155

Dublin – The Fitzwilliam Park, No5 Fitzwilliam Square, Dublin 2, Tel: 00 353 1 6628 280

Kilkee (Co Clare) – Halpins Hotel & Vittles Restaurant, Erin Street, Kilkee, Tel: 00 353 65 56032

Killadeas (Irvingstown N.Ireland) – The Inishclare Restaurant, Killadeas, Co Fermanagh BT94 1SF. Tel: 013656 28550

Killarney (Co Kerry) – Earls Court House, Woodlawn Junction, Muckross Road, Co Kerry Tel: 00 353 64 34009

Kilmeaden (Co. Waterford) – The Old Rectory – Kilmeaden House, Co Waterford Tel: 00 353 51 384254

Letterkenny (Co Donegal) – Castle Grove Country House, Ramelton Road, Letterkenny, Co Donegal Tel: 00 353 745 1118

Riverstown (Co Sligo) – Coopershill House, Riverstown, Co Sligo Tel: 00 353 71 65108

Skibbereen (Co.Cork) – Liss Ard Lake Lodge, Skibbereen, Co.Cork Tel: 00 353 28 22365

Sligo (Co Sligo) – Markree Castle, Colooney, Co Sligo Tel: 00 353 71 67800

Wicklow (Co Wicklow) – The Old Rectory, Wicklow Town, Co Wicklow Tel: 00 353 404 67048

CHANNEL ISLANDS

Guernsey (Fermain Bay) – La Favorita Hotel, Fermain Bay, Guernsey GY4 6SD. Tel: 01481 35666

Guernsey (St Martin) – Bella Luce Hotel & Restaurant, La Fosse, St Martin, Guernsey, Guernsey Tel: 01481 38764

Herm Island (Guernsey) – The White House, Herm Island, Guernsey GY1 3HR. Tel: 01481 722159

Jersey (St Aubin) – Hôtel La Tour, Rue de Croquet, St Aubin, Jersey, JE3 8BR. Tel: 01534 43770

PREFERRED PARTNERS

Preferred partners are those organisations specifically chosen and exclusively recommended by Johansens for the quality and excellence of their products and services for the mutual benefit of Johansens members, readers and independent travellers.

AT&T Global Services

Classic Malts of Scotland

Diners Club International

Dunhill Tobacco

Ercol Furniture Ltd

Hildon Ltd

J&H Marsh & McLennan

Knight Frank International

Honda UK Ltd

Moët Hennessy

NPI

Pacific Direct

To enable you to use your 1999 Johansens Recommended Traditional Inns, Hotels & Restaurants Guide more effectively, the following four pages of indexes contain a wealth of useful information about the establishments featured in the Guide. As well as listing them alphabetically, by region and by county, the indexes also show at a glance which properties offer certain specialised facilities. The indexes are listed as follows:

- Alphabetically by region
- By county
- With a swimming pool
- With fishing nearby
- With shooting locally
- With conference facilities for 100 delegates or more
- Double rooms for £50 or under
- Johansens Preferred Partners
- Inns accepting Johansens Privilege Card

1999 Johansens Recommended Traditional Inns, Hotels & Restaurants listed alphabetically by region

ENGLAND

WALES

SCOTLAND

CHANNEL ISLANDS

By county

ENGLAND

Berkshire

SCOTLAND

Aberdeenshire

Banffshire

Clackmannanshire

Dumfriesshire

Fife

Inverness-shire

Isle Of Skye

Perthshire

Stirlingshire

Wester Ross

CHANNEL ISLANDS

Jersey

With a swimming pool

ENGLAND

SCOTLAND

CHANNEL ISLES

With fishing nearby

ENGLAND

WALES

SCOTLAND

CHANNEL ISLANDS

With shooting nearby

ENGLAND

WALES

SCOTLAND

With conference facilities for 100 delegates or more

ENGLAND

SCOTLAND

With double rooms for £50 per night or under

ENGLAND

SCOTLAND

Accepting Johansens Privilege Card

10% discount, room upgrade where available, VIP service at participating establishments. Full Terms & Conditions available on request.

ENGLAND

WALES

Johansens Preferred Partners

Play the role of Hotel Inspector

At the back of this book you will notice a quantity of Guest Survey Forms. If you have had an enjoyable stay at one of our recommended hotels, or alternatively you have been in some way disappointed, please complete one of these forms and send it to us FREEPOST.

These reports essentially complement the assessments made by our team of professional inspectors, continually monitoring the standards of hospitality in every establishment in our guides. Guest Survey reports also have an important influence on the selection of nominations for our annual awards for excellence.

'Diversity and excellence for the independent traveller'.

MOËT
BRUT IMPÉRIAL
BRUT IMPÉRIAL
MOËT & CHANDON
CHAMPAGNE
BRUT
ÉPERNAY FRANCE
FONDE EN 1743
The first choice at
every Johansens
Recommended Hotel

Guest Survey Report

Your own Johansens 'inspection' gives reliability to our guides and assists in the selection of Award Nominations

Name/location of hotel: ______________________ Page No: __________

Date of visit: ______________________

Name & address of guest: ______________________

______________________ Postcode: __________

Please tick one box in each category below:	Excellent	Good	Disappointing	Poor
Bedrooms				
Public Rooms				
Restaurant/Cuisine				
Service				
Welcome/Friendliness				
Value For Money				

PLEASE return your Guest Survey Report form!

Occasionally we may allow other reputable organisations to write with offers which may be of interest.
If you prefer not to hear from them, tick this box ☐

To: Johansens, FREEPOST (CB264), 43 Millharbour, London E14 9BR

Guest Survey Report

Your own Johansens 'inspection' gives reliability to our guides and assists in the selection of Award Nominations

Name/location of hotel: ______________________ Page No: __________

Date of visit: ______________________

Name & address of guest: ______________________

______________________ Postcode: __________

Please tick one box in each category below:	Excellent	Good	Disappointing	Poor
Bedrooms				
Public Rooms				
Restaurant/Cuisine				
Service				
Welcome/Friendliness				
Value For Money				

PLEASE return your Guest Survey Report form!

Occasionally we may allow other reputable organisations to write with offers which may be of interest.
If you prefer not to hear from them, tick this box ☐

To: Johansens, FREEPOST (CB264), 43 Millharbour, London E14 9BR

ORDER FORM

Call our 24hr credit card hotline FREEPHONE 0800 269 397

Simply indicate which title(s) you require by putting the quantity in the boxes provided. Choose your preferred method of payment and return this coupon (NO STAMP REQUIRED) to: Johansens, FREEPOST (CB264), 43 Millharbour, London E14 9BR. Your FREE gifts will automatically be dispatched with your order. Fax orders welcome on 0171 537 3594

PRINTED GUIDES

	Qty	Total £
A Hotels – Great Britain & Ireland 1999 ....£19.95		
B Country Houses and Small Hotels – Great Britain & Ireland 1999 ....£10.95		
C Traditional Inns, Hotels and Restaurants – Great Britain & Ireland 1999 ....£10.95		
D Hotels – Europe & The Mediterranean 1999 ....£14.95		
E Hotels – North America, Bermuda, Caribbean 1999 ....£9.95		
F Historic Houses Castles & Gardens 1999 *published & mailed to you in March '99* £4.99		
G Museums & Galleries 1999 *published & mailed to you in April '99* £8.95		
H Business Meeting Venues 1999 *published & mailed to you in March '99* £20.00		
I Japanese Edition 1999 ....£9.95		
J Privilege Card 1999 ....£20.00 *You get one free card with you order, please mention here the number of additional cards you require*		

TOTAL 1

CD-ROMs

	Qty	Total £
K The Guide 1999 – Great Britain & Ireland *published and mailed to you in Nov 98* £29.95		
L The Guide 1999 – Europe & North America *published and mailed to you in Nov 98* ..£19.95		
M Business Meeting Venues 1999 *published and mailed to you in April '99* £20.00		

TOTAL 2

SPECIAL OFFERS

	Qty	Total £
SAVE £7.85 — 3 Johansens guides A+B+C ..~~£41.85~~..£34		
In a presentation box set add £5		
SAVE £12.80 — 4 Johansens guides A+B+C+D ....~~£56.80~~..£44		
In a presentation box set add £5		
SAVE £14.75 — 5 Johansens guides A+B+C+D+E ....~~£66.75~~..£52		
In a presentation box set add £5		
+Johansens Suit Cover		FREE
+P&P		FREE
SAVE £10.90 — 2 Johansens CD-ROMS K+L ~~£49.90~~..£39		
SAVE £10 — Business Meeting Pack H+M.....~~£40~~..£30		

TOTAL 3

Postage & Packing

UK: £4.50 or £2.50 for single orders and CD-ROMs
Ouside UK: Add £5 or £3 for single orders and CD-ROMs.

TOTAL 4

One Privilege Card — FREE
10% discount, room upgrade when available,
VIP service at participating establishments

TOTAL 1+2+3+4

Name (Mr/Mrs/Miss)

Address

Postcode

Prices Valid Until 31 August 1999
Please allow 21 days for delivery

Occasionally we may allow other reputable organisations to write to you with offers which may be of interest. If you prefer not to hear from them, tick this box. ☐

☐ **I enclose a cheque for £** ____ **payable to Johansens**
☐ **I enclose my order on company letterheading, please invoice (UK only)**
☐ **Please debit my credit/charge card account (please tick).**
☐ **MasterCard** ☐ **Diners** ☐ **Amex** ☐ **Visa** ☐ **Switch** (Issue Number)

Card No

Signature **Exp date**

J14

ORDER FORM

Call our 24hr credit card hotline FREEPHONE 0800 269 397

Simply indicate which title(s) you require by putting the quantity in the boxes provided. Choose your preferred method of payment and return this coupon (NO STAMP REQUIRED) to: Johansens, FREEPOST (CB264), 43 Millharbour, London E14 9BR. Your FREE gifts will automatically be dispatched with your order. Fax orders welcome on 0171 537 3594

PRINTED GUIDES

	Qty	Total £
A Hotels – Great Britain & Ireland 1999 ....£19.95		
B Country Houses and Small Hotels – Great Britain & Ireland 1999 ....£10.95		
C Traditional Inns, Hotels and Restaurants – Great Britain & Ireland 1999 ....£10.95		
D Hotels – Europe & The Mediterranean 1999 ....£14.95		
E Hotels – North America, Bermuda, Caribbean 1999 ....£9.95		
F Historic Houses Castles & Gardens 1999 *published & mailed to you in March '99* £4.99		
G Museums & Galleries 1999 *published & mailed to you in April '99* £8.95		
H Business Meeting Venues 1999 *published & mailed to you in March '99* £20.00		
I Japanese Edition 1999 ....£9.95		
J Privilege Card 1999 ....£20.00 *You get one free card with you order, please mention here the number of additional cards you require*		

TOTAL 1

CD-ROMs

	Qty	Total £
K The Guide 1999 – Great Britain & Ireland *published and mailed to you in Nov 98* £29.95		
L The Guide 1999 – Europe & North America *published and mailed to you in Nov 98* ..£19.95		
M Business Meeting Venues 1999 *published and mailed to you in April '99* £20.00		

TOTAL 2

SPECIAL OFFERS

	Qty	Total £
SAVE £7.85 — 3 Johansens guides A+B+C ..~~£41.85~~..£34		
In a presentation box set add £5		
SAVE £12.80 — 4 Johansens guides A+B+C+D ....~~£56.80~~..£44		
In a presentation box set add £5		
SAVE £14.75 — 5 Johansens guides A+B+C+D+E ....~~£66.75~~..£52		
In a presentation box set add £5		
+Johansens Suit Cover		FREE
+P&P		FREE
SAVE £10.90 — 2 Johansens CD-ROMS K+L ~~£49.90~~..£39		
SAVE £10 — Business Meeting Pack H+M.....~~£40~~..£30		

TOTAL 3

Postage & Packing

UK: £4.50 or £2.50 for single orders and CD-ROMs
Ouside UK: Add £5 or £3 for single orders and CD-ROMs.

TOTAL 4

One Privilege Card — FREE
10% discount, room upgrade when available,
VIP service at participating establishments

TOTAL 1+2+3+4

Name (Mr/Mrs/Miss)

Address

Postcode

Prices Valid Until 31 August 1999
Please allow 21 days for delivery

Occasionally we may allow other reputable organisations to write to you with offers which may be of interest. If you prefer not to hear from them, tick this box. ☐

☐ **I enclose a cheque for £** ____ **payable to Johansens**
☐ **I enclose my order on company letterheading, please invoice (UK only)**
☐ **Please debit my credit/charge card account (please tick).**
☐ **MasterCard** ☐ **Diners** ☐ **Amex** ☐ **Visa** ☐ **Switch** (Issue Number)

Card No

Signature **Exp date**

J14

Guest Survey Report

Your own Johansens 'inspection' gives reliability to our guides and assists in the selection of Award Nominations

Name/location of hotel: ______________________ Page No: ________

Date of visit: ______________________

Name & address of guest: ______________________

______________________ Postcode: ________

Please tick one box in each category below:	Excellent	Good	Disappointing	Poor
Bedrooms				
Public Rooms				
Restaurant/Cuisine				
Service				
Welcome/Friendliness				
Value For Money				

PLEASE return your Guest Survey Report form!

Occasionally we may allow other reputable organisations to write with offers which may be of interest.
If you prefer not to hear from them, tick this box ☐

To: Johansens, FREEPOST (CB264), 43 Millharbour, London E14 9BR

Guest Survey Report

Your own Johansens 'inspection' gives reliability to our guides and assists in the selection of Award Nominations

Name/location of hotel: ______________________ Page No: ________

Date of visit: ______________________

Name & address of guest: ______________________

______________________ Postcode: ________

Please tick one box in each category below:	Excellent	Good	Disappointing	Poor
Bedrooms				
Public Rooms				
Restaurant/Cuisine				
Service				
Welcome/Friendliness				
Value For Money				

PLEASE return your Guest Survey Report form!

Occasionally we may allow other reputable organisations to write with offers which may be of interest.
If you prefer not to hear from them, tick this box ☐

To: Johansens, FREEPOST (CB264), 43 Millharbour, London E14 9BR

ORDER FORM

Call our 24hr credit card hotline FREEPHONE 0800 269 397

Simply indicate which title(s) you require by putting the quantity in the boxes provided. Choose your preferred method of payment and return this coupon (NO STAMP REQUIRED) to: Johansens, FREEPOST (CB264), 43 Millharbour, London E14 9BR. Your FREE gifts will automatically be dispatched with your order. Fax orders welcome on 0171 537 3594

PRINTED GUIDES

	Title	Price	Qty	Total £
A	Hotels – Great Britain & Ireland 1999	£19.95		
B	Country Houses and Small Hotels – Great Britain & Ireland 1999	£10.95		
C	Traditional Inns, Hotels and Restaurants – Great Britain & Ireland 1999	£10.95		
D	Hotels – Europe & The Mediterranean 1999	£14.95		
E	Hotels – North America, Bermuda, Caribbean 1999	£9.95		
F	Historic Houses Castles & Gardens 1999 *published & mailed to you in March '99*	£4.99		
G	Museums & Galleries 1999 *published & mailed to you in April '99*	£8.95		
H	Business Meeting Venues 1999 *published & mailed to you in March '99*	£20.00		
I	Japanese Edition 1999	£9.95		
J	Privilege Card 1999 *You get one free card with you order, please mention here the number of additional cards you require*	£20.00		

TOTAL 1

CD-ROMs

	Title	Price	Qty	Total £
K	The Guide 1999 – Great Britain & Ireland *published and mailed to you in Nov 98*	£29.95		
L	The Guide 1999 – Europe & North America *published and mailed to you in Nov 98*	£19.95		
M	Business Meeting Venues 1999 *published and mailed to you in April '99*	£20.00		

TOTAL 2

SPECIAL OFFERS

Save	Offer	Qty	Total £
SAVE £7.85	3 Johansens guides A+B+C ~~£41.85~~ £34		
	In a presentation box set add £5		
SAVE £12.80	4 Johansens guides A+B+C+D ~~£56.80~~ £44		
	In a presentation box set add £5		
SAVE £14.75	5 Johansens guides A+B+C+D+E ~~£66.75~~ £52		
	In a presentation box set add £5		
	+Johansens Suit Cover		FREE
	+P&P		FREE
SAVE £10.90	2 Johansens CD-ROMS K+L ~~£49.90~~ £39		
SAVE £10	Business Meeting Pack H+M ~~£40~~ £30		

TOTAL 3

Postage & Packing

UK: £4.50 or £2.50 for single orders and CD-ROMs
Ouside UK: Add £5 or £3 for single orders and CD-ROMs.

TOTAL 4

One Privilege Card **FREE**
10% discount, room upgrade when available,
VIP service at participating establishments

TOTAL 1+2+3+4

Name (Mr/Mrs/Miss)

Address

Postcode

Prices Valid Until 31 August 1999
Please allow 21 days for delivery

Occasionally we may allow other reputable organisations to write to you with offers which may be of interest. If you prefer not to hear from them, tick this box. ☐

☐ I enclose a cheque for £ ____ payable to Johansens
☐ I enclose my order on company letterheading, please invoice (UK only)
☐ Please debit my credit/charge card account (please tick).
☐ MasterCard ☐ Diners ☐ Amex ☐ Visa ☐ Switch (Issue Number)

Card No

Signature

Exp date

J14

ORDER FORM

Call our 24hr credit card hotline FREEPHONE 0800 269 397

Simply indicate which title(s) you require by putting the quantity in the boxes provided. Choose your preferred method of payment and return this coupon (NO STAMP REQUIRED) to: Johansens, FREEPOST (CB264), 43 Millharbour, London E14 9BR. Your FREE gifts will automatically be dispatched with your order. Fax orders welcome on 0171 537 3594

PRINTED GUIDES

	Title	Price	Qty	Total £
A	Hotels – Great Britain & Ireland 1999	£19.95		
B	Country Houses and Small Hotels – Great Britain & Ireland 1999	£10.95		
C	Traditional Inns, Hotels and Restaurants – Great Britain & Ireland 1999	£10.95		
D	Hotels – Europe & The Mediterranean 1999	£14.95		
E	Hotels – North America, Bermuda, Caribbean 1999	£9.95		
F	Historic Houses Castles & Gardens 1999 *published & mailed to you in March '99*	£4.99		
G	Museums & Galleries 1999 *published & mailed to you in April '99*	£8.95		
H	Business Meeting Venues 1999 *published & mailed to you in March '99*	£20.00		
I	Japanese Edition 1999	£9.95		
J	Privilege Card 1999 *You get one free card with you order, please mention here the number of additional cards you require*	£20.00		

TOTAL 1

CD-ROMs

	Title	Price	Qty	Total £
K	The Guide 1999 – Great Britain & Ireland *published and mailed to you in Nov 98*	£29.95		
L	The Guide 1999 – Europe & North America *published and mailed to you in Nov 98*	£19.95		
M	Business Meeting Venues 1999 *published and mailed to you in April '99*	£20.00		

TOTAL 2

SPECIAL OFFERS

Save	Offer	Qty	Total £
SAVE £7.85	3 Johansens guides A+B+C ~~£41.85~~ £34		
	In a presentation box set add £5		
SAVE £12.80	4 Johansens guides A+B+C+D ~~£56.80~~ £44		
	In a presentation box set add £5		
SAVE £14.75	5 Johansens guides A+B+C+D+E ~~£66.75~~ £52		
	In a presentation box set add £5		
	+Johansens Suit Cover		FREE
	+P&P		FREE
SAVE £10.90	2 Johansens CD-ROMS K+L ~~£49.90~~ £39		
SAVE £10	Business Meeting Pack H+M ~~£40~~ £30		

TOTAL 3

Postage & Packing

UK: £4.50 or £2.50 for single orders and CD-ROMs
Ouside UK: Add £5 or £3 for single orders and CD-ROMs.

TOTAL 4

One Privilege Card **FREE**
10% discount, room upgrade when available,
VIP service at participating establishments

TOTAL 1+2+3+4

Name (Mr/Mrs/Miss)

Address

Postcode

Prices Valid Until 31 August 1999
Please allow 21 days for delivery

Occasionally we may allow other reputable organisations to write to you with offers which may be of interest. If you prefer not to hear from them, tick this box. ☐

☐ I enclose a cheque for £ ____ payable to Johansens
☐ I enclose my order on company letterheading, please invoice (UK only)
☐ Please debit my credit/charge card account (please tick).
☐ MasterCard ☐ Diners ☐ Amex ☐ Visa ☐ Switch (Issue Number)

Card No

Signature

Exp date

J14

ORDER FORM

Call our 24hr credit card hotline FREEPHONE 0800 269 397

Simply indicate which title(s) you require by putting the quantity in the boxes provided. Choose your preferred method of payment and return this coupon (NO STAMP REQUIRED) to: Johansens, FREEPOST (CB264), 43 Millharbour, London E14 9BR. Your FREE gifts will automatically be dispatched with your order. Fax orders welcome on 0171 537 3594

PRINTED GUIDES

		Qty	Total £
A	Hotels – Great Britain & Ireland 1999 ....£19.95		
B	Country Houses and Small Hotels – Great Britain & Ireland 1999 ....£10.95		
C	Traditional Inns, Hotels and Restaurants – Great Britain & Ireland 1999 ......£10.95		
D	Hotels – Europe & The Mediterranean 1999 ....£14.95		
E	Hotels – North America, Bermuda, Caribbean 1999 ....£9.95		
F	Historic Houses Castles & Gardens 1999 *published & mailed to you in March '99* £4.99		
G	Museums & Galleries 1999 *published & mailed to you in April '99*....................£8.95		
H	Business Meeting Venues 1999 *published & mailed to you in March '99* £20.00		
I	Japanese Edition 1999 ....£9.95		
J	Privilege Card 1999 ....£20.00 *You get one free card with you order, please mention here the number of additional cards you require*		

TOTAL 1

SPECIAL OFFERS

		Qty	Total £
SAVE £7.85	3 Johansens guides A+B+C ..~~£41.85~~..£34		
	In a presentation box set add £5		
SAVE £12.80	4 Johansens guides A+B+C+D ....~~£56.80~~..£44		
	In a presentation box set add £5		
SAVE £14.75	5 Johansens guides A+B+C+D+E ....~~£66.75~~..£52		
	In a presentation box set add £5		
	+Johansens Suit Cover		FREE
	+P&P		FREE
SAVE £10.90	2 Johansens CD-ROMS K+L ~~£49.90~~..£39		
SAVE £10	Business Meeting Pack H+M.....~~£40~~..£30		

TOTAL 3

CD-ROMs

		Qty	Total £
K	The Guide 1999 – Great Britain & Ireland *published and mailed to you in Nov 98*......£29.95		
L	The Guide 1999 – Europe & North America *published and mailed to you in Nov 98* ..£19.95		
M	Business Meeting Venues 1999 *published and mailed to you in April '99* £20.00		

TOTAL 2

Postage & Packing

UK: £4.50 or £2.50 for single orders and CD-ROMs
Ouside UK: Add £5 or £3 for single orders and CD-ROMs.

TOTAL 4

One Privilege Card **FREE**
10% discount, room upgrade when available,
VIP service at participating establishments

TOTAL 1+2+3+4

Name (Mr/Mrs/Miss)

Address

Postcode

Prices Valid Until 31 August 1999
Please allow 21 days for delivery

Occasionally we may allow other reputable organisations to write to you with offers which may be of interest. If you prefer not to hear from them, tick this box. ☐

☐ **I enclose a cheque for £** ______ **payable to Johansens**
☐ **I enclose my order on company letterheading, please invoice (UK only)**
☐ **Please debit my credit/charge card account (please tick).**
☐ **MasterCard** ☐ **Diners** ☐ **Amex** ☐ **Visa** ☐ **Switch** (Issue Number)

Card No

Signature **Exp date**

J14

ORDER FORM

Call our 24hr credit card hotline FREEPHONE 0800 269 397

Simply indicate which title(s) you require by putting the quantity in the boxes provided. Choose your preferred method of payment and return this coupon (NO STAMP REQUIRED) to: Johansens, FREEPOST (CB264), 43 Millharbour, London E14 9BR. Your FREE gifts will automatically be dispatched with your order. Fax orders welcome on 0171 537 3594

PRINTED GUIDES

		Qty	Total £
A	Hotels – Great Britain & Ireland 1999 ....£19.95		
B	Country Houses and Small Hotels – Great Britain & Ireland 1999 ....£10.95		
C	Traditional Inns, Hotels and Restaurants – Great Britain & Ireland 1999 ......£10.95		
D	Hotels – Europe & The Mediterranean 1999 ....£14.95		
E	Hotels – North America, Bermuda, Caribbean 1999 ....£9.95		
F	Historic Houses Castles & Gardens 1999 *published & mailed to you in March '99* £4.99		
G	Museums & Galleries 1999 *published & mailed to you in April '99*....................£8.95		
H	Business Meeting Venues 1999 *published & mailed to you in March '99* £20.00		
I	Japanese Edition 1999 ....£9.95		
J	Privilege Card 1999 ....£20.00 *You get one free card with you order, please mention here the number of additional cards you require*		

TOTAL 1

SPECIAL OFFERS

		Qty	Total £
SAVE £7.85	3 Johansens guides A+B+C ..~~£41.85~~..£34		
	In a presentation box set add £5		
SAVE £12.80	4 Johansens guides A+B+C+D ....~~£56.80~~..£44		
	In a presentation box set add £5		
SAVE £14.75	5 Johansens guides A+B+C+D+E ....~~£66.75~~..£52		
	In a presentation box set add £5		
	+Johansens Suit Cover		FREE
	+P&P		FREE
SAVE £10.90	2 Johansens CD-ROMS K+L ~~£49.90~~..£39		
SAVE £10	Business Meeting Pack H+M.....~~£40~~..£30		

TOTAL 3

CD-ROMs

		Qty	Total £
K	The Guide 1999 – Great Britain & Ireland *published and mailed to you in Nov 98*......£29.95		
L	The Guide 1999 – Europe & North America *published and mailed to you in Nov 98* ..£19.95		
M	Business Meeting Venues 1999 *published and mailed to you in April '99* £20.00		

TOTAL 2

Postage & Packing

UK: £4.50 or £2.50 for single orders and CD-ROMs
Ouside UK: Add £5 or £3 for single orders and CD-ROMs.

TOTAL 4

One Privilege Card **FREE**
10% discount, room upgrade when available,
VIP service at participating establishments

TOTAL 1+2+3+4

Name (Mr/Mrs/Miss)

Address

Postcode

Prices Valid Until 31 August 1999
Please allow 21 days for delivery

Occasionally we may allow other reputable organisations to write to you with offers which may be of interest. If you prefer not to hear from them, tick this box. ☐

☐ **I enclose a cheque for £** ______ **payable to Johansens**
☐ **I enclose my order on company letterheading, please invoice (UK only)**
☐ **Please debit my credit/charge card account (please tick).**
☐ **MasterCard** ☐ **Diners** ☐ **Amex** ☐ **Visa** ☐ **Switch** (Issue Number)

Card No

Signature **Exp date**

J14

NO STAMP NEEDED

Johansens
FREEPOST (CB264)
43 Millharbour
London
E14 9BR

NO STAMP NEEDED

Johansens
FREEPOST (CB264)
43 Millharbour
London
E14 9BR